WATER, LAND, AND
LAW IN THE WEST

DEVELOPMENT OF WESTERN RESOURCES

The Development of Western Resources is an interdisciplinary series focusing on the use and misuse of resources in the American West. Written for a broad readership of humanists, social scientists, and resource specialists, the books in this series emphasize both historical and contemporary perspectives as they explore the interplay between resource exploitation and economic, social, and political experiences.

John G. Clark, University of Kansas, Founding Editor
Hal K. Rothman, University of Nevada, Las Vegas, Series Editor

WATER, LAND, AND LAW IN THE WEST

The Limits of Public Policy, 1850–1920

Donald J. Pisani

Foreword by Hal K. Rothman

 University Press of Kansas

Published by the University Press of Kansas (Lawrence, Kansas 66049), which was
organized by the Kansas Board of Regents and is operated and funded by Emporia
State University, Fort Hays State University, Kansas State University, Pittsburg State
University, the University of Kansas, and Wichita State University

Library of Congress Cataloging-in-Publication Data

Pisani, Donald J.
    Water, land, and law in the West : the limits of public policy, 1850–1920 /
Donald J. Pisani ; foreword by Hal K. Rothman.
        p.   cm. — (Development of western resources)
    Includes bibliographical references and index.
    ISBN 0-7006-0795-1 (alk. paper)
        1. Water-supply — Government policy — West (U.S.) — History. 2. Water rights
— West (U.S.) — History. 3. Riparian rights — West (U.S.) — History. 4. Land
use — Government policy — West (U.S.) — History. 5. Conservation of natural
resources — Government policy — West (U.S.) — History. 6. Water — Law and legislation — West (U.S.) — History. 7. Conservation of natural resources — Law and
legislation — West (U.S.) — History.   I. Title.   II. Series.
    HD1695.W4P57 1996
    333.91'00978—dc20   96-14093

British Library Cataloguing in Publication Data is available.

Printed in the United States of America

10 9 8 7 6 5 4 3 2 1

For Richard Lowitt,
model historian and esteemed friend

CONTENTS

FOREWORD

Donald J. Pisani has compiled a remarkable body of work. In addition to two major scholarly volumes that focus on agriculture, water and water law, reclamation, public policy, and natural resources in the American West, Pisani has written more than two dozen important and pathbreaking articles, which have been published in diverse places across the scholarly landscape. This diffuse dissemination has meant that a wide range of scholars has seen parts of this corpus but few have had the opportunity to consider how the pieces relate to each other. This volume brings together ten of these pieces, the ones the author deems most important, in one place for the first time. Divided into four parts—"Water Law," "Land," "Forests, Conservation, and Bureaucracy," and "Federal Reclamation"—the chapters attest to the breadth of the topics Pisani has addressed.

Even to the most casual observers of western, legal, and environmental history, this is work of great significance. Rooted in impressive archival scholarship in the tradition of the venerated Paul Wallace Gates, Pisani's work has contributed to shaping the way in which historians view a range of natural resource–related topics. Pisani uses a grass-roots research strategy; his generalizations come from volumes of data, built piece by piece from the ground up. In Pisani's construction of the world, the local drives the state and the federal; the decisions made at the local level ignite the process that forms the building blocks of legal and cultural institutions. A fragmented West, divided by local rather than regional or national allegiances and battling against itself for economic gain in a zero-sum equation, emerges from Pisani's work. Local elites play a formative role, shaping law, policy, and local and regional society to their advantage and battling to retain that advantage in changing cultural, legal, and economic climates.

There is a declensionist tone to Pisani's work, yet it differs from the more typical views of decline that pervade the historical writing of the later twentieth century. Pisani does not see the fall from grace so characteristic of the perspective of our era, nor does he routinely engage in irony. Instead, the weakness and malleability of American institutions provide the overriding themes in Pisani's work, the myriad ways in which law and policy fail to achieve the ends for which they are created. In particular, the gap between the ideals of American society and the instruments of their implementation and the realities of life in places where institutions have not yet entirely coalesced is evident. In this gap between idea and ideal, between theory and practice, is where Pisani articulates his message, where he shows how ideas failed, were transformed, and sometimes even used to create entirely different situations than their authors intended.

This meeting of law, policy, and values is one of the major contributions of Pisani's work. The basic premises of our society, the painstaking details of the formation of law and its application to the lives of people, are delineated in these chapters. They debunk myth and add new layers to our understanding of the process of the formation of institutions. In environmental history, this focus on institutions is a crucial concept, one in the process of being explicated.

Yet Pisani is scrupulous in his efforts to understand that the people of the past inhabited a different world than the people of today. Pisani seeks to uncover that world, complete with its value systems and premises, and use it to understand the decisions of the past. He neither excuses nor condemns the past; he analyzes the past for what it was, a different place than the present with an integrity of its own, ways of looking at the world that are not our own, and an entire matrix of rules, regulations, and operations that remain unique to time and place.

In this volume, some of the major emphases of the environmental history of the American West are played out. Pisani reveals to us how natural resources are regarded, how they are claimed, how institutions that adjudicate them form and change, and how the process comes apart. The chapters reveal patterns in the development of the institutions of American society in the settlement of the West, the consequences of good intentions as well as of bad, of avarice as well as of public service. Thus they serve as a model for understanding the underlying premises of a society and its relationship to the physical world.

Hal K. Rothman

PREFACE

The idea for reprinting these essays originated with my friend and colleague Richard Lowitt. He observed that many of my published articles were closely related and that students of the law, public policy, natural resources, and western U.S. history would profit from having them under one cover. The University Press of Kansas tested the idea on two outside readers with good results. I selected what I consider the ten most significant and useful pieces for this volume, divided them into four parts, and prepared brief introductions for each group.

The ten essays were published between 1982 and 1994. They originally appeared in the journals listed in the back of this book as "Source Note" and appear here substantially as first published. I have tinkered with the prose in places but only for the sake of clarity; the interpretations remain the same. Some note formats have also been changed slightly.

The essays have much in common. They are stories of tarnished dreams; all deal with failures to achieve justice, equity, or efficiency in the administration of natural resources. They also reflect the weaknesses of public policy in the United States, including the American desire to develop the nation's latent wealth as rapidly as possible; the national aversion to planning; the tendency of federalism to disperse power through many levels of government; and the absence of a "career bureaucracy" in Washington capable of providing leadership or direction to natural resource policies.

There is no attempt to glorify or romanticize the "opening" or "taming" of the West, nor do these pages provide any prescriptions for improving public policy in the future. Indeed, most of the barriers to effective and just resource administration—from uncertain objectives, to bureaucratic infighting, to the power of Congress—afflict late-twentieth-century resource managers as much as they did those in the last century. I do not, however, impugn the motives of previous generations of policymakers; they lived in a world driven by different values and different concerns. Professional historians have an obligation to learn from the past, but we must avoid making history a whipping post for the anxieties and frustrations of our own times.

Among the people who deserve thanks are the editors of the journals in which the chapters in this book first appeared. They have my gratitude for granting permission to reprint and for the care they took in preparing the manuscripts for publication the first time around. Others who merit recognition include Charlotte Gregory, who did an expeditious job of retyping the articles, and Brad Raley, my talented and valued research assistant, who spent many tedious hours proofreading and puzzling through the idiosyncracies of WordPerfect. His patience, good humor, and sound judgment are much appreciated. Cynthia Miller and Mike Briggs of the University Press of Kansas strongly supported the project and provided encouragement and good advice. The indefatigable Hal Rothman, editor of the press's series on natural resources in which this volume appears, kindly agreed to write the Foreword. Thanks also to the chair of my history department, H. Wayne Morgan, for many stimulating conversations and for his commitment to affairs of state. Finally, I am honored and grateful, as holder of the Merrick Chair in Western American History at the University of Oklahoma, for the generous and indispensable financial support that position has given to my study of the American West.

PART ONE
Water Law

The triumph of prior appropriation—the legal principle that the first to put water to a "beneficial use" has the paramount right to the future use of that water—is a complicated but compelling part of the history of the American West. At the beginning of the nineteenth century, a form of prior appropriation replaced or displaced the traditional doctrine of riparian rights in parts of Massachusetts, New York, and other eastern states. Under the riparian doctrine, the use of water was reserved to those people who owned land bordering streams. Those rights were incidental to land ownership, and they were "correlative" rather than absolute. That is, they existed only in relationship to each other—as a pool of conditional rights. Riparian owners could use water to drive mills or to sustain people or live-stock, but they could not so diminish the flow or quality of water as to injure downstream users. Industrialization placed new demands on the rivers of New England. Textile mills depended upon a uniform flow of water to drive spindles, looms, and other machines, and industrialists refused to build factories without first obtaining an exclusive right to dam streams and regulate their flow.[1]

Prior appropriation was not invented in the American West, but it was the first part of the country in which water could be used far from the channel of a living stream and became a commodity that could be bought and sold like coal, timber, or land. (The New England textile mill owners demanded "in-stream rights"—the right to use water within the existing channel rather than to divert it.) Without prior appropriation, the capital needed to transform the West into a region of dams and canals could not have been raised, and it is easy to forget that private capital reclaimed most of the West's irrigated land. (As late as the 1980s, only about one in four irrigated acres was watered by the federal government.) The three chapters in this part deal with water rights. The first provides an overview of west-ern water law in the nineteenth century, the second explores the origins of prior appropriation in two California mining districts, and the third dis-cusses the Bureau of Reclamation's attempts to limit state control over water in the first decades after passage of the Reclamation Act in 1902.

Since the 1970s, the doctrine of prior appropriation has come under increasing criticism from environmental groups, lawyers, and other

1

social critics. Prior appropriation creates absolute rights and provides little incentive to conserve water. Indeed, users are encouraged to consume more water than they need so they can maintain a claim to the largest supply possible. This misuse, in turn, leads to waterlogged fields, the buildup of alkali and salts from excessive irrigation, abandoned farms, the pollution of surface- and groundwater from pesticide runoff, damage to fish and wildlife from excessive diversion, an increased use of underground water, inadequate land use planning, and the neglect of the water needs of Native American communities. Even though the right to use water was given away for nothing by the federal government or states, prior appropriation does not recognize a "public interest" in how water will be used.[2]

The principle of first in time, first in right resolved disputes over many natural resources, including land and grazing rights. But as it applied to water, prior appropriation meant that the individual or group willing and able to produce the greatest amount of wealth in the short run should have as much water as he or it could use—even all the water in a stream—regardless of the long-range consequences for the development of agriculture and stable agricultural communities. For some decades after the California Gold Rush, older systems of water law, particularly the riparian doctrine and Hispanic communal rights, challenged prior appropriation. Initially, prior appropriation applied only to mining, but in the 1870s and 1880s, as the mining industry declined and the West's population grew, prior appropriation rapidly spread to farming and other activities. This change occurred despite warnings from many western engineers that the monopolistic character of prior appropriation posed great dangers to the region's future.

Until fairly recently, most historians of the American West assumed that prior appropriation was the by-product of an arid climate. The conversion of water into private property had a powerful appeal to earlier generations of Americans who saw the resource mainly as potential capital, which comfortably fit with Frederick Jackson Turner's view that the frontier pulverized existing law and reformed it to meet new conditions. In *The Great Plains* (1931), Walter Prescott Webb popularized the notion that climate best defined the American West, though he borrowed most of his ideas about water law from the great legal scholar, C. S. Kinney. By the time Webb wrote, the vast majority of western water lawyers considered prior appropriation the most equitable and efficient allocation system possible.[3]

Obviously, large parts of the West are arid, but there are many problems in claiming that aridity alone defined the nature of western water law. The message of both "Enterprise and Equity" and "The Origins of Western Water Law" is that culture counts for more than climate—after all, aridity did not produce prior appropriation in the Mexican communities of the Southwest. Nor did all miners support priority rights. Prior appropriation resulted from large-scale hydraulic mining in the mid-1850s and after; it was not the choice of *all* miners.[4] Miners wanted the law to serve the kind of operations they conducted at a particular time in a particular place, and they were quite comfortable with riparian rights when that doctrine best met their needs—which it often did.[5] Some miners strenuously resisted the spread of prior appropriation, and it triumphed, not because of its inherent logic or greater efficiency, but because of changing technology: the exhaustion of easily accessible placer deposits transformed the industry from a collection of independent businesses to a handful of huge companies. Prior appropriation was far from inevitable. Until a substantial number of miners became the employees of hydraulic mining companies, most favored prior appropriation only when local control over water could be sustained. It took many years for prior appropriation to sweep away alternative systems of water allocation.

Prior appropriation did not triumph in the courts of the West until the 1870s and 1880s, at a time when Congress provided little leadership or direction in the management of natural resources on the public domain. The states assumed the responsibility for administering the allocation of water almost by default—California did so for more than half a century before Congress passed the Reclamation Act of 1902. The question of what residual or inchoate rights the federal government retained in western waters—particularly on the public domain and in interstate streams—did not become a hot issue until the twentieth century. "State vs. Nation" discusses the Reclamation Service's attempt to define and assert federal water rights after 1902. The Reclamation Act raised the prospect that the federal government might take control of all the West's surplus or unclaimed water, at least in the interstate and boundary streams. Just as miners opposed private monopolies of water by capitalists, western politicians, land developers, and farmers feared that a government water monopoly would unsettle existing rights and reduce land values. Public monopoly was no less feared than private monopoly. Both were signs of an economy in poor health; both were threats to economic liberty.

Most westerners believed that government should foster and encourage the construction of dams and canals, as it fostered the development of railroads and industry, but it should not impose a direct regulatory cost on the public. Prior appropriation reflected the late nineteenth-century assumption that self-seeking individuals and corporations could best serve economic development, and that discrete decisions made in the marketplace generally contributed to the greater good. Applicants for water could not be denied if their use of water served a useful purpose. It did not matter if a junior appropriator worked better land, or raised higher value crops, or used the water for a purpose that created greater wealth, or even that a senior diversion limited urban development. Water rights were a matter for the courts to decide, not state engineering offices or other administrative agencies, but the courts had no way to determine how much water was being used or to what effect other than through the testimony of the water users themselves.

When westerners began clamoring for the construction of storage reservoirs in the 1880s and after, there was no absolute shortage of water. The main problem was that senior appropriators monopolized the summer runoff. Most western streams carried their greatest volume in late April, May, and June, while most irrigation occurred in July, August, and early September. Therefore, dams solved the fundamental hydrologic problem of how to use water from the spring thaw in the late summer, when it was most needed. The construction of storage reservoirs, like the twentieth-century use of underground water, begged the issue of conservation, bypassing the need for reform in water laws by augmenting the existing supply rather than by reallocating it.

There were three major attempts to reform prior appropriation in the nineteenth century. In the 1870s and 1880s, a handful of California reformers argued that the only way to repair prior appropriation was for the state to condemn private water rights, assume the operation of all dams and canals, and sell or lease water to individual consumers. At least in theory, this proposal gave all users equal access to the variable supply. A state system would eliminate "rights" in the traditional sense of the word—absolute and perpetual grants would cease—and this allocation system would be elastic enough to adapt to new needs and conditions. The campaign for a centralized state system was part of the backlash against the growth of large corporations in California during the 1870s, land and water companies as well as railroads. Yet most Californians feared overlarge government as much as overlarge business, and the threat to established rights, as well as the cost of maintaining the administrative bureaucracy needed to allocate water, limited the appeal of a state system.[6]

The irrigation district offered a second alternative. As a result of the long battle between prior appropriation and riparian rights in the San Joaquin Valley, the California Supreme Court offered water users the option of organizing into districts and controlling their own water rights.[7] The California legislature followed the court's lead by adopting the Wright Act in 1887, which allowed district residents to tax all property within their borders to pay for extending old irrigation systems and building new ones. The Wright Act's basic objective was to finance arid land reclamation, but many proponents of the law thought that by giving districts the power to condemn *all* water rights, riparian or appropriative, the law would also quiet litigation. Stockton's *Daily Independent* noted that the Wright Act would prevent "all schemes for the wholesale seizure of the running water of the State under any claim of law whatever. If it will accomplish this, as it will do, it will preserve the water for the use of those who need it. . . . The Wright bill is all that stands between the rich water monopolist and the poor farmer."[8]

The Wright Act did little to temper prior appropriation, nor did a third alternative to unrestricted prior appropriation: state administrative control over water, which became increasingly popular in the late 1880s and 1890s. Although Wyoming adopted an ambitious model water code in 1890, when it entered the Union, it could do so only because irrigation was limited there and gold and silver mining had had relatively little impact on that state's economy. In California, Colorado, and other states where irrigation was common, those who favored administrative control did so to improve the system of filing and recording water rights—in effect, to make prior appropriation more efficient—not to increase state regulatory control over who used water or how it was used.[9]

The Reclamation Act of 1902 gave the federal government the job of building western irrigation projects, and at the time it was adopted, supporters estimated that federal reclamation would reclaim from 50 to 150 million acres. This never happened, in part because of divided control: the federal government administered the public domain, but, even on national irrigation projects, control over the issuance and administration of water rights remained with the states. The Reclamation Bureau tried but failed to assert paramount national rights in court. It also failed to persuade the states to adopt model water laws sympathetic to the needs of the Bureau of Reclamation. In the end, it was forced to carry its case to friendly federal courts and support interstate water compacts, by which the states divided interstate streams among themselves with the blessing of Congress and federal agencies. Yet because the Reclamation Bureau never formally repudiated national water rights, it left a legacy of suspicion in the West that fueled frequent campaigns to transfer part or all of the remaining public lands to the states so that control over land and water could be unified.

Prior appropriation and state control over water rights were profoundly decentralizing forces in a federal system of governance. Perhaps there was no real alternative. Historian Donald Worster has argued that the administration of water rights was best left to farmers themselves, organized in the autonomous irrigation districts favored by John Wesley Powell.[10] I have suggested that national control was another alternative. Without the interposition of the federal government, it seems unlikely that individual farmers could have protected their rights from land and water speculators.[11] Yet we would agree that prior appropriation had and has severe weaknesses. Eventually, prior appropriation must give way to a new allocation system that pays as much attention to protecting the physical environment as to protecting vested rights, and to protecting common interests as well as individual needs. Nevertheless, in the 1990s prior appropriation remains the rule of law in most parts of the American West.

CHAPTER ONE

Enterprise and Equity:
A Critique of Western Water Law
in the Nineteenth Century

Half a century ago, Walter Prescott Webb devoted twenty-one pages in *The Great Plains* to a discussion of western water law.[1] Webb became the first American historian to explore water law systematically. For all its flaws, some of which are mentioned in this chapter, his work raised vital questions about the adaptation of institutions to the physical environment and the relationship of law to economic development. Unfortunately, historians of the western half of the nation have been slow to follow his lead. Most surveys of the nineteenth-century West pay scant attention to water and none at all to water law. Recently, a handful of scholars have provided good descriptions of many of the laws and have analyzed important legal conflicts. But they pay inadequate attention to the antecedents, purposes, and economic consequences of western water rights as they evolved in the last century. They have neglected the critical relationship between the law and economic growth.[2]

This chapter is not a systematic summary of western water law. It is built around five arguments rather than a central thesis. These are: first, that economic needs and conditions determined the shape of water law more than aridity or any other single physical factor; second, that prior appropriation[3] grew logically out of an adaptable common law and appeared in New England years before it developed in the West; third, that while the doctrine of prior appropriation stimulated economic development, it suffered from profound weaknesses and ultimately may have worked against the "common good"; fourth, that in many parts of the nineteenth-century West, riparian water rights[4] and Spanish or Mexican communal water laws offered viable legal alternatives to prior appropriation; and, fifth, that the desire of old-timers to bolster their interests in competition with newcomers best explains water law reform in the late nineteenth century. At the heart of the chapter are two assumptions: that the law is a conscious product of many discrete economic choices, not simply an elaboration of abstract legal principles; and that the initial dependence of the West on mining prevented greater legal consideration of the just and efficient allocation and distribution of water to agriculture. Not all these ideas are "revisionist" or original nor can they be explored fully in one chapter. But taken together, I hope they provide a useful overview and suggest a new, broader way of looking at the role of water law in western history.

In virtually every study of western water law, statutes and court decisions appear in isolation, the product of immaculate conception, with no apparent kinship to law in the eastern half of the nation. The work of the nation's most prominent legal historians has had little influence on the study of water law even though it suggests that nineteenth-century property laws developed from the same assumptions in all states. For years, James Willard Hurst, probably the nation's foremost legal historian, has called for a functional or "instrumental" approach to the law. Hurst maintains that in most state courts time-honored legal postulates and dogma played little part in deciding how to allocate natural resources. As early as 1950, he declared that "[w]e shall get a more realistic grasp of the part law has played in United States history if we keep in mind the readiness of Americans to use it as a means to bring about immediate practical results." A decade and a half later, in his magisterial history of the nineteenth-century lumber industry in Wisconsin, he noted that Americans cherished the belief that "it was common sense and it was good, to use law to multiply the productive power of the economy." To the notion that Americans saw the law "more as an instrument for desired immediate results than as a statement of carefully legitimated, long-range values," what he called "the release of energy," Hurst added many ancillary ideas. He believed that nineteenth-century law promoted economic growth and did not just remove legal restrictions or limit the state's regulatory powers. Hurst asserted that the state used its power to affect the economy positively as much in the nineteenth-century heyday of laissez-faire as in the twentieth-century era of administrative regulation. He believed that trial and appellate court decisions revealed better the symbiotic relationship between the economy and legal system than U.S. Supreme Court judgments. And finally, Hurst recognized that government allocates property in many ways, not just through taxing and spending but also through the distribution of public lands, the issuance of franchises, or the manipulation of the money system. Hurst worked "at the borderland of law and economic history," as one of his admirers aptly noted. His consideration of how government allocated resources through the operation of the law broke new ground for a generation of scholars.[5]

Other legal historians, including Harry Scheiber and Morton Horwitz, have made significant contributions to Hurst's instrumentalist interpretation of property law.[6] Horwitz has described how the changing economy of New England in the early nineteenth century forced a redefinition of water rights in common law. After 1815 the proliferation of large-scale integrated cotton mills dramatically increased the need for water power. The eighteenth-century assumption that the law was a fixed, unchanging standard that judges simply sought to discover and interpret, and that attention to legal precedent assured that judges would not stray from pre-existing laws and principles, worked well in a stable, rural, agricultural society where nature limited wealth largely to profits derived directly from the land. But the dawn of a new economic order challenged old assumptions and, according to Horwitz, "the evolving law of water rights had greater impact than any other branch of the law on the effort to adapt private law doctrines to the movement for economic growth."[7]

The common law originally reflected the belief that rivers were part of God's plan as revealed in nature. God not only determined the course of streams, He dictated that, in Blackstone's words, water was "a moving, wandering thing," whose very nature defied conversion to property. Consequently, any attempt to dam or divert a stream was at the least an unnatural act. The construction of mills and factories produced several new kinds of legal conflict: actions by downstream riparian owners against landowners whose dams upstream interfered with the natural flow; suits by mill owners whose operations had been curtailed by downstream dams which, by backing up water, made the flow upstream sluggish and unpredictable; and, finally, riparian owners whose land had been flooded by dams. Between 1820 and 1831, the productive capacity of New England cotton mills increased six times. More water rights cases were decided in the decade between 1824 and 1833 than in the entire history of the common law. "By the middle of the nineteenth century," Horwitz concludes, "the legal system had been reshaped to the advantage of men of commerce and industry at the expense of farmers, workers, consumers, and other less powerful groups within the society." The law had "actively promoted a legal redistribution of wealth against the weakest groups in the society."[8]

The growth of factories in the East posed as much of a challenge to traditional riparian rights as the development of mining and irrigation in the West. In 1844 Massachusetts Chief Justice Lemuel Shaw declared that "[the] proprietor who first erects his dam for such a purpose has a right to maintain it, as against the proprietors above and below; and to this extent, a prior occupancy gives a prior title to such use." This decision, erected on the principle of "first in time, first in right," placed economic development ahead of equal access. Water had become property detached from the land, and prior appropriation offered businessmen a monopoly subsidy just as special franchises and charters did.[9]

Webb can be forgiven for declaring that there was "little occasion" to modify water rights in the East before 1850, but students of western water law have continued to suggest that common law water rights constituted a relatively changeless, static system.[10] Many western judges and legislators—cut off from adequate law libraries and a community of lawyers—did rely heavily on obsolete, traditional expositions of the law. They were simply unaware of how eastern courts modified the common law before the Civil War. Nevertheless, western courts often applauded the adaptability and sufficiency of common law principles. In an 1857 case, the California Supreme Court noted that in the absence of "direct precedent, as well as without specific legislation, we have been compelled to apply to this anomalous state of things the analogies of the common law and the more expanded principles of equitable justice." In an 1872 Colorado case upholding appropriation, the court maintained that the "principles of the [common] law are undoubtedly of universal application." And in 1907 the Arizona court proclaimed that "[t]he essence of the common law is flexibility and adaptability. It is not a body of fixed rules, but is the best product of human reason applied to the premises of the ordinary and extraordinary conditions of life. . . . Should the common law become so crystallized that its expressions take the same form, wherever the common-law system prevails, irrespective of physical, social, or other conditions peculiar to the locality, it would cease to be the common law of the history, and would be but an inelastic and arbitrary code."[11] Not only did many court decisions proclaim the flexibility of the common law, but some early decisions freely mixed elements of riparian rights and appropriation.[12]

The failure to recognize the adaptability of common law has contributed to the assumption that nature dictated the evolution of western water law. Robert Dunbar, the foremost student of western water law, flatly declares, "Climate has been the determining factor in the development of western water law." And Gordon Bakken, who has written the best general surveys of law in the West, states, "Pioneer legislators and judges in the Rocky Mountain States created the law of prior appropriation to deal with this problem of aridity."[13] Certainly, many court decisions sustain this interpretation.[14] It is also reinforced by the fact that the driest states in the West—Nevada, Arizona, Utah, Colorado, Wyoming, Idaho, and New Mexico—recognize only prior appropriation, while the states with humid as well as arid and semiarid sections—California, Kansas, Montana, Nebraska, North and South Dakota, Oregon, Texas, Washington, and Oklahoma—recognize riparian as well as appropriative rights. Nevertheless, aridity is, at best, half an answer to why prior appropriation was embraced with such ardor in so many parts of the West.

The affection of western courts and legislatures for prior appropriation can only be understood in light of regional economic conditions in the last half of the nineteenth century. Aridity was a problem, but western agriculture was in its infancy in the 1850s and 1860s, and farmers had little influence in state or territorial legislatures. Moreover, most mining was conducted in the region's major mountain ranges where there was plenty of water, although not always in the right places. Lawmakers perceived the region as an economic wilderness punctuated by oases of human activity. Transportation was poor, investment capital limited, and labor scarce. Most who went west in search of gold or silver saw the region's potential solely in economic terms, and many did not intend to stay. The West had its share of boosters from the beginning, but the golden dream of an empire on the Pacific seemed visionary to most residents of the region. The West's economic promise was in mining and perhaps stock-raising. Not surprisingly, in 1855 the California Supreme Court declared that "[t]he Legislature of our State in the wise exercise of its discretion has seen proper to foster and protect the mining interest as paramount to all others," a judgment it reiterated in 1875 when it proclaimed that prior appropriation had been adopted "to distribute the bounty of the government among the greatest number of persons, so as most rapidly to develop the hidden resources of this region."[15]

Western courts and legislatures faced the fundamental problem of how to stimulate a fledgling industry whose activities were confined largely to the public domain. Here *was* a problem very different from those encountered by eastern courts. Initially, miners needed to turn away water to expose streambeds and get at placer deposits. But within a few years, especially in California, they began to divert water and transport it great distances to wash away topsoil in search of ancient streambeds. Before the 1870s, virtually all water suits pertained to mining and milling on government land, not to agriculture on private lands. Irrigation was very limited, and farmers often used water provided by mining companies to raise crops sold in mining camps.

There could be no riparian rights where the federal government owned the land, and by the mid-1850s it still had not defined the rights of miners. Hence, all privileges were as between individuals, not absolute. Not only did prior appropriation allow water to be treated as private property, which the mining industry demanded, but it was the only possible solution that followed the well-established precedent of disseisin rights, the right of a landholder to evict a trespasser when title to the land was held by a third party. Since miners on the public lands were disseisors of the United States, the earliest possession took priority, in both water and mineral claims.[16]

California courts warned repeatedly that prior appropriation had not and could not replace the riparian doctrine. In an 1859 case, the state supreme court declared that prior appropriation was "undoubtedly . . . a very convenient rule," but it denied that the privilege constituted a grant from the federal government, which had not spoken on the water rights issue. Therefore, prior appropriation was a makeshift which could be over-

turned by Congress at any time. Even more important, the court emphasized that "this exceptional privilege is, of course, confined to the public
domain." It reiterated this maxim in its 1884 *Lux v. Haggin* decision.
"After carefully examining all the cases bearing on this question," it declared,
"we are unable to find one in which it is held, or even suggested, that outside of the mining districts the common-law doctrine of riparian rights
does not apply with the same force and effect in this state as elsewhere."
Some states, led by Colorado and Wyoming, did not accept this premise.
But California was not unique. The Montana Supreme Court maintained
that "[i]t is not claimed that the decision of any court, either in this Territory or California, has pretended to establish the doctrine of prior appropriation . . . to agricultural lands."[17]

The mining legacy boxed Congress into a corner. Its members knew
even less about water than they did about mining. State courts took the
absence of congressional legislation dealing with mining claims on the
public domain as tacit acceptance of their judgments. Finally, in 1866, 1870,
and 1877, Congress enacted measures recognizing the right of settlers to
tap streams flowing through the public lands for mining, agriculture, and
other purposes so long as water users conformed to local customs and procedures.[18] In fact, the 1877 legislation, the Desert Land Act, formally
restricted water use to "bona-fide prior appropriation." Many legal scholars
have assumed that Congress was, in effect, voting for appropriation over
riparian rights or rejecting riparian rights as inapplicable to the West. But
since California and other states had encouraged appropriation, the lawmakers had little choice but to honor these rights.

State legislatures and courts extended prior appropriation to agriculture by applying questionable precedents culled from mining cases. This
process has never been adequately examined by historians. Nevertheless,
since the 1870s, if not before, plenty of farmers, lawyers, and land and
water companies preached the doctrine's virtues, and many students of the
law followed their lead. In 1911 a political scientist proclaimed riparianism
as "hopelessly inadequate," but dignified appropriation as "the only doctrine suited to an arid agriculture." Walter Prescott Webb declared that
"history . . . makes clear the necessity of . . . prior appropriation." In 1935
Carey McWilliams lauded appropriation as "the fairest and most economical and the fullest use of an inadequate water supply," and in 1953 Wallace
Stegner declared it "an essential criterion" in an "irrigating country."[19]

Many nineteenth-century scientists and engineers did not share this
enthusiasm. By mandating prior appropriation on the public lands, the
Desert Land Act touched off a mad scramble by speculative land and
water companies to claim water for new projects, many of which were
chimerical. In his famous 1878 report on the arid lands, John Wesley
Powell warned that private ditch companies demanded monopolistic

control over the region's water supply. Once they gained a foothold, "evils will result therefrom that generations may not be able to correct, and the very men who are now lauded as benefactors in the [arid] country will, in the ungovernable reaction which is sure to come, be denounced as oppressors of the people." This fear did not abate. When Powell spoke to the constitutional convention of Dakota Territory in 1889, he urged: "If you fail in making a constitution in any other respect, fail not in this one. Fix it in your constitution that no corporation—no body of men—no capital can get possession and right of your waters. . . . Such a provision will prevent your agricultural resources from falling into the hands of a few." Powell rejected both riparian rights and appropriation. Instead he proposed the creation of autonomous water districts whose boundaries conformed to natural drainage basins rather than to county or state lines. Within such districts, farmers could tailor-make water laws to suit their particular needs.[20]

No state better illustrated the dangers of prior appropriation than California. At the south end of the San Joaquin Valley, the Kern County Land and Water Company—the largest irrigation enterprise in the West—pieced together an empire of 300,000 acres and claimed three times more water from the Kern River than the stream had ever carried. Control over the river allowed the company to buy up smaller ditches and build new canals until it established a water monopoly in the county. In the 1870s the company was hailed for making the desert blossom—though largely by farmers whose land appreciated in value as it was provided with water. But during the 1880s, the enterprise became increasingly unpopular. Irrigators who complained about the cost of water often had their supplies reduced or cut off. In addition, the company filed more than 100 suits against farmers who refused to sell their water rights, forcing many to give up their land and flee the county. It also used local officials, including judges, sheriffs, and tax assessors (who were owned or controlled by the company), to harass recalcitrant settlers. Little wonder that William Hammond Hall, California state engineer from 1878 to 1889, advised his colleague, Elwood Mead of Wyoming: "I do not believe in the distribution or acquirement of water rights by *appropriation*. It is a word which should never have been admitted into Water Rights Legislation. . . . To 'appropriate' presupposes that the thing taken is without ownership, like a wild beast of the forest or of the plain . . . to be shot down and dragged out by the first brute that came in sight of it."[21]

Prior appropriation provided great economic incentives and opportunities for investors in irrigation projects, but it was grossly inefficient as a tool to parcel out a scarce resource. In most western states during the nineteenth century, appropriators had to meet only one condition—put their diversion to a "beneficial use." Gordon Bakken has commented that without a "beneficial application the asset remained open to subsequent use by the numerous operatives vying for the valuable commodity." But this apparent limitation was largely ineffective because, as one legal scholar recently noted, "[p]ractically all of the farmers, miners, manufacturers, power companies, and cities of the West met this test when they took the water, since each had a practical wealth-producing use in mind. Each use advanced the development of the resources of the country."[22] Farmers routinely used far more water than they actually needed because beneficial use did not mean either reasonable or economical use. Moreover, use varied year by year, so, of necessity, rights had an elastic quality in court. Farmers might not irrigate at all in wet years, and in dry years might leave a field fallow. Courts generally recognized claims for more water than was actually needed if an irrigator expected to expand his delivery system. The farmer who claimed water to irrigate 160 acres, but initially watered only 60 acres, usually received the full amount if he presented well-conceived plans to cultivate the entire acreage eventually. Until the water was needed, he could sell the surplus. Moreover, "paper claims" could be maintained for years through minimal work on ditches, which explains why the Salt River in Arizona had been appropriated 25 times over by 1900 and the San Joaquin River 172 times over.[23]

The courts had neither the expertise nor revenue to gather stream flow data, check to see how much water was actually being used, or determine the quantity actually needed to raise different crops in different soils. Nor could they call on state officials to provide impartial information. The courts relied almost exclusively on the testimony of interested witnesses, and extravagant claims often received the benefit of the doubt. For example, during the 1880s Colorado water decrees promised as much as five times the volume of water ditches were capable of carrying.[24] To make matters worse, different courts granted different amounts of water to irrigate the same kind of land and crops. Such allocations promoted expensive and inconclusive litigation. In 1893 John Norton Pomeroy, one of the few scholars of western water law sympathetic to riparian rights, concluded that prior appropriation had been "a most fruitful cause of litigation in California . . . but this is a feeble illustration of the litigation and controversy which must arise from the statutes of Colorado and of the various territories when they come into full operation upon an increasing population." Pomeroy recognized that litigation resulted as much, if not more, from conflicts between rival appropriators as from contests between appropriators and riparian owners.[25]

Comprehensive studies of the optimum amount of water required to raise different crops in different soils did not begin until the late 1890s; meanwhile, most farmers simply assumed that more was better. They had far more incentive to waste water than to save it. The courts recognized use as the basic criterion for determining how much water to award individual claimants, even if the amount used was excessive. By diverting the largest amount possible, farmers could reserve water either for future use or sale. Moreover, companies often sold water by the number of acres irrigated rather than by the volume of water actually used, and farmers claimed far more water than they applied to the land because nineteenth-century irrigation systems were grossly inefficient and lost tremendous quantities of water through seepage and evaporation. The longer and smaller the canal, the greater the loss. In 1903 Secretary of Agriculture James Wilson estimated that canals which carried 100 cubic feet per second lost about 1 percent of their volume per mile while those carrying 25–50 c.f.s. lost over 5 percent per mile.[26]

Given these weaknesses in the doctrine of prior appropriation, what legal alternatives did westerners have to allocate the region's water? For decades historians have charged that riparian rights hindered western economic development.[27] Robert Dunbar maintained that riparian rights were "poorly suited to irrigation-based communities" because they "deprived millions of prospective farms of water."[28] Yet the riparian doctrine had many advantages over appropriation, particularly in the nineteenth century before massive reservoir projects dramatically increased the supply available for irrigation. The region's most productive land was the alluvial soil adjoining streams, and it was also the cheapest to irrigate. Riparian land did not require long canals, nor did riparian owners face the high cost of condemning land for canal rights-of-way. Moreover, the irrigation of riparian land permitted maximum "return flow," water that seeped back into streams from saturated land. And since riparian titles permitted only the reasonable use of water, rather than an absolute property right, riparian rights easily expanded or contracted in response to seasonal fluctuations in the water supply. They were "correlative" because they had no existence apart from each other. Riparian owners had an unquestionable right to sufficient water for domestic uses and stock; all other diversions existed at the sufferance of riparian neighbors.

Many early western courts recognized these virtues. Despite inconsistencies in its early decisions, the California Supreme Court never completely lost sight of common-law principles. In 1853 it declared prior appropriation "impracticable in application." "The right of property in water is *usufructuary*, and consists not so much of the fluid itself as the advantage of its use. The owner of land through which a stream flows, merely transmits the water over its surface, having the right to its reasonable use during its passage. The right is not in the *corpus* of the water." In 1855 it proclaimed: "The right to water must be treated in this State as it has always been treated, as a right running with the land . . . and as such, [it] has none of the characteristics of mere personalty." In the following year the court insisted that common law principles had "abundantly sufficed for the determination of all disputes which have come before us . . . we have neither modified its rules, nor have we attempted to legislate upon any pretended ground of their insufficiency." And in an 1865 case, the court summarily rejected "the notion, which has become quite prevalent, that the rules of the common law touching water rights have been materially modified in this state. . . . This notion is without substantial foundation."[29]

Nor was California unique. In 1871 the Nevada Supreme Court rejected the argument that in a hot, arid climate like Nevada's, riparian appropriators ought to be able to divert an entire stream for irrigation. It defended the rights of other riparian owners on the stream "who have an *equal need and an equal right.*" In the following year the same court held that riparian rights gave "the greatest right to the greatest number, authorizing each to make a reasonable use of [the water], providing he does no injury to the others equally entitled to it with himself; whilst the rule of prior appropriation here advocated would authorize the first person who might choose to make use of or divert a stream to use or even waste the whole, to the utter ruin of others who might wish it." In 1890 a dissenting Idaho opinion questioned whether appropriators should be permitted to sell water to others and thereby prevent riparian owners from using water that flowed by their property. And in 1903, Nebraska's Supreme Court proclaimed: "[W]e doubt whether a more equitable starting point for a system of irrigation law may be found [than the riparian doctrine]." John Norton Pomeroy echoed this judgment in his survey of water law in the Pacific Coast states. Pomeroy maintained that no law could "tend to the peace and prosperity of society which attempts to violate and override natural laws and natural rights, immutable truths which exist in the regular order of nature." He urged that smaller streams be reserved entirely for riparian irrigation, and that prior appropriation should be permitted on larger streams only after the needs of riparian farmers had been satisfied.[30]

Virtually all the cases cited above were decided before the dramatic growth of private irrigation projects in the late 1870s and 1880s. During those decades, traditional riparian rights were abandoned in Nevada, Colorado, and Idaho and restricted in many other states. Nevertheless, common law principles lived on. In Utah the Mormon church initially doled out water, and the state did not formally acknowledge appropriation until 1880 or 1897.[31] Mining played no part in the formulation of water rights and water laws; irrigation took precedence from the beginning. Church control over natural resources, and the dominance of agriculture in the state's economy, permitted the attachment of water rights to the land. As Utah's population grew, state courts recognized a form of prior appropriation, but established two categories of rights, primary (early) and secondary (later). Secondary claims were honored only in years there was sufficient water to serve all primary rights. And in each category, water was distributed equally, not according to strict priority; in dry seasons each user's supply was cut back. In effect, rights were correlative, and Robert Dunbar correctly observes that "the Utah water right was a blend of the appropriative and the riparian."[32]

The Utah example is more evidence that the nature of the local economy, rather than aridity, did most to shape western water law. The early courts and legislatures of Utah, Idaho, Montana, Colorado, and Wyoming all tried to balance riparianism and appropriation. In 1861 Colorado's territorial legislature authorized diversions for irrigation, but limited irrigation to riparian land and provided for the appointment of water commissioners to divide the water "in a just and equitable proportion" during dry spells.[33] In the following year, the lawmakers declared that "there shall be at all times left sufficient water in said stream for the use of miners and farmers along said stream," suggesting once again that riparian users had the strongest rights.[34] The 1864 legislature acknowledged the preeminent needs of mining when it ordered that no stream could be diverted "to the detriment of any miner, millmen or others along the line of said stream, who may have a priority of right." However, it tempered this restriction by repeating that "there shall be at all times left sufficient water in said stream for the use of miners and agriculturists along said stream."[35]

The principles contained in the Colorado laws spread throughout the mountain West, but, as in Colorado, they were gradually debased and diluted. In 1865 Montana's first irrigation statute limited diversions to riparian landowners and provided for local commissions to apportion water in times of scarcity. Ten years later, Wyoming created commissions and charged them with dividing the water in lean years "as they may in their best judgement think best for the interests of all parties concerned." However, the watermasters were required to observe "the legal rights of all" and nothing in the law could "impair the prior vested rights of any mill or ditch owner, or other person to use the water of any . . . water course." The nature of these "prior rights" was not explained or defined; neither prior appropriation nor riparian rights were mentioned directly. Local justices of the peace appointed Montana's commissioners, and the county courts selected Wyoming's. But when Idaho passed its first agricultural water law in 1881, it allowed private water companies to appoint the commissioners. No water could be diverted without permission from a watermaster or his deputy, but the law pledged to respect "the vested rights of individual companies or corporations . . . to the use and control of water which is or may be their private property." In the 1860s, when plenty of unclaimed water remained in most western streams, legislators could easily put community needs first. And at least a few jurists saw the implications of these laws. For example, Justice C. J. Wade of Montana maintained that the 1865 territorial law—which was overturned by the territorial supreme court in 1870 on grounds that only the courts could decide what was a "just and equitable" distribution of property—had been designed "to utterly abolish and annihilate the doctrine of prior appropriation, and to establish an equal distribution of the waters of any given stream in the agricultural districts of the Territory."[36]

Riparian rights were not the only casualty of the corporate irrigation boom of 1877–1893; laws inherited from Mexico suffered a similar fate. The nature of Spanish and Mexican water law has not been well understood. The Mexican government occasionally made exclusive water grants to individuals, but these carried no clear priority and were revocable by the government. Prior appropriation did not exist as a system, and community needs took precedence over individual rights, including the rights of riparian landowners.[37] The basic purpose of Mexican law was not to stimulate private enterprise but to irrigate the maximum acreage. "Legal rights, whether they be corporate or individual, did not constitute a single, overbearing consideration in the adjudication of water disputes," Michael Meyer has written. "[J]udges were at pains to indicate to their superiors that their verdicts had been rendered with the common good in mind." Mexican water law derived from long-established principles inherited from Spain: that running water belonged to the king or state; that its use was common to all; that irrigation was permissible only with the approval of the government; that wherever possible irrigation should be a community endeavor; and that which lands to irrigate should be decided according to the feasibility of getting water to them, not on their date of settlement.[38]

Surprisingly, major scholars of water law such as Kinney, Wiel, and Dunbar never discuss the Spanish and Mexican legacy, perhaps because it was so antagonistic to *both* riparian rights and prior appropriation. In 1854 the California legislature ratified a community control system that had prevailed in southern California since the Mexican period. It authorized the creation of water commissions in townships within the agricultural counties of San Diego, San Bernardino, Santa Barbara, Napa, Los Angeles, Solano, Contra Costa, Colusa, and Tulare. These commissions were required "to examine and direct such water courses, and apportion the water thereof among the inhabitants of their district, determine the time of using the same, and upon petition of a majority of persons liable to work upon ditches, lay out and construct ditches." The commissioners could condemn land for rights-of-way, levy taxes to pay for maintenance and construction, and apportion water. The law contained two significant restrictions: it did not apply to counties where mining was the major industry, and it prohibited diversions that interfered with the rights of downstream riparian owners.[39]

This law served community needs well. At the time, most irrigation works were inexpensive—constructed by groups of farmers, much as county roads were laid out in the nineteenth century. All available capital poured into mining, so the 1854 stature provided a useful tool to develop California's agricultural resources. It did not sanction absolute individual rights to water. The legislature, or at least the Los Angeles legislator responsible for drafting the law, must have recognized that prior appropriation would serve no useful purpose.

Little is known about how the 1854 law operated, but it was promising enough to be amended and expanded many times as the legislature tried to tailor the public control principle to particular counties.[40] In San Bernardino County, which had the largest community irrigation system outside Los Angeles, the law prohibited new settlers from taking up land along streams already fully committed to irrigation. Perhaps the most "revolutionary" aspect of the legislation, though it simply reaffirmed Mexican practices, was that it reserved all water in certain streams to public use. Unfortunately, after 1862, when the legislature granted private irrigation companies the right to condemn land for canal rights-of-way, these laws were emasculated. In 1866 the Tulare County water commission lost the power to levy taxes and appoint independent watermasters to allocate water; now all appointees had to be drawn from nominees proposed by the county's private water companies. Two years later the legislature formally subordinated communal water rights to those acquired under prior appropriation.[41]

By the late 1870s, as corporate irrigation spread to nonriparian land, conflicts erupted between riparian owners and appropriators in many parts of the San Joaquin Valley, and the system of public control was all but forgotten. Its demise suggests that while California's courts took the lead in molding prior appropriation to fit mining, after 1862 the legislature fitted appropriation to new uses on lands outside the public domain. One cardinal principle of constitutional law is that vested rights require protection even if the foundation of those rights is shaky. So the California Supreme Court accepted statutory property rights even though it preferred the riparian doctrine.

This same transformation occurred in New Mexico and Texas, though at a slower rate. Since few Anglo-American settlers entered New Mexico until the 1860s, the assembly blocked any change in the status quo and repassed many laws that prevailed before 1846.[42] In 1851 and 1852 it reaffirmed the system of community acequias. Statutes adopted in 1861, 1863, 1866, and 1880 reinforced and expanded these laws, even though the legislature also granted private companies the right to run irrigation ditches in 1874. The lawmakers proclaimed irrigation the primary use of water in the territory; for example, no mills could be constructed that reduced the value of a stream to farmers. All owners of tillable land were required to provide labor to maintain community water systems in proportion to the size of their farms, cultivated or not. Justices of the peace called landowners together each year to elect one or more overseers or watermasters. The watermasters were required to distribute water—in the words of the 1852 law—"with justice and impartiality," according to the acreage farmed and the crops cultivated by each settler. No one could tap into an acequia without permission, and those who wasted water, or shirked their responsibility to maintain the ditches, faced stiff fines.[43]

Texas differed from New Mexico, Arizona, and California in that mining played little part in its economy, the state contained no national public domain, and irrigation was unnecessary in the heavily settled, humid, eastern section.[44] Nevertheless, as in much of the American Southwest, traditional patterns of use persisted.[45] Lawmakers from San Antonio and El Paso, where most irrigation occurred in the nineteenth century, enacted a community irrigation statute in 1852. Because irrigation played only a small part in Texas agriculture during the nineteenth century, the legislature did not adopt appropriation until 1889, and the 1852 law was not repealed until 1913.[46]

The Mexican system eventually disappeared, but prior appropriation might still have been remodeled. In the late nineteenth century, critics of appropriation recommended that the western states grant more authority over the allocation of water to state administrative officials. They proposed the creation of state engineering offices to measure streams, administer the filing of claims, maintain centralized records of rights, and supervise diversions. They also asked that rights be attached to the land as an alternative to absolute ownership; that domestic use take precedence over all other water uses; that no water be diverted without formal permission from the state; that the amount granted be based on immediate rather than anticipated needs; and that, in times of scarcity, some provisions be made for rotation of diversions. Reform first came to Colorado and Wyoming, then spread to Nebraska in 1892, Idaho in 1895, Utah in 1897, and by 1913 to virtually every other western state including California. However, the degree of reform varied. Colorado's constitution declared that all water not previously appropriated belonged to the state while Wyoming's provided that *all* water belonged to the state. Wyoming water laws also permitted administrative officials to reject water claims not deemed in the public interest, while in Colorado, and most western states, insufficient water was the only justification for turning down a claim. Only Wyoming and Nebraska successfully tied water rights to the land; in the other states water could be bought and sold independently. They were also the only two states to permit the adjudication of water rights by administrative commissions rather than by the courts.[47]

Most legal scholars have seen the expansion of formal state administrative control over water as a substantial reform. Moses Lasky, one of the twentieth-century West's prominent water lawyers, declared, "[T]he methods and machinery of administration adopted to enforce the doctrine of prior-appropriation were themselves an admission of the failure of the doctrine and resulted in a change from it." Unquestionably, these reforms were motivated in part by a quest for efficiency and a desire to limit the authority of the courts. Gordon Bakken concludes that the "reconstruction" of prior appropriation symbolized the erosion of frontier individualism. "Lawmakers not only shifted legal direction away from first users but also acknowledged the wasteful practice born on the frontier and tried to maximize the efficient use of water." To use Bakken's phrases, "distributive administration" displaced "individual appropriation."[48]

Bakken's conclusion does not draw a careful enough distinction between the letter of the law and the application of the law. In most states water law reform did not so much represent an assertion of power against "the interests" as an attempt by the interests to shore up their rights, especially against newcomers. This was particularly obvious in Colorado. There, most water laws enacted in the 1870s and early 1880s grew out of conflicts along the Cache La Poudre, a stream tapped first in 1865, then by the Greeley Colony in 1870. A major drought in 1874 underscored the need for an orderly method to divide the water between farmers in the colony and more recent settlers upstream. At the state constitutional convention in January 1876, a resolution was introduced calling for state ownership of water and laws "to secure a just and equitable distribution of the water" and "promote the greatest good to the greatest number of citizens." The resolution said nothing about appropriation and received no support. As finally adopted, Article 16, Section 5, of the Colorado Constitution not only confirmed and protected existing claims; it restricted all future rights to appropriation.[49]

That Wyoming went far beyond other western states in drafting laws that put "public needs" first was partly due to Elwood Mead, who wrote the provisions on water in its constitution and served as its first state engineer. But Wyoming water law was also the result of economic conditions legal historians have largely ignored. First, Wyoming had a much larger supply of unappropriated water than other western states and a relatively small population. Second, unlike California and Colorado, mining had never been extensive, so prior appropriation had not put down deep roots. Third, the range cattle industry, upon which Wyoming was so dependent, suffered a severe blow from the blizzard of 1886–1887 and drought of the late 1880s; the state's future seemed bleak unless it could attract small farmers by guaranteeing them an adequate, cheap water supply. Finally,

Wyoming did not have large, established communities of farmers with vested water rights, such as those at Greeley in Colorado or Fresno in California. In short, the whole economic context was different. That the "Wyoming Idea"—which granted substantial quasi-judicial powers to the state engineer and water commission—could be adopted enthusiastically in Wyoming but win so little support elsewhere becomes understandable when we look at the different economic conditions throughout the arid and semiarid West. In states or territories with an established, flourishing irrigation industry, comprehensive water law reform—even in the name of justice and efficiency—posed more of an economic threat than opportunity. While many states borrowed *parts* of the Wyoming system, only Nebraska, the Dakotas, and Oklahoma adopted it whole. In none of these was irrigation a vital part of agricultural development. The arid states created new administrative bureaucracies, but most left the ultimate power to allocate and distribute water in the hands of local courts and the water users themselves.

By 1900 prior appropriation was firmly fastened on the West, though it coexisted with riparian rights in the Pacific Coast and Great Plains states. Robert Dunbar has maintained that appropriation, "[f]orged as an adaption [*sic*] to the arid west, . . . continues to be shaped by western needs and pressures."[50] But his own book raises doubts. For example, on the Cache La Poudre River priority has not proven flexible. The three major ditches date from 1865, 1870, and 1878. In spring, when the river carries its largest volume, all three get a full supply of water. But by mid-summer, the "newer" diversions are often cut back. Priority of claim, not efficiency or justice, determines which farmers receive water and which do not. The law does not answer the important question of why a few months or years of prior use should give such a vital advantage over those with equal needs. Moreover, while some communities, such as Phoenix, have been able to buy up agricultural water rights relatively easily, Tucson, Denver, San Francisco, and Los Angeles have all faced expensive court challenges from agricultural interests. Finally, Dunbar acknowledges that by exhausting streams, appropriation often threatens recreational uses of water, particularly sport fishing. Recreational uses have a vast economic potential in certain parts of the West. Although some states now recognize the maintenance of minimum flows as a beneficial use of water, recreational needs still take a back seat to traditional water uses.[51] In 1961 a U.S. Senate committee concluded: "The present system of water rights, which provide for diversions first in time to have the most secure rights, provides little stimulus toward more efficient use of water, and, in fact, may promote inefficient and wasteful use of water in order to perfect larger rights. As the demands on the water resources of the West grow, it may well be an economic necessity for some of the Western States to review their water laws with a view to changes which will bring about more efficient use of water, or else accept a ceiling on their potential growth."[52]

In 1839 the Kentucky Supreme Court upheld the right of a railroad to run trains through Louisville even though the noise constituted a public nuisance. "The onward spirit of the age must, to a reasonable extent, have its way," the court noted. "The law is made for the times, and will be made or modified by them. The expanded and still expanding genius of the *common law* should adapt it here, as elsewhere, to the improved and improving conditions of our country and countrymen."[53] In the nineteenth century the courts adapted to canals, railroads, steam power, telegraphs, telephones, and a multitude of other technological innovations that had a profound effect on the structure of the American economy. The law exalted personal rights and individualism, defining freedom largely as economic opportunity.

Western courts tried to balance opportunity against the perceived need to develop resources as rapidly as possible; in addition, they attempted to lay a foundation for future settlement in the West.[54] The courts often took a broader view of economic development than state legislatures, which were much more susceptible to political and economic pressure. John Guice has called the territorial judges of Colorado, Montana, and Wyoming "the real heroes of the period [1861–1890]" because they were able to assure "maximum economic development . . . through the establishment of order in mining and agriculture, no mean accomplishment."[55] Perhaps so. But the courts were neither omniscient nor omnipotent. Whatever changes occurred in prior appropriation as it spread from mining to agriculture, two principles remained inviolable: that the chronological priority of a use transcended the value of a use, and that rights to water were exclusive and absolute. In 1902, Frederick Haynes Newell, first director of the United States Reclamation Service (now Bureau), prophesied that "there must come a time when water must be apportioned with justice to all, and a century or more hence we will have it distributed not upon priority rights, but upon technical rights. We cannot have a farmer getting more water than he is entitled to, because his great-grandfather or somebody else happened to secure the water right two months ahead of somebody else. Water must ultimately be conserved in the most just manner for the general welfare of all citizens."[56] That time never came. The pursuit of wealth took precedence. Enterprise triumphed over equity.

The Origins of Western Water Law: Case Studies from Two California Mining Districts

Historians have long recognized that California water law was in flux during the 1850s. They have attributed this to inherent ambiguities in the common law, to the legislature's simultaneous endorsement of traditional "riparian rights" and the novel customs of the mining camps, to the ignorance and eclecticism of judges new to the arid West, to rapid turnover on the California supreme court bench, and to that court's reluctance—given the risk that the rules of property they enumerated might later be rejected by Congress—to legislate for the public domain. Attention has focused too narrowly on the state legislature, the state supreme court, and Congress. Economic conditions within the mining camps, as well as the values, ideals, and views of law held by the miners, have been neglected. This chapter looks at the origins of western water law through the experience of two California mining districts, one near Weaverville in far northern California, the other at Columbia, east of Stockton in the central part of the state. It suggests that the doctrine of "prior appropriation"—which was destined to become the dominant principle of water allocation throughout the arid and semiarid West—emerged gradually, amidst conflict, as a response to the rise of the private corporation and to new techniques of mining. Prior appropriation was not, as some historians have suggested, universally favored by the first generation of placer miners.[1]

The mining district of Columbia, east of Stockton, was discovered in 1849, and by April 1850, six to eight thousand miners clustered in and around the town. An early historian of Tuolumne County remarked that "[i]t was seen [by miners] that there was not a foot of ground upon the immense flat, from Santiago Flat to Tim's Springs, and from Shaw's Flat to the hill overhanging the Stanislaus, but was rich enough to pay for working, if water could be obtained for that purpose." The first argonauts laboriously transported paydirt to springs or carried barrels of water to their claims. During the heavy rains that fell during Christmas 1851, a stream formed in Columbia's main street. Fifty sluice boxes or "long toms" were quickly erected to utilize nature's gift; miners used the water over and over again as large parts of the new town were excavated in the frantic search for gold.[2]

It cannot be too strongly emphasized that the first California mining companies were joint-stock ventures owned and administered by the miners themselves. They were not corporations dominated by outside capital. Like many antebellum Americans, miners feared and resented monopoly when it did not serve the common good, and they regarded business corporations as inherently elitist, undemocratic, and monopolistic. In 1850, claim holders near Columbia pooled money and labor to divert water from the Tuolumne River, exposing rich placer deposits in the streambed; by April the *Stockton Times* counted twenty-four dams in one eighteen-mile stretch.[3] However, the gold in and adjoining streams was quickly exhausted, and attention then turned to ancient placer deposits far removed from living streams. Several small water companies appeared in the fall of 1850 and spring of 1851, but they relied on ephemeral sources and served only twenty or thirty miners for a few days before their supply was exhausted.[4] Consequently, in June 1851, two Columbia bankers, James and Darius Mills—the latter destined to become one of California's leading financiers—formed the Tuolumne County Water Company. They raised $250,000 in and around the town and in July began building a new water system. In May 1852, the company delivered water from the south fork of the Stanislaus to Columbia, and by August their ditch reached the surrounding diggings. "Hundreds of claims will be supplied with water through the enterprise of this company that could never be sufficiently [supplied] in any other way," the *Columbia Gazette* crowed.[5] Miners in more remote diggings continued to provide themselves with water, but most of the three thousand miners who worked claims within two miles of town were entirely dependent on the new company.[6]

Once the company completed its first water system, the increased value of its stock permitted the directors to borrow another $250,000 to complete a reservoir to feed the ditches during the six to eight weeks each summer when the flow of the Stanislaus gave out.[7] A turning point had been reached. This capital was raised *outside* Columbia; control over the local water supply was passing from miners to capitalists and the business of providing water had been split off from the act of mining.

The dry winter of 1852–1853 produced the first criticism of the company. At a protest meeting held in January 1853, miners complained that the Tuolumne County Water Company (TCWCo.) charged much higher rates at Columbia than it did at Shaw's Flat, where it faced competition from a joint-stock operation, the Sullivan's Creek Company. They also accused the company of cutting off water to those who publicly complained about poor service or extortionate rates.[8] The TCWCo. had been founded by local miners, not capitalists, critics charged, and most of them assumed that the revenue from water sales had already more than compensated the outside investors who now dominated the enterprise. (In August, as if to underscore the miners' charges, the *Alta California* reported that the company was debt-free and returned a four percent dividend *per month* on its stock.) Miners considered the rates doubly onerous because profits from placer mining declined sharply during the latter months of 1852 and the early months of 1853.[9]

In the summer of 1853, the miners asked the company to reduce rates by at least 50 percent, claiming that the price of water often exceeded the value of the gold it produced. They now hoped that competition from a rival private company, the Tuolumne Hydraulic Company,[10] would drive down rates, but the new company ran out of money, partly as a result of litigation over water rights pressed by the TCWCo., and most of its aqueduct system was absorbed by the older company.[11] Consequently, in the fall of 1854, disgruntled argonauts launched their own project, the Columbia and Stanislaus River Water Company (C&SRWCo.), and began constructing a twenty-mile canal and flume system from the Stanislaus to Columbia and Sonora.

Originally, the C&SRWCo. planned to divert the south fork of the Stanislaus River. Although the TCWCo. claimed an older right to that stream, the miners assumed that providing water for use took precedence over providing water for sale. Nevertheless, the threat of litigation, and the fact that the flow of the south fork had proven very erratic, persuaded the new company to extend its ditch and flume network an additional twenty-two miles to the river's main channel. By doing so, friends of the new system also hoped to avoid the cost of building an extensive reservoir system. Subsequently, several thousand angry miners organized to boycott the TCWCo. in March 1855, vowing never to pay more than four dollars a day for water—which rate the company claimed would return only 2 percent a month on the actual cost of its water system. Since Columbia bankers had invested heavily in the new company, the miners also urged their fellows to deposit any surplus money "in the iron safe of some friendly merchant, so that it will be impossible for it to be used against us by the controlling cormorants of this monster monopoly with which we are now at war." Miners who did not honor the strike, the leaders warned, would have their names published in the newspaper. The boycott did not result in violence, but it did generate tremendous support for the rival Columbia and Stanislaus River Water Company, especially because the miners had used their free time to help build this new water system, taking stock in exchange for labor.[12]

In October 1854 the *Columbia Gazette* reported that "[a]ll classes of [the] community feel the importance of the undertaking, and are seizing hold of it with an alacrity and zeal highly commendable." It tried to pacify directors of the "foreign" Tuolumne County Water Company by insisting that a ready market awaited all the water both companies could provide. The *Weekly Columbian* described the new project as "one of the most magnificent achievements of enterprise which the records of California industry can produce!"[13] Nevertheless, the Tuolumne County Water Company's directors made every effort to crush its new rival, first, by attempting to gain control of its stock, second, by challenging its water rights in court, and, finally, by trying to buy out wealthy miners who had loaned the C&SRWCo. money in exchange for mortgages on its works.[14] In retaliation, miners frequently sabotaged the Tuolumne Water Company's hydraulic works.

By the end of 1855, the miner-controlled Columbia and Stanislaus River Water Company delivered more water than did its older rival, and in 1856 competition helped lower the price to two dollars a day. By the end of that year, thirty-five miles of the C&SRWCo. aqueduct had been completed at a cost of $150,000.[15] Miners working on the ditch supplied their own provisions for months on end, and local merchants loaned the company money to see the job through to completion. In the minds of virtually all the miners, greed and the absence of competition—not the necessarily high cost of hydraulic projects—kept water prices high. "No community can prosper where so essential an auxiliary to their prosperity as is water . . . is in the hands of any one co.," the *Weekly Columbian* observed. It charged that the Tuolumne Water Company was "an enemy that would take from you the proceeds of the sweat of your brow, the bread you eat, the clothes you wear, and your last shilling." The *Columbian* denied that depressed economic conditions were due to the boom-and-bust nature of mining. Hard times were a legacy of monopoly, it insisted, not the result of a decline in the supply of accessible gold.[16]

The ditch was finally completed in November 1858. In all, the C&SRWCo. works included sixty miles of flume and canal, as well as a 3,100-foot tunnel. When the first water from this quasi-public utility reached Columbia, residents celebrated with a huge public dinner, fireworks, bonfires on hills surrounding the town, and a ball at the local theater. Not since the gold strike of 1855 had more people filled the streets. The miners had invested their spirit, along with their money and labor, in the project, and on November 29 they paraded into town triumphantly bearing the tools used to build the great ditch, "all held as proudly aloft as if they had been precious war trophies, won from opposing legions on fiercely contested fields," one participant later recounted. Many also carried battered beanpots, symbols of the sacrifices made in what they considered a battle for survival. The whole procession conveyed an impression of solemnity and dignity. A correspondent to San Francisco's *Alta California* confidently proclaimed that the festivities had been "in honor of the commencement of a new era in the prosperity of our country." With the death of the "monster monopoly," as the TCWCo. was frequently called, the glory days of the early 1850s would return.[17]

The miners had won a great battle against long odds, exhibiting courage, self-sufficiency, independence, and resourcefulness—qualities deeply respected by Americans. The physical obstacles alone were formidable; blasting the tunnel and erecting flumes that ran forty or fifty feet above the ground had been filled with danger and uncertainty. The moral fervor of the celebration spoke volumes about the resentment most miners felt toward the apparent tyranny of corporations. They won despite the financiers and high-priced legal talent arrayed on the side of the Tuolumne County Water Company. Their aqueduct was a symbol of what free men in a free society could accomplish. In that sense, completing the C&SRWCo. ditch was a deeply patriotic act.

Of course, the miners were too late; nothing, not even free water, could have rescued the Southern Mines from decline. The Central Mines—those in Nevada, Plumas, and Sierra counties, north of Grass Valley and Nevada City—hung on much longer. They drew abundant water from high mountains. The water supply in the Sonora region, by contrast, had always been erratic, and the most elaborate flumes and canals did no good when streams ran dry. The Central and Northern Mines also had the advantage of deep tertiary gravels missing in the Sonora region, along with a larger supply of better quality lumber. "By the middle of the 1850s the population decline of the southern mines reflected the basic change in California gold mining," one historian of California mining has written, "the shift from rich shallow diggings to deep tertiary gravels and quartz veins. Added to this, the return home of large numbers of foreign miners, due to numerous causes of which the Foreign Miner's tax was one of the most important, and it is easy to understand the population decline of the southern mines." The year 1858 witnessed the great migration to the Fraser River in British Columbia and the advent of hydraulic mining in Tuolumne County. In 1859, another group of miners abandoned the Southern Mines—this time for Nevada's Comstock Lode.[18]

Meanwhile, as the total cost of its water system reached $500,000, the Columbia and Stanislaus River Water Company's debts accumulated. During the last stages of construction, the company had been forced to borrow $150,000 from several large investors, led by Edwin Davis. Now it could not pay the interest, let alone the principal on that debt. Davis promised not to foreclose on his mortgage if the company turned over half its income from water sales until the debt had been erased. The trustees refused. Davis's demand favored large investors who had provided financial support only when the project was certain to be completed. Their contribution, the trustees argued, was much less than that of the miners, merchants, and other small stockholders who had supported the company from the beginning, often at great sacrifice, by taking stock in exchange for labor and supplies. All the investors, the trustees decided, should profit or suffer alike. As a result, Davis sold his mortgage to the only bidder, the Tuolumne County Water Company. That gave the TCWCo. the leverage it needed to buy out its competitor for a small fraction of what the new system had cost. The water monopoly had been restored.

The C&SRWCo. had not been badly managed, but it was launched at a time when miners were capable of paying two or three times as much for water as they could in 1859 or 1860. The company had failed to secure a reliable water supply during the summer months of dry years, and it had been forced to pay investors like Davis 3 to 8 percent a month in interest. Not surprisingly, the disappointed miners who remained in the Columbia diggings turned to litigation and violence to save the Columbia and Stanislaus from buyout. Friends of the C&SRWCo.—and they constituted the bulk of miners—bitterly complained that under cover of law, the old company had used deceit and fraud to outwit its rival. In July 1860, the *Columbia Times*, now a staunch supporter of the Tuolumne County Water Company, fretted that "a band of lawless men" had promised that if a last-minute suit to preserve the C&SRWCo. failed, they would hold the ditch in defiance of the law, "or, if not able to hold it by force, that they will then destroy all the ditches in the county." The *Times* warned that capitalists would never invest new money in the region under such conditions, and that destroying the ditches was counterproductive because it simply added to the price of water. Nevertheless, vandalism continued,[19] and the paper chided citizens time and again for not helping local law enforcement officials apprehend those responsible.

In reprisal, the private water company threatened to cut off water to all miners, but the miners charged that the company itself had sabotaged the hydraulic works to reduce the value of the C&SRWCo. and make it unattractive to outside investors. "That the law attaches no penalty to robberies of this class," a group of thirty protestors wrote to the directors of the Tuolumne County Water Company in August 1860, "does not in the least palliate the crime which you have committed. There are crimes of such an inhuman nature as not to be thought of or conceived by the makers of laws. . . . [Y]our only incentive was the avaricious greediness of your sordid minds."[20]

Little more than a year later, in 1861, a correspondent of the *Sacramento Daily Union* reported that "a good feeling is now being cultivated between miners and the Water Company." That was because the most disgruntled miners left the county in that year, after title to the public water company passed to its rival; only a handful of gold seekers remained to work the diggings surrounding Columbia. The private Tuolumne Water

Company had pieced together six hundred miles of ditches and flumes, including one flume eleven miles long and one ditch sixty miles long, but its hard-won monopoly constituted a pyrrhic victory.[21] It was forced to slash its rates as the supply of gold dwindled, and it could not escape the high fixed costs of maintaining ditches and flumes that were often damaged by ice, snow, rock slides, and simply routine use.

Large-scale mining came early to the Columbia diggings, but not to Weaverville. Nevertheless, miners in the Northern Mines looked at water in the same way—as an aid to the act of mining rather than as a separate species of property. Three months after James Marshall's famous find at Coloma in January 1848, gold was discovered seven miles south of Weaverville, in what would later be Trinity County. The Trinity mines were among the most inaccessible in the state; it took ten days to reach the diggings from the headwaters of the Sacramento River through steep, nearly impassable mountains. Nevertheless, by 1851 the entire county had been explored, and in the following year miners took up scattered claims along its major streams. In 1853, the county contained no more than a thousand white residents, most of whom were concentrated along a seventy-five-mile stretch of the Trinity River and a few of its tributaries. As in California's other mining districts, Trinity County argonauts quickly discovered that cooperation paid. In 1850, sixty men formed a company to divert the Trinity into an old channel, exposing three-quarters of a mile of stream bed. One observer, who arrived on the scene in 1850, later recounted that these miners averaged an ounce of gold per pan "and never less than a dollar to the shovelful." Not surprisingly, when heavy spring rains washed out the diversion dam, thirty miners hastily formed a joint-stock company and pledged a thousand dollars apiece to rebuild it.[22]

In the following year, the increasing number of miners forced most newcomers to work deposits farther from water. This touched off conflicts between "ditchers" and "anti-ditchers." The debate concerned more than mining techniques. The ditchers, who worked in larger groups, wanted to exploit placer deposits in "dry diggings" by bringing water to the isolated areas. They insisted on the right to mine as much ground as their ditches could supply with water. The "antis" worked alone or in groups of two or three, as miners had since 1848. They wanted to restrict the size of claims to provide opportunity to the largest number of miners, regardless of how much effort or capital an individual or group could muster. They argued for equal access to the wealth of the public domain; only the discoverer of a mineral deposit deserved any special privileges.[23]

Some conflicts were impossible to resolve. The story of William Ware's ditch is a case in point. Ware had been a dentist in Wilmington, Delaware, before he came to California in 1849. He first went to Tuolumne County, then migrated to the Trinity mines in June 1850. That fall he cut the region's first water "race," or ditch, and in the following spring dug the West Weaver Canal to carry water into McKenzie's Gulch, a few miles from Weaverville. In all, Ware built three major ditches out of the East and West Weaver rivers (two of the Trinity River's largest tributaries). They were among the largest and most costly in the county, covering eleven miles at a reported cost of twelve thousand dollars.[24] Since most early ditches and flumes were cooperative ventures by which groups of miners delivered water to themselves at cost, only a few, like Ware's, provided water for sale. They posed no danger during the wet years of 1851 and 1852, but that changed following the dry winter of 1852–1853. In the spring of 1853, Ware turned almost the entire stream into his ditch, depriving miners who worked the banks of the West Weaver below the diversion of their livelihood.[25]

The conflict that erupted during the drought of 1853 was as much between upstream and downstream ditchers as between ditchers and anti-ditchers. Ware and another canal owner, James Howe, maintained, in the words of Trinity County's first historian, that "the priority of possession conferred a perfect and perpetual right."[26] However, not all miners agreed that the principle of "first in time, first in right" should define claims to water, and even those who accepted that dictum disagreed as to how it should be interpreted. Mining camp law had always ranked claims according to age, but mineral rights also depended on continuous occupation and use. Although Ware's main ditch had been completed in the spring of 1851, most miners who bought water from him did not arrive in Trinity County until 1852 or 1853. The dentist-turned-miner-turned-entrepreneur argued that he provided a necessary service, that the mineral region would never be fully developed until the rights of capital were recognized, and that the date a ditch was completed, and its capacity, should take precedence over when individual miners began to buy the water. Thus, according to Ware, *all* miners who purchased water from him deserved a priority of 1851.

Ware's customers accepted this logic; their claims would have been worthless otherwise. Channel miners downstream from his diversion, however, pointed out that they had arrived in the county first. In any case, they reasoned, those who mined in or along the bed of a living stream should have a stronger right to water than those who labored on claims far removed from the channel. Water used within a river basin remained in the channel, subject to reuse by miners downstream. Moreover, little was lost to evaporation or seepage (compared to the amount that disappeared from lengthy ditches and flumes).

Following several futile attempts to arbitrate the dispute, 120 of the downstream miners—armed with rifles, pistols, axes, and shovels—descended on Ware's wooden dam, burned it, and chopped down the diversion flumes so that the water of the West Weaver could reach their claims. In Cox's words, the army of miners "left not a vestige," and—mocking the new custom of posting notice of diversion to establish chronological priority—they posted their intention to tear down any new dam.

Ware filed complaint against nine miners, who were arrested and jailed. The conflict then took on comic-opera qualities as over one hundred additional miners, many of whom had helped to destroy the dam and race, marched into Weaverville and informed the sheriff that they were as guilty as those in jail. He should either free the nine or lock them all up. The sheriff dutifully stuffed the new arrivals into his hewn log jail, which was no more than eighteen-by-twenty-feet square.

The conflict deepened as hundreds of additional miners rushed into town to demand that the prisoners be released from the cramped, poorly ventilated jail or confined in more hospitable surroundings. If the sheriff refused to act, the miners promised to tear down the jail. Subsequently, he moved the prisoners to the county courthouse, but within a couple days let them go because the county could not afford to feed them. The dispute continued, as several of those who had been jailed launched a conspiracy to assassinate Ware. As one county historian concluded, "it galled them terribly to think that they should be committed to prison for contending for what they thought to be their rights as Americans, hence their banding together to do that rash act."[27]

The conspirators abandoned their plan when they discovered that William Ware was a fellow Mason, but the conflict over water rights continued. On June 7, 1853, a meeting of pro-Ware miners from Sidney and McKenzie gulches adopted a resolution deploring the "wanton destruction of property" and pledging that "[i]t becomes us as Americans and good citizens to protect one another in our rights and privileges." By a seven-to-one vote, they repudiated "any and every such spirit of agrarianism [anarchy] as has so lately manifested itself in the burning of the reservoir and cutting of Dr. Ware's Race." They promised to help rebuild Ware's aqueduct and to sort out the rights of the various ditch companies "according to the priority of their right." Nevertheless, the miners insisted that at all times four tom-heads of water be permitted to flow in the creek for use by those downstream.[28]

A few weeks after this meeting, the *Shasta Courier* published an angry letter from "West Weaver," an anonymous spokesman for the riparian claimants. Until the summer of 1852, he pointed out, there had been sufficient water in the West Weaver to serve everyone. When periodic shortages occurred, reason and simple justice dictated that the miners closest to the stream received preference. The arbitrators appointed at the meeting of Sidney and McKenzie gulch miners had no authority to divide up the water, the correspondent insisted, nor had they acted fairly. Evaporation would reduce the four tom-heads of water to almost nothing by the time it

reached the downstream claims. "West Weaver" claimed that an offer by
the channel miners to share the stream equally with those who relied on
the Ware and Howe races had been rebuffed. "Now . . . the miners of West
Weaver are as quiet and well disposed as any to be found in California,"
he noted, but "they were told that, that which of right belonged to them
they should not have, and were further told that their diggings were
worthless, and that as the diggings of Sidney were rich, that Sidney of
course should have the water. Not only insulting our poverty, but robbing
us because we were poor." The West Weaver rights, he insisted, would be
"strictly maintained and the insults fully repaid."[29]

Another round of meetings followed in December 1853. Ware's supporters met, in the words of an obviously biased record of the meeting, "to
investigate the existing difficulties between Dr. Ware and a mob of miners
on West Weaver, who, without any apparent cause and in violation of all
laws of the country and of honor, have destroyed his property . . . and as
we are creditably informed are now holding water by force of arms that is
justly the property of Ware and others."[30] The meetings were held in
response to Ware's petition to the California legislature to confirm his
water claims. The downstream miners appealed to the lawmakers to dis-
tinguish between the right to sell water and the right to use it:

Very great difficulties have arisen between miners and ditch companies, with regard to the water of many mining streams, and gulches in
many of the mining districts of this state, and particularly in this
county, which difficulties have arisen solely from the manifestly
unjust and monstrous assumption of an absolute fee simple title to
running water by certain ditch companies—such ditch companies
intending and endeavoring thereby to deprive all miners of their natural, legal, and inalienable rights to make use of such water as would
naturally flow through the gulch or valley of the stream in which they
worked, and which is necessary to work their claims. . . . Also, such
difficulties have been the cause of much annoying, expensive and
vexatious litigation, the said ditch companies having, by the influence
of their money, caused criminal prosecutions to be commenced
against all and any miners who dare boldly to assert the natural and
legal rights guaranteed to him or them as miners and American citizens, and attempting by all possible means to so overawe, intimidate
and crush the mining spirit generally, that they . . . might with
impunity and an utter disregard of all natural and legal rights [ripar-
ian rights] effectually carry out their scheme.

The channel miners insisted that allowing entrepreneurs to claim water
apart from the land violated the de facto federal policy that the mines

should be open to all and that the public domain was exclusively under the supervision of Congress. In any case, custom dictated that water could only be used in common; no one could claim an exclusive right.[31]

When the West Weaver conflict reached the newly established Ninth Judicial District Court for Trinity County in 1854, the judge simply upheld the prior appropriation doctrine, which by that time served the interests of the largest number of miners on the stream, those who relied on William Ware's water system. "The question and rights involved in this case are of great importance to the mining population of this as well as the other mining counties of this State," Judge J. W. McCorkle proclaimed, "and upon their equitable and fair adjustment depends not only the quiet and peace of the community, but to a great extent the prosperity and success of the miners and the full development of the vast mineral resources of the country." Mining in Trinity County changed dramatically in the mid-1850s. Huge water wheels, some as large as forty feet in circumference with as many as eighty eighteen-gallon buckets attached to the rim, fed Trinity River water into flumes that served nearby river bars, and once hydraulic and drift mining began in 1859 and 1860, small-scale operations disappeared almost entirely. At the end of 1859, the *Alta California* reported that the rocker and tom had all but vanished in the mines adjoining Weaverville and had "given place to immense flumes and powerful hydraulics. . . . The flume of Jones & Howe in McKenzie's Gulch is not surpassed by any like work in the State, and it is not hazardous to predict that three years hence the owners will be the wealthiest men in Northern California."[32]

The time had passed when almost anyone could earn five to twenty dollars a day using simple tools. In California, the water shortage of late 1852 through 1854 recurred frequently during the next few decades, but by the 1860s mining in Trinity County had passed into the hands of larger congregations of miners as well as private companies. McCorkle justified his pro-Ware decision on grounds not just that prior appropriation was needed to attract capital, but also because, in his words, "[t]he beds of most of the creeks and streams in the mineral regions have been worked out, while extensive gold fields lie unoccupied and untouched yet, for want of water, but which by the construction of canals . . . will yield good wages to the miners for years to come, and furnish thousands with constant employment, who otherwise would be compelled to lay idle, except during the rainy season."[33]

McCorkle responded to immediate economic interests rather than to the dictates of doctrinal purity or consistency. Nevertheless, when Isaac Cox published his *Annals of Trinity County* in 1858, the author reported that the emergence of prior appropriation in California had been hard for many residents of his county to swallow. "While it is admitted by all that Dr.

Ware's enterprises are of the highest order of importance to sustain our mining interests," Cox reported, "it is painful to record the fact that the fellow-citizen whose life we have before us, and his labors, seems to be the target of a power bent on destroying what beneficial uses thus have been wrought."[34]

The Trinity County story was not unusual; it was repeated in countless mining districts during the middle 1850s. Almost everywhere the quest for individual wealth clashed with the demands of investors in corporate ventures. California differed from other mining states both in the size of its placer deposits and the scale of its hydraulic mining operations; the mining laws of most other states focused on shaft mining, which posed entirely different legal problems. Nevertheless, most western states had surface mining as well, and many early miners assumed the dominance of riparian water rights. In Alder Gulch, Montana, for example, miners declared in 1864 that water "shall belong exclusively to the miners of that creek or gulch" and guaranteed each claim "one sluice-head of water of not less than twenty inches" and as much more as necessary once everyone had received this amount. They declared "the right to the possession of the land and water thereupon inseparable and indivisible," forbade all exclusive rights or privileges to water, and branded any flume or ditch that deprived downstream miners of water "a public nuisance."[35] On Pritchard and Eagle creeks in Shoshone County, Idaho, as well as in the Coeur d'Alene District, miners first on the scene held superior rights to water, but only if they returned what they used to the natural channel of the stream for reuse by those below.[36] Throughout the West, the miners first on the scene argued that the law should provide equal access to water. Eventually, the courts confirmed the rights of private corporations, but only after small-scale operations had dramatically declined. In the 1850s, courts spent more time trying to balance existing rights than encouraging new capital investment. Nevertheless, since western miners accepted the principle that the law could and should adapt to new economic opportunities, they had little ammunition once large-scale hydraulic mining became dominant.

Miners throughout California exhibited the same antimonopoly spirit that prevailed among farmers and workingmen in the eastern United States and would later animate midwestern farmers in their attacks against banks and railroads. Argonauts saw the tentacles of monopoly everywhere. Two very different conceptions of law were at stake in California during the 1850s: one that the law should work to provide the greatest opportunity for the largest number of individual economic actors, the other that the law should encourage the most rapid development of natural resources and generate the greatest possible wealth (at least in the short run). In such a climate, it is easy to understand why many miners harbored deep fears of prior appropriation, at least as the principle was employed by private water companies.

Prior appropriation eventually triumphed in the mining camps, but it never completely displaced the riparian doctrine. The mining camps produced a medley of laws; they did not uniformly embrace prior appropriation. As a result, California court decisions reflected local needs much more than broad legal principles or dicta. Mining districts were often isolated and relatively autonomous, district courts were few and far between. And since district judges were elected rather than appointed, public opinion had a powerful influence on the bench. The background, personality, and training of judges were less important in shaping the outcome of water rights decisions than were the specific location of a court and the nature of mining operations within its jurisdiction. Miners often ignored supreme court decisions, not just because they believed in popular sovereignty rather than "revealed law" or because they doubted that any practical comprehensive water laws could be drafted, but because they questioned whether the legislature or the state's highest court had any right to allocate the resources of the public domain.

The law was very much the creature of the changing technology and organization of an inherently unstable industry. Until the late 1850s, few Californians could have guessed that hydraulic and shaft mining would completely displace simpler forms of mining; and the size of "Tertiary deposits"—those ancient gold-bearing gravels hundreds of feet thick in Nevada and Placer counties—was unknown until the 1860s. Moreover, as techniques to extract gold improved, many miners returned to sites first worked in 1849 or the early 1850s and revived mining in or adjoining river channels, albeit on a limited scale. Large mining and water companies appeared by the middle of the 1850s, but their dominance was not seen as inevitable, particularly in counties where gold deposits did not warrant large-scale investments. In short, prior appropriation was not predestined to displace traditional riparian rights.

Nevertheless, this new system of water law was remarkably consistent with the American ideal of limited government. Prior appropriation was one of the greatest nineteenth-century legal subsidies in that it allowed public property (water on public land) to be taken for free. The federal government might have mined government lands itself; it might have chartered private companies to do so, retaining a share of the proceeds; it might have charged individual miners for the privilege by issuing licenses; or it might have formed "mixed enterprises" to do the job—as many eastern states had done early in the nineteenth century by investing public funds in banks and transportation projects. It did none of these things; they were never considered realistic options. Prior appropriation fitted well with the American expectation that government should provide economic incentives without attempting to regulate industries or fit them into an overall economic plan. Indeed, one of prior appropriation's great attractions was that it imposed no expense on the state and required no bureaucracy or commission to implement. As such, it encouraged Americans to see the value of water in terms of the labor costs needed to develop or exploit it, not in the resource itself. Yet we should not forget that while prior appropriation outlived most of its critics, it did not triumph without conflict.

CHAPTER THREE

State vs. Nation: Federal Reclamation and Water Rights in the Progressive Era

In 1955, the U.S. Supreme Court revived a legal controversy which had been dormant, if not forgotten, for decades. In *Federal Power Commission v. Oregon*, the court authorized the F.P.C. to build the Pelton Dam on the Deschutes River despite opposition from the state of Oregon.[1] Since the dam would be constructed entirely on public land, argued the court, federal officials did not have to apply to the state for either a construction permit or the right to impound water. Though federal water rights were not directly at issue, a majority of the justices ruled that Congress had never relinquished control over water flowing through the public domain to the states, as had been widely assumed in the West. Justice William O. Douglas strongly dissented. "In the West," he wrote, "the United States owns a vast amount of land. If by mere Executive action the federal lands may be reserved and all the water rights appurtenant to them returned to the United States, vast dislocations in the economies of the Western States may follow."[2] Eight years later Douglas's fears intensified when the U.S. Supreme Court, in *Arizona v. California*, seemed to promise federal officials virtually all the water they needed to improve the public lands.[3]

The two decisions shocked westerners and prompted their representatives in Congress to introduce more than fifty bills to limit federal water rights. Much was at stake. About 700,000,000 acres of land in the arid West—an estate seven times the size of California—remained under federal control, and 59 percent of the region's water supply originated in national forests or parks. The perceived threat to future state water projects, and the fear that the federal government might confiscate water rights established under state laws without paying adequate compensation, kept this controversy at white heat into the 1970s and 1980s.

Both the Pelton Dam case and *Arizona v. Colorado* reflected the federal government's expanding role in developing western water resources after World War II. But the "reserved rights doctrine," as it came to be called, was not a new legal phenomenon.[4] Its roots stretched back to the federal reclamation program launched in 1902. From the beginning, the United

States Reclamation Service found itself mired in a dilemma. It desperately needed to secure a water supply for the twenty-five irrigation projects authorized by 1907,[5] but the Reclamation Act of 1902 required it to work in conformity with muddled and anachronistic state water laws that recognized no prior federal water right. Between 1902 and 1907 Reclamation Service officials helped devise a theory which asserted the paramount authority of the federal government over western waters and initiated a chronic jurisdictional conflict between state and nation.

Until after the Civil War, the federal government remained the unchallenged proprietor of the public domain. Then, in 1866, 1870, and 1877, Congress recognized the right of settlers to use streams flowing through the public lands for mining, agriculture, and other purposes so long as water users conformed to local customs and procedures.[6] These statutes laid the foundation for state administration of water rights. Many westerners assumed that the same laws tacitly deeded *ownership* of the water to the states; Colorado and Wyoming even wrote this principle into their constitutions.[7]

In the early years of the twentieth century, there emerged a strong "state party" led by Elwood Mead, head of the Office of Irrigation Investigations in the Department of Agriculture. Mead saw pitfalls in the principle of state sovereignty—especially in the enforcement of state water laws on federal lands and interstate streams—but he predicted that any attempt to impose a comprehensive water code on the West would unsettle existing rights and lead to economic chaos. Wide variations in western climates, soils, crops, and geography made a uniform national code impractical, and since most Washington bureaucrats were easterners with little knowledge of "desert" agriculture, such a code would be poorly administered. Mead prodded the arid states to modernize their water laws in a series of publications discussing the inadequacies of those statutes.[8] He advocated such reforms as the creation of state engineering offices to record old water rights and supervise the acquisition of new ones; the use of watermasters to parcel out water, especially in dry years; and the adjudication of contested water claims by state administrative commissions modeled after the board of control he created when he drafted Wyoming's water code in 1889 and 1890.[9]

In 1901, while Congress debated the measure that became the Reclamation Act a year later, the state engineers of Colorado, Idaho, Nebraska, Utah, and Wyoming—all friends and supporters of Mead—met at Cheyenne and drafted a bill to protect state sovereignty. The legislation provided, in the words of its sponsor, Senator Francis E. Warren of Wyoming, "[t]hat construction, supervision, control or sale of irrigation works and storage, diversion, disposal and distribution of stored water, shall be in the engineer's office of each state or territory accepting the benefits of Government aid; the feasibility of all plans subject, however, to the Secretary of the Interior." Warren and the Wyoming state engineer tried, but failed, to win President Theodore Roosevelt's support for that bill, or for a more modest proposal that would have permitted the states to decide where federal reservoirs would be built.[10] Nor was the president persuaded by such strong proponents of federal reclamation as William Ellsworth Smythe and Hiram Martin Chittenden, who urged that the federal government construct reservoirs but leave the design of projects and the distribution of water to the states.[11] Mead was especially disappointed. Most new reservoirs, he argued, would capture "flood water" at the headwaters of streams already heavily used for irrigation. Since the public lands destined for reclamation were generally far removed from the storage sites—often in another state or states—the new water supply would have to pass by existing ditches on its way downstream and would doubtlessly be "pilfered" by established farmers.[12]

Mead recognized that the Reclamation Act of June 1902 represented many shortsighted compromises and failed to clarify or define federal and state rights and responsibilities. Congressman George W. Ray of New York, who led the floor fight against the legislation in the House, echoed many of Mead's arguments. "What laws are to govern and apply in the execution of this bill?" Ray asked. "The laws of the State in which the water, in which the reservoirs, or in which the canals may be? . . . The United States Government surrenders all control [in this bill and] . . . I simply point this out to you, gentlemen, because when this law is written on the statute book it will be impossible of execution." An earlier version of the bill expressly transferred control over water rights to the states, but that provision was stricken from the final legislation. On the other hand, a proposal to give Congress "absolute jurisdiction and control of the previously unappropriated waters of [interstate] rivers and streams . . . necessary for the purposes of navigation or irrigation" won little support. As adopted, Section 8 declared that "nothing in this act shall be construed as affecting or intended to affect or in any way interfere with the laws of any State or Territory relating to the control, appropriation, use, or distribution of water used in irrigation, but State and Territorial laws shall govern and control . . . the waters rendered available by the works constructed under the provisions of this act." The law placed one restriction on state administrative control. Rights to all water delivered by federal irrigation works "attached" to the land watered and could not be bought, sold, or monopolized as a commodity separate from the land.[13]

Congress had given the Reclamation Service a difficult job, for in 1902 state water laws varied markedly. Only three states west of the Mississippi—Colorado, Wyoming, and Nebraska—had established formal administrative procedures to regulate the acquisition of new water rights, and only Wyoming and Nebraska possessed administrative machinery to adjudicate conflicts between water users. Disputes over rights usually ended up in the courts—a slow, expensive, and rarely conclusive process—or were resolved (often only temporarily) through informal agreements. Besides this legal quagmire, the Reclamation Service had to contend with scanty knowledge concerning the volume of water available for federal projects. The "surplus" supply could not be determined simply by adding up claims filed with county recorders or state engineers because many states allowed farmers to establish titles without filing a formal claim. Some permitted irrigators to file for more water than they could put to "beneficial use," a practice that led to countless legal battles among "old" and "new" appropriators on a stream. Then, too, in states that recognized riparian rights, a precise determination of surplus water was impossible because such rights were indeterminate by law.

As early as July 1902, the Reclamation Service responded to the confusion at the state level with a warning from Director Frederick Haynes Newell: "The people who have conflicting rights in any stream or body of water must get together; they must compromise their differences . . . or we will be able to do nothing."[14] This threat proved empty. The 1903 legislative sessions in the arid states tested the willingness of western leaders to cooperate with the Reclamation Service, but only Nevada proved to be an eager partner in reform.[15] No state needed federal reclamation more than Nevada, whose population and economy had declined steadily since the end of the silver boom in the late 1870s. Nevada Senator Francis G. Newlands advised Newell, "All I want is a bill which will give your Dept. as free a hand as possible in this state." A Reclamation Service official reported that most of the state's lawmakers favored "the largest measure of national control and administration that the Federal Government can be prevailed upon to undertake." Some Nevada legislators were even ready to abandon the cherished principle of state sovereignty over water. This was not done, but in creating the new office of state engineer, the legislature required the governor to appoint a person recommended by the secretary of the interior or director of the U.S. Geological Survey. (The initial appointee, A. E. Chandler, came from the ranks of the Reclamation Service and remained on the federal payroll.) The legislature also attached all water rights to the land, limited farmers to three acre-feet of water per acre irrigated, and ordered the state engineer to determine the state's surplus water supply and prepare lists of appropriators ranked in order of priority. The legislature failed to provide enough money for a full-scale investigation of water rights, and it also neglected to give the engineer authority to review future claims, but the statute clearly represented an expansion of national power in the Silver State. Not surprisingly, the first federal irrigation project was opened in Nevada in June 1905.[16]

Newell and his aides were disappointed that no other states followed Nevada's lead. They feared a "backlash" if they tried to dictate reform and reluctantly decided not to demand new laws as a prerequisite to the construction of federal irrigation works. Nevertheless, an opportunity to further their aims arose in August 1904 when a bistate commission, created by Washington and Oregon to overhaul their water laws, appealed to the Reclamation Service for guidance. Newell asked Morris Bien, head of the service's Lands and Legal Department, to draft a model water code suitable not only for Washington and Oregon but for the entire arid West. As both a lawyer and civil engineer, with many years experience in the U.S. Geological Survey and General Land Office, Bien was well suited for the job.[17]

In early 1905, Bien unveiled his plan. Many of its features resembled Mead's proposals. The new code rested on the principle of public control over water and included a state engineer's office as the capstone of each state's administrative structure. It required a centralized record of all rights, vested the courts with responsibility for resolving conflicts over rights, and limited riparian rights to beneficial use. Except for leaving the adjudication of water rights to the courts, these reforms could be endorsed by those who favored stronger state control over water in that they reflected the ideals of efficiency, technical expertise, and conservation. But the Bien plan also promised important new privileges to the federal government. Reclamation Service officials could order the state engineer to "reserve" all the unclaimed water within a river basin for their use, and that supply would remain off-limits to other claimants until surveys had determined the service's precise needs—a process that could take years. Even after such surveys, federal claims could be reduced only with the approval of the secretary of the interior.[18]

In most of the arid West, Bien's model water law was seen as a threat to established rights and to the principle of state sovereignty over water.[19] He left the adjudication of rights in the state courts, but westerners feared that the code's failure to provide for state *administrative* settlement of water controversies suggested that ultimately the Reclamation Service would assume that responsibility and bypass the states entirely. According to Bien's critics, the resulting bureaucracy would be cumbersome, expensive, inefficient, and inequitable. Even those less suspicious of the Reclamation Service noted that any attempt to determine the supply of surplus water and reconcile conflicting rights would lead to expensive litigation. Opposition also came from fledgling hydroelectric companies, which feared any limitation on riparian rights. Among the critics, one question loomed above the rest: Would the new law adequately protect private property rights? Could federal, state, and private reclamation projects "coexist" side by side? Most westerners feared they could not.

After the Reclamation Service filed claims to all of Oregon's surplus water, the *Portland Oregonian* testily commented: "Oregon must sit by for three years for the filing . . . of final plans for the [irrigation] works, and wait further to see if the United States 'authorizes the construction of the proposed work.' This last operation is final. No date is set even for the commencement of the works."[20] Eventually, only North Dakota, South Dakota, and Oklahoma adopted the Bien code, and those states contained few suitable reservoir or project sites.

Bien's failure to persuade the West to adopt his water code prompted him to consider a new strategy—the assertion of paramount federal water rights. During the late 1890s, an unstable foundation had been laid for such a theory by both Congress and the courts. The General Appropriations Act of June 4, 1897, in a section devoted to forest reserves, specified that all water appurtenant to such reservations could be used for "domestic, mining, milling, or irrigation purposes, under the laws of the state wherein such forest reservations are situated or under the laws of the United States and the rules and regulations established thereunder."[21] This language implied that Congress had relinquished only part of its control over western waters in the statutes of 1866, 1870, and 1877. In addition, during the 1890s, state and federal courts in Washington and Montana ruled that the federal government, as owner of the public domain, could dispose of its land and water either together or separately, and had always been able to do so. Even after public lands passed into private ownership, and thus fell under the police power of the state, the federal government did not automatically surrender title to the water serving those lands. Ownership either remained with the nation or passed to the individual water user. "The right to such waters, after the national government has disposed of them," the Circuit Court for Montana ruled in 1898, "must always be a question pertaining to private persons."[22]

These decisions pertained to specific circumstances in particular states. But on May 22, 1899, the United States Supreme Court expanded the foundation of federal rights in *United States v. Rio Grande Dam and Irrigation Company*. The case hinged on the question of whether states or territories could grant water to irrigators if diversions threatened the navigability of a stream. In delivering the majority opinion, Associate Justice David Josiah Brewer noted that "in the absence of specific authority from Congress a State cannot by its legislation destroy the right of the United States, as the owner of lands bordering on a stream, to the continued flow of its waters; so far at least as may be necessary for the beneficial uses of the government property."[23] This declaration was little more than a postscript to a decision primarily concerned with federal control over navigable streams, but by 1904 and 1905 Newell and Bien recognized the far-reaching implications of Brewer's words.

Fearful of losing political support in the West, Reclamation Service officials rarely discussed federal water rights in public and they filed for water under state laws just as individual appropriators did. Nevertheless, Bien and Newell never doubted that the nation enjoyed sovereignty over the West's unappropriated water. Bien maintained that the federal government, as original owner of the public domain, had also owned the water supply appurtenant to the land. Ownership of the water antedated the creation of territories and states, and even the Desert Land Act of 1877—which reserved the public domain's surplus water "for the appropriation and use of the public irrigation, mining, and manufacturing purposes subject to existing rights"—did not limit or surrender federal sovereignty.[24]

The government, according to Bien, deeded land to individuals and permitted the states to parcel out water to make the land productive. But title to the water passed directly from the nation to individual appropriators. The states never "owned" the water within their borders; they simply provided administrative systems to record water rights and prevent conflicts among users. Section 8 of the Reclamation Act, Bien explained, had been drafted "in order that the State records of water appropriations shall not be rendered useless by the failure to make record of the appropriation of the relatively large proportion of the water supply which would be used by the United States in any drainage area in which it may construct works." In short, Section 8 merely sought continuity in confirming and recording rights; federal officials could restrict or abrogate state control at any time. "The water being part of the land," Bien noted, "it is difficult to see any ground for the theory of State control. Where the United States has disposed of the land it has either transferred the water with it to the new owner or retained its right to it."[25] Director Newell made Bien's arguments his own. "The States are recognized by the Federal Government as in control of the regulation of the use of water merely because the Federal Government has not undertaken to regulate such matters," he observed in 1904. "The court in the Rio Grande case made it plain that the State laws must give way if ever the Federal Government undertook to resume control."[26]

Bien and Newell were overconfident. The legal foundation for federal sovereignty over the West's surplus water rested on ambiguous laws and court decisions which raised more questions than they answered. In particular, the character and extent of riparian rights remained poorly defined. Reclamation Service officials opposed the riparian doctrine because they believed it increased litigation over water rights, prevented a determination of the water available for reclamation in several states, and imperiled the storage of "flood water" at the head of the West's many interstate streams. In the absence of a federal tribunal or commission empowered to condemn water in one state for use in another, and faced with the enormous cost of buying up rights wholesale, the service's legal staff challenged the riparian doctrine directly. Bien argued that the Desert Land Act had tacitly abrogated that species of water rights in 1877, or at least restricted riparians to beneficial use. The 1877 law said nothing about such rights but did encourage the appropriation of water on the public domain. It applied exclusively to land still part of the national estate, but it also implied "residual" federal authority over water *outside* public lands. In theory, within those states which honored the riparian doctrine, one riparian owner at the end of a stream could block all appropriations above him. However, Congress had never sanctioned riparian rights, and, as mentioned above, several federal court decisions ruled that the federal government had retained control over the arid West's unused water supply even after deeding away the land.

Ironically, this interpretation of the Desert Land Act limited the usefulness of the Supreme Court's decision in the Rio Grande case. That ruling suggested that federal agencies could use as much water as they needed to develop government lands, but it failed to discuss the origin or nature of federal water rights, basing those rights on ownership of "lands bordering on a stream." Reclamation Service officials argued that this phrase did not imply the existence of a federal riparian right but simply identified the land most susceptible to improvement; obviously the West's streams did not carry enough water to improve *all* government land. Still, the Rio Grande decision could not be added to the Reclamation Service's arsenal of legal weapons without raising the "ghost" of riparian rights. Just as vexing, the Court had failed to make clear whether a federal agency could claim the entire surplus of a stream— even though it had no *immediate* need for the water—or whether it could divert water from one river basin into another for use on nonriparian lands. Thus, in 1905 federal authority was as cloudy as it had been in the nineteenth century.

Bien hoped that the Supreme Court would define federal water rights in the case of *Kansas v. Colorado*, which was finally decided in 1907.[27] This suit involved a conflict between Kansas and Colorado over the Arkansas River, which originated in Colorado but flowed through Kansas, Oklahoma, and Arkansas before emptying into the Mississippi. Colorado built its case on state sovereignty, claiming an absolute right to all the water within its borders. Kansas—whose laws recognized riparian as well as appropriative rights—argued that upstream diversions threatened downstream riparian rights. Neither position squared with the objectives of the Reclamation Service. Colorado's brief threatened the principle of federal control over unappropriated water and Kansas's claim jeopardized the government's plans to dam the Arkansas River in the service of future reclamation projects upstream.[28]

The U.S. Attorney General's office entered the case specifically to protect the Reclamation Service. Federal attorneys hoped to abrogate the riparian doctrine by arguing that riparian rights were inapplicable to the arid West and had been overturned by state and federal statutes. Prior appropriation alone should apply on interstate streams. The issue of federal sovereignty over unappropriated water was not raised. Instead, the government based its case on the Constitution's commerce clause, which vested the nation with authority over navigable streams.[29]

At the same time the Justice Department was preparing its brief in *Kansas v. Colorado*, it was composing arguments in still another case that the Supreme Court had agreed to hear—*Winters v. United States*.[30] In June 1898 the agent for the Fort Belknap Indian Reservation in Montana filed for water from the Milk River, which served as the reservation's northern boundary. Then, in 1905, diversions upstream from the reservation combined with a drought to dry up the Indian water supply. At the urging of the reservation superintendent, federal officials in Washington directed the U.S. attorney for Montana to file suit. He hoped to defend the Indian claims as senior to other appropriations but discovered that some defendants held rights established prior to 1898. Reluctantly, the lawyer decided to argue that the waters of the Milk River were "part and parcel" of the reservation and "*never were, and never became public waters* subject to appropriation by any person under state or federal laws." The Indians, he maintained, were riparian owners with the right to demand an unimpeded flow in the river, and—citing the Rio Grande case—he insisted that the United States had, in creating the Indian reservations, "reserved" as much water as necessary to develop them. Indian water rights existed even if the Indians had never filed for water under state or territorial laws and had never used the water. "The Indian case is exceptional," noted the solicitor general of the United States, "and their rights antedate [the] modern evolution of the law of waters." In August 1905 the Montana District Court granted an injunction blocking the diversions, and upstream farmers promptly lodged an appeal that eventually reached the U.S. Supreme Court.[31]

The Reclamation Service bitterly opposed the Justice Department's brief in the Winters case, and Director Newell carried his arguments directly to Theodore Roosevelt. The suit might have been used to justify extending federal water rights to cover public land within national irrigation projects, but Bien considered that course dangerous. He worried about the perceived inconsistency of the Justice Department "endeavoring to sustain the doctrine of riparian rights" on Indian reservations at the same time it advocated the curtailment or elimination of such rights in *Kansas v. Colorado*. The federal position in the Winters case, he argued, was "antagonistic to the *possibilities of irrigation development*, both private and national," and "beneath the dignity of a great nation." Reservation Indians, he believed, would be better off claiming water under the doctrine of prior appropriation because downstream riparian owners posed more danger to the development of reservation land than appropriations upstream. Bien did not understand the nature of Indian water rights as sketched in the Winters case, but he recognized that the assertion of such rights would severely reduce the water supply of federal reclamation projects.[32]

The Winters decision, handed down in 1908, did not sustain the riparian argument advanced by the U.S. attorney, but it had far-reaching implications because it affirmed the indefinite and open-ended nature of Indian water rights. The ruling's full implications were not recognized until the 1960s and 1970s, and hence it posed no direct threat to the fledgling national reclamation program. In any case, the Reclamation Service's legal staff had little time to digest the Winters verdict; it was preoccupied with the bombshell decision in *Kansas v. Colorado,* issued by the Supreme Court in 1907.

The latter opinion, read by the same judge who presented the court's ruling in the Rio Grande case, rejected the arguments of all parties to the suit and called instead for an "equitable division of benefits" between the two states. It recognized federal authority over navigation in interstate streams but did not acknowledge a special federal right to sufficient unused water to reclaim the arid lands in interstate river basins. The U.S. attorney general observed tersely in his annual report: "The Supreme Court entered a decree dismissing the petition of the intervenor [the federal government], on the ground that Congress has no power to control the flow of waters within the limits of a State except in a matter affecting the navigation of the stream." Morris Bien suspected that the decision was "intended as a warning that the court will construe the Reclamation Act within narrow limits." Equally disappointed was A. E. Chandler, one of the service's chief legal advisers and a well-known expert in western water law, who concluded that the federal government "must abide by State regulations and decrees in irrigation matters, and prosecute its work as if it were an ordinary corporation. It has no preferred rights."[33]

The 1907 decision in *Kansas v. Colorado* had profound consequences for the Reclamation Service. By throwing out the government's arguments and refusing to discuss the origin or nature of federal water rights, the Supreme Court strengthened the champions of state sovereignty. Morris Bien—who remained head of the service's legal staff until his retirement in July 1924—never abandoned his belief in federal sovereignty.[34] But in the years after 1907 his agency no longer expected any direct help from the Supreme Court, and it relied on other tactics to secure water—tactics which proved to be extremely unpopular in the arid West. Even prior to 1907, the service had purchased water claims in conflict with its own, but this course proved extremely expensive. It also tried to checkmate or stall the construction of state and private irrigation projects by withdrawing from entry potential reservoir sites on the public domain and by making "blanket" claims to water. From 1902 to 1904, the Reclamation Service set aside over 40,000,000 acres even though it expected to reclaim less than three percent of that area. The service "locked up" both the Rio Grande and the Colorado River until the late 1920s, earning fierce criticism in Colorado, Utah, and Wyoming. It claimed ten times the average flow of the Colorado and persisted in that claim even though it had no immediate plan to use the water. Farmers served by these streams often complained that the nation's ostensible commitment to comprehensive river-basin planning translated into a "no development" policy.[35]

The tactic of withdrawing public lands to reserve a water supply worked only where most land within a river basin remained part of the public domain. Elsewhere, the Reclamation Service turned to "friendly" federal courts for help, hoping to win concessions at the lower level that it had not been able to secure from the Supreme Court. In 1912, the Justice Department appointed two attorneys to represent the service in suits affecting federal irrigation projects. By 1926, thirty cases were pending in Arizona, New Mexico, Colorado, and California. As the attorney general noted in his annual report for that year, "the initial litigation is both expensive and slow, but there seems no other way of determining the rights of the parties in interest."[36]

In the years after 1907, most federal irrigation projects suffered from persistent water shortages, and legal suits offered almost the only opportunity to secure a reliable supply. The experience of western Nevada's Truckee-Carson Project was typical. By 1913 only about 20 percent of the 232,000 acres within project boundaries were being irrigated, and no additional land could be reclaimed without more water and new reservoirs. In that year the Justice Department filed suit against nonproject irrigators along the Truckee River, claiming all the stream's unappropriated water. John F. Truesdell, the attorney who represented the Justice Department and Reclamation Service, denied that the Supreme Court had repudiated federal sovereignty in *Kansas v. Colorado*. "In practice we only use the theory of Federal ownership as an anchor to the leeward," he explained to the manager of the Truckee-Carson Project in 1918. "We strive strenuously to show that we have complied with every State law and therefore our rights are good upon that theory; but we say that even if we have failed in some particular, they would be good anyway because the Government does not have to comply with State statutes."[37]

The government's competitors for Truckee River water emphasized that the nation was subject to the same legal restrictions—particularly beneficial use—as applied under state law to other appropriators. If the Reclamation Service refused to limit itself to the water actually needed for the land already settled, then it should use its decreed share within a certain period or forfeit the remainder. On February 13, 1926, thirteen years after the Justice Department filed suit, the federal district court in Reno issued a temporary decree awarding the Reclamation Service all the Truckee's surplus water with a priority of 1902. In effect, the government won the right to withdraw unappropriated water just as it withdrew public lands. However, the decision then—as well as in 1944 when a less generous decree was issued—proved to be of dubious value. The court did not consider the theoretical foundation upon which the federal right rested. It simply determined the amount of water needed by each claimant outside the project, listed those amounts, then "deeded" the remaining water to the nation in recognition of the "blanket claims" to the Truckee filed by the Reclamation Service in 1902.[38]

The Reclamation Service's part in the federal-state jurisdictional conflict over water rights is significant for several reasons. Originally, the government expected to use virtually all the West's unclaimed water on its irrigation projects. But by failing to make water law reform a precondition for federal aid, and by rushing to open as many projects as possible in the years from 1902 to 1907, it severely limited the effectiveness of national reclamation. So did the Supreme Court by refusing to define federal water rights outside Indian reservations. The court's decisions were narrow and ambiguous, much less conclusive than they appeared to be in 1899, 1907, or 1908. Long after *Kansas v. Colorado*, Reclamation Service officials clung tenaciously to the principle of federal sovereignty—even though their careful compliance with state water codes indirectly strengthened the champions of state sovereignty. The service won some concessions from sympathetic federal courts, but it never secured a water supply sufficient for comprehensive river-basin development.

Nevertheless, the legal arguments prepared by Morris Bien and his staff—along with the Supreme Court's decision in the Winters case—are echoed in the vexing doctrine of federal reserved rights rediscovered after World War II. What the future holds for that doctrine and western water users is far from clear. Regardless of what occurs, however, the outcome will be of monumental significance.

PART TWO
Land

Americans living in large cities at the end of the twentieth century can hardly imagine the power and significance of land in the history of the United States. In the mid-eighteenth century, Cadwallader Colden, the surveyor-general of New York, observed that "[t]he hopes of having land of their own & becoming independent of Landlords is what chiefly induces people into America & they think they have never answer'd the design of their coming till they have purchased land which as soon as possible they do & begin to improve ev'n before they are able to mentain themselves." England and her North American colonies differed in many ways, but perhaps the biggest difference was the relationship between land and labor. In England land was dear and labor abundant; in the colonies, the equation was reversed, which had a profound effect on the economy, society, and politics of pre-Revolutionary America and the United States.[1]

Long before Frederick Jackson Turner delivered his famous 1893 address, "The Significance of the Frontier in American History," most Americans recognized that what made the United States different from Europe was its great size and abundance of fertile land. Free or cheap land helped the nation to escape feudalism, a landed aristocracy, and the twin despotisms of monarchy and an established church. When low-priced land was hard to find, potential settlers looked for the cause in a perversion of American institutions. As a Maine frontier lawyer observed in 1808: "The most prominent feature in their [settlers on the Maine frontier] character is a violent and implacable hatred to the law. The sheriff of the county and his officers they have marked out and doomed as victims for sacrifice and the hated name of execution [of writs in ejectment proceedings] is to terrify them no more. They declare the profession of law must come down, that lawyers must be extirpated and their offices prostrated with the dust. The court house they say must fall and the gaol share a similar fate."[2]

Widespread hostility to large proprietors and land companies helps explain why the new government of the United States did not reward heroes of the Revolution with gifts of public land. Congress soon backed away from its post-1785 policy of selling land at public auction in blocks of 640 acres or larger. After 1800, the minimum parcel dropped to 320 acres, and in 1804 to 160 acres. Purchasers could take up to four years to pay for land, and the price eventually settled at a modest $1.25 an acre. To a large extent, federal policy was driven by the actions of the states and land companies. Private companies often sold land on credit, and many of the original states had land of their own to sell and flooded the market from the 1780s to the War of 1812.

Settlers claimed a natural right to land and insisted that their labor, not formal paper titles or arbitrary boundary lines, gave land value and established ownership. This belief translated into the principle of preemption, established by Congress as a general policy in 1841, by which squatters on the public domain won the right to purchase a 160-acre homestead at the minimum government price once that land had been surveyed.[3] On the frontier, claims clubs proliferated to prevent any challenge to preemptive rights. The clubs permitted members to claim as much as 640 acres— four times the amount specified by the Preemption Act of 1841.[4]

Preemption, however, did not help in those instances where two or more persons claimed title to the same land. This situation was the central issue addressed in "Squatter Law in California, 1850–1858," an article that built on the work of the great land historian Paul Wallace Gates, particularly his essays on land policy in California and possessory rights or "betterment laws" in Kentucky during the 1790s and after.[5] Carey McWilliams called California "the great exception," and that fairly characterizes its land policy. In the 1850s, the state was covered by Mexican land grants that encompassed nearly 9 percent of its total area, and much of the remaining land was desert, mountains, or inaccessible. The generous pro-settler land policy followed by the United States government in Oregon and other frontier states in the 1830s and 1840s did not prevail in California, and in no state was the gulf between past experience and present circumstance, or ambition and opportunity, greater.

I became interested in squatters while reading the works of California historians, including Hubert Howe Bancroft and Josiah Royce. Their histories were in part morality plays that exhalted the passing of the frontier and the triumph of order and righteousness. Bancroft and Royce claimed that swarms of squatters attempted to steal and extort land from Mexican claimants or their assignees and thus were responsible for much of the "lawlessness" that characterized California during the 1850s. The squatter became an indispensable symbol of the dark side of the frontier. Yet he was also vital to the march of progress. Without lawlessness, there could be no civilization; without chaos, there could be no order; without vice, there could be no virtue; and without greed and dissipation, there could be no redemption by the righteous pioneer class that would one day write the history of early California to its own advangage.

Squatters were neither more nor less virtuous than other Californians, and few if any sought to become independent yeoman farmers.

Nevertheless, they were animated by a powerful natural rights view of law rooted in popular sovereignty. With the notable exception of Gates, most historians took these arguments as a smoke screen to obscure the theft of land from bona fide landowners. But the real deception was perpetrated by a set of pioneers who consciously and unconsciously used squatters as scapegoats to hide their own extensive, and often illegal, land dealings. Much of the best land in California was granted by Mexican authorities in the two decades preceding American statehood, and most squatters could not believe that Congress and the courts would confirm Mexican claims that averaged 17,000–19,000 acres apiece. The Mexican claimants, they insisted, had not lived up to the conditions imposed by the Mexican government at the time of the grants; therefore, those who held Mexican grants deserved a homestead, but no more. By the mid-1850s, the squatters became a potent force in California politics. They failed to accomplish most of their objectives, but they had a powerful effect on California property law.

"Land Monopoly in California" takes up the California story where the essay on squatter law ends. In 1989, I was asked to participate in a session honoring Professor Gates at the 1990 Economic History Association Meeting in Montreal. Recognizing Gates's enormous contribution to the agricultural and economic history of the United States, I happily agreed. Gates recognized that California was very different from the midwestern states he had studied earlier in his career. In the Midwest the family farm flourished; in California it languished. As Gates observed, the foundations of land monopoly were laid long before agribusiness fastened its hold on the state. And, he recognized, unlike midwestern states, where rampant land speculation characterized the *initial* phase of settlement but soon gave way to small farms, in California monopoly became more rather than less entrenched as time passed. According to Gates, the family farm never had a chance in California, and by the 1870s, if not earlier, rural California exhibited great extremes in wealth and poverty.

Nevertheless, Gates's analysis had two major weaknesses: he did not devote enough attention to the marked differences between California's economy and those of midwestern states, and he did not discuss how irrigation agriculture, particularly in the San Joaquin Valley, affected patterns of landholding. Gates underplayed the fact that the Golden State was too far removed from markets to raise anything but wheat for export, and that wheat did not lend itself to family farming. Moreover, California's population in the 1850s and 1860s was highly migratory, composed largely of young males who hoped to escape California as soon as possible and return home wealthy. Even when their hopes of quick riches were dashed, California's large cities offered potential farmers many occupational alternatives to agriculture. California was strikingly urban from the 1850s on, and it had little or no resemblance to the Midwest.

Gates ignored water policy, and I try to show that water did as much to dictate farm size as land. With the decline of mining, capital poured into irrigation projects in the 1870s and 1880s. Irrigation companies allied with land companies because it was far easier to sell land than water; water gave the land most of its value. Large landholders attempted to monopolize both. The best example was the Kern County Land and Water Company in the southern San Joaquin Valley around Bakersfield, destined to become a stronghold of twentieth-century agribusiness. In some places irrigation contributed to the breaking up of large holdings—particularly around Fresno—but usually the reverse was true.[6]

The piece on "George Maxwell, the Railroads, and American Land Policy, 1899–1904" also concerns the interplay of land and water policy. It focuses on a little-known but important figure in the history of the American West. Water lawyer, publicist, conservationist, and progressive gadfly, George Maxwell was pompous, self-righteous, moralistic, blindly devoted to the causes he espoused, and an extraordinary worker who knew how to inspire and how to organize. In the 1890s, he was hired by California landowners who opposed having their land included, and taxed, within irrigation districts. At a time when investment capital had dried up in the West, the irrigation district offered the only hope of smashing the great estates of the Central Valley and replacing them with family farms. Maxwell became the paid advocate of large landowners, who were often speculators. He failed to get the district legislation ruled unconstitutional, but he helped to discredit the districts and to frighten off investors.

That done, in 1896 Maxwell turned to federal reclamation as the best way to create renewed demand for private land in California. Three years later, he formed an alliance with many of the nation's land-grant railroads. The depression of 1893 had lifted by 1899, but the West's economic future still looked bleak. Several railroad lines owned large amounts of land, particularly the Great Northern, which in 1902 held between 13 and 14 million acres in Montana and millions more in western North Dakota and Washington state. Maxwell sold federal reclamation as a pump-priming measure to build up the carrying trade of these railroads, drive up the price of their land, and encourage private capital to invest in new water projects. In 1902, many friends of federal reclamation expected the policy to start a new land rush as 60 million to 100 million acres of virgin land were opened to the plow.[7]

The most important point raised by the article is one historians of western water use have long ignored: the 1902 Reclamation Act was incomplete by itself. If the West was to become home to the small farmer, then something had to be done to protect the irrigable public lands. Once the depression of the 1890s lifted, millions of acres of these lands were taken up each year, by livestock companies as well as by dry farmers. Between 1898 and 1922, the federal government reclaimed only a few million acres by irrigation in the western half of the nation, while between 130 and 140 million acres—twice the amount of land taken from the public domain between 1868 and 1897—were claimed for dry farming. Much of that land was irrigable, and as it passed into private ownership the prospects for government irrigation projects in the northern Great Plains dimmed. Federal reclamation became a self-defeating proposition. Since the funds initially available for reclamation came from sales of public land, not from the general treasury, the more land that was sold, the less remained to be irrigated.

"George Maxwell, the Railroads, and American Land Policy" is also about the dissolution of the fragile coalition that pushed the 1902 Reclamation Act through Congress—a coalition Maxwell created. The Reclamation Act grew out of the depression of the 1890s, and Progressive Era prosperity reduced the interest of easterners in the national program, particularly the labor unions and manufacturing associations that had strongly favored the measure. Maxwell conceived of federal reclamation as a *national* reform, an effort to move land-less men to man-less land, but by the time construction began, the fears of the 1890s had dissipated. In most parts of the West, the livestock industry took precedence over farming—although the two were not necessarily incompatible—and some land could be farmed without irrigation. California and Colorado needed federal reclamation far less than their poorer neighbors because private capital was very active in those two states. In California the best public land had long since been taken. To further complicate matters, most states looked at the region's economic development in mercantilist terms; their neighbor's success was perceived as their loss. Support for federal reclamation was particularly weak on the Great Plains, which had a great need for water but offered few rivers or canyons to dam.

Maxwell's campaign for federal reclamation depended heavily on financial support from the railroads, which bankrolled his publicity mill from 1899–1905. But within a few years of the Reclamation Act's passage, railroad executives recognized that a new land rush was under way and that federal reclamation had little to do with it. Moreover, executives from the northern lines became suspicious that federal reclamation—with Maxwell's encouragement—would result in turning the tide of settlement from Montana and the northern Great Plains to the Southwest. Federal reclamation did little to benefit railroad lands.

Once the Reclamation Act took effect, Maxwell sought to abolish the Desert Land Act (1877), the Timber and Stone Act (1878), the use of land scrip, and all other legislation that allowed cattle, timber, mining, and other companies to monopolize public land. Private companies freely used these laws, along with the commutation clause of the Homestead Act (1862), to acquire land.[8] In 1903, Theodore Roosevelt created a Public Lands Commission to recommend revisions in the land laws, but he quickly backed away from reforming those laws after he discovered that powerful Republican U.S. senators from the West—including Francis E. Warren (Wyoming), Henry Teller (Colorado), and H. C. Hansbrough (North Dakota)—thought that reform would paralyze land prices and discourage immigrants from moving into their states. Roosevelt was more concerned with the 1904 election than with eliminating the worst features of the nation's land laws or even with ensuring the long-term success of the Reclamation Act. Nor did the commission—which consisted of William Richards (commissioner of the General Land Office), Gifford Pinchot (head of the forest office in the Department of Agriculture), and Frederick Haynes Newell (director of the Reclamation Service)—demonstrate much enthusiasm for reform. Not until the 1930s was the public domain closed to entry, and by that time little public land of value remained. The dream of turning the West into a region of family farms was all but dead.

CHAPTER FOUR

Squatter Law in California, 1850–1858

On June 29, 1850, Sacramento's *Placer Times* warned that the city was on the verge of revolution. The editor lashed out at the "turbulent and misguided body of men" who had "imposed upon their fellow citizens a monstrous perversion of public law and moral right." Squatters occupied much of the city; they had staked out lots, erected fences, pitched tents, and established a claims club to survey plots and register titles. These men sought, in the words of the *Times*, to "terrify their opponents into submission" by provoking anarchy and class conflict. The remedy was clear: "For ourselves, when the law has become powerless, and the public authority is derided, when all existing sanctions in the state are disregarded, we know of no other power than the law of arms." Six weeks later, war broke out in Sacramento. Before it was over, the city assessor, sheriff, and a half dozen residents had been killed. The 1850 squatter uprising is one of the most famous in western history—and one of the most misunderstood. It was hardly an instance of "lawlessness" or irrational violence.[1]

This essay takes a fresh look at squatters by focusing on the relationship between law and politics and the efforts of public officials to reconcile the legal values of different groups of frontier residents. My purpose is not to glorify or to romanticize the squatters, but rather to suggest that there was far more to this phenomenon than most historians have recognized. The squatters blended greed and idealism, self-interest and a passionate devotion to natural rights. They assumed that some legal principles were immutable, and they challenged constituted authority only when law and right appeared to part company. They operated within a well-defined legal culture that enabled them to win strong public sympathy. Initially, the California legislature and courts extended substantial support to the squatters, not just because they were numerous, and not just because they had considerable political influence, but because their arguments had a powerful logic and appeal. To be sure, the squatters had plenty of enemies, particularly among businessmen, but the squatters called upon such time-worn legal principles as popular sovereignty, preemption, and equal access to wealth to justify their actions. Only in the mid-1850s, after the U.S. Supreme Court paved the way for the wholesale approval of Mexican land grants, did the squatters' legal position erode. Then their values collided with calcifying formal law.

Sacramento's squatter war was inextricably tied to the career of one of California's most notable pioneers and heroes, John Augustus Sutter. Sutter's early life provided many clues to his later career—a tendency toward bravado and extravagance; a warm, outgoing personality; and a richly romantic imagination. Born in Germany (1803) and raised in Switzerland, Sutter's Burgdorf dry-goods business failed in 1834. Faced with the prospect of debtor's prison, he fled to New York, leaving his family behind. He spent the next five years wandering from St. Louis, to Santa Fe, to Oregon, to Honolulu, and to Sitka, before arriving in California in 1839. By that time, he had become "Captain Sutter, formerly of the Swiss Guard of France"—a fabricated title for fabricated service. The merchant was becoming a prince. After Sutter assumed Mexican citizenship, the governor of Alta California awarded him eleven square leagues of land (about 49,000 acres) at the confluence of the Sacramento and American rivers. There he established a kind of feudal barony, "New Helvetia" as he called it, using Indian labor. The centerpiece of New Helvetia was Sutter's Fort, which consisted of adobe walls 3 feet thick and 18 feet high enclosing a courtyard 300 feet long by 160 feet wide. Cannons capped the northeast and southeast corners. Just who the fort was built to protect *against* is subject to conjecture, but it was an unmistakable symbol for a would-be aristocrat. It became the terminus of the overland trail to California, and Sutter became the benefactor of many hard-pressed immigrants. In 1845, Sutter received an additional twenty-two leagues of land from the governor, completing his California empire. Thereafter, he became "General" Sutter, presumably in exchange for services rendered to the Mexican government. After some hesitation, he supported the Bear Flag Revolt, independence, and eventually statehood for California. Like many who went West, Sutter created a persona to match his dreams.[2]

At the beginning of the Gold Rush, Sutter hoped that Sutterville—a town he laid out in January 1846, three miles south of the fort on high ground that never flooded—would succeed Monterey as the capital of Alta California. But the Mexican War intervened and Sutter was more and more besieged by his creditors. In October 1848, desperately trying to avoid the attachment of his property, he transferred title to his son, John A. Sutter, Jr., who had just arrived in California. The twenty-one-year-old younger Sutter quickly discovered three things about the father he had not seen for fourteen years: his father's financial records were hopelessly jumbled and poorly maintained; his father was at least $80,000 in debt; and his father was—by modern standards at least—an incurable drunkard whose judgment was impaired for days or weeks on end and who gave away his property with reckless abandon. It was not unusual for the elder Sutter to spend $1,000 providing friends with an evening's supply of champagne, wine, food, and cigars.[3] He had already deeded away large parts of Sutterville to friends. Therefore, during the winter of 1848–1849, the merchant Sam Brannan—who then ran a combination cantina/trading post out of Sutter's Fort—persuaded the younger Sutter to lay out a new town between Sutter's Fort and the Sacramento River embarcadero. Many merchants, Brannan argued, could not find space to rent in Sutter's Fort and would snap up Sacramento lots because that city would have better dock facilities and more direct access to the gold country. And since the elder Sutter still owned most of the land within the proposed city, the growth of Sacramento would do more to extricate him from debt than the growth of Sutterville. Brannan became the first businessman to set up shop in the new city. Sutter, Jr., hired Peter Burnett—destined to become California's first governor—as his attorney and agent. Burnett subsequently became responsible for marketing town lots and, by his admission, received 25 percent of all proceeds. At this time, Sutter senior still favored Sutterville over Sacramento, but Burnett went to San Francisco to lure newly arrived argonauts to Sacramento.[4]

Sacramento's new residents found a far different city from those they had known back home. From 1848 into the early 1850s, most of the city's inhabitants camped under the stars or lived in canvas tents; wooden buildings were rare and brick buildings nonexistent. One early observer described the city as "a huge American camp meeting." As land soared in value, the incentive to buy and sell town lots increased, particularly in the business district near the waterfront. Sutter eventually resumed control over what remained of his Sacramento holdings and delegated the responsibility for selling it to Sam Brannan, Burnett, and other agents. In the months that followed, speculators bought most of Sutter's land, and many lots changed hands several times. Indeed, some were wittingly or unwittingly sold two or more times by different agents—which produced a flood of litigation against Sutter. In March 1849, after renting out the fort— by this time a decaying adobe structure surrounded by mounds of whiskey, champagne, and beer bottles left by the miners who congregated there—Sutter retired to Hock Farm near Marysville. A year later, in July 1850, Sutter transferred all his land, save for Hock Farm, to a fledgling real estate company. He received only $6,000 and one-sixth of the net proceeds. Among others, the firm included John McDougal, California's second governor. Sutter later recounted that "the better part of the profits flowed into the pockets of unscrupulous agents," and few of his "friends" passed up the opportunity to cheat him. Another golden opportunity presented itself in the summer of 1850, when the younger Sutter left California and granted Brannan and others power-of-attorney over the last large block of lots in Sacramento.[5]

Sacramento, not Sutterville, won the devotion of land speculators, but when a massive flood hit Sacramento at the end of 1849, Sutter's preference for Sutterville was vindicated. The rains that began in November 1849 continued with brief respites into the new year and by mid-January the Sacramento River covered 80 percent of the city with four feet of water. The streets that were not flooded became impassable, and many merchants lost everything as barrels, boxes, ledger books, and dead animals floated through the city. Now the title to lots became even more muddled because the flood swept away the city's tent cabins, forcing residents near the river to flee to high ground twenty blocks east of the waterfront. Property values and rents plummeted. Simultaneously, heavy snows in the Sierra drove many miners out of the hills and into Sacramento. The unusually large snowpack kept the rivers too high for placer mining until late July. As the city filled up with disgruntled argonauts, many of whom had just arrived in California, the demand for mining supplies fell and many businesses collapsed.[6]

Word that the war with Mexico had ended reached California at the beginning of 1849, at which time most Sacramento residents assumed that the military government headed by Bennett Riley had ended.[7] Thereupon, at a public meeting Henry A. Schoolcraft (yet another of Sutter's agents) was elected "First Magistrate and Recorder for the District of Sacramento," mainly to register deeds. The first state legislature did not convene until December 1849, and Sacramento did not elect its first mayor and town council until April 1850. On December 11, 1849, Sutter begged Riley to send a company of soldiers to Sacramento to protect the city from the growing number of squatters who threatened, in Sutter's words, the "worst consequences." Riley ignored Sutter's request, and no sustained attempt was made to marshal the law against the squatters until May 1850, when the new city government was in place. Meanwhile, the squatters' association filled the institutional void.[8]

In December 1849, a group of Sacramento squatters begged relief from Congress, explaining that the speculators charged bona fide settlers prohibitive prices and rents. They asked Congress "so to apportion the public domain to actual settlers only as shall preclude the gambling speculators now so rife amongst us, and assist the rights of occupants of the soil in conformity with the laws of our country."[9] Sutter had never received formal title to his grant from the government in Mexico City and its boundaries were uncertain. At the time he applied for the land, Sutter specifically asked Mexican officials to exclude the alluvial land that regularly flooded, and the speculators to whom he sold did little or nothing to improve or occupy their lots. Those who attempted to settle within the city limits balked at the prevailing high prices—particularly because they could not be sure that Sutter and his assignees were the rightful owners. If Congress or the U.S. Supreme Court confirmed Sutter's Sacramento grant, the squatters' association promised to honor that decision. But Sutter's agents, as well as those who bought from the agents, feared that it would take years for Washington to act, during which time they would lose all profits from use of the contested land. The longer the delay in evicting the squatters, moreover, the greater the likelihood that possessory rights would ripen.

The squatters were harassed by lawsuits and eviction notices, and slowly city officials tightened a legal noose. First—in an attempt to undermine the activities of the extralegal claims club—the city council proclaimed that no one but the city surveyor could mark off lots within the city. Then, with the full approval of city officials, the probate judge who heard local trespass cases decided that evicted squatters had no right of appeal to the courts. In the eyes of the dispossessed and their allies, these actions made the existing city government "extra-legal." It had violated basic precepts of unwritten law, and, consequently, its edicts were null and void. In a manifesto adopted in August, the squatters promised to "disregard all decisions of our courts in land cases and all summonses or executions by the sheriff, constable, or other officer of the present county or city touching this matter." They took great care, however, to legitimize their actions, pledging to be "governed by martial law." The property rights of those Sacramento residents who did not take up arms against the squatters "will be sacredly regarded and protected . . . but the property and lives of those who take the field against them will share the fate of war"—that is, become contraband.[10]

Charles Robinson, who drafted the manifesto, would one day sit in the California legislature and assume the governorship of Kansas, and another squatter leader, James McClatchy, founded the Sacramento *Bee* in 1857. McClatchy, according to historian Walton Bean, "brought an Irishman's hatred of land monopoly to his leadership of the squatters in the gold rush period and then to the *Bee's* editorial columns."[11] Neither man fitted the characterization of squatters purveyed by the state's leading periodicals. Few newspaper editors recognized any differences among squatters or attempted to understand or publicize their legal arguments. California's newspapers circulated widely in the East, and reports of violence, let alone sympathy for squatter rights, frightened away potential residents and retarded the advance in land values.[12] Then as now, newspapers supported themselves through advertising, and businessmen shunned journals that questioned their property rights or challenged their moral authority within the community. Historians who later pored over the pages of these periodicals shared this bias. Hubert Howe Bancroft, Josiah Royce, and others emphasized the lawlessness of the frontier but paid little attention to squatter perceptions of the nature of law, the source of law, or the moral authority of law. The frontier became the antithesis of civilization: a place beyond family, beyond church, and beyond the conventions and mores of civil society. In order for good to triumph over evil, and for the "pioneer generation" to rescue California from the turmoil of the 1850s—as, for example, many historians claimed it had through San Francisco's vigilance committees of 1851 and 1856—the frontier had to appear as wild and disorderly as possible, as a place where morality broke down and where parasitic types preyed on the law-abiding and righteous. Squatters had to be shorn of any legal or moral justification for their conduct; otherwise, the history of early California was simply the triumph by force of one group of white settlers over another.

The Bancrofts and Royces sympathized with the Mexican grantees and regarded what they called "squatterism" as a particularly pernicious form of lawlessness. In the eyes of the first generation of California historians, society had virtually collapsed before the law-abiding rose up to restore order. Writing in the 1880s, Bancroft concluded that the squatter was the antithesis of the rule of law. "Squatterism" was "only a phase of mob law." "Popular sovereignty," according to Bancroft, was no more than a brazen attempt to sidestep or subvert long-established legal principles. What made squatters so dangerous was their numbers. Unscrupulous politicians and jurists pandered to the "squatter element." They captured political parties, local offices, the courts, and even the legislature. Sutter's claim, according to Bancroft, was "beyond all question valid." After all, Sutter was first on the scene, and he had lived on it, cultivated it, and raised flocks and herds on it. Unlike most Mexican claimants, he enjoyed title through deed as well as document. Bancroft brushed aside the American faith in preemption and gave no credence to the squatter arguments.

Josiah Royce, a much more thoughtful observer than Bancroft, essentially agreed. "Every moral force," he remarked in his history of the state, "every force, namely, that worked for the real future prosperity of the new commonwealth, was ipso facto against these lawless squatters." Like most Californians of the late nineteenth century, Royce argued that the state's future depended on attracting a class of hard-working, thrifty, and pious small farmers. Mining and uncertain land titles had branded the state with a permanent stain of social irresponsibility and contributed to a chronic restlessness and instability. As long as agriculture languished, California's social, economic, intellectual, and moral development would be stunted.[13]

Most twentieth-century historians shared this view. Of the major historians of California, only Paul Gates attempted to understand the squatter point of view.[14] One of John Sutter's biographers linked the "squatter spirit" to Manifest Destiny and the "demagogic bait of untold square miles of uninhabited land to be added to the public domain."[15] Another traced the squatter impulse to an atavistic leveling tendency—resentment that Sutter had succeeded in amassing a huge estate while many miners had stumbled in the pursuit of wealth. "From remote ages," he explained, "man has been, as he still is, inclined to suspect those who rank him in wealth and preferment. This, we think, was clearly evidenced in this era." He conceded that some squatters were "actuated by conscientious motives," but they were "led astray by the overpowering influence of designing men. The moral obliquity of the leaders in this trouble, it occurs to me, is pronounced."[16] The index of Mary Floyd Williams's history of the San Francisco vigilance committee of 1851 defined "squatters" as "lawless settlers," and land historian Roy Robbins noted in his brief discussion of land titles in early California that "[n]ever before had there been such a total disregard for law and order" in the United States. More recently, John Caughey's history of California portrays squatters as greedy men bent on defying authority and obstructing justice.[17]

The "rule of law" is something more than equity or even due process. It is a "law-mindedness" rooted in the conviction that, ultimately, "the people" have a greater right to define and interpret the rules they live by than legal experts. This view of law predominated in all parts of the United States in the nineteenth century. Historians of the West have observed it in the Iowa Claims Clubs, on the Oregon Trail, and in the California gold camps.[18] "Popular Sovereignty" reinforced a deep suspicion of centralized authority; an abiding faith in localism; and the conviction that land was the foundation of opportunity, freedom, and independence. Jefferson had argued that liberty could flourish only in a society dominated by small, independent family farmers. During the Jacksonian period sympathy for squatter rights increased as the last property qualifications for voting and holding office disappeared, as common schools proliferated, as the states ended imprisonment for debt and humanized penal codes, and as hostility to judges and lawyers—whom many Americans perceived as all-too-willing agents of the new forces of industry—became widespread.

Many political thinkers of the second quarter of the nineteenth century regarded the monopolization of money, natural resources, goods, and services as a perversion of law and government by self-serving elites. It was not the natural or inevitable by-product of a nascent market economy. Special charters to corporations (especially banks), direct or indirect government subsidies to private companies, and tariff concessions all reflected a society out of balance.[19] So did squatters. A vast body of land and a burgeoning population found expression in the national preemption laws of 1830, 1834, 1838, and 1841. By the 1830s, the minimum price per acre for public land became the established price, and after the Depression of 1837, Congress faced increasing pressure to provide free land. This pressure came mainly from eastern workers, but squatters and western politicians made the same demand. They argued that human beings had a natural right to a livelihood; that "virgin land" had no value until it was occupied;

that the Spanish had drained off settlers by granting free homesteads; that the cost of clearing, breaking, and fencing land—along with the burden of building schools, roads, and paying the expenses of government—already imposed too great a burden on residents of the frontier; and that many urban problems could be traced to land monopolies.[20]

The states also responded to squatter demands. Kentucky and Virginia claimed much of the same trans-Appalachian frontier, and between 1795 and 1820 they granted it to two sets of settlers. Kentucky's legislature promised preemptioners the right to as much as four hundred acres (at twenty dollars for each one hundred acres). It ordered all nonresident owners to list their lands for taxes on pain of forfeiture; imposed a 50 and later 100 percent penalty on delinquent taxes; and excused occupants from paying rents or profits from the use of contested land prior to the filing of ejectment suits. In such suits, the occupant could demand restitution for his improvements *if* their value exceeded 75 percent of the price of the land alone. As an alternative, he could buy the tract by paying the assessed value without improvements. (If the improvements were worth less than 75 percent of the land's value, the legal owner had the choice.) And if a settler lived on land for seven years and paid taxes thereon, he automatically won a possessory right to that parcel. The Kentucky experience established two precedents: the right of occupants whose title was rejected by the courts to the value of their improvements, and the right of title through uncontested use.[21]

Although the U.S. Supreme Court ultimately upheld the rights of Virginia's grantees against those claiming under Kentucky laws, the special privileges extended to actual settlers were sustained repeatedly by Kentucky's courts.[22] Other states, moreover, copied Kentucky and promised evicted squatters the value of their improvements, less the profits derived from the land after the commencement of an eviction action. Ohio enacted occupancy laws in 1810, 1816, and 1843; Illinois in 1810; Indiana in 1818; Missouri in 1834; Alabama in 1836; Arkansas and Michigan in 1838; Iowa in 1839; Mississippi in 1836; Wisconsin in 1849; Minnesota in 1851; Oregon in 1854; and Kansas in 1855. Except in Kansas, these privileges were limited solely to those who had "color of title," not to anyone who had occupied and improved the land.[23] Therefore, squatter rights remained in dispute when California entered the Union.

Mexican-American residents of California were ill-prepared for the battles over land that raged during the 1850s and 1860s. Alta California was isolated—as remote from Mexico City as it was from Boston, New York, and Washington, D.C.—and it contained few farms. In the 1830s and 1840s, limited local markets for agricultural products, combined with the dominance of the hide and tallow trade with New England, reinforced a pastoral economy based on "large" ranchos and the open range. Land was abundant and relatively worthless—save for the grasses it produced. The economic imperatives of frontier California—where cattle required as much as thirty acres of grazing room apiece—made 4,000- or 5,000-acre ranches modest enterprises. Few title disputes arose, despite the imprecise boundaries of Mexican grants; and since much of the land had been awarded in exchange for military or civilian service—few grants were made to encourage colonization—landowners felt little need to conform to the specific terms of their awards.[24] Yet the old economic order began to crumble even before the Gold Rush. Involvement in the hide and tallow trade turned the Californios into a debtor class, and they had no way to extricate themselves save by selling cattle and mortgaging their land. As William Robert Garner observed at the beginning of 1847, "The creditors are already making preparations for the recovery of money due to them by individuals in every part of California; they are appointing attorneys, who will act with vigor in the performance of their obligations, and there is little doubt that many a noble tract of land will have to change its owner under the hammer."[25]

The loose legal system of Alta California rested on fundamentally different principles from those embraced by the Anglo-Americans who flooded into the state in the 1840s and 1850s. Mexican California contained few lawyers, no law libraries, no formal body of law, no elaborate legal rules, and no enforcement system. Alcaldes decided most legal disagreements without resorting to formal jurisprudence. Mexican law was designed to prevent litigation rather than encourage it, and when litigation occurred local officials paid far more attention to community mores than to abstract legal principles; they sought to heal social wounds and maintain group cohesion as well as to resolve specific disputes. Such principles as prompt bail, public confrontation of an accuser, and trial by jury were unknown in Alta California. Americans were used to a system that drew sharp lines between executive, legislative, and judicial authority, but the office of alcalde combined the three functions and seemed to concentrate arbitrary power. Moreover, Americans saw legal contests in adversarial terms. Trials were occasions during which each side presented itself in the best light and portrayed the opposition in the worst light. They were designed to determine a clear winner and loser. This kind of confrontation, with formal cross-examination of witnesses by professional lawyers, was alien to Mexican California. American law was obsessed with predictability and consistency; Mexican law with accommodation and conciliation.[26]

Before 1846, Spanish and Mexican authorities made over eight hundred grants covering between 13 and 14 million acres of the state's best arable land. After California became a state, Congress created a special land commission to review those claims. Each grantee or assignee was required to file a claim with the commission within two years. The commission's decisions could be appealed first to a federal district court and, if necessary, to the U.S. Supreme Court. The claims averaged between 17,000 and 19,000 acres apiece, but several Mexican families held estates in excess of 300,000 acres. Hearings before the commission lasted from 1852–1856, though the last appeal was not decided until the 1870s. In all, the commissioners confirmed 553 grants covering 8,850,000 acres. Over 75 percent of the claims were upheld.[27]

Although the land commission has often been portrayed as an institution designed to rob Mexican Americans of their patrimony,[28] at least initially the board was highly sympathetic to the Mexican grantees. The commission was a concession to precedent—a throwback to the process by which Spanish grants in Louisiana, Florida, and Missouri had been reviewed. Its great weakness was that it focused exclusively on disputes between claimants and the United States, not between the claimants themselves. It did nothing, for example, to quell litigation among those whose grants overlapped. In any case, there was no feasible alternative to this method of adjudication. Thomas Hart Benton proposed a blanket confirmation of Mexican claims, reserving a right of appeal to those who opposed particular grants. This, he argued, would spare claimants with incontestable titles the time and expense of securing documentation and legal counsel to present their case. But such a policy might well have led to enormous bloodshed. Given the relatively small number of Mexican claimants and the army of squatters, Benton's proposal was as unrealistic as the frequently heard squatters' demand that no Mexican grant should exceed 160 or 320 acres.[29]

Squatters hoped that the land commission would repudiate most of the Mexican claims. In 1853 and 1854, Congress opened to preemption all unsurveyed land outside Mexican grants, and all claims disallowed by the land commission. This convinced many newcomers to California that the land commission would hold grantees to the letter of Mexican, if not American, law. They assumed that Congress, the commission, the state legislature, and the courts would limit even the valid Mexican claims and transfer the surplus land to the public domain. The sheer mass of cases, and the fact that none of the original members knew much about land laws or read or spoke Spanish, made the commission cautious.[30] It issued its first rulings in August 1852, all of which favored the Mexican claimants. The proceedings of the commission, regularly published in northern California newspapers, convinced many Californians that the panel had violated a public trust. The issue extended far beyond the Mexican grants. Residents of the mining camps feared that the commission would set an unhealthy precedent: if it ignored squatter rights, Congress might use its decisions as an excuse to evict miners from the public lands or force them to pay rent or purchase licenses. Not surprisingly, some politicians suggested abolishing the commission and turning over the review of Mexican grants to the U.S. District Court, which, it was hoped, would show less sympathy to the claimants.[31] The principle of preemption was also undermined by President James Buchanan's decision to dump 11 million acres of the best public land in the Sacramento and San Joaquin valleys on the market following the depression of 1857. Many of the 11 million acres were taken for cash or scrip, often by speculators, but it remained unsold for more than a decade, during which time it was closed to preemptioners and homesteaders. To make matters worse, by 1861 only 20 to 25 percent of the state's public land had been surveyed, almost all of it in barren and remote parts of the state, far removed from transportation and markets.[32]

Not surprisingly, Jacksonian debates over monopoly, special privilege, and corruption in government reached their peak in frontier California.[33] Many settlers assumed that the United States, having won California on the field of battle, should treat *all* land within the new state's borders as the spoils of war.[34] The federal government had tacitly condoned the trespassing of miners on government land and had followed a "pro-settler" policy on virtually every earlier frontier. Mining codes provided all white males with equal access to wealth, and in the absence of certain conditions, particularly continuous use, mining claims were subject to forfeiture. If the argonauts could create mining districts and establish rules to regulate the use of one part of the public domain, why could not agriculturalists do the same thing elsewhere on the public domain? The emphasis mining law placed on rapid development of mineral resources reinforced the principle of maximum use central to squatter law. Finally, the adoption of increasingly liberal preemption laws during the 1830s and 1840s, as well as the need to attract residents to California—owing to its isolation and vulnerability to foreign attack—suggested that Congress would reward actual settlers in every way possible.

The argonauts represented a culture steeped in the philosophy of Harrington and Locke, a culture that regarded private property as the foundation of most basic rights. Human beings were endowed with an instinct for property closely linked to an instinct for liberty. Property rights were not absolute. Government could impose limits on private property in various ways—such as through eminent domain, taxation, and police power—but no society could flourish that thwarted the acquisitive impulse.[35] The Mexican grants were incompatible with the family farm, with the concept of equal access to wealth, and with the Anglo-American presumption that no property rights were absolute. Squatters knew that the Treaty of Guadalupe Hidalgo conferred certain "inviolable" rights. But that treaty had to be construed in light of American as well as Mexican standards of justice. Who could believe that American lawmakers would uphold the right of an individual or family to thousands of acres that had never been surveyed, occupied, or improved? When squatters lost out in title contests, moreover, they should receive restitution for their improvements, if only because those improvements usually drove up the price of the land. Squatters bought and sold land, but they considered their brand of speculation different from that practiced by land monopolists. Speculation was necessary to secure the "grubstake" needed to acquire tools, livestock, seed, and lumber and to tide a farmer over until his first crops came in. It also provided the capital necessary to pay the cost of litigating boundaries and titles.

Preemption and Manifest Destiny took on added importance because many Mexican grants were questionable. The number of ranchos increased from one hundred in 1836 to five hundred a decade later, and half these grants were approved during the 1840s. Many squatters assumed that, anticipating war, the last Mexican governors had given away as much land as possible to prevent the United States from enjoying the fruits of victory. In a report published in 1850, Henry Halleck, California's secretary of state during the late 1840s, surveyed the Mexican grants and concluded that most were "very doubtful, if not entirely fraudulent." He warned that a large percentage of land had already fallen into the hands of non-Mexican speculators. A published report by William Carey Jones, an agent for the Interior Department, reached the opposite conclusion, arguing that the Mexican grants were "mostly perfect titles." But this document was widely perceived as self-serving. In the late 1840s, Jones had acquired thousands of acres of Mexican claims, and he was the attorney and agent for John C. Frémont, who held the huge Mariposa grant east of present-day Modesto and Merced. Both men were married to daughters of powerful U.S. Senator Thomas Hart Benton of Missouri, and as mentioned earlier, Benton favored the wholesale confirmation of the Mexican grants.[36]

Frémont's claim was widely regarded as unjust if not fraudulent, and the more lenient the policy followed toward the Mexican grantees, the greater the chance that his grant would be approved. In 1844, Governor Micheltorena awarded ten square leagues in what would become Mariposa County to Juan Alvarado, and Frémont bought it three years later for $3,000. When gold was discovered there in the spring of 1849, the land rapidly advanced in value. Frémont hired Jones to present his case to the land commission, and the claim was confirmed in January 1853. Alvarado never saw the land and did not comply with a single condition of Mexican law: the tract had not been surveyed; it contained no permanent residence; it had never been occupied by whites; and it had not been improved. Not surprisingly, no grant was more unpopular than that held by John C. Frémont.[37]

There were, of course, many different kinds of squatters in Gold Rush California. Some entered land with the complicity, or at least forbearance, of claimants or assignees who knew that settlement generally drove up property values. Others trespassed solely in the hope of being "bought out" by the bona fide owner, and speculators often hired entrymen to locate on rural or urban land, then purchased their "claims." There were plenty of squatters who had no desire to own land because with ownership went taxes. Some used the land to graze cattle stolen from the herds of Mexican grantees. Others engaged in mining, hunting, trapping, or lumbering. Those later evicted—and the process of removing a squatter often took years—might sow several crops of wheat or raise a fine herd of livestock during the period of trespass. In 1852, nine families claimed preemption rights to parts of Thomas O. Larkin's rancho on the Sacramento River and stripped away its best timber. Eventually, both the land commission and district court sustained Larkin's claim. In the meantime, however, he bought out many of the squatters, perhaps fearing reprisals if they were chased off at gunpoint, perhaps hoping that conciliatory treatment would persuade them to purchase the land once he had secured clear title.[38]

Not all squatters wanted something for nothing. Many made a valiant effort to buy their land, some paid twice (for example, when two Mexican claimants held overlapping grants), and some incurred enormous legal expenses as they struggled to build their homes. Since most land that was clearly part of the public domain was far removed from the state's population centers and markets, would-be farmers had little choice but to settle next to Mexican grants, and since most of those grants had not been surveyed and had indefinite boundaries, trespass was inevitable.[39] The fact that neither urban nor rural squatters did much to improve their claims has been taken as prima facie evidence that they were basically extortionists. But what incentive did settlers have to build homes, fence land, and plant crops unless they could be sure of a possessory right?[40]

Preemptioners who squatted on or near Mexican grants ran great risks. If they settled on a Mexican claim in the hope it would be disallowed, they faced the prospect of losing their improvements. But if they purchased land from a claimant whose boundaries were subsequently adjusted, or whose application was subsequently rejected, they might lose the cost of the land as well as the value of their improvements. The land commission posed a threat to grantees and to squatters alike. Even if the land commission eventually rejected most of the grants, that process could take years. Meanwhile, the value of the valid claims would increase— along with the price squatters would have to pay eventually. Most squatters were willing to pay what their land was worth in 1849 or 1850, but not the inflated prices of 1853 or 1854. Obviously, the longer the confirmation process took, the greater the chance of litigation and violence.[41]

Litigation was only part of the problem. In 1850 and 1851, frequent and bitter clashes over real estate in Sacramento and San Francisco raised the fear that squatters—swelled by the large number of miners who wintered in town—would torch and pillage the business districts and seize the institutions of local government. Between May 1850 and June 1851, five major fires swept through large parts of San Francisco, and the Vigilance Committee of 1851 charged that these conflagrations had been touched off by arsonists bent on plunder. The fact that the fire of May 4, 1851, occurred on the first anniversary of another major fire appeared to be more than coincidence. The number of organized squatters far exceeded the number of law enforcement officers. To make matters worse, many police sympathized with (or at least condoned) their demands. California's court system was as yet undeveloped; there were no county or state prisons; most counties lacked the tax revenue to pay for institutions of local government; district attorneys were young and inexperienced; and justice was often cheated because witnesses to crimes rarely stayed long in any one place.[42]

Squatters received plenty of initial encouragement from the state legislature, the state supreme court, and the federal district court that heard appeals from the land commission. Three years before Congress sanctioned preemption in California, the first legislature (1849–1850) took the law into its own hands by awarding preemption rights to those "now occupied and settled upon" up to 160 acres of public land. The boundaries had to be clearly marked, the parcel had to be continuously occupied, and claimants had to spend at least $100 on improvements. The legislature did not require the land to be surveyed or fenced, but leaving it for longer than three months constituted abandonment and the forfeiture of all rights.[43] A second law prohibited legal actions against trespassers for the recovery of land unless the plaintiff had purchased or occupied the land within five years prior to the ejectment action. Squatters could acquire a possessory right through cultivation and improvement or the erection of a "substantial enclosure"; or use of the land to supply fuel, fencing materials, timber, pasture, "or for the ordinary use of the occupant." When a "known lot or simple farm" had been "partly improved," the remainder of a claim was deemed to have been "occupied," even though it had not been enclosed, cleared, or improved in any way. In short, the legislature shifted the burden of proving title from the occupant of land to the nominal owner.[44]

The California Supreme Court—elected by the first legislature—encountered a host of thorny problems as it attempted to reconcile the Mexican and American systems of jurisprudence and define the law in a new land. Its greatest challenge was to win the respect of a public that had little faith in lawyers and judges. In February 1850, the Senate Committee on the Judiciary noted that it was a "popular doctrine" that common sense was

entitled to higher consideration than the reflection and ripe experience of the most profound jurist. . . . In short, reduced to its simplest terms . . . the proposition is, that the man who is entirely ignorant of a multifarious subject, is more competent to form a just and correct judgment concerning it, than the man who has made it the business of his life to comprehend it in theory and understand it in its minute and practical details.[45]

The paramount legal question in 1850—for squatters and Mexican claimants alike—was, what constituted the possession of land? Did a landowner have to erect a house and occupy it? Was he responsible for erecting fences to warn *off* trespassers? Or was it sufficient to clear the land of brush and drive stakes around the perimeter? To complicate the problem, the act of laying claim to farmland differed from that required to hold urban lots. Rural landowners could establish a possessory right by cutting down trees, planting crops, fencing, or digging a well—in many cases without living on the land.

Two important cases testing possessory rights came before the California Supreme Court in 1850. Recognizing their importance, Justice Nathaniel Bennett asked that they be argued twice. In the first, an ejection suit, a squatter named Hepburn had occupied vacant land near San Jose. The plaintiffs had once lived on the land, but at the time of Hepburn's entry it was unfenced, uncultivated, and showed no sign of ever having been used. Therefore, Hepburn erected a house, hoping to establish a preemption right. In 1844, the land had been granted to an "emancipated" Indian identified in the 1850 reports only as "Roberto." The original grant prohibited Roberto from selling or encumbering it. The Indian, however, became indebted to a man named Sunol in 1847 and deeded him the ranch to satisfy that obligation. Sunol, in turn, sold part of the property to the other plaintiffs in December 1849. Justice Bennett supported the trespasser. To eject Hepburn, he concluded, the plaintiffs would have to demonstrate that they were in actual possession at the time Hepburn built his house. Bennett acknowledged that Sunol's horses and cattle once grazed upon the 160-acre tract in question, but he decided that this was of no consequence unless the animals had been confined to that land. Equally important, Bennett insisted that *the terms of Mexican grants had to be strictly adhered to*. The proviso that Roberto could not sell or encumber the land was, in Bennett's judgment, intended to protect Indians from themselves and from unscrupulous whites. The wisdom of this policy was obvious: Roberto had disposed of an estate worth perhaps $100,000 to erase a debt of $500.[46]

It would, indeed, be an unfortunate state of things if a person in the actual possession of land, having entered without violence and in good faith and under a title, which to say the least is equally good with that under which his adversary claims, could, after having made valuable improvements on the premises, be thrust out of possession upon such loose and indefinite acts as those upon which the plaintiff relies. Were that so, then indeed would there be no security to the possessions of most of the people of the city of San Francisco.

In these cases Bennett established two principles sympathetic to squatters: Mexican grantees and assignees were bound strictly by the terms of their original charters, and the burden of proof in eviction proceedings rested on the plaintiff rather than on those who occupied the land.[47]

The California Supreme Court overturned *Woodworth* in 1853, but it did so on the grounds that the American alcalde had the same right to grant land within the city's boundary as his Mexican predecessor.[48] Justice Bennett's major argument remained intact: in order to perfect title to land granted by Mexico, all conditions of that grant had to be complied with. In 1852, the court ruled that the Mexican Congress had decided in 1824 and 1828 that no title could vest until the territorial assembly had approved it and the proper documents had been recorded and filed. The mere award of land, without further compliance with the conditions set forth in a grant, constituted at best an inchoate title, and such titles were insufficient to sustain an ejectment action. As the court noted in passing judgment on a grant from Governor Alvarado: "There is no map attached, no survey, record, or evidence that the plaintiffs have ever been put in judicial posses-sion. . . . But that these requisitions must be fully complied with, this court has no doubt, without which . . . the title did not pass to the grantees, but remained in the government of Mexico." Subsequently, the court con-cluded, the particular land at issue in the 1852 case became part of the public domain of the United States.[49]

The crisis came to a head in the mid-1850s. By 1853, California squat-ters held the balance of power between the Democratic, Whig, and Know-Nothing parties.[50] In 1854, a sharp recession hit California, as mineral production and migration into the state fell off. The value of the state's tax-able property, which had steadily risen from 1851 to 1854, shrank by 5 per-cent in 1855.[51] Displaced miners flooded into the cities, and trespassing incidents soared, particularly in San Francisco. There, eviction actions and squatter riots resulted in many deaths and injuries and in June 1854, led to the formation of an "Association for the Protection of the Rights of Prop-erty, and the Maintenance of Order."[52] Then, at the end of that year, the U.S. Supreme Court stunned squatters by upholding the infamous Fré-mont grant in an opinion that proved to be the turning point in the battle for squatter rights.

The Frémont case was filled with irony. The land commission con-firmed the grant in December 1852, but a year later the District Court for Northern California overturned that ruling. Thereupon Frémont appealed and the U.S. Supreme Court issued its decision in December 1854.[53] The same man who claimed a baronial estate of 44,000 acres would soon become the first presidential candidate of the new Republican Party—a party pledged to free labor and the family farm.[54] Many Republicans went beyond the principle of preemption to embrace free land, and Congress had debated several homestead bills in the years following the Mexican War. And while Chief Justice Roger B. Taney and the other Democratic members on the high court had close ties to Frémont's father-in-law, Senator Thomas Hart Benton of Missouri, they also feared aristocracies, monopoly, special privilege, and all things Mexican. Nor could they have been comfortable with Frémont's antislavery stance. Most important, they gave far more weight to written than to customary law.[55] The high court had ruled on dozens of contested titles within Louisiana and Florida, and in those cases the judges fell into two groups. The majority emphasized the paramount right of American settlers to establish title to unoccupied land through preemption; the minority emphasized the sanctity of the Spanish grants.[56]

As late as 1850, the U.S. Supreme Court had, like the California high court, insisted that compliance with Spanish and Mexican law was necessary to perfect land titles within territory acquired by the United States.[57] In the Frémont case, however, Chief Justice Taney, speaking for the majority, decided that the California land grants were different from those in Louisiana and Florida. In Louisiana and Florida, he argued, grants had been made to encourage settlement and constituted only a survey right. That right ripened into title only after the survey had been completed and filed with the proper authorities. In California, however, the land was awarded solely to benefit individual grantees. There the grant preceded the survey. It followed that the Alvarado claim vested "in the grantee a present and immediate interest." The fact that Alvarado failed to comply with the conditions stipulated by the Mexican government was relatively unimportant; the grant was not contested during the period of Mexican rule, nor did it specify a forfeiture procedure. Moreover, Taney reasoned, Alvarado had good reason not to live up to the terms of the award. The Mariposa Valley was inhabited by hostile Indians who made it impossible to survey, use, or reside on the land. Nor could Alvarado be faulted for the territorial legislature's failure to confirm the grant. That body met irregularly—perhaps only once after the award was made—and it was too preoccupied with other matters, including the war with the United States, to pay any attention to land that was then relatively worthless. As for Alvarado's sale to Frémont (also ostensibly prohibited by Mexican law), Taney insisted that by prohibiting entail in 1823, the Mexican Congress made any such limitation illegal. In any case, since Frémont had purchased the land in 1847, *after* the American conquest, Alvarado's sale to Frémont was perfectly legal.[58]

Justices Catron—who had written most of the opinions pertaining to titles within the Louisiana Purchase—and Campbell filed impassioned dissents. The Spanish, they observed, had ruled out Indian hostilities as an excuse for failing to comply with the terms of land grants. If hostile Indians had posed such a great danger, why did not Mexican authorities include an "escape clause" in the original grant? "Alvarado manifestly took the grant at his own risk," Catron reasoned, "and if he did not intend to perform the condition of inhabitation, or could not do it, he must bear the consequences. To hold otherwise would be to subvert the manifest design of the colonization laws of Mexico, by reserving indefinitely, to single individuals, large bodies of uncultivated and unoccupied lands." Equally important, the Mariposa grant was distressingly vague, and by opening the door to the wholesale approval of virtually all Mexican grants, it undermined the intent of Congress in setting up the land commission. If the Frémont claim was upheld, Catron insisted, "all others must likewise be . . . as no balder case than the one before us can exist in California, where the grant is not infected with fraud or forgery." California was filling up with people who had filed for preemption rights, and they had as much right to legal protection as the Mexican grantees. Congress had extended preemption to California in 1853 as an incentive "to populate the country, which is yet in progress." If land did not have to be surveyed as a condition of title, then the boundaries of floating grants could be drawn arbitrarily to include preemptioners, a large percentage of whom lived next to the Mexican tracts. Justice Campbell agreed. The Mexican government could, he reasoned, excuse a failure to live up to the conditions of charter obligations because the land had little value in the 1830s and 1840s. But American courts were morally obligated to consider the contests over land that had erupted *since the conquest*, not just conditions prior to the American occupation. He saw no valid distinction between Spanish and Mexican grants in Louisiana, Florida, and California.[59]

The federal district court and the California Supreme Court accepted the Frémont decision, but not before California Chief Justice Murray issued a stinging rebuke to Taney. Murray, like Catron and Campbell, was certain that the earlier U.S. Supreme Court decisions pertaining to land grants in Florida and Louisiana also applied to California:

At the risk of exposing myself to the ridicule or censure of many, for what may be considered temerity on my part in questioning the soundness of these decisions, I cannot refrain from the opinion that . . . the Supreme Court [has] taken a new departure, and entirely disregarded their previous decisions.[60] It is, however, a matter of congratulation to myself to know that this wholesale abandonment of principles, so long and satisfactorily settled, was not unanimous, and that one of the Judges on that Bench, better acquainted probably than any of his associates with this class of cases, and who has almost given shape to the law of this subject, together with another Judge, second to none in point of ability upon that or any other Bench in the United States, both dissented from the opinions in the case of Fremont, and for reasons substantially the same as those which influenced the decisions of this Court.[61]

The Frémont decision cast a long shadow over the 1855 and 1856 California legislatures. One firmly established principle of American law was that squatter rights dated only from the time the legal owner of property received formal title. Many California squatters, however, erroneously believed that the 1850 law discussed earlier barred all ejectment actions not undertaken within five years of the date of that legislation. In fact, the five-year period of adverse possession mandated by the 1850 legislature ran only from the time a grantee or assignee gained the right to sue. By 1855, squatter sentiment was so strong, and elective judges so sympathetic to settler rights, that Mexican grantees and assignees feared that the squatters would use the 1850 law as a pretext to seize their land even before the land commission finished its work. The legislature tried to compromise by rescinding the 1850 law reaffirming the five-year statute of limitations. Now, however, no possessory right could antedate the 1855 legislation.[62] Small wonder that the *Democratic State Journal* observed that "if the people were to utter their sentiments on this subject, there would not be found one in fifty in favor of the proposed alteration in this statute of repose."[63] A whole set of land titles that had seemed close to confirmation were once again up in the air. Squatters thought that the clock had been rolled back to 1850, and that the property of one class of citizens had been confiscated to shore up the monopolistic holdings of Mexican-American land barons and EuroAmerican speculators.[64] The Democratic Party, headed by Governor John Bigler, had repeatedly pledged itself to land law reform but accomplished little.[65] In June and July 1855, squatters throughout the state met to elect delegates to a state convention and to formulate statements of principle to guide the candidates they supported in the fall elections. The *Alta California* remarked that "[l]arge bodies of settlers have convened lately throughout the State. The settlers element will be a powerful one in the future politics of California."[66]

The land commission had, as a group of San Francisco settlers put it, "lost the entire confidence of the people of California, whose rights and interests they were sent here to protect."[67] When the legislature met in December 1855, the most popular pro-squatter reforms were included in the most ambitious squatter bill ever considered in the United States.

Sponsored by Senator William Shaw, head of San Francisco's most prominent settlers' association, the bill took on added urgency when John C.
Frémont received a formal patent to the Mariposa claim in February 1856.
By presuming that all land in the state was open to preemption until
proven otherwise, and by denying to lawful owners any compensation
from squatters until they received a patent, the legislation was designed to
undermine or nullify the rulings of the land commission. (This was no
small matter because five or ten years free use was often worth more than
the land itself.) The Shaw bill reduced the statute of limitations on real
estate from five to two years, prohibited the sale of land unless the owner
had resided on that land for at least one year prior to the date of sale, and
required that all squatters who occupied a piece of land for a year or more
be compensated for their improvements by the lawful owner. The requirement that squatters receive restitution for improvements was tantamount
to confiscation because the value of improvements frequently exceeded the
value of the land itself.[68]

The Shaw proposal had strong support in the assembly, but far less in
the senate, where southern California's Hispanic population was better
represented. One member of the legislature, General Covarrúbias, proposed renaming the Shaw bill "An Act to Annul the Treaty of Guadalupe
Hidalgo and Amend the Constitution of the United States," but opponents
of the legislation put up less fight than might have been expected. Many
denied that the legislature had the constitutional power to interpret treaty
rights, and, they insisted, defining property rights was a job for the courts.
The radical nature of the legislation played into the hands of its opponents.
As the *Nevada Journal* remarked, "some of the provisions of the Act are of
so outrageous and monstrous a nature, that the Supreme Court of the U.S.,
if not some lesser tribunal, will declare the law unconstitutional."[69]

Early in March, the Senate Committee on Public Lands favorably
reported a substitute bill, promising that the committee had "examined
similar statutes in other States and the judicial decisions upon them, and
find that the Act [proposed] . . . is more favorable to the possessor
[squatter] than any they have seen, and grants all to the settler that
under those decisions could be given him. An attempt to do more
would be futile."[70] Senate debate over the measure came in mid-March
1856. The strongest spokesman for the Mexican grantees was Senator De
La Guerra of Santa Barbara. He argued unsuccessfully for an amendment to pay owners for the "use and occupation" of their land from the
time a patent was issued and tried to exclude from the act all land that
had been assessed for taxation in 1851 and each year thereafter. This was
just, he insisted, because no one would pay taxes unless they had color
of title. Moreover, the great mass of squatters had taken up the land they
held in 1853 and 1854.[71]

As adopted, the Shaw bill applied to all Mexican grants not yet confirmed by the land commission and the courts. It proclaimed that "actual and peaceable possession of land shall be prima facie evidence of a right to such possession," and it promised that no ejectment action could be pressed unless done so within two years of the issuance of a formal patent. The right of parties claiming land would begin from the date of their patents; nothing could be recovered for the previous use or enjoyment of that property. When a jury decided in favor of the plaintiff in an ejectment suit, the defendant could ask the jury to determine the value of the land (including improvements, growing crops, and the cost of the use of the land from the time the patent was issued). In such cases, the plaintiff had six months to pay the rent and the value of all improvements (including interest). If he refused, the *defendant* had six months to purchase the land at a value determined by the jury.[72]

The California Supreme Court, following the lead of the U.S. Supreme Court in the Frémont case, quickly acted to invalidate the legislation. In two related cases pertaining to town lots in Sacramento, the court overturned pro-squatter decisions from that city's Sixth Judicial Court. It reaffirmed the principle of the 1855 statute of limitations: adverse possession began when a formal title was issued, not from the date a squatter entered the land. Moreover, it declared unconstitutional that part of the 1856 Settlers' Law that gave squatters the right to apply the value of their improvements against the value of the land itself and then purchase the land for the reduced price.[73] Chief Justice Murray—who had questioned the Frémont decision—recognized that since many Mexican grants had been surveyed to include squatter improvements, the grantees and their assignees were often as guilty of confiscating property as squatters. He denied, moreover, that the settlers' law violated the promise to protect the property rights of Mexican citizens contained in the Treaty of Guadalupe Hidalgo. Nevertheless, the 1856 statute was unconstitutional for two reasons. First, it was confiscatory because bona fide owners who refused to pay for improvements could lose their land along with the improvements, and second, it denied lawful owners rents and profits that had accrued before the issuance of a formal patent (even though the patent itself merely confirmed a preexisting property right rather than created a new one). No settler law in American history had gone so far. "We have examined them all," Justice Murray proclaimed, "and . . . believe that we are warranted in saying that there is no case to be found like the present; . . . in none was it held that the Legislature could authorize one man to intrude upon the lands of another, or offer a premium to fraud and violence."[74]

Legislatures had the unquestioned power to abridge property rights and impair contracts, but they could not violate natural law— which dictated that government was created to preserve human life and to protect property—and they could not act in an arbitrary fashion. Murray noted:

> The supreme power cannot take from any man his property without his own consent, for the preservation of property being the end of government, and that for which men enter into society, it necessarily supposes and requires that the people should have property and be protected in it, without which they must be supposed to lose by entering into society, the very thing which was the end and design of the social compact to secure, and for the attainment of which they entered into it.

If by retrospective legislation lawmakers could abolish rights already vested, then there was no limit to legislative discretion.[75]

In a strong dissent, Justice Terry argued that this decision threatened the balance of power between the legislature and judiciary created by the state constitution. There were no fixed rules to help judges determine the character and extent of Murray's natural laws. If, as John Locke had insisted, the right to define natural justice resided with the people, then ultimately government was impotent. Anglo-American jurisprudence rested on the principle that courts were bound to accept statutes that did not violate federal or state constitutions—even those laws they considered unpalatable or dangerous. "Our authority to judge," Terry reasoned, "is derived from the Constitution and laws of the State; we can know no power superior to the Constitution, nor acknowledge any higher law than a statute duly enacted pursuant to its provisions." While Murray used Locke to establish the natural right to property, Terry used Locke to assert legislative supremacy and to argue that the value of land in California came largely from the energy and labor of the occupant. Squatters who had resided on the land for five years or more had taken it up under the assumption that it was a portion of the public domain. Terry concluded:

> Under these circumstances we may well doubt whether it would be a greater violation of natural justice to deprive hundreds of citizens and their families of the homes erected by the labor of years, without making any compensation for the improvements which constitute a great part of the value of those homes, or to permit them to retain possession of them upon paying to the owner of the soil the full value of all that is really his own. It appears to be settled that the Legislature may enact laws by which private property may be taken for private purposes in cases where the general good would be thereby promoted. The propriety, policy, and expediency of such acts, can be properly determined only by the Legislature.[76]

The California Supreme Court's rejection of the 1856 Settlers' Law did not end the controversy over squatter rights. There were many more settlers' conventions, many more court cases, and much more bloodshed.[77] In 1858, in response to public demands for new legislation to protect squatters, the legislature required that any person evicted by an owner whose claim was approved by the land commission but subsequently rejected or reduced in size by the courts could sue to recover the land and all rents and profits that had accrued from the time he was ousted, along with court costs.[78] In the same year, in an attempt to stimulate the lagging migration to California, the legislature sent two unsuccessful petitions to Congress. The first asked the national government to provide 160 acres of free land to each settler; the second asked it to survey all land grants in California, confirmed or unconfirmed, along with the private holdings adjoining those tracts. The legislators noted that "our future prosperity and greatness, and the character and perpetuity of our institutions depend mainly upon the number and permanency of our population."[79]

Public sympathy for squatter rights did not disappear following the California Supreme Court's rejection of possessory rights, but conflicts over land titles gradually became more rural and localized. In 1850, California was the land of the small operator, and institutions of business and finance were in their infancy. By 1856 or 1857, new methods of placer mining, laborsaving machinery, large-scale investment, and exhaustion of the most accessible gold deposits had revolutionized the mining industry. The number of miners declined sharply, and most of those who remained in the gold region worked for hydraulic mining companies. The fear that animated so many squatter conventions in 1850 and 1851—that the federal government would require miners to purchase or rent their claims—had abated. Robbed of much of their autonomy and independence, the miners who remained were far less likely to exhibit strong sympathy for squatters. The prospect that urban and rural squatters would join hands to seize the institutions of government through ballots or bullets all but disappeared by the end of the decade.

Although California squatters did not attain their immediate objectives, they had a significant impact on western law, particularly on statutes of limitations. The first statute of limitations was adopted during the reign of Henry VIII. It fixed the period of occupancy necessary to establish title to land at sixty years, a period shortened to twenty years during the reign of James I. Most eastern states adopted this term, but Missouri, Texas, and New Mexico shortened it to ten years; Arkansas and Utah to seven years; and California, Colorado, Nevada, Arizona, Idaho, and Montana to five years. This was not just a sop to squatters. In mining states—where the population was highly mobile and transitory—a twenty-year period was highly impractical. As the author of one nineteenth-century treatise on lim-

itations put it, "if parties will not settle their business matters within reasonable periods before human testimony is lost and human memory fails,
on pain of losing the right to a remedy thereon, not the law, but the party is
responsible for the hardship entailed." In short, everyone, including the
legal establishment, benefited from shorter periods of adverse possession.
Squatters gained title in less time, and the shorter term reduced the number of capricious suits against formal titleholders, protecting the plaintiff in
new states where sympathy for squatters was very strong.[80]

This was no small reform. It encouraged investment in land, and it
also promoted the expansion of irrigation (because statutes of limitation
applied to all real property, water no less than land). In California, riparian
owners at the end of a stream could, theoretically, block all upstream
diversions. However, if an upstream farmer turned water onto his land
continuously for five years, without protest from riparian owners, he automatically gained title to that water. This was a significant abridgment of
traditional property rights. Riparian owners could sue to block these
diversions, but only at the risk of a full-scale water war. Even when they
knew about "illegal" ditches, they often permitted diverters to purchase a
right to use the water rather than take the offending party to court. This
expansion of squatter rights kept the peace in one way, but undermined it
in another. Since "prescriptive" rights (rights established through use)
could exist with no formal record, they seldom surfaced until a local court
issued a judicial decree dividing a stream. Consequently, prescriptive
rights were a major source of litigation.[81]

Several conclusions emerge from this study. California during the
1850s offers one of the best opportunities in American history to see how
law was formed and defined on the frontier—in the city and countryside
as well as in the mining camp. It demonstrates that nineteenth-century law
was never monolithic, consistent, or even entirely "rational." Nor was it
the captive of any "dominant" economic class. In the California of 1850 or
1860, no such class existed because the interests of businessmen were not
harmonious or consistent. In the early 1850s, the courts might have
rejected squatter arguments in favor of "commercial interests" in Sacramento and San Francisco, arguing for the absolute sanctity of private property. But some businessmen were squatters, many were speculators, and,
most important, the alternative vision that economic development
depended on the stability of a society's agricultural foundation was compelling. Judges had many economic visions or alternatives to choose from,
and they could not predict how their decision would influence economic
behavior. In any case, courts are always reluctant to question the dominant
legal values of an age, and public officials tried to balance economic interests that were often incompatible, knowing full well that law must be
enforceable to be effective.

Nineteenth-century western courts tried as hard to define the public interest as legislatures. In fact, in articulating squatter sentiment, the courts may have been more "democratic" than the legislature, not less. The legal battles in California pitted preemption against the sanctity of treaty rights in a rapidly changing economic context. The squatters were victims as well as victimizers, and it is not easy to sort out winners and losers when two or more visions of law collide. Neither side found it possible to win a clear victory. The squatter story leaves us with a fundamental question: how much of what historians have taken as lawlessness really represented the clash of fundamentally irreconcilable legal principles? Historians need to ask whether in some cases the frontier suffered from too much law rather than too little.

Finally, this story raises important questions about the foundation myth at the heart of western history—the story of pioneers triumphing over frontier lawlessness.[82] John Sutter certainly suffered at the hands of trespassers who stole horses, cattle, pigs, and timber from his farm near Marysville. "The squatters are loose in my fields; all is squatted over," he observed in 1853. "I am in debt and cannot sell a foot of land at present. Our government did not act right with us Californians," he lamented.[83] When an incendiary burned his house to the ground in 1865, Sutter lost his library, correspondence, mementos, and the memoirs he had begun to write, along with his home. He had no insurance, and the desperate act of an arsonist—a vagrant who Sutter had caught stealing and had whipped—reinforced the image of California's turbulent society.[84]

This was obviously the stuff of which martyrs are made. As early as 1853, the aging squire of the Sacramento Valley was appointed as a major general in the California militia, a post that called for brilliant uniforms, pomp, and lavish display—all in keeping with the Sutter tradition. Unfortunately, the new honor also called for more champagne, cigars, and celebration—which Sutter could ill afford to provide his legions of admirers. Now both prince and pauper, Sutter was called upon to give frequent speeches and receive the adoration of his followers, especially on Admission Day. In the 1854 celebration, he rode a beautiful horse at the head of California's first regiment, and orators linked him to the greats of all ages—the man who would forever be credited with the opening of the Far West. A year later, a speaker rhapsodized:

Especially let us dwell with admiration upon the history of one of the oldest and most notable of that [pioneer] band—pure in heart—dispensing his hospitality with the prodigality of God's gift to men—comforting the wayworn and weary immigrants— ministering to the wants of the dying—bestowing the last words of respect upon the dead—once the owner of a princely domain—

in his old age harassed and beset by pecuniary and other worldly difficulties: always, however, through every change, in every phase of varied fortune, the same lofty, stainless, and genial nature: Let us regard the venerable Sutter as a model worthy of our imitation, an object deserving our sincerest esteem.[85]

At about this time the argonaut Joseph Warren Revere—a descendant of Paul Revere—said of Sutter, "In times past men have been deified on slighter grounds."[86]

Inevitably, fledgling pioneer societies got hold of Sutter. By the 1870s, the Associated Pioneers of the Territorial Days of California held annual reunions. When the group met in 1877, Sutter was guest of honor. According to Sutter's most perceptive biographer, the group was "an admiring and sympathetic circle, whose atmosphere was balm to his wounded heart." When he was introduced, round after round of toasts followed, and thunderous acclaim shook the walls of the hotel. So choked with emotion did Sutter become that when he rose to acknowledge the greeting, all he could say was, "It is not possible." In the following year, the "general" was elected president of the organization, at which time he observed, "We are now hastening onward to our final resting place but the romance of our history as California pioneers, with its reverses and successes, will tend, for ages, to stimulate the energy of our posterity." It is important to recognize, of course, that if the members of the Associated Pioneers of the Territorial Days of California used Sutter, he used them as well. Sutter frequently asked the group—which included such notables as Mark Twain and William Tecumseh Sherman—to put pressure on Congress to vote him a pension to compensate for the land he had lost. Occasionally, of course, the voice of a skeptic broke through the adoration. In 1877, for example, a speaker at San Jose claimed that those who had arrived in California before 1841 were mainly adventurers and charlatans. But Sutter responded that he had come to California to "settle in" the region and as "a missionary to tame and civilize the wild Indians."[87]

The pioneer societies created a usable past out of shared memories, shared hopes, and denial. California had been saved from outlaws and Indians; civilization had replaced savagery; virtue had triumphed over evil; and prosperous farms and cities now stood where once there was wilderness. The religious appeal of such stories of renewal and redemption is obvious. But the creation of a heroic past was more than an appeal to myth or religion. Sutter's most perceptive biographer, James P. Zollinger, noted in passing: "These celebrations were an ingenious ruse to draw up public opinion and public sentiment opposed to the 'squatter interests.'"[88]

The real past was obscured by Sutter's halo and the halos of other pioneers, and the judgment of many who lived at the time of the Sacramento squatter riots was forgotten. Those who wrote about him in 1850 were far less charitable. "Sutter is a good-meaning pleasant man," the Sacramento merchant William Prince wrote to his wife a few days after the Sacramento squatter riots, "but [he is] the most sappy headed fool you can conceive of & excited with wine usually & half his time half drunk & the Yankees have used him & flattered him & made him believe that he owns the greater part of Califa [California]. . . . [T]he Am'n Speculators have got him to give Deeds for all [his property] except Hock Farm, which he deeded to his wife & it is these Speculators many of whom will be ruined if they cant sell the lots, that are so deadly against Squatters." At about the same time, the Frenchman Ernest de Massey met Sutter and concluded:

> If he had more of the Yankee in him he today would be one of the richest capitalists in the whole world; but unfortunately much of the vast fortune that seemed to turn his head got away from him. His followers have tricked, deceived, and plundered him; taking advantage of his weakness for drink they have persuaded him into making transactions involving land-concessions which contain clauses so cunningly worded that they have brought on ruinous and endless litigation. According to local opinion within a few years he will be completely ruined by those whom he formerly aided.[89]

Who were the mysterious men who had victimized Sutter? One was certainly Sam Brannan, who cheated both Sutter and his son. Brannan has long been recognized as one of the rogues of western history, though his land dealings have never been carefully examined. He led a party of 238 Mormons to California in 1846 and then freely embezzled church property—a practice that historian Walton Bean described as "not far from robbing the almsboxes." This led to the first jury trial in California and a hung jury. In 1850, John Sutter, Jr., sold Brannan the last large block of town lots in Sacramento for $125,000, but through artful stalling Brannan eventually forced the naive younger Sutter to settle for a few thousand dollars. Deals like this made Brannan rich. "Young Sutter was publicly pillaged," according to Zollinger. "Some of these practitioners [Sutter's agents and business associates], like Sam Brannan, . . . wore the mask of Puritanism and of patriotism to wage war upon the small-fry bandit and were themselves wholesale robbers and despoilers of the law. To read of their tactics against Augustus Sutter is enough to make one cry aloud with pain even today." Is it any wonder that Brannan—his reputation purified and his past all but forgotten—would help organize the San Francisco Vigilance Committee of 1851 and lead the forces of righteousness? Is it any wonder that later he would organize the Society of California Pioneers? And is it any wonder that another of Sutter's trusted lieutenants, Peter Burnett—California's first state governor—would, after a very successful career as president of the Pacific Bank in San Francisco, retire with a fortune and spend his declining years writing a book entitled, *Why We Should Believe in God, Love God, and Obey God* (New York, 1884)?[90] The history of the United States is filled with pioneers who sought to justify their actions and divert attention from the seamier side of their past.

Plenty of amateur historians were taken in by the pioneer glitter, but not Hubert Howe Bancroft. Bancroft's politics influenced his history in countless ways, but he was no fool. In the year of the American Centennial, 1876, Bancroft went east in an attempt to take down Sutter's memoirs. "You fill an important niche in the history of the western coast," Bancroft remembered telling Sutter. "Of certain events you are the embodiment—the living, walking history of a certain time and locality. Often in my labors I have encountered your name, your deeds, and let me say that I have never yet heard the former mentioned but in kindness, nor the latter except in praise." On saying this, Bancroft recalled, "Tears came into the old man's eyes, and his utterance was choked, as he signified his willingness to relate to me all he knew." Sutter listened with rapt attention to Bancroft's plan to write a history of the Far West, and subsequently the old man poured out his recollections ten hours a day over the next five days. Bancroft concluded that Sutter had "a kind heart, unaffected and sincere." If "not the shrewdest," he was an "inborn gentleman" with the manners of a "courtier."[91] Yet when Bancroft came to describe Sutter in print he was brutal and contemptuous:

> None of the pioneers named in this register has received so much praise from so many sources; few have deserved so little. . . . He was but an adventurer from the first, entitled to no admiration or sympathy. . . . He was great only in his wonderful personal magnetism and power of making friends for a time of all who could be useful to him; good only in the possession of kindly impulses. His energy was a phase of his visionary and reckless enthusiasm; his executive ability did not extend beyond the skillful control of Indians and the management of an isolated trading post. Of principle, of honor, or respect for the rights of others, we find but slight trace in him. There was no side of any controversy that he would not readily adopt at the call of interest; nationality, religion, friendship, obligation, consistency, counted for little or nothing. There were no classes of his associates, hardly an individual, with whom he did not quarrel, or whom in his anger he did not roundly abuse. . . . He never hesitated to assume any obligation for the

future without regard to his ability to meet it; he rarely if ever paid a debt when due; and a general, vague, and kindly purpose to fulfill all his promises in the brilliant future but imperfectly excuses his short-comings.[92]

In his own way, Bancroft was as much of an industrialist as Collis P. Huntington. One suspects that he loathed Sutter's carelessness and lack of discipline as much as Sutter's tendency to temporize and vacillate. He knew that in the end Sutter had been his own worst enemy. Yet sooner or later speculators got to almost all the Mexican grantees. As early as 1851, even before the land commission began reviewing the Mexican claims, George McKinstry, formerly Sutter's business manager, observed, "I could fill a fools cap sheet with the names of the old guard bust community, including your humble servant." Sutter was not alone.[93]

The significance of the squatter story extends beyond California and the West. For generations historians have debated the question of "western uniqueness," but there has been surprisingly little research into how the law reflected the special economic circumstances, opportunities, and aspirations of westerners. The questions of whether the treaty rights of Mexican grantees transcended the natural rights of Gold Rush squatters, or whether custom and tradition took precedence over formal written laws, are vital to an understanding of the frontier West. Yet legal history should be more than a matter of sorting out winners and losers—more than determining "who-gets-what-when" or deciding which sets of human beings achieve dominance over others. Deeply embedded in American culture, it serves as a prism on that culture. And because the law represents a menu of social options, its implications extend far beyond legal doctrines and the shape of the economy. The "squatter commonwealth" represented one vision based on equal access to property and widespread ownership. This clashed with a competing vision that emphasized the most rapid development of wealth. The squatter story represents a seam, or perhaps fault line, in the historical record. The principle of preemption looked to the past, to a Jeffersonian society of small operators in which widespread land ownership was the law's paramount goal. The Homestead Act (1862) symbolized the culmination of that ideal. But California in the 1850s anticipated the future of American society in its large cities, concentration of capital, and the number and size of its business corporations. What happened in California during the 1850s would recur in many other parts of the West and the nation over the following decades as industrialization and urbanization transformed the nation.

CHAPTER FIVE

Land Monopoly in Nineteenth-Century California

In no American state was land monopoly more of a perceived problem than in nineteenth-century California. Many social critics considered it prima facie evidence that wealth and privilege had triumphed over equity and the general welfare. They saw the symptoms of this disease in retarded immigration rates; in the concentration of people in cities; in the growth of what they took to be a lazy, unproductive aristocratic class whose "artificial" wealth was based on rents and speculative profits; in the volatility of a "boom and bust" economy; in suitcase farming and worn-out soils; and in the emergence of an agricultural caste of "wage slaves," which undermined the independence and security of free labor. Monopoly was inimical to the small farm, which, it was assumed, produced food at cheaper prices, stimulated the growth of transportation, strengthened public education, and provided markets to fledgling industries. Even more important, boosters assumed that small farms strengthened the family and that an egalitarian, democratic society could not survive without widespread landownership. The small freehold was at once the source of economic stability and the wellspring of republican virtue.[1] This chapter examines the "problem of monopoly," how it originated and why it became a permanent feature of California agriculture. Although it builds on the superb work of Paul Wallace Gates—who echoed many of California's nineteenth-century social critics—it argues that the state's scarcity of water and the nature of irrigation agriculture contributed even more to the concentration of ownership than venal, shortsighted, and carelessly drawn national and state land laws.

In March 1876 the *San Francisco Chronicle* lamented that "[t]here never has been a State on the continent in which the land laws were so well devised for monopoly and so directly against settlement and production, in which titles were as much clouded, and where it has been as difficult as here for men of small means to obtain a clear title, at a reasonable cost, to a homestead and farm."[2] An 1872 California legislative report showed that each of 122 individuals and companies owned more than 20,000 acres. These landowners were cattlemen, wheat farmers, and a wide variety of speculators, including former state officials. Bixby & Flint held 334,000 acres; Miller & Lux, 328,000; William S. Chapman and associates, 277,600; Edward F. Beale, 173,000; Isaac Friedlander, 107,000; and Dibble & Hollister, 101,000. Perhaps even more alarming, 2,298 people owned more than 1,000 acres, and the 620 largest farms and ranchos in California averaged 22,000 acres.[3] By the 1870s, the state's easily arable land was gone, and the legislature—which had done much to encourage monopoly in the 1850s and 1860s—debated ways to break up giant holdings through massive levies on unimproved land; graduated land taxes; the elimination of taxes on crops, buildings, and other improvements; direct limitations on the size of farms; and restrictions on the amount of land that could be inherited. None of these proposals, however, won widespread support among the lawmakers.

No explanation of the concentration of land ownership in the two decades after statehood is possible without considering the work of Paul Wallace Gates.[4] Historians have criticized Gates's studies of state and national land policies for idealizing the family farm and small farmers, for not recognizing the varieties and social benefits of land speculation, for not realizing that in parts of the Midwest tenantry was a passing phase that helped some farmers eventually to own their own land, for placing too much emphasis on formal land policies and not enough on the changing nature of agriculture or local economic conditions (such as the availability of capital), and for not acknowledging that the perversion and abuse of land policies was part of a broad-based threat to the "small operator" which accompanied the emergence of the corporate state. (If the small farmer was victimized, one argument runs, so were millions of workers, small businessmen, and even corporations.) These are fair criticisms, though many of Gates's critics have been more concerned with agricultural productivity and "efficiency" than with his concern for social justice and democratic values. Moreover, they have largely ignored California, which was the subject of Gates's most penetrating essays.[5]

Gates's fascination with California was understandable. It was a state where monopoly was far more persistent than in the Midwest or New York, and it was a state where the baneful effects of concentrated, nonresident ownership were painfully obvious in the almost complete absence of a rural society and stable communities. From Henry George to Paul Taylor, Walter Goldschmidt, and Carey McWilliams, social critics had warned of the dangers of concentrated landownership, but none understood the land system like Gates. Unlike the experience of older states, such as New York and Ohio, land monopoly in the Golden State became more, rather than less, virulent as time passed; the family farm as it was known in New England and the Midwest never had a chance.

The problem began, Gates argued, with an 1851 law that provided a process to confirm the Mexican land grants made before 1846. That statute required every titleholder to file a claim with a federal commission within two years. The commission's decisions could be appealed first to a district court and then to the United States Supreme Court. The commission and the courts were required to observe not just the Treaty of Guadalupe Hidalgo, but also United States laws, court decisions, and principles of equity. In all, Spanish and Mexican authorities made 750 grants that totaled between 13 and 14 million acres—13 or 14 percent of the entire state. They ranged in size from less than 20 acres to the 115,000 acres included within the former San Fernando Mission. Many families held multiple claims—for example, the De la Guerra family had the title to 326,000 acres confirmed and the Carillo family 320,000. The Mexican grants covered the sites of California's largest cities and much of its best farmland outside the San Joaquin Valley.[6] The board reviewed its first application in January 1852 and approved the first claim in August. Most titles were confirmed within a few years, and over 75 percent were upheld—553 grants covering 8,850,000 acres.[7]

Gates boldly rejected the judgment of an earlier generation of California historians who regarded the Land Act of 1851 as institutionalized theft, a pretext by which land-hungry Anglo-Americans robbed Mexican Americans of ancestral estates. Instead, he insisted, the law was a "statesmanlike measure" that *favored* the original grantees.[8] It was not unprecedented; Congress had anticipated the legislation in earlier laws designed to confirm claims in the states of Louisiana, Florida, and Missouri. Moreover, the problem was not that the land commission moved too slowly, but just the reverse. Congress and the residents of California wanted fast action; consequently, the commission confirmed some highly doubtful claims, including the Limantour tract in the heart of San Francisco, which was later overturned in the courts but not before it created chaos in the city's business district. The commission finished its work in 1856, though some claims wandered through the courts for years thereafter. Mexican grantees hired the state's most skilled lawyers, and some San Francisco title companies specialized in gathering information in Mexican and Spanish archives and finding witnesses for the claimants. The commissioners, however, were political appointees. None knew much about land law, nor did they read or speak Spanish, and their staff was hopelessly overworked as it tackled the 813 cases. Only after the emergence of three overlapping claims to San Francisco did Congress arrange for the hiring of Edwin M. Stanton to provide a defense equal to the legal talent arrayed on the other side. Meanwhile, the lure of higher salaries persuaded some of the government's best attorneys to defect to the grantees. Not surprisingly, the courts reversed over 35 percent of the commission's decisions.[9]

The Mexican claims were the wellspring of monopoly, according to Gates, but he also demonstrated that Congress did little to reserve Califor-

nia's remaining public lands for bona fide settlers. Long before passage of
the Homestead Act (1862), early settlers in Florida and Oregon had been
given a quarter or half section free as an inducement to settle there. California Senator William Gwin recommended that the same policy be followed in his state, but, given the flood of miners, Congress saw no need to
provide special incentives.[10] It paid scant attention to California until after
the Civil War, and federal agencies did little better. For example, although
land surveys began in 1852, the General Land Office ran most of its early
township and section lines in remote and desolate parts of the state, such
as the Mojave Desert, and the Coachella, Imperial, and Owens valleys.[11]
By 1861 only one-fifth to one-fourth of the state's land had been surveyed,
little of which possessed any value. Consequently, most settlers squatted
on or near Mexican grants or purchased land from the grantees.

In 1853 Congress opened all unsurveyed land outside the Mexican
claims to preemption. Simultaneously it granted California lieu lands to
compensate for school sections contained within the Mexican grants. Subsequently, the state sold—in violation of federal land laws—lieu warrants
that permitted purchasers to enter *unsurveyed* public land. It also allowed
claimants under the 500,000-acre grant to locate on unsurveyed land.[12]
Since California did not establish a land office until 1858 and left the onerous job of recording claims and collecting fees to its counties, two or more
parties often demanded the same acreage—one filing in a federal land
office, the other in a county. The records of county surveyors were notoriously inaccurate and unreliable, and those officials, in company with the
state surveyors general, speculated on a grand scale. To compound the
problem, following the depression of 1857 President James Buchanan
dumped 11,000,000 acres of California land—including some of the choic-
est tracts in the Sacramento and San Joaquin Valleys—onto the market to
raise money to offset declining federal revenues. It sold for $1.25 an acre
cash in unlimited quantities, or for depreciated military bounty warrants
and other forms of scrip. But it remained off-limits to preemptioners and
homesteaders even after 1862. Most of this land sold between 1867 and
1871, long after the financial crisis had passed.[13]

The state's best efforts to aid would-be small farmers failed; ironically,
the only squatters whose claims received protection were those holding
large tracts.[14] The 1851 law promised that all Spanish and Mexican grants
rejected by the courts would become part of the public domain, and, as
mentioned above, legislation adopted in 1853 subjected them to preemption. But the U.S. Supreme Court's 1862 rejection of the Suscol claim to an
84,000-acre block of rich land in Solano and Napa counties, north of San
Francisco, changed that. The high court's decision touched off a land rush
to Suscol. Squatters tore down fences, erected huts and shacks, and staked
out farms in the hope of preempting a quarter section. However, in 1863 a

handful of San Francisco investors, who had purchased the land from the original grantee prior to the Supreme Court's decision, persuaded Congress to permit them to preempt as much land as they held in 1862 at the standard government price of $1.25 an acre. (Ten of them possessed more than 1,000 acres and one claimed 5,000).

Armed with the new law, these holders began evicting the 250 settlers who had taken up residence on the Suscol Rancho after the Supreme Court's decision. In the early months of 1865, the preemptioners retaliated by destroying farm equipment and firing into the homes of the largest landowners. Not only did the decision stand, but in 1864 and 1866 Congress extended the Suscol principle to cover other tracts that had changed hands prior to their confirmation or rejection. The General Land Office and the courts interpreted these laws as permitting preemption claims as large as 5,000 acres *whether the land had been improved or not.* The homestead principle had lost again.[15]

Meanwhile, the Morrill Act of 1862 became yet another pillar of monopoly. According to Gates, cattlemen and speculators, aided by compliant judges and politicians, thwarted Congress's intention to encourage small farming, foster democracy, and promote the rapid settlement of the West. Lawmakers in Washington specified that agricultural college scrip could be used only to secure "offered land," and no individual could claim less than 160 acres or more than three sections within any township. But California officials ignored these restrictions. They permitted scrip holders to file on newly surveyed land for thirty days *before it was opened to other claimants;* to acquire parcels of *unsurveyed* land as small as forty acres; and to enter the double-minimum-priced sections within railroad land grants by paying an additional $1.25 an acre. As a result, the scrip sold for as much as five to eight dollars an acre and became enormously popular with large speculators.[16]

The best evidence of the failure of federal land policy, Gates concluded, was that from 1868–1873, when about 6,000,000 acres of public land were taken in California, Homestead Act entries covered only 809,621 acres.[17] By the 1870s, according to Gates, the concentration of ownership was greater in California than in Ireland. Although California railroads acquired most of their 11,500,000-acre subsidy after 1870, and although the Desert Land Act (1877) and Timber and Stone Act (1878) also contributed to monopoly, Gates considered the 1850s and 1860s as the critical decades.[18]

The implications of Gates's work are vast. He demonstrated that by the 1870s and 1880s—long before the rise of "agribusiness" as we know it—California agriculture was characterized by giant "factories in the fields," by suitcase farming, by a large number of tenants, and by a rural "underclass" of seasonal workers. He showed how monopoly corrupted

California politics and undermined respect for the law as well as for the courts and legislature. ("Long after the titles had been confirmed, the surveys finally accepted, and the patents issued," Gates poignantly noted, "squatters continued their battle for justice. Even the law, the courts, and the sheriffs could not persuade them to abandon their hopes.")[19] The whole society suffered. For example, in the 1880s owners of the state's 5,000,000 acres of improved rural land paid taxes at a rate eight or ten times greater than those who owned the 21,000,000 acres of unimproved land. Moreover, the small farmers who held 20 percent of the cultivated land paid 75 percent of the total taxes collected on agricultural real estate. County officials quickly learned that large landowners could paralyze county government by refusing to pay taxes, and the need for income often forced them to accept payments far lower than the rates provided by law. The Constitution of 1879 promised equal assessment of land through a state board of equalization, but the power of county assessors and boards of supervisors remained substantial, and they were under the thumb of the monopolists. "California's tax structure for years penalized intensive development of land and made feasible continuation of large ownership," according to Gates. "Land-tax reform was one of the major objectives of the land-reform group but its political clout, though on the surface strong, was ineffective in the legislature."[20]

Gates was right, but his analysis contained two basic flaws: He did not devote enough attention to the nature of the California economy in the nineteenth century and he failed to recognize the impact of aridity on agriculture and landholdings.[21] California was, in Carey McWilliams' words, "the great exception." During the first two decades after statehood, it was isolated and suffered from a multitude of problems, ranging from the high cost of living to its image in the eastern press as a desert infested with outlaws to bad government. Its early economic development was far different from that of the agricultural states Gates had previously studied.[22] California's mining industry contributed to the growth of ports and supply towns, which concentrated capital and furnished miners and former miners with jobs during the off-season. The first generation of immigrants found plenty of alternatives to farming. Most had no intention of making the state a permanent home anyway; they would have rejected farming as an occupation even had cheap land been available. Speculators found it easy to engross large estates because most of the population was migratory, with no commitment to the soil, and the legislature gave preference to the traditional California industry of stock-raising rather than farming.[23]

From the beginning the state relied heavily on exports: wheat and cattle during the 1860s and 1870s, as well as citrus fruit by the 1880s. Wheat farming was ideally suited to the rich, flat terrain of the Central Valley. It required little preparation of the land, little labor, and almost no experience on the part of the farmer himself—and no house, barn, or even bunkhouse for farmhands during the harvest. California's spring and winter rains, and its long, hot, dry summers, also made the cultivation of cereals attractive. Wheat was a crop that lent itself to mechanization—such as the header, which came into use around 1860—and it promised immediate and substantial returns. (Those who raised more labor-intensive crops often had to wait years for the first returns on their money and labor.) Finally, squatters or renters could engage in wheat farming with relatively little capital and without making improvements that might later be lost to rival claimants. Nevertheless, profitable wheat farming and cattle ranching demanded large estates. Both industries were strong allies of monopoly.[24]

Neither land laws nor the nature of agriculture fully explain why monopoly flourished in California. Any explanation must look at what made the state unique. From the beginning, California's farms were tributary to its cities, not the reverse. Despite a dramatic decline in the number of miners during the 1860s, the percentage of farm workers increased only modestly—from 16 percent to 20 percent during that decade. Even more surprising, in the 1870s, after completion of the first "transcontinental" and during the years when the Southern Pacific built its line through the San Joaquin Valley, the rural populace continued to shrink in relation to the number of urban dwellers. Metropolitan counties consistently grew faster than rural counties. As early as 1860, a decade after statehood, 21 percent of California's people lived in communities of 2,500 or more. (Ten years after Ohio statehood only 1 percent of its people lived in towns larger than 2,500, and a decade after Illinois entered the union, that state did not contain a single community that large.) Until about 1880, California's population center was San Francisco, which contained over 40 percent of the state's residents.

It is easy to forget—given California's spectacular *urban* growth in the twentieth century—that from 1870 to 1890, eight of the arid West's eleven states and territories grew faster than the Golden State and during the 1890s, nine did.[25] Even the population boom touched off by the Gold Rush had precedent. (Wisconsin had fewer than 30,000 residents in 1840, and more than 300,000 in 1850—figures similar to California's—and Minnesota's population grew by twenty-nine times during the 1850s.) The Golden State's numbers grew by 47 percent in the 1860s, by 54 percent in the 1870s, and by 40 percent in the 1880s, faster than the national average. But those statistics did not match the record of other new *agricultural* states. Kansas grew by 240 percent in the 1860s and by 173 percent in the following decade; Minnesota by 155 and 77 percent in the same two decades; and Nebraska by 355 and 270 percent. During the nineteenth century, California grew at a much slower rate than Ohio from 1800 to 1850, or Illinois from 1810 to 1860, or Iowa from 1840 to 1890.[26]

No sharp line can be drawn between the industries of country and city. We know little about the relationship of land speculation to banking— even though William Ralston's loans to land barons contributed to the Bank of California's collapse in 1875. (Isaac Friedlander owed the bank $500,000 and William Chapman $214,000; neither had provided any collateral.) Moreover, fraudulent land titles and litigation became an added cost of doing business, contributing to high interest rates and San Francisco's large number of business failures. Gates noted that frightened squatters— many of whom were prominent businessmen—paid Jose Limantour from $100,000 to $300,000 before his claim to a large part of San Francisco was disallowed. And since there were at least nineteen major private claims to parts of the city, along with the city's extensive claim, the cost of uncertain titles must have been enormous. Much of the violence in frontier California—the highwaymen, vigilantism, squatterism, and racial and ethnic conflict—resulted in part from what were perceived to be inequitable land policies. The absence of cheap land may also have hastened urbanization; miners flooded into cities in part because they had little access to arable public lands.[27]

That said, the most important question is not why large landholdings were so common, but why they persisted. In other states stock-raising and wheat farming gave way to more diversified family farms as the population increased and land prices rose. The big difference in California was that in most parts of the state irrigation and water law reinforced early patterns of land tenure. Irrigation entered its "take-off" phase during the 1870s and 1880s, as investors turned their attention from mining to the fertile alluvial soil in the Central Valley.[28] Few businesses in the arid West offered the potential profits of reclaiming virgin desert land. The 1890 census estimated that the average price per acre of irrigated land nearly tripled during the 1880s. Moreover, while the cost of watering that land averaged about eight dollars an acre, the average per-acre value of irrigated crops was nearly fifteen dollars an acre. The value of the water rights alone was over three times the per-acre cost of providing water.[29]

Irrigation had widespread appeal because it promised to protect large ranchers and grain farmers from drought at the same time it posed as the enemy of concentrated ownership.[30] Some social reformers argued that as the value of land increased, soaring taxes would force monopolists to sell out even if the lure of fat profits did not. Unfortunately, private companies could water land only by monopolizing it. They needed large blocks to facilitate the acquisition of canal rights-of-way and to place water rights on an equal footing. Otherwise, established settlers would appropriate any new supply of water without paying a cent, and conflicts would arise between pioneers and newcomers. Irrigation canals had to be built in *anticipation* of population, and a large supply of water had to be held in reserve for later use. Nominally, the doctrine of prior appropriation[31] restricted water users to "beneficial use," that is the amount of water actually needed to achieve an immediate objective. But large ditch projects took months or years to complete, and private water companies often encountered extortionist "paper claims" filed by individuals or rival companies. Courts permitted claims to far more water than was immediately needed. This contributed greatly to land monopoly, because most land in California's Central Valley and south of the Tehachapi Mountains had little value without water. Such practices discouraged investors and drove up the price paid by bona fide settlers for farms.

One example speaks volumes: the 40,000-acre empire of the Kern County Land and Water Company adjoining the town of Bakersfield at the south end of the San Joaquin Valley. In the 1870s James Ben-Ali Haggin, William Carr, and Lloyd Tevis, San Francisco capitalists, used a medley of land laws, including the Desert Land Act (1877), to secure most of the readily irrigable land in the valley. What they could not acquire from the state or the nation they purchased from the Southern Pacific Railroad. Professor Gates has shown how state and federal land policies contributed to the formation of this baronial domain,[32] but he neglected an equally important story: the promoter's efforts to secure control of the Kern River and other local water sources.

Settlers streamed into Kern County in the early 1870s, anticipating completion of the Southern Pacific line, which reached Bakersfield in mid-decade. One of the driest, most isolated parts of the state, Kern County still contained plenty of government land. By 1873, Haggin, Carr, and Tevis had completed six ditches covering 5,000 acres. They tried to buy up *all* existing water rights, but many farmers refused to sell. Subsequently, they encouraged irrigators to incorporate their ditches and sell stock to outside investors. This would, they promised, increase land values and provide capital to improve, consolidate, and expand the delivery system. Small-fry speculators quickly took the bait, but regretted their lack of caution after the three entrepreneurs secured majority control in the Buena Vista, Pioneer, and Stine canals, among others. In 1875 the men claimed 3,000 cubic feet per second from the Kern River, about three times more water than the stream had ever carried. Then they formed the Kern County Land and Water Company and began to build new canals, including the Kern Island and Calloway canals. By 1878, Carr, Haggin, and Tevis controlled all the county's major ditches.

The Kern County Land and Water Company used a variety of tactics to intimidate "uncooperative" farmers. It cut off water or provided shoddy service. It filed over 100 suits challenging the water rights of those who refused to sell out to the company. And because it enjoyed great political influence within Kern County, the company pressured local officials—

including sheriffs, county judges, and tax assessors—to help secure its objectives.[33] In January 1878, after the Bakersfield Grange bitterly protested to the legislature that the Kern County Land and Water Company wasted water and discriminated against farmers who challenged company policies, the *San Francisco Chronicle* recommended that the legislature reform the state's water laws because the company had forced "poor men to sell their lands at a low price, or failing in this . . . freeze out or dry out all those who may have the temerity to wish to hold on to the homes acquired after years of toil and hardship."[34]

The Kern County Land and Water Company's ultimate objectives remain a mystery. Haggin insisted that he was a public benefactor. "My object has not been, nor do I wish to monopolize large bodies of land," he proclaimed in 1880, "but I desire to make valuable and available that which I have by extending irrigation ditches over my lands, and when these lands are subject to irrigation to divide them up and sell them . . . in small tracts with the water rights necessary to irrigation."[35] He explained that after 1877 he did little to improve the land or to lure new settlers into Kern County because the drought of that year touched off a storm of litigation—including the famous case of *Lux v. Haggin*.[36] If the supreme court limited or redefined prior appropriation in California, and Haggin claimed his water under prior appropriation, the value of his property would plummet.

Many bona fide settlers regarded this argument as subterfuge. They charged that Haggin, Tevis, and Carr had used the water rights issue as a ruse to win public support in the battle to overturn riparian rights in California and to crush the rival livestock company of Miller & Lux. The trio did everything possible to appear "pro-settler" and to enlist "friendly" judges and juries in their cause. By opposing riparian rights, they appeared to be antimonopoly. In reality, they were just monopolists of another kind. The Kern County Land Company's holdings were part of 1,400,000 acres the cattlemen owned in Arizona, New Mexico, and California. The company needed alfalfa for its stock, but water rights acquired under the doctrine of prior appropriation required that the water be diverted continuously, on pain of forfeiture. (Private companies could not "stockpile" water for future use.) If the Kern County Land and Water Company had sold its land outright, water rights would have vested with the freeholders, reducing the company's water supply along with its political clout. By leasing, the company maintained control over both water and land.[37] It made no serious effort to subdivide its vast holdings until the 1890s, *after* the California Supreme Court had affirmed the primacy of riparian rights in Kern County. Population statistics told a grim story. While the county's population more than doubled from 1870 to 1877, the number of children in the county dropped from 649 in 1879 to 246 in 1886. Many families were replaced by single male renters and leaseholders.[38]

In Kern County irrigation served as the ally of monopoly. Elsewhere, at least for a time, it led to the breakup of large estates, as critics of wheat farming had hoped. Gates did not pay sufficient attention to the diversity of California farms in the nineteenth century. Taken as a group, irrigated holdings larger than 160 acres averaged 547 acres in 1890—even bigger than irrigated ranches in such grazing states as Nevada and Wyoming. Nevertheless, the average irrigated farm *under* 160 acres numbered only 30 acres, smaller than those in all western states and territories save Utah.[39]

Fresno County's experience underscored the difference. Irrigation evolved very differently there, in the Kings River Valley, than it did in the Kern Valley, one hundred miles to the south. During the 1890s, as irrigated land in Kern County decreased from 154,549 to 112,533 acres, irrigated land in Fresno County nearly tripled, expanding from 105,665 to 283,737 acres.[40] During the 1860s, before Fresno existed and before the alternate sections were granted to the Southern Pacific, speculators acquired huge, unbroken chunks of the public domain.[41] This dramatically reduced the cost of purchasing and developing the land. So did the method of settlement. The Fresno speculators tried to attract *groups of colonists* rather than individuals or families. They formed companies that competed for buyers by offering plenty of inducements, such as putting out vines and supplying expert agricultural advice to former urbanites who lacked agricultural experience. They also planted shade trees, built roads, set up dairies, and sold the land on credit. Colonies provided instant communities. They also provided compact and efficient settlements. The sale of land in large units to groups of settlers, rather than in individual farms, reduced advertising costs, commissions paid to salesmen, and interest charges. ("Overhead" expenses constituted about half the cost of irrigating virgin land.) The first colony was established south of Fresno in 1875, and within a decade twenty-one colonies covered 45,000 acres. They provided homes for 1,500 families, about 7,500 people, and served as one of the few examples of successful planned agricultural development in the nineteenth-century American West.[42]

Fresno was located between the Kings and San Joaquin rivers, and it usually received plenty of water. The Kings carried two or three times more water than the Kern during summer months, when the latter often ran dry, and Fresno received almost twice the average annual rainfall than Bakersfield.[43] These were substantial natural advantages. During the 1870s, courts in Fresno and adjoining counties issued many injunctions to protect riparian owners downstream in the Mussel Slough section of the Kings River from the increasing number of diversions upstream around Fresno. However, most appropriators simply ignored the court orders. The stream rarely dried up completely, and the riparian owners realized that angry diverters would defy any injunction. Compromise promised the only solution. Many sold their riparian rights to upstream interests, as California courts abandoned the timeless principle that such rights were inalienable and appurtenant to the land. Kings River developers recognized the hopelessness of litigation, so the conflict between prior appropriation and riparian rights did not limit agricultural development there as it did elsewhere in the San Joaquin Valley. As E. B. Perrin, one of the principal speculators and irrigation promoters in the Fresno region, commented, "The news soon spread all over the country that the water for the Fresno colonies was the most secure and plentiful in the State, and this created the biggest land boom in Fresno County." The companies sold water at very low rates. They still faced suits by downstream appropriators, but none of those claims were open-ended like the riparian rights claimed by Miller & Lux in Kern County. As Arthur Maass and Raymond Anderson have shown so well, Kern County would have been far better off had it attracted the same species of speculator which flourished in Fresno County.[44]

As in Fresno, the history of Los Angeles demonstrated that small farms thrived only where there was an abundance of water.[45] However, Fresno and Los Angeles were not typical. During the 1870s, many critics of land monopoly maintained that large holdings would be broken up only when the state condemned and extinguished all private water claims and leased or rented the water itself. In October 1873 California's leading agricultural periodical, the *Pacific Rural Press*, concluded:

> The people have of late been everywhere so mercilessly plucked by corporations that there is a universal distrust of associated capital, and an effort will be made to keep all the water possible in the hands of the State, and away from monopolists. All these corporations want the people or the Government to give them something for nothing, in order that they may sell it back shortly after to the people at an immense profit. Millions of acres of lands have come into the possession of certain companies on this principle, which the people have lately come to the conclusion is a wrong one. . . . The common opinion prevails that the State should own, or at least control these canals. That there should be a comprehensive system of irrigation, which would be applicable to the whole [San Joaquin] valley, not to a particular section. That at all events the farmers should not get their water from any corporation whatever, which may, if it chooses, discriminate between certain persons, or by sharp practices, get possession of the land. The evil of having a number of companies competing on adjacent lands, each with an independent system, has been shown up in older countries.[46]

If the hostility to "associated capital" was strong, so was the fear of government. Neither riparian rights nor prior appropriation required close supervision by public officials. In effect, these two doctrines assigned the cost of resolving disputes to the courts, where the water users themselves paid the price of uncertainty, rather than to a state bureaucracy, where water rights could be treated as a matter of concern to all Californians. Among the arguments used against a comprehensive state water system and state administrative control over water rights was that the new bureaucracy would build up corrupt political "rings," that government was inherently wasteful and inefficient (much unnecessary work would be done), that some sections would be taxed to pay for improvements in others, and that hydraulic miners would use state irrigation to justify massive new state aid to the moribund hydraulic mining industry.[47]

The pervasive suspicion of large institutions, public or private, and the incapacity of the courts to plan or to govern, left one last weapon against water monopoly, the irrigation district. Beginning in the early 1870s, the California Grange sponsored legislation to encourage farmers to pool money to build irrigation works and maintain local control over water. In this way, it was hoped, agriculture could avoid overreliance on either private water companies or the state. In 1876 the legislature approved two bills to create limited districts within the San Joaquin Valley, but the courts emasculated the new statutes because they sought to tax *all* district residents, stockmen and town-dwellers as well as farmers. Not until 1887, after the California Supreme Court proclaimed irrigation a "public use" of water in *Lux v. Haggin* (1886), paving the way for the condemnation of private dams, ditches, and water rights by public corporations, did the legislature enact a *comprehensive* district law.[48]

The Wright Act of 1887 was prompted not just by the triumph of riparian rights in 1886, but by the rapid expansion of irrigation during the 1880s, which resulted in new demands on almost all the state's unclaimed water. The law empowered locally elected boards of directors to purchase or condemn water rights, draft plans for delivery systems, supervise construction, and monitor distribution. No water rights were absolute because the water belonged to the district, not to individual farmers. Water was allocated according to the value each tract of land bore to the total assessed value of district property. Not surprisingly, the *San Francisco Chronicle* predicted that "[w]hatever may be the defects of the Wright bill, it will have the effect of shutting off all schemes for the wholesale seizure of the running water of the State under any claim of law whatever. If it will accomplish this, as it will do, it will preserve the water for the use of those who need it. . . . The Wright bill is all that stands between the rich water monopolist and the poor farmer." Farmers, it hoped, would soon see the end of costly and protracted litigation.[49]

The Wright Act promised many other benefits: coordinated, efficient water systems in place of the wasteful works constructed by private enterprise; the distribution of water at cost, with no discrimination among users; and home rule. But the most important benefit was indirect: by driving up taxes on the unimproved land held by speculators, wheat farmers, and stock growers, the law would encourage the sale of land to small farmers. Land monopoly would die a natural death—not at the hands of the state, but as a result of evolutionary market forces.

Unfortunately, this legal weapon proved ineffective. In the eight years following 1887, forty-nine irrigation districts covering 2,000,000 acres were organized under the Wright Act—about 2 percent of the entire surface of the state. However, opposition from large landholders—mainly wheat farmers in the Sacramento Valley and stockmen in the San Joaquin— proved fatal. Their main objection was well-expressed in a letter written by a Sacramento Valley resident to a Colusa newspaper:

> That the irrigation law is a blow aimed directly at large land holders is as apparent as a nose on the face. In Colusa county there could not be formed an irrigation district of any considerable dimensions without including one or more small burghs or towns. Now what we want to know is this. Is it right for the many men of small holdings who generally hang around those little villages and the men with no holdings at all except a cigarette holder, to waltz up to the polls on election day, and cast their vote, and thereby become the dictator to the man with his thousands of acres of land? There is only one way to construe the matter. It places the whole army of men with small holdings, the laborer, the tramps and the paupers on one side and the landlords with their thousands of acres on the other. And the former say to the latter, "we will build an irrigation ditch here or there as we please and we'll make you foot the bills."[50]

Large landowners challenged virtually every feature of the Wright Act in court, from the process of organization to the issuance of bonds. The U.S. Supreme Court upheld the legality of districts in 1896,[51] but the pall of litigation, bad management, and speculation that hung over most of these quasi-public entities limited bond sales. As of 1910, only 174,000 acres within the original districts were irrigated—about 5 percent of the irrigated land in the state. Ironically, when the irrigation district was revived during the second decade of the twentieth century, it became the ally of agribusiness rather than the family farm. The Kern County model triumphed.[52]

Irrigation agriculture did not expand as rapidly in nineteenth-century

California as in arid states with less potential, such as Utah and Colorado. The century ended with a severe drought, and prominent northern Californians appealed to the U.S. Department of Agriculture to conduct a survey of water rights in California. "Great sums have been lost in irrigation enterprises," the petitioners warned. "Still greater sums are endangered. Water titles are uncertain. The litigation is appalling."[53] San Francisco bankers, realtors, investors, and manufacturers were particularly concerned. Some held the bonds of defunct irrigation districts and others owned heavily mortgaged land in the Sacramento Valley, in parts of which the rural population sharply declined in the 1890s. All were keenly aware that the tide of immigration to northern California that had given that portion of the state its political and economic preeminence in the nineteenth century had receded. If San Francisco was to survive as the queen city of the West, something had to be done to stimulate small farming in its hinterland, the Central Valley.

Elwood Mead, head of the Office of Irrigation Investigations in the Department of Agriculture, conducted the survey. He concluded that the insecurity of water claims had seriously impeded the growth of small farming in California:

> There are few places in the world where rural life has the attraction or possibilities which go with the irrigated home in California, yet immigration [to California] is almost at a standstill and population in some of the farmed districts has decreased in the past ten years. It is certain that some potent but not natural cause is responsible for this, and this cause seems to be a lack of certainty or stability in water rights which has given an added hazard to ditch building and been a prolific source of litigation and neighborhood ill feeling. Farmers who desire to avoid the courts and live on terms of peace and concord with their neighbors avoid districts where these conditions prevail.[54]

For Mead the question of who owned the land or built the irrigation works was far less important than who owned the water. The two most glaring weaknesses in western water law, he believed, were the failure to attach rights to the land irrigated—titles to water could be bought and sold like any commodity, hence they could "float" from one part of a river basin to another—and the state's lack of administrative control over the remaining, "surplus" water. Each of six individuals or corporations had claimed the *entire* San Joaquin River, and the remaining claims to that stream—many of which had never been filed with county recorders—constituted eight times its greatest volume and 172 times its average flow.[55] Not surprisingly, water law reform was high on the agenda of the California Progressives.[56]

Technology permitted irrigation to expand dramatically in the early decades of the twentieth century despite concentrated ownership in land and water.[57] Conservation, including lining canals with concrete and improving irrigation techniques, made the existing supply go further. Moreover, dams captured previously unclaimed "flood water" wasted when the snow melted in the spring, and new steam and gasoline pumps began to tap the vast supply of water under the floor of the San Joaquin Valley. Irrigation promoters were much more successful at expanding the existing supply than in eliminating monopolistic claims. Irrigated land returned enormous profits per acre, but only to those capable of paying far more for improved land than in the East or South. The average California farm tripled in value from 1900 to 1920.[58] A quarter section of land "under ditch" cost as much as $10,000 to $15,000 in southern California, and the cost of irrigating virgin land soared as the size of dams and canals expanded to serve land ever further from water. The outlay for irrigation, added to the many other expenses of getting started in agriculture, pushed the price of an 80- or 160-acre farm far beyond the means of most small farmers or urban workers. California reformers tried valiantly to reproduce familiar patterns of landownership that prevailed in the Midwest and New England. Their task was hopeless. In patterns of agriculture as in so many other ways, the Golden State would remain exceptional.

This chapter can only begin to suggest the ways irrigation affected patterns of land tenure in California and, by implication, other states in the arid West. It is not meant to be definitive. But it points to one major conclusion. Even though the percentage of land irrigated in the nineteenth-century West was small compared to today, and even though the nature and impact of irrigation varied from county to county and state to state, in California it was destined to become a firm ally of monopoly and agribusiness. Historians must not discount the impact of the land laws Professor Gates explained so well, but water laws were no less important. Gates was wrong to suggest that monopoly had become a *permanent* feature of California agriculture by the 1870s. In the years from 1870 to 1920, many champions of irrigation hoped to use that new institution to break up large holdings and produce stable agricultural communities. They were no less important than Henry George and others who wanted to tax unimproved land at higher rates or place limitations on the amount of land that individuals and corporations could own. In the far West, the failure of the Wright Act—which was widely copied in the arid region—to achieve its original objectives was even more important than the failure of the Homestead Act. It became the servant of the very monopolists it was designed to destroy.

CHAPTER SIX

George Maxwell, the Railroads, and American Land Policy, 1899–1904

On April 17, 1899, George Maxwell and Elwood Mead met with officials of the Northern Pacific, Great Northern, Santa Fe, Southern Pacific, and Union Pacific railroads in the office of the second vice-president of the Great Northern. The meeting followed in the wake of the depression of 1893–1898 and during a drought that lasted from 1898 until 1901, sharply reducing the carrying trade of the northern lines. Maxwell, a lawyer and journalist from California, and Mead, head of the Office of Irrigation Inquiry in the Department of Agriculture and formerly Wyoming's state engineer, outlined a plan to unite the grazing and agricultural interests of the West. The railroad executives had several objectives: They wanted the states and national government to construct storage reservoirs in the arid and semiarid West to protect against future droughts. They also wanted Congress to lease public grazing lands and to allow the railroads to swap the land they had been granted for government tracts (so that the consolidated holdings would form unbroken blocks of land more desirable to stockmen, who wanted to fence and segregate herds and thus protect pure-blooded cattle).

At the end of the meeting, the leaders of four railroads granted Maxwell a subsidy of $30,000—$500 a month from each line—to mount a publicity campaign to put pressure on Congress to adopt the desired legislation. (The Union Pacific initially balked but later joined the others.) "It was the consensus of opinion that the railroad companies could accomplish little or nothing . . . appearing in it for themselves," an official of the Northern Pacific wrote to President C. S. Mellon, "but that they would have to furnish the sinews of war for at least the first year. . . . We believe [that] if the single bill could be passed by which Government lands would be leased that this company would be benefited many times annually the expense incurred."[1] The railroads continued Maxwell's subsidy for six years, during which time American land and water policies received close attention from Congress. Railroad support and pressure unquestionably contributed to passage of the Reclamation Act in 1902,[2] but the more ambitious objective of reforming the nation's land laws—which followed hard upon the reclamation crusade—failed.

Although the public domain within the humid half of the nation had all but disappeared by 1870, the population of the United States doubled between 1870 and 1900. The secretary of the interior noted in his 1896 report that while 620 million acres of land had passed into private hands in the century prior to 1883, in the thirteen years thereafter 326 million acres were taken. (Cultivated land within the United States increased from 81 million acres in 1865 to 211 million acres in 1890.)[3] When the Depression of 1893 ended, the demand for land became even more intense. In 1898, 8.5 million acres were patented; in 1899, 9 million; and in 1903, 22.5 million. In six years an expanse of public land equal to the area of California passed into private ownership.[4] The production of cattle and sheep had become a big business, and most of the land claimed during this period was for pasture. The fear that the West was becoming the prisoner of railroads, cattle companies, land speculators, and sundry other interests that would stifle individual economic opportunity deepened during the protracted economic depression. "The density of population is approaching, in parts of the country, the conditions of Europe," a writer in *Forum* warned in 1892, "and the child is now living who will perhaps see in the fertile portions of the United States a population almost equal in density to that of England or France. Our statesmen can find no greater field than this for the exercise of statesmanship."[5]

The land crisis provided a perfect opportunity for George H. Maxwell.[6] Born and educated in California, Maxwell began his professional career as a court stenographer, then entered Hastings Law School in San Francisco and was admitted to the bar in 1883. He specialized in water rights cases and became so successful that when California adopted the Wright Act in 1887—a law that authorized groups of farmers and promoters to form irrigation districts and tax *all* the property within a designated area to pay for the construction of dams and canals (or for the consolidation of old water systems)—landowners throughout the state hired him to defend their property rights. The fifty districts contained nearly 2 million acres, and by the middle 1890s that land carried a bonded debt of $16 million. However, only 100,000 acres were irrigated and only half a dozen districts contained practical irrigation projects. Critics claimed that the works cost many times what they should have, that district management was corrupt and inefficient, and that speculation and fraud had been common. Maxwell carried their case all the way to the U.S. Supreme Court. As he wrote in the *California Advocate*, a journal he established to focus public opinion and apply pressure to the California legislature, "The Wright Irrigation District Act is a menace to every one contemplating settlement in California, warning them that any newcomer to the State may, at any time, against his will, have his property embraced in an irrigation district and taxed even to confiscation to provide irrigation for others."[7] Nevertheless, in 1895 the high court upheld the constitutionality of the 1887 legislation, which forced Maxwell to adopt a new strategy to bail out the district landholders.[8]

Maxwell remained in the employ of landowners within the Poso, Browns Valley, Central, Tipton, Alta, Big Rock Creek, Escondido, and Jamacha districts, and after 1895 he made a valiant attempt to remove bondholder liens from property owned by his clients. His sudden conversion to the cause of federal reclamation in that year was also motivated, at least in part, by the situation in California. The migration west, which had been so large in the 1880s, all but disappeared in the 1890s; something had to be done to create a new land rush. "If we get migration started," Maxwell wrote in August 1900, "people will go west faster than the government will build reservoirs, and lands already on the market and provided with water [such as land within California irrigation districts] will be salable at fair prices when it is practically impossible at present to find a purchaser." Since Maxwell's clients often paid him in land, he would benefit along with district landowners. In September 1900, he wrote to his soon-to-be law partner, noting that in the Poso District, landowners had promised Maxwell 5,000 acres to clear their titles. "I think land in this district is a good subject of speculation," he noted, "and worth getting hold of as a fee even though there was no cash in it at the present time." Federal reclamation raised the prospect of soaring land prices—as well as the possibility that the central government would buy up the district bonds, eliminating the outstanding debt within defunct districts.[9]

In 1896, Maxwell attended a meeting of the National Irrigation Congress in Phoenix, where he made a strong appeal for federal construction of reservoirs. He understood the need to unify East and West, as well as economic interests within the West. He gravitated toward Senator Francis E. Warren of Wyoming. At that time, most western politicians considered "free silver" the paramount political issue facing the region, but the Wyoming senator was more interested in attracting new settlers and rescuing the livestock industry from the depression. Because of the economic slump and the failure of the Carey Act,[10] from 1895 to 1898 Warren favored the unconditional cession of all or part of the public domain to the states as the most practical way to solve the West's land and water problems. Cession was attractive to those westerners who believed that Congress would never authorize the construction of reservoirs, and that if it did the states would fall into endless quibbling for meager appropriations. Moreover, since the states exercised de facto control over the West's water supply, any federal construction program would result in attempts to assert federal control over water, unsettling property values. Nevertheless, in 1897 or

1898 Warren changed his strategy. He now favored federal construction of dams in a handful of western states, using river and harbor appropriations. Cession to the states of the remaining public lands would eliminate the central government's responsibility to promote western economic development, and Warren feared Congress's unwillingness to legislate on western issues even more. In any case, by holding out for direct appropriations and by threatening to filibuster bills important to easterners, the western senators might force Congress to approve cession, if nothing more. Wyoming would win in either case.[11]

By 1898, Maxwell and Mead—Warren's chief adviser on land and water matters—had agreed on the plan sold to the railroads in April 1899. It included the construction of storage reservoirs by the Army Corps of Engineers, as recommended by Hiram Martin Chittenden.[12] These would be built in thinly populated states mainly to serve private lands, such as those owned by the railroads. The impounded water would be distributed free under state laws; the users or the states would build distribution canals. In more densely populated parts of the West, where agriculture was already well established, the federal government would construct reservoirs with the understanding that the farmers who benefited would repay the cost of construction. Maxwell variously estimated that his program would cost $143 or $200 million. Spent over ten years, this amount would reclaim 74 million acres. Much of this money, he promised, would be quickly returned because the remaining—and then unsalable—public land would soar in value. The leasing of public grazing land would provide yet another source of revenue to construct dams and canals. But it could also pay for pumping projects, education, or operating state governments—not just dams and canals. Maxwell gave the midwestern states—which offered few promising damsites—a strong incentive to support his program.[13]

At the beginning of June 1899, the Trans-Mississippi Commercial Congress met in Wichita, Kansas. At that meeting, Maxwell announced the creation of the National Irrigation Association—without, of course, revealing who had bankrolled the organization. It was significant that he ignored the established political parties; he sought to rise above partisanship just as he sought to make land and water law reform a national rather than sectional issue. The organization's headquarters were in Chicago, middle ground between East and West. From that locale, Maxwell published several magazines and leaflets (most notably the *National Advocate*) that were distributed to newspaper editors and members of Congress as well as to those who paid the five-dollar-a-year NIA dues.

Shaping public opinion was only one of his goals; Maxwell also wooed businessmen and industrialists in all parts of the nation (including manufacturers associations, trade associations, and chambers of commerce). On the back of the National Irrigation Association's stationery was a map of the United States with a black line bisecting the nation. While over 58 million lived east of that line, little more than 4 million lived in the western half of the nation. "The purpose of the National Irrigation Association is to put this [surplus] population there [in the West]," a legend on the letterhead explained, "and to create in Arid America new opportunities for millions of Workers and Home-Builders, and enormously increase the Home Markets for American Merchants and Manufacturers." His California experience taught him the value of "networking." Asking businessmen to lobby their representatives in Washington in support of reclamation and land reform as general propositions had little effect. Therefore, Maxwell provided members of the NIA with position papers on pending legislation and urged them to write in support of the bills he (the NIA) favored. In December 1900, he advised a friend on how to organize the merchants of Great Falls, Montana. First, every businessman sympathetic to reclamation and land reform should make a list of the firms from which he purchased goods. Second, he should write a personal letter to those who were NIA members thanking them and asking for continued support. Third, he should send membership materials to every eastern merchant and manufacturer from whom he purchased goods who was not a member of the NIA, explaining how the development of the West would drive up their profits. Meanwhile, he should trade only with merchants who joined the NIA. "The merchants of the west," Maxwell concluded, "should understand that the National Irrigation Association is nothing more nor less than a central channel through which the combined and united influence of all the western merchants can be brought together and driven with the force of a rifle ball against some one specific proposition."[14]

In 1898 and 1899, land reform and federal reclamation went hand in hand; irrigation and stock-raising complemented each other. At that time, railroad leaders did not see the full potential of irrigation, nor could they anticipate the land rush that would occur on the northern plains early in the twentieth century. With labor unrest and the protracted depression much on their minds, they were unable to envision Montana as an agricultural state and eager to sell or lease their land to cattlemen. Why, after all, should farmers come to Montana when there was better farmland and a longer growing season in California, Colorado, and other parts of the West?

As the depression lifted, the railroad's program changed. Maxwell's main motive in allying with Mead was to defeat ceding the arid lands to the states—which the railroads strenuously opposed because it would be much harder to shape land policies in a multitude of state legislatures than in Congress. The leasing compromise was particularly brittle. The Mead-Maxwell proposal—federal administration with revenue granted to the states—did not fully satisfy either man. By promising lease revenue to the states, it eliminated one source of revenue Congress might use to pay for the construction of dams and canals. Maxwell wanted to restrict leasing to land adjoining agricultural tracts in quantities no larger than the farm itself and to make leases unassignable. This ran counter to a bill secretly written by Mead in late 1899 or early 1900 and introduced by Wyoming's congressman, Frank Mondell. The Mondell bill—which never became law—promised the states up to 2 million acres of grazing land apiece in tracts of up to 3,000 acres. In theory, the leased land would remain open to entry under the Homestead Act, with proceeds earmarked for public education and arid land reclamation. All leases, however, would last for five years—Maxwell favored annual leases—and those who took up grazing land under the Homestead Act would have to pay the lessee for all improvements.[15]

By the end of 1900, Maxwell was convinced that Mead had betrayed him and that the needs of grazing and agriculture could not be reconciled; the leasing provision was stricken from the constitution of the National Irrigation Association. "We have to-day not only to overcome the opposition of some mis-guided leaders of eastern agriculturalists," Maxwell wrote to Montana's U.S. Senator Paris Gibson, "but the treachery of false friends in the west, who, while pretending friendship to our movement, are seeking to damn it with faint praise or to ambush it or steer it on rocks where it will go to pieces."[16] Thereafter, Maxwell severed ties with the grazing states and forged a new alliance with Frederick Haynes Newell and Francis G. Newlands, who favored dedicating the proceeds from public land *sales* to reclamation. He abandoned the leasing issue and turned his back on river and harbor appropriations as too uncertain and too likely to result in the Corps of Engineers being given exclusive control over arid land reclamation. Meanwhile, Mead became convinced that the federal reclamation program envisioned in the offices of the United States Geological Survey had the objective of reasserting federal authority over water in the West. Once that was done, the arid states would virtually cease to exist as viable political units. Mead, Warren, and most other politicians in the grazing states insisted that all irrigation works erected by the federal government should be approved by the states in which they were located and that each state should retain full control over the water.[17]

The events leading to adoption of the Reclamation Act of 1902 are well documented,[18] but the link between that program and land law reform is not. The Reclamation Act of 1902 was not complete in and of itself. Its success—at least as measured by the railroads whose subsidy to Maxwell contributed so much to passage of that legislation—depended on reforming the nation's land laws. Otherwise, the arable lands would quickly fall into the hands of speculators and grazing interests. James J.

Hill's Great Northern was built without a federal land subsidy, but in 1902 he also controlled the Northern Pacific, which owned between 13 and 14 million acres in Montana and millions of additional acres in Washington state and western North Dakota. Moreover, as late as 1905 there were still 56 million acres of public land left in the northern Great Plains, including 41 million in eastern Montana, 6.3 million in western North Dakota, and 8.9 million in western South Dakota. Like most railroad leaders, Hill wanted to dispose of his land as rapidly as possible to avoid taxes and to blunt public criticism that the railroads retarded settlement by monopolizing prime farmland.[19]

The Jeffersonian Hill quickly absorbed Maxwell's message: irrigation was a panacea that would benefit farmers, railroads, and the nation alike. Hill thought that the United States faced two major problems: a lack of readily arable land and a rapidly increasing population. Only irrigation would permit the intensive cultivation of desert land and promote family farming. "The largest area for cheap irrigation in the United States is south of the Sweet Grass Hills and in the Milk River Valley on our line, in northern Montana," Hill noted in private correspondence in May 1902. "At an expense of five or six dollars an acre, covering a period of say, eight or ten years, four or five million acres can be put under a full supply of water. . . . That district, with a good supply of water, would produce nearly as much grain as is produced on our entire System at the present time." The railroad would benefit in two ways: land previously leased to grazers would sell for $15 to $25 an acre once it was provided with water from government ditches, and the additional freight traffic would permit the Great Northern to lower rates and still increase profits.[20]

In Montana, Hill relied heavily on the counsel of Paris Gibson, a close business associate whom he had known since the 1870s.[21] Gibson opposed national legislation to lease the public lands to stock owners or to turn them over to the states. In California, he reasoned, such legislation might work because there many farmers opposed the open range and combined raising stock with the cultivation of alfalfa and other crops. In Montana and most of the rest of the West, however, leasing or cession would reinforce the status quo and limit growth. Established cattlemen, rather than new settlers, would inevitably receive preference in any leasing scheme, and those cattlemen would monopolize the land adjoining streams or surrounding springs, as they had in the past. There was no way, Gibson repeatedly warned Maxwell, to write proper safeguards into a state leasing policy as long as cattlemen retained such great power in the legislatures. Far better to delay. At least ten years would be required to determine what land in Montana was arable. At the end of that period, but not before, Montana would contain a sufficient number of farmers to warrant leasing legislation.[22]

Moreover, the value of the Reclamation Act of 1902 in Montana would be severely limited unless the Desert Land Act (1877), Timber and Stone Act (1878), and the commutation clause of the Homestead Act were repealed.[23] "Unless they are repealed," Gibson informed Maxwell, "there will be no further reclamation by the federal government of lands in Montana beyond the St. Mary's Lake enterprise, for there will not be less than three million acres taken up the present year in the State of Montana, and, as you well know, the tide of immigration has not yet begun to set in our state." Virtually all this land, Gibson charged, was appropriated by stockmen who had no intention of improving it.[24] Gibson believed that the arable West would prove to be much larger than the estimates made in 1902. Instead of 60 to 100 million acres, Gibson predicted that as much as 135 or even 150 million acres would eventually be watered. Since irrigated land required less and less water over time, the water supply would cover far more land than the estimates made for virgin land. Moreover, California and other western states had vast and as yet largely untapped supplies of subterranean water, and hardy grains and forage crops from the steppes of eastern Europe and Asia would grow where other plants would not.[25]

Within months of passage of the Reclamation Act, George Maxwell and his National Irrigation Association undertook the cause of land reform on behalf of the railroads, and Gibson, as a member of the Public Lands Committee, became the champion of reform in the United States Senate. Maxwell, like Gibson, assumed that "reforms in the land laws . . . are absolutely essential to the continued existence of a national irrigation policy." Since 20 million acres had been taken from the public domain in fiscal year 1902, Maxwell feared that within a few years the 100 million acres of irrigable land would be lost.[26] Maxwell and Gibson thought that any attempt to correct abuses of the land laws "by an increased field force as recommended by the Commissioner of the General Land Office is simply foolish."[27] They wanted to repeal all legislation except the Homestead Act (shorn of its commutation clause) and prohibit the use of land scrip, *then* have a special commission propose new land laws. Obviously, years might elapse between the repeal of the old laws and the adoption of new ones. Meanwhile, all public grazing lands outside the national forests and Indian reservations should be set aside as permanent "range reserves" subject to annual leases.[28]

The Public Lands Commission, created in October 1903, was established to deal with illegal fencing of the public domain, the leasing question, and the abuse of land laws by stock growers, but many of its supporters also hoped that it would reserve and protect the remaining irrigable lands. It consisted of W. A. Richards, commissioner of the General Land Office and a former governor of Wyoming; Frederick Haynes Newell, director of the Reclamation Service; and Gifford Pinchot, head of the Forestry Office in the Agriculture Department.[29] Through extensive hearings, interviews, and correspondence, the commission found that while most of the land laws had been abused, those abuses benefited actual settlers as well as speculators. The real problem, Senator Henry C. Hansbrough of North Dakota informed Pinchot, was that the laws had not been enforced. Given the increasing number of claims, western land offices inspected only contested entries and took affidavits and the sworn statements of neighbors at face value. The Desert Land Act, Hansbrough insisted, was necessary to induce private enterprise to reclaim land in places not suitable for large federal reclamation projects. He admitted that the commutation clause of the Homestead Act had been misused by some livestock companies, but the greatest abuses occurred where farming was impossible. Elsewhere, farmers successfully challenged illegal entries. Moreover, the commutation clause was indispensable in an age when the cost of farming was rapidly increasing. By permitting farmers to purchase their land as early as six months after entry, rather than waiting the five years for clear title required under the Homestead Act, it enabled them to borrow money using their land as collateral. In this way they could purchase farm machinery, tools, seed, stock, and other necessities. And by opening the land to taxation, the commutation clause contributed to community development through the construction of roads, schools, and other permanent improvements.[30]

Even critics of the land laws were forced to agree. In the spring of 1904, Newell sent C. J. Blanchard, the Reclamation Service's chief statistician, to Montana to investigate Gibson's charges. He found that 90 percent of all Homestead Act entries in the Minot Land Office had been commuted and that most commuters were speculators rather than settlers. The commutation clause, he proclaimed in a letter to Newell, was a "license to steal." Nevertheless, he agreed with Hansbrough's judgment that perversion of the laws was due more to lack of enforcement than to loopholes in the statutes themselves; there was little respect for the law anywhere in the state. "What impresses me most in my investigation of the settlement of Montana lands," he noted, "is the strange indifference not only of the people as a whole but particularly of those in mercantile and commercial pursuits and [the] domination of the land sharks in legislative, financial and business lines is supreme." Reform had no constituency in Montana.[31]

Newell and Pinchot found plenty of confirmation when they visited northern Montana in September 1904. Among other discoveries, they found that the number of land patents issued was far greater than the number of new homes created. They recognized, however, that conditions differed too much within the West, and even within each state and territory, to warrant blanket reforms. In a preliminary report to the president in March 1904, they noted that the states and territories which contained the largest amount of public land were "progressing rapidly in population and wealth." They recommended repeal of the Timber and Stone Act and amendments to the Desert Land Act to require proof that the land was actually being irrigated, but little more.[32] The final report of the commission, issued in 1905, did not go much further. In addition to repeal of the Timber and Stone Act, it urged that the remaining public domain should be inspected to segregate and protect the agricultural land; that the Lieu Land Act of 1897 (which permitted those who held claims to land within national forests to choose equivalent acreage elsewhere) should be rescinded; that the commutation clause should be limited to those who had resided on the land for a minimum of three years; that the area subject to entry under the Desert Land Act should be limited to 160 acres; and that Congress should empower the president to create grazing districts and the Department of Agriculture to supervise a leasing system. Except for revoking the lieu-land provision, Congress ignored these recommendations. Despite strong support for leasing in western Nebraska, the pro- and anti-leasing forces in the West tended to cancel each other out. Moreover, the fact that the West was enjoying an economic boom, and the fear that tightening up land laws would drive prospective settlers into Canada, undermined public support for reform.[33]

Maxwell interpreted the Public Land Commission's caution as timidity. Like many progressives, he saw politics and life in black-and-white terms. "The great strength of any movement before the public," he wrote to a friend in January 1903, "is the profound and absolute conviction in the minds of its advocates that *it is right,* and that every opposition to it is totally or utterly wrong, and the assumption of a compromise position always weakens the general fight in the minds of the public." Maxwell was convinced that he had Theodore Roosevelt's ear, as he had in the fight over reclamation legislation a year earlier. After meeting with the president at the beginning of March 1903, he observed: "Above all things that I admire is a man with backbone, and he [TR] certainly has one. The land grabbers can neither fool him nor phase him a particle. I called on him Saturday . . . to show him the majority report of the Senate Committee on Public Lands. . . . When he read the last paragraph on page 7, which says there should be but one land law and that a genuine homestead act, he tapped his finger on it very emphatically, and said, 'that's right, that's right.'" Later in March, Maxwell confided to Paris Gibson that Roosevelt was "a man who cannot be swerved from what he believes to be right by mere matters of political expediency." Gibson was equally optimistic. In a meeting with Roosevelt on January 8, 1903, the president assured him that if the bills he had introduced to repeal the Desert Land Act and commutation clause did not pass Congress in 1903, he would push them through in 1904—despite opposition from many parts of the West. Gibson reported that the president insisted that "we must 'standpat' for the repeal of those land laws by which so much of the public domain is being taken by land speculators."[34]

Nevertheless, by the summer of 1903 the president had decided that the West was deeply divided over repeal. The Public Lands Commission appointed in October 1903, had done nothing. Gibson and Maxwell concluded that TR was stalling and might secretly support the enlarged homestead legislation and leasing schemes favored by their enemies. Both believed that TR was too concerned with the 1904 election—and keeping the peace with such powerful western Republican senators as Francis Warren of Wyoming, Fred T. Dubois of Idaho, and Henry Teller of Colorado, all of whom opposed repeal—to provide effective leadership. On December 7, 1903, Gibson fumed that the decision to appoint an investigatory commission was "the weakest thing he [TR] has done since he assumed the position of President," and a few weeks later confided that he was "completely disgusted" with the president and hoped he would "lose his job." Owing to the president's indecisiveness, support for repeal evaporated in the House.[35]

The president was only part of the problem. The composition of the land commission was equally important. As historian Paul Gates has observed, "a reading of the two reports of the commission suggests that it was created to give support to views already well crystallized in the minds of Pinchot and Newell."[36] Newell had mixed feelings toward reform. He shared Maxwell and Gibson's desire to keep the irrigable land open to settlers rather than speculators. On the other hand, the Reclamation Fund created in 1902 to pay for reclaiming the arid and semiarid lands within government irrigation projects came from the sale of lands elsewhere in the West. If all land laws were repealed save for the Homestead Act shorn of the commutation clause, the fund would quickly dry up. Maxwell recognized this problem and suggested that the sale of timber from government land would compensate for the lost revenue.[37] However, Pinchot balked at this idea because he hoped to use this revenue to expand forestry operations.[38]

The leasing of grazing lands was another divisive issue. In order to win support for transferring administrative control over the national forests from Interior to Agriculture, Pinchot courted large livestock associations in 1903 and 1904. Stock interests were split over leasing, but those who supported it wanted long-term permits, while Maxwell and Gibson favored one-year grants that could be canceled any time the land was found valuable for agriculture. Here, again, Newell had mixed feelings. Since western farmers often raised livestock as an adjunct to growing alfalfa and other forage crops, and since stock-raising often provided an income during the lean years following the initial settlement of "virgin" land, he wanted to keep the range open to the new farmers within federal irrigation projects. Newell realized that any leasing system would be dominated by the large operators Pinchot had courted. Nevertheless, the fees from grazing permits might also provide additional revenue to the Reclamation Fund. Finally, as dedicated supporters of Theodore Roosevelt, Pinchot and Newell were well aware of the political implications of their actions. Since repeal had only a small constituency within or without the West, doing nothing was the safest political course.[39]

Maxwell's failure to reserve the public domain for actual settlers coincided with a much more personal defeat in Montana's Milk River Valley. Months before passage of the Reclamation Act, the United States Geological Survey withdrew seventy-seven townships from settlement in the Milk and Marias valleys, which led Great Northern officials to assume that one of the first, if not *the* first, government irrigation projects would be built in Montana.[40] James J. Hill and Great Northern officials wanted to dam the outlet of St. Mary's Lake and divert that water into the Milk River via a twenty-seven-mile canal. The augmented river would carry the water 150 to 200 miles east—including 100 miles within Canada—until it reached 250,000 acres of railroad and public land near Chinook and Malta which Hill thought was unusually well-suited to sugar beet and alfalfa production.[41] But despite the fact that a Milk River Project was one of the first five government water projects authorized by the secretary of the interior in 1903, there were repeated delays.

The Milk River was an international stream, and the Reclamation Service refused to begin construction until a treaty had been signed defining each nation's share of the water. To complicate matters, in 1905 an adjudication of rights to the stream within the United States became imperative when the U.S. attorney filed suit claiming that white farmers upstream had diverted water that properly belonged to Indians on the Fort Belknap Reservation between Havre and Malta. These delays afforded enticing opportunities for land speculators who quickly discovered—using "leaks" from railroad officials—where the government project was likely to be located. This forced Newell to propose a cheaper scheme to serve 200,000 acres of public domain between Great Falls and Havre, which largely excluded railroad land.[42] The interests of the Great Northern and Reclamation Service overlapped but were not identical. "If we could be freed from the pest of petty speculators and amateur lobbyists who are taking up the time of the responsible men [in the Reclamation Service]," Newell complained to Maxwell in March 1904, "we could make far more rapid progress. I trust you will use every effort in your power to keep this thing out of the public press and to avoid discussion of it during the present critical situation."[43]

By the time an agreement was reached with Canada in 1909, Hill and other railroad leaders had lost interest in federal reclamation and land reform. Railroad support for Maxwell had always been shaky because some lines stood to benefit more from federal reclamation than others.[44] Initially, Collis P. Huntington of the Southern Pacific was Maxwell's strongest ally among the railroad barons, but Huntington died in 1900 and thereafter James J. Hill became his leading patron. Soon after passage of the Reclamation Act, rumors circulated that Maxwell was speculating in Arizona land and that both he and Newell were far more interested in the Salt River Project in Arizona than in the Montana projects. Since sales of public land in Montana and North Dakota returned large sums to the Reclamation Fund, railroad executives felt betrayed. "I have come to the conclusion that Mr. Maxwell is no longer of much service or use to us in irrigation matters," Louis W. Hill (James J. Hill's son and vice-president of the Great Northern) wrote in March 1904, "and I do not see why we should continue to pay him each month for his services. So far as I can see he does not keep posted on conditions along our line and work to the interest of our territory. . . . I believe with the right man looking after these matters we should get work started on at least one irrigation scheme this summer."[45]

In March 1905, the senior Hill acknowledged that "local selfishness" had been responsible for some problems faced by the Reclamation Service in Montana, but now he believed that "it would have been much better if what we had done towards National Irrigation had been done in the Milk River Valley. We then would have had something to show for it; at present there is nothing." The five leading railroads—each of which had contributed $5,000–$6,000 a year to Maxwell's National Irrigation Association since the late 1890s—decided that Maxwell had lost his touch in Washington. They cut off their subsidies at the end of 1904.[46]

Maxwell's policies had already become fair game in Congress. In late March and early April 1904, the Senate considered a land reform bill introduced by Paris Gibson.[47] "I firmly believe," Gibson proclaimed, "that by means of our existing public-land policy, and the efforts of men and companies occupying large tracts of land for stock raising to prevent the settlement of the Rocky Mountain states, not one acre in forty of all the land of those States suitable for agriculture will be taken by home makers."[48] Gibson denied "emphatically" that the railroads were the driving force behind repeal. When Hansbrough charged that they had paid Maxwell a "princely salary" during the past five or six years to drive up the value of their lands, Gibson admitted the relationship but insisted that the National Irrigation Association had "a very diverse membership" composed of merchants and industrialists from many different states; it was not a "star chamber concern." In any case, Gibson noted disingenuously, the Great Northern was not a land grant line and had never owned any land. It contributed to Maxwell's war chest solely because James J. Hill believed in the same reforms Maxwell advocated: the importance of the family farm and "reclaiming and populating the arid domain." This argument did not satisfy Hansbrough, who pointed out that the NIA did not hold regular meetings and that all its executives were appointed by Maxwell.[49]

The western senators were more than ready for Gibson. In floor debate on the repeal bill, Senator Clark of Wyoming warned that "if this bill should become a law it would absolutely stop the development of the whole arid and semiarid country, which even now labors under many and serious disadvantages." Clark and Senator Dubois of Idaho argued that land scrip—most of which was held by a few railroads—was a far greater danger to the homesteader than the land laws. After 1897 the railroads secured vast quantities of scrip in exchange for government land originally promised to them but included in forest reserves. Since the scrip allowed holders to select land *anywhere* within the public domain, in some places the railroads had been able to monopolize landownership by consolidating railroad and government sections. If the land laws were repealed, the scrip would become much more valuable, as would all railroad land.[50]

Warren of Wyoming pointed out that three out of the four western states that had enjoyed the greatest population growth since 1890—Idaho, North Dakota, and Wyoming—were also states where stock-raising was the dominant business. This proved, he reasoned, that the range cattle industry had not retarded settlement or stunted economic development. Moreover, over 90 percent of the farms in these three states were operated by their owners, a tenancy rate much lower than the national average. No institution—according to Warren—had contributed more to land monopoly than the railroad. Indeed, the economic power of Montana's livestock industry derived in no small measure from the fact that the Northern Pacific Railroad had in the late 1890s and after sold millions of acres to cattlemen and sheepmen. These men—and others who held large blocks of land—stood to profit enormously from repeal.[51]   H. C. Hansbrough argued that only 30 million acres had passed into private hands between 1881 and 1902 under the Desert Land Act, Timber and Stone Act, and commutation clause, but 77.5 million had been taken under the Homestead law without resort to the commutation provision and another 64 million acres had been granted to the railroads. The railroad grants had done far more to promote monopoly than the Desert Land Act, which more than any other law had encouraged western reclamation. The increase in commuted Homestead Act entries suggested that the cost of setting up a farm was too expensive, or too many poor families were moving West, not that most of the commuted claims were falling into the hands of speculators.[52]

Senator Henry Teller of Colorado entered the debate just hours before Congress adjourned. As a former secretary of the interior, Teller knew more about the public domain and national land laws than any other senator. He returned to the theme raised at the beginning of the debate a month earlier: repeal was the brainchild of George Maxwell, whose publicity mill churned out stories about the weaknesses of federal land laws and the need to protect irrigable land for actual settlers solely because the land-grant railroads paid him to do so. These companies were not acting out of public spirit, as Gibson suggested, but "by their own interests in the property they want to sell." "Repeal the homestead law, repeal the desert-land law, and you will make it impossible for a man to get land anywhere unless he owns scrip."[53]

The congressional debate destroyed whatever chance for repeal remained. At the time, hostility towards Roosevelt and Pinchot's reservation policy ran high in many parts of the West. From 1902 to 1905, over 26 million acres were added to the national forests, and many of the reserves contained good grazing and agricultural land. No westerner could be sure where the process would end. Because they threatened to limit access to the public domain, both repeal of the land laws and reservation were perceived as threats to economic opportunity. Congress's public exposure of the relationship among Maxwell, the railroads, and land reform made Theodore Roosevelt even more cautious. The president's antitrust policy, as well as his desire to bring the railroads under public scrutiny and control, prevented him from supporting any land policy championed by James J. Hill and his corporate allies. Ten days before the debate over Gibson's bill began, the U.S. Supreme Court upheld the dissolution of the Northern Securities Company—a holding company that controlled the Great Northern, Northern Pacific, Union Pacific, and Burlington lines. TR was understandably wary of jeopardizing this triumph by joining the railroads in pushing for a reform that would win him few votes.[54]

As it turned out, the railroad's interest in reform was just as shaky as Roosevelt's. Late in 1904, the Northern Pacific—which had already disposed of most of its land in North Dakota—withdrew from sale the 6.75 million acres it still owned in Montana between the Missouri River and the Rocky Mountains. Then, in consultation with the U.S.D.A. and the state of Montana, it set up experimental farms along the lines of the Northern Pacific, Great Northern, and Chicago, Milwaukee & St. Paul to study the crops best suited to Montana. The land was not returned to the market until 1908.[55]   Meanwhile, the railroads threw themselves wholeheartedly into the campaign for "dry farming" that was sweeping the Great Plains, and their earlier support for irrigation evaporated. At the 1909 Dry-Farming Congress held in Billings, Louis W. Hill, by this time president of the Great Northern, advised his listeners that "it is desirable to start with a good impression, and do not give the people whom you expect to come here an impression that they are going to a dry country which perhaps has rain and perhaps has seasons of great drought. Those of us who are acquainted with the country for 20 years or longer know that there is no reason on earth why this land cannot be cultivated with just as good an opportunity and as good a chance to harvest a crop with as great a certainty as in any of the states east of the Mississippi River. . . . Montana is neither arid nor dry." The northern railroads purchased nearly 40 percent of the 10,500 memberships in the 1910 Dry-Farming Congress.[56]

The dry-farming movement spread rapidly in the first and second decades of the twentieth century. The annual precipitation in most parts of the northern Great Plains fell below fifteen inches in only three years, and only in 1910 was drought severe. Moreover, national and international markets for grain remained strong, profits from cattle steadily declined from 1900 to 1913, and the price of farmland quadrupled between 1900 and 1920. With the help of the Enlarged Homestead Act of 1909 and the Stock-Raising Homestead Act of 1916, nearly twice the amount of public land was taken between 1898 and 1922 than the 70 million acres that passed into private ownership between 1868 and 1897. By the end of World War I, the railroad and government land in the northern Great Plains had disappeared, and the West's last great land rush was over.[57]

The role of the railroads in shaping land and water policy—at both the state and federal levels—deserves much more study. In the case of land reform, the railroads demonstrated a stronger commitment to modernizing outdated laws than the progressives. Their leaders had mixed motives, but there is little reason to doubt that Hill and Huntington thought their efforts would benefit the nation as well as their companies. In many parts of the West, the railroad served almost as a surrogate government—both because its great power undermined the effectiveness of state and local institutions and because those institutions were too poor to perform vital public services.[58] That said, railroad executives were no wiser or more farsighted than leaders in government. In 1899, the livestock and mining industries seemed destined to predominate in Montana and many other parts of the West for the foreseeable future. No one could anticipate that Montana's population would more than double between 1900 and 1920, as homesteaders took up land on its northern and eastern plains. At the dawn of the new century, James J. Hill and others recognized the promise of irrigation; federal reclamation might revive the family farm and shore up republican values, as well as inflate railroad land prices and increase rail traffic. But when the Reclamation Service failed to provide the expected aid, the railroads changed course again, this time to support dry farming. In short, they reacted to events far more than they molded them. (It is significant that the railroads were unwilling to build irrigation projects on their own.)

The quest for land law reform demonstrates that by 1903 many of the old Jacksonian arguments against monopoly had lost their sting, and the "land problem" was no longer an important part of the nation's political agenda, as it had been in the 1860s, 1870s, and 1880s. Much of the public domain remained, but not much land worth fighting over. And with the depression gone, one of the prime justifications for reform disappeared. The Reclamation Act of 1902 was enacted in large part because the migration west had dried up during the 1890s. Unless the federal government took direct action, argued those like George Maxwell, the West would remain an object lesson in arrested economic development. The days of haphazard, unplanned settlement seemed over. Now the federal government would take the lead. However, the surprising flood of immigrants into Montana and other parts of the West during the first two decades of the twentieth century showed that the pessimists were wrong; the West was growing rapidly despite all the dire predictions. That made the job of reformers doubly difficult. For in the absence of a demonstrated need for change, federal power was no less to be feared than that of predacious private enterprises. If land law reform meant more and more national forests or permanent grazing reserves, most westerners wanted nothing to do with it.

PART THREE

Forests, Conservation, and Bureaucracy

No book has had a greater influence on the history of natural resource policy in the United States than Samuel P. Hays's pathbreaking *Conservation and the Gospel of Efficiency* (1959), which looked at the influence of professionalization and bureaucratization on national resource politics and policies in the "Progressive Era." Hays denied that the conservation movement was a broad popular movement, or that it was directed against the private corporation, as some historians had argued in the 1940s and 1950s. In the three decades from 1890 to 1920, battles over presidential power preoccupied the president, Congress, and the executive agencies. The creation of such bureaus as the Forest Service and Reclamation Service, led by experts in new disciplines like hydrology and silviculture, symbolized the advent of a new kind of politics. "Conservationists envisaged," Hays declared, "even though they did not realize their aims a political system guided by the ideal of efficiency and dominated by technicians who could best determine how to achieve it."[1]

Much as it has taught us, Hays's thesis has serious weaknesses, ranging from its imprecise definition of such critical terms as "science" and "efficiency," to its neglect of conservation organizations outside government, to its disregard of state conservation laws and policies. "Forests and Conservation, 1865–1890" and "Forests and Reclamation, 1891–1911" challenge the Hays thesis from several directions. The first chapter makes the point—hardly original with me—that conservation originated in the decades following the Civil War and that it was more an emotional and moral response to perceived abuses of nature than a quest for efficiency or "scientific planning."[2] The second chapter argues that the bureaucratic unity and scientific approach to resource management Hays attributed to the Reclamation Service and Forest Service were more apparent than real. The interests and ambitions of the two bureaus often clashed. Both attempted to achieve financial independence from the hurly-burly of annual congressional appropriations—by securing control over revenue from public land and timber sales and grazing permits—but Congress quickly reined in the two agencies. Within and between them, by the end of Theodore Roosevelt's second term, it was politics as usual. Once in power, the Progressive Era bureaucrats did not behave much differently from those who administered bureaus in the nineteenth century.

Long before the depression of the 1890s, conservationists began to question how long the material progress of the United States could be sustained. The campaign to save the forests was motivated in part by the fear that the United States was running out of timber. Yet it was also a form of jeremiad, a ritual or litany. George Perkins Marsh's *Man and Nature* (1864)—perhaps the single most influential book on conservation and ecology ever published in the United States—warned that once forested land fell to less than a certain percentage of a nation's land mass, a process of "desertification" was both inevitable and irreversible. In effect, Marsh replaced the wrath of God with the wrath of Nature, urging nineteenth-century Americans to repent and mend their profligate ways or face terrible punishment.

Although Marsh invested human beings with a tremendous power over nature, that power was not unlimited. Some laws could not be broken with impunity. We know surprisingly little about the relationship between religion and conservation in the history of the United States, particularly how the concept of stewardship tempered the biblical injunction to subdue the earth and finish God's Creation. The settlement of the Midwest and Far West deeply worried the conservationists. Marsh's message was the antithesis of Frederick Jackson Turner's. Turner emphasized the evolution of civilization from Native American, to fur trapper, to herdsman, to farmer, to towns devoted to commerce, industry, and civilization. Marsh suggested that this process could also be reversed.

Nineteenth- and early twentieth-century science was as much moralism as empirical observation. To be sure, a new relationship between government and science developed in the decades after the Civil War. The U.S. Geological Survey, Biological Survey, Bureau of Forests, and other natural resource agencies dated from the 1870s and 1880s, and many of their employees became active in such fledgling scholarly organizations as the Philosophical Society of Washington, the Anthropological Society of Washington, the National Geographic Society, and the Cosmos Club. "By the 1890s," Michael Lacey has noted, "Washington's bureaucracy had become by far the nation's most active publisher of scientific work, in fields ranging from agronomy and anthropology to geography, geology, education and social statistics. The *National Geographic* magazine came out of the Washington circle, as did the *American Anthropologist*. For many years *Science* magazine, the period's most important source of reporting on science and civic affairs, was dominated editorially by members of the Washington community; in fact, it was funded by one of them."[3]

Nevertheless, much of what passed for science in the nineteenth century consisted of fact-gathering, statistical compilation, and observation rather than laboratory experimentation, and the line between pure and applied science was blurry. Indeed, the technology of the time had only a limited capacity to test and verify hypotheses. Nature was not studied independent of human beings; mankind was at the center of the scientific universe. In an 1883 address on evolution, John Wesley Powell warned physical scientists about maintaining the proper perspective: "When a man loses faith in himself, and worships nature, and subjects himself to the government of the laws of physical nature, he lapses into stagnation, where mental and moral miasma is bred." The object of science was not to describe nature in some disinterested, impartial way, but to use the lessons of nature to benefit human beings. Indeed, "scholarly detachment" posed great danger if it distracted scientists from that basic goal.[4]

Historians often forget that scientific ideas are the creatures and creations of a particular culture. They are not "timeless truths" discovered by a class of uniquely "objective" human beings. As the environmental historian Donald Worster has observed, most histories of science disregard "the fact that science is always, in some measure, involved in matters of value and moral perception."[5] In nineteenth-century colleges and universities, there were powerful pressures on the faculty *not* to specialize and *not* to do research. Biologist David Starr Jordan, who was destined to become president of Stanford University, began his career at Lombard University in Illinois teaching classes in natural science, political economy, German, Spanish, literature, and "evidences of Christianity." Scientists were expected to contribute to the liberal arts, and their basic job was to produce the well-educated man. Graduate programs, research institutes, endowed chairs, specialized scientific journals, and federal grants were far in the future.[6]

Science is not just a "body of knowledge" or a collection of disciplines; it is a set of ideas that characterize and define an age. Unfortunately, historians rarely discuss ideas as they impinge on public policy. The nineteenth-century conservation movement was built on many ideas including the assumption that nature preferred forested land to deserts; that year-round rainfall was the norm and aridity abnormal; and that nature aspired to order and regularity.

Science became more empirical in the early decades of the twentieth century, and the fear of human arrogance that permeated the work of George Perkins Marsh and his followers largely disappeared. Nevertheless, much of the moralism remained. Conservation's most important leaders, including John Wesley Powell, Henry Gannett, C. S. Sargent, Bernhard Fernow, and Gifford Pinchot, looked at forests in different ways, but none among them had much empirical evidence to support his views. Sargent, a professor of aboriculture at Harvard and editor of *Garden and Forest*, and later Pinchot, insisted that forests were nature's reservoirs. Chopping them down led to a wide variety of baneful results, including erratic stream flows, drought, flooding, and soil erosion. On the other hand, Powell had no sympathy for the creation of national forests or for the protection of forested land. In 1878, he suggested that there was plenty of timber left in the American West and that forested land could best be protected as private, rather than public, land. He recommended that control over the forests be given to those who lived within the river basin in which the forests were located. He suggested, moreover, that trees wasted rather than saved water. By soaking up moisture and returning it to the atmosphere they retarded the spread of irrigation in the West.[7]

The conflict among these "conservationists" erupted in the late 1880s and continued through much of the 1890s, but the two sides buried their differences in 1899 and formed a shaky partnership that rendered arid land reclamation and forest protection not just compatible but symbiotic. Without this new alliance, passage of the Reclamation Act of 1902 and the transfer of control over the forest reserves from Interior to Agriculture in 1905 would have been much more difficult, if not impossible. Nevertheless, even though many conservationists in the federal bureaucracy were good friends—particularly Frederick H. Newell of the Reclamation Service and Gifford Pinchot of the Forest Service—they competed for scarce resources and public favor.

Bureaucratic conflicts originated in the nineteenth-century rivalry between the Interior and Agriculture departments. At a time of low crop prices, Powell's desire to expand western irrigation agriculture met little favor in Agriculture, which largely represented eastern farmers. Nevertheless, the Agriculture Department refused to be outflanked by Interior. In the 1890s, it created an Office of Irrigation Inquiry, and later an Office of Irrigation Investigations, which directly challenged the U.S. Geological Survey's attempt to monopolize the federal government's study of water in the United States. After 1902, F. H. Newell, head of the Reclamation Service, feared that the Bureau of Plant Industry and the Bureau of Soils would undermine the work of the Reclamation Service. Once he became head of the Forest Service in 1905, Pinchot attempted to temper and restrain criticism of federal reclamation, but other officials in Agriculture consistently charged that the Reclamation Service paid too much attention to the construction of dams and canals and not enough to the practical problems of desert farming.

There were many additional sources of tension. The reservation of more than 100 million acres of public domain as national forests, national parks, national monuments, mineral reserves, water power sites, and for other purposes during Theodore Roosevelt's presidency reduced the amount of salable land and limited the size of the reclamation fund. It also raised the question of how to regulate grazing within the rapidly expanding national forests. Pinchot favored large stockmen. They exercised great power in most western legislatures and in Congress, and it was easier for the Forest Service to enforce grazing regulations through contracts with large operators. Newell, on the other hand, was more interested in securing access to the forests for small farmers. Many government projects adjoined forest reserves, and the farmers they served depended on the sale of livestock to survive during the first years of breaking ground, when their land returned little revenue. Range rights, like water rights, were generally based on chronological priority, and the Forest Service's permit system rewarded established livestock companies at the expense of settlers on the irrigation projects.

The history of conservation in the Progressive Era is much in need of revision. Not only had "conservation"—as an impulse or ethic, if not a movement—been around since the 1860s and 1870s, but the creation of new agencies contributed to bureaucratic fragmentation and made the development of a *coherent* natural resources policy more rather than less difficult. Jay N. "Ding" Darling, head of the Biological Survey during the mid-1930s, remarked: "Conservation as a national principle has no substance or co-ordination. . . . Fourteen agencies in the Federal Government and forty-eight states with some semblance of an official organization in charge of conservation! But they are like so many trains running on single-track roads, often in opposite directions and without any train dispatcher or block system. Collisions are frequent, wrecks are a daily occurrence, and the destruction is greater than the freight delivered at the specified destination." The evidence suggests, contra Hays, that bureaucratization inhibited rather than encouraged unified, coordinated, rational planning.[8]

CHAPTER SEVEN

Forests and Conservation,
1865–1890

Let me say to you that the laws of nature are the same everywhere. Whoever violates them anywhere, must always pay the penalty. No country ever so great and rich, no nation ever so powerful, inventive and enterprising can violate them with impunity. We most grievously delude ourselves if we think we can form an exception to the rule.

—Carl Schurz, speech to the American Forestry Association, October 15, 1889

Historians have largely ignored the growth of conservation sentiment during the decades following the Civil War.[1] They have examined such important subjects as American attitudes toward nature and the wilderness, federal land policies, the national parks idea, the crusade to create national forests, and fish and wildlife protection, but concern over the abuse of natural resources has been treated as a twentieth-century phenomenon, a legacy of "progressivism."[2] The popular scientific thought concerning land use in the nineteenth century has been overlooked, particularly the ideas espoused by those who worried about the nation's forests. This chapter examines the persistent fear of timber famine after the Civil War and basic assumptions regarding the value of woodlands. Those assumptions demonstrate that a conservation "ethic"—if not a unified, coherent movement—existed long before Progressive reformers popularized conservation. That ethic derived from the fear that abuse of the land threatened the future of American civilization. Late nineteenth-century conservationists were as often moralists and philosophers as scientists, and in many ways their beliefs differed from the ideology preached by such men as Theodore Roosevelt, Gifford Pinchot, W J McGee, Frederick Haynes Newell, Richard T. Ely, and Charles R. Van Hise. But they also anticipated the later conservationists, especially in exploring the interrelationship of different natural resources and their uses.

In the nineteenth century, legislative interest in conserving the nation's forests was limited. Until late in the century, little was done to classify or to segregate public lands according to different values and uses. Not until 1878, in the ill-conceived Timber and Stone Act, did the national government provide for sales of woodlands separate from agricultural and mineral lands, and initially that law applied only to California, Oregon, Washington, and Nevada. At both the state and the federal levels, bills were considered during the 1870s and 1880s to protect forests from fires, foraging livestock, lumbermen, farmers, miners, manufacturers, and other wood users. Some measures called for the creation of state or national forests, but those proposals enjoyed little success outside New York and Pennsylvania. True, section 24 of the March 3, 1891, General Revision Act authorized the creation of national forests. But despite strong support from the American Forestry Association and the secretary of the interior, it would have failed as a discrete bill. As part of an omnibus measure to reform notoriously inadequate land laws, it was overshadowed by provisions repealing the Timber Culture Act of 1873 and the preemption acts and by others that attempted to plug loopholes in the Homestead (1862) and the Desert Land (1877) acts. Though the 1891 statute provided for the withdrawal of forests to protect farms, pastureland, and communities from drought and spring floods, it said nothing about how those forests should be used, nor did it appropriate money to administer them. Between 1891 and 1897 Congress considered twenty-seven bills pertaining to management of the reserves, but comprehensive regulations were not adopted until the twentieth century. Nineteenth-century state and federal forest legislation did not constitute a coherent, consistent policy to protect the environment or even a policy to promote the most efficient use of the nation's timber.[3]

That should not suggest that the public or the scientific community lacked interest in the woodlands. Concern for the future of American forests antedated the Civil War. For example, in both *The Pioneers* (1823) and *The Prairie* (1827), James Fenimore Cooper lamented the destruction of trees. In *The Pioneers*, Judge Temple, who personified reason and social responsibility, warned that Americans were "felling the forests as if no end could be found to their treasures, nor any limits to their extent. If we go on this way, twenty years hence we shall want fuel." And Francois André Michaux, who in 1819 published in French the first systematic study of American forests (revised and issued in English in 1849 as *Northern American Sylva*), noted an "alarming destruction of the trees . . . which will continue to increase in proportion to the increase in population. The effect is already felt in a very lively manner in the great cities, where they complain more and more every year, not only of the excessive dearness of firewood, but even of the difficulty of procuring timber for the various kinds of building and public works."[4] Michael Williams asserts that "in 1840 probably 95 percent of America's energy requirements for heating, lighting, and motive power were supplied by wood; coal hardly entered into the picture at this time." Cities along the eastern seaboard grew dramatically during the early decades of the nineteenth century, and farmers—particularly in New York and New England—supplemented their incomes by cutting firewood for urbanites. The increasing use of steam engines by riverboats and railroads also drove up the demand for wood; in 1850 a typical 400-ton boat burned 660 cords on an eleven-day round-trip between Louisville and New Orleans. In some places, particularly New York and northern Ohio, forests were burned to produce ashes used in the production of potash and pearlash; that industry often went hand in hand with clearing land for agriculture or grazing.[5]

The first extended warning of timber famine came from Frederick Starr, Jr., whose essay "American Forests: Their Destruction and Preservation" appeared in the *Report of the Commissioner of Agriculture for the Year 1865*, published in 1866. Starr alerted his readers to "an impending national danger, beyond the power of figures to estimate, and beyond the province of words to express." He calculated that from 1850 to 1860 about 30 million acres of heavily forested land had been stripped to produce new farms. If the nation's population continued to grow at the rate of the 1850s, more than 100 million acres of timber would be cleared during the 1860s and each succeeding decade for farming alone—an area the size of California. The danger extended far beyond the lumber supply. Starr observed that "there is no one thing in our land which has more certainly caused the present high rates of labor than the high price of fuel for all domestic and manufacturing purposes, the high rents for the industrial classes, and the high price of the raw material upon which nearly one-half million of our industrious, intelligent mechanics labor for their bread." Economic prosperity depended on "cheap bread, cheap houses, cheap fuel and cheap transportation for passengers and freights." Since the forests of New England and the Middle Atlantic States had been severely depleted, the cost of transporting lumber from ever greater distances was as significant as the total quantity of available timber. As the price of building materials rose, the urban poor enjoyed less and less hope of escaping crowded tenements for homes of their own. Starr implied that since most republican virtues and values depended on widespread property ownership, the foundation of the Republic was threatened.[6]

Starr recognized that a significant turning point in the nation's use of timber was reached as settlers poured onto the Great Plains. The population of Kansas grew by 240 percent during the 1860s and by 173 percent during the 1870s, while Nebraska's increased by 355 percent and by 268 percent during the same decades. The absence of timber on the plains resulted in the opening of pine forests surrounding the Great Lakes to logging. Communities along the eastern seaboard adjoined timber supplies—unlike the farms and cities of the plains, which were located on the edge of what had long been known as the Great American Desert.[7]

The nation's rapidly expanding rail network also contributed to the destruction of forests. New lines exposed previously inaccessible tracts of land to the axe and the plow, and many railroads owned and operated lumber companies. The railroads consumed enormous quantities of wood for cars, stations, fuel, fences, and especially crossties. One historian has calculated that from the late 1870s to about 1900, the railroads used 20 to 25 percent of the "annual timber product." In 1890 *Scientific American* estimated that 73 million ties were needed each year to construct new roads and to maintain old ones. (Before chemical treatment for insect damage became common, ties had to be replaced every five to eight years.) Additional demands came from rapidly expanding cities and industries, especially as factories converted from water to steam power.[8]

Forest fires also endangered the timber supply. Farmers had traditionally used fire to clear forests and to burn dead grass to improve pasturage. But the opening of the arid West to mining and stock-raising in the 1860s and 1870s resulted in the invasion of virgin forests by grass fires touched off by sparks from locomotives, campfires of careless hunters, and fires purposely set by sheepmen. In 1882, following a fire that destroyed about 2,000 square miles of forested land in Michigan, one writer concluded: "The destruction of the great pine-forests of the Northwest, of Michigan and Wisconsin, rapidly as it is carried forward by the lumberman's axe, is hastened by the fires lighted, in some cases, by the lumberman's carelessness . . . fires consume more than are cut down by the axe."[9]

The destruction of timber was particularly rapid around the Great Lakes, in the Rocky Mountains of Colorado, and in California. In 1866 the commissioner of the General Land Office observed that the dwindling forests of the Great Lakes were a "serious concern," an alarm echoed by the United States commissioner of mining's statistics for the Rocky Mountain forests in 1870. California was particularly vulnerable. The mining industry used enormous quantities of wood for ore reduction and shaft timbers, and the rapid growth of San Francisco, Oakland, Sacramento, and other communities kept the demand for building materials high. Since most Sierra Nevada forests remained inaccessible until the 1880s and 1890s, the lumber industry was for several decades limited to a few heavily logged counties along the coast from Eureka to Monterey. Nevertheless, in the late 1860s the California State Board of Agriculture predicted that one-third of the state's timber had already been cut and that at the current rate the state's entire supply would disappear within forty years. The United States commissioner of agriculture was even more pessimistic. In 1872 he warned that "requirements of the State for forest products will be at least ten times greater for the next twenty-two years." As the decade wore on, estimates became gloomier. In 1874 a writer in the *Overland Monthly* stated that within twenty years California would be importing most of its wood from Alaska; and in an 1878 editorial titled "The Abuse of Nature and Its Penalties," the *Sacramento Daily Union* cautioned that at the current rate of logging, "the exhaustion of the forest growth of the Sierra is only a question of some ten years, and . . . if the rate of consumption is increased the catastrophe will occur considerably sooner." Those fears continued well into the 1890s.[10]

Estimates of the nation's timber supply were equally alarming. They varied enormously because students of forestry differed as to what constituted accessible timber, especially given the rapid construction of railroads in the western half of the nation during the decades following the Civil War. They also disagreed about units of measurement and about what species of trees were usable or desirable for factories, houses, furniture, fuel, and other needs. In his report for 1877, Secretary of the Interior Carl Schurz warned that at the existing rate of consumption, within twenty years the supply would "fall considerably short of our home necessities." For the first time, the Census of 1880 contained a survey of the nation's forests. Charles Sprague Sargent, professor of aboriculture at Harvard University, compiled the report largely from published documents, statements of timberland owners, and information provided by state land agents. Such important western species as Douglas fir and ponderosa pine were not considered. In an article in *North American Review*, Sargent reassured readers that the forests were "still capable of yielding a large amount of material, and of continuing to do so for many years." His census report, however, predicted that the most common source of sawtimber, the white pine, would be used up in about eight years and that the most likely substitute, California redwood, would disappear soon thereafter. The report prompted *Forest and Stream*—the most prominent popular forestry journal in the country—to forecast a twenty-five-year overall supply. Later in the decade Bernhard E. Fernow, chief of the Forestry Division of the United States Department of Agriculture, estimated a fifty-year supply. But in 1889 Schurz warned that "men whose hair is already gray will see the day when in the United States from Maine to California and from the Mexican Gulf to Puget Sound there will be no forest left worthy of the name."[11]

Passionate warnings of timber famine reflected a fear deeper than that of the overuse of an essential natural resource. Schurz, and many others, worried that Americans had violated fundamental laws of nature and faced dire consequences. Ironically, arguments against deforestation assumed that while nature operated according to immutable, relentless laws, man had a profound effect on nature. Human beings were not just prey to forces beyond their control; because natural laws were so predictable, man could often mold the environment to his advantage.

The foundation of that thinking was the assumption that, under "normal" conditions, the environment was humid and wooded; grasslands and deserts were "abnormal." *Forest and Stream* explained in 1873: "That all these arid plains, thousands of years ago, were covered with trees seems to be highly probable. From their laying flat, the forests, once on fire, were consumed to the very last tree." Fernow suggested that the entire earth would have been covered with forests, "save only a few localities," had man and other animals not interfered with nature's norm. The Great Plains had been turned to vast, barren prairies by forest and grass fires; the devastation was completed by herds of hungry, tramping buffalo that destroyed new seedlings. "You must remember," Fernow told a reporter in 1891, "that the entire earth is a potential forest." As late as 1899 Charles E. Bessey, a professor at the University of Nebraska, suggested in a paper before the American Association for the Advancement of Science that, where not impeded by towns or fields, pine trees had spread across Nebraska and parts of the Black Hills of South Dakota "with a good deal of rapidity."[12]

Not only were forests considered the norm, so was abundant year-round rainfall; and the two went hand in hand. Years before the Civil War, writers observed that deforestation rendered the local climate more severe, subject to greater extremes of heat and cold. Noah Webster noted in 1799 that in the wake of extensive logging in New England's forests, the "warm weather of autumn extends into the winter months, and winter into summer months." Farm journals in New England embraced the idea that forests influenced climate and made it almost commonplace by the Civil War.[13]

The corollary that forests produced or at least increased rainfall also antedated the Civil War, but it had little meaning for residents of the humid half of the nation. Not until settlers reached the semiarid plains did the idea gain wide currency. Then it was endorsed not just by land speculators—who never tired of painting the Great Plains as a potential Garden of Eden—but also by respected scientists ranging from geologist Ferdinand V. Hayden, head of the United States Geographical and Geological Survey, to the nation's foremost student of the forests during the 1870s and 1880s, Franklin B. Hough. In 1874 the *Pacific Rural Press,* California's leading farm journal, bluntly declared that "the fact that forests have a beneficial effect on the surrounding country, by producing an increase of rain, is indisputable." In 1888, *Scientific American* confidently proclaimed that the correlation between forests and rainfall was "thoroughly well established." Nor was the influence restricted to the forested area. In 1885 *Nature* observed that "forests exercise an influence on climate which does not cease on their borders, but extends over a larger or smaller adjacent region according to the size, kind, and position of the forest." A few years later, the editor of *Science* concluded that "so often has it been asserted that the growth of forests promote rainfall, that it has almost become an axiom in science as well as among the people."[14]

Many theories were offered to explain how forests stimulated rainfall. One held that tree roots tapped groundwater and released it into the atmosphere through leaves or needles. This moisture, added to that carried by passing clouds, produced precipitation. Another explanation was that forests were canopies that prevented or reduced the escape of radiant heat from the soil. Lower temperatures in or near forests lowered the dew point and encouraged atmospheric condensation. A third hypothesis was that winds moved much faster over open ground than over trees. Forests provided more resistance to air, so rain clouds backed up over the trees, concentrating the moisture. Another argument maintained that forests caused upward wind drafts, compressing the air above the trees until it became saturated with water, which fell as rain or snow. Because trees were pointed, and often bore sharp needles, some scientists assumed that forests were nature's assembled lightning rods and attracted thunderstorms much better than did flat or round objects. Clouds were positively charged with electricity and trees carried a negative charge, hence forests could force rain clouds to alter their course and to congregate above the trees.[15]

Many scientists denied that forests had any significant effect on rainfall or on the climate generally.[16] But other forest influences were more widely accepted. The relationship of forest to farmland had long been of interest to farmers, and not just because trees had to be cleared before crops could be planted. Forests offered a hospitable habitat to a richer variety of game than either grasslands or deserts. They also produced rich soils. In 1885 *Forest and Stream* editorialized:

Forests are . . . on certain soils an essential preliminary to agriculture, and of essential benefit on all soils. Their function is to elaborate the organic elements in compounds readily assimilable by plants, which cannot draw them directly from the atmosphere; and to decompose certain insoluble forms of lime and potash into soluble salts, the presence of which in the cereals is necessary to the support of man and beast.

In short, soil, no less than climate, depended on the forest. The relationship was governed, according to *Popular Science Monthly*, by a "universal law."[17]

Estimates of the ideal ratio of forest to farm varied widely. Hayden suggested 10 or 15 acres of trees on each 160 acres. Felix L. Oswald maintained that when the ratio of forested area to cropped land fell to less than one acre in six, irrigation and artificial fertilization were required to produce good harvests. The danger was greatest where forests gave way to fields of grain, less harmful where orchards replaced the indigenous trees. Nathaniel H. Egleston suggested that the best harvests came from land 25 percent forested, with trees left "in masses." Many scientists, however, insisted that the optimum percentage of forest cover varied from region to region and from country to country. George Perkins Marsh noted that European silviculturists had recommended 32 percent forest cover for France and 23 percent for Germany. Marsh refused to state a ratio for the United States, but since the western half of the nation was much drier than France or Germany, he concluded, "I greatly doubt whether any one of the American States, except, perhaps, Oregon, has, at this moment, more woodland than it ought permanently to preserve." Fernow was more specific. He advocated at least 25 percent forest land and warned that the agricultural states of Ohio, Indiana, and Illinois and the Rocky Mountain states all had less than 15 percent.[18]

Trees were as important to city dwellers as to farmers. Before the Civil War the issue of whether forests were healthful or dangerous generated considerable debate. The prevalence of malaria, chills, and a wide variety of fevers prompted Americans to consider the cause and transmission of disease. Malaria was assumed to derive from a toxic gas, or "miasma," that issued from moist, decaying animal and vegetable matter. In an address to the American Philosophical Society in 1700, Hugh Williamson stated that forests preserved swamps and marshes, blocked the purifying rays of the sun, and exuded an atmosphere "constantly charged with gross putrescent fluid." Jeremy Belknap, in his *History of New Hampshire* (1792), acknowledged that "whilst one condemns the air of woodland as destructive to life and health, another celebrates it as containing *nutritive* particles." Belknap himself believed that forest air was "remarkably pure." As evidence he cited the "vigorous and robust" health of those on new plantations and the "great age" of the first planters. The forest absorbed "noxious vapors" and transmitted healthful breezes while a "profusion of effluvia from the resinous trees imparts to the air a balsamic quality which is extremely favourable to health." Nevertheless, many frontiersmen noted that once the forests had been cut and burned, and the marshes drained or filled, the incidence of fevers dropped sharply.[19]

Those who worried about the pernicious effects of the woodlands did not disappear after the Civil War, but their voices were drowned out by those who promised therapeutic benefits. For example, in California the Southern Pacific Railroad introduced the fast-growing *Eucalyptus globulus,* or blue gum, from Australia. It was expected to curb malaria epidemics in the swampy Central Valley as well as to provide lumber (particularly for railroad ties), fuel, and windbreaks. The slim, stately trees would slow the winds that carried disease gases. They would also absorb moisture from the soil, retarding the process of vegetative decay. The eucalyptus leaves contained a volatile oil whose strong odor was thought to disinfect the air—as well as the ground once the leaves fell. The eucalyptus had unique health-giving qualities, but all trees were assumed to absorb dangerous gases and to screen or to filter fungi and bacteria. The forests themselves did not produce disease gases. "Since cholera, typhus, yellow fever and malaria are soil diseases of miasmatic origin," explained Fernow,

> the forest soil becomes important. . . . The vegetable matter in the forest soil is deficient in albuminoids, potash, phosphates and nitrates, and is therefore less nutritive for bacteria than field, garden or city soil. Temperature and moisture conditions in the forest soil are also different and less favorable to microbe life, which thrives best with certain temperatures and an alternation of dry and wet as is found in unshaded fields.

The forests thwarted such bacteria from entering the atmosphere by preventing the ground from drying out and turning to dust—which was easily carried by the wind. Fernow favored the creation of large urban parks as well as the preservation of forests. The parks would reduce disease by bringing forest influences to the city.[20]

Forests were assumed to serve many purposes besides promoting rainfall, protecting agriculture, and preventing disease. As *Forest and Stream* noted in 1882, "no woods, no game; no woods, no water; and no water, no fish." Not everyone worried about the supply of fish and game, but everyone had a stake in the forests' alleged ability to conserve water. Forests captured water in the spongelike humus as well as underground. Their shade and equable temperatures helped prevent evaporation. Forests also retarded the melting snow in the spring, limited erosion in the mountains, and prevented flooding in the valleys and plains below. And since they released water at a gradual rate, rather than in torrents, they served as natural reservoirs for farmers who irrigated. J. B. Harrison, secretary of the American Forestry Association, warned in 1889:

> If forest-conditions are destroyed on the mountains . . . evil and destructive forces which no human power can control will be liberated and set in motion. The soil will be carried down from the mountain slopes. . . . The streams will be ruinous torrents for a short time each year . . . and their channels will be dusty chasms during the season when water is most needed. The air will be filled with dust from the perpetual erosion of the hills. . . . The laws and forces of nature will not make exceptions in our favor, though we are a great country.

Sargent was one of the staunchest critics of the idea that forests changed the climate, but he agreed that Americans faced "great disasters . . . unless the safeguards which nature has furnished are respected and preserved."[21]

Those "disasters" were severe indeed. In 1876, *Scientific American*, in an editorial titled "Timber Waste a National Suicide," predicted that "a period, so near as to be practically tomorrow . . . is at hand when our existence as a nation will end." Writer after writer concluded that the violation of nature's laws threatened the material and spiritual foundation of American civilization. Americans, so the critics charged, had behaved as spendthrifts, squandering resources accumulated over centuries. The obsession with short-term profit blinded them to the truth that the essence of civilization was its debt to future generations. "A people can only justify its claim to be called civilized," wrote Charles Eliot Norton, "by so using the free gifts which it has received from Nature and its own predecessors as to transmit them undiminished and improved to its successors."[22]

Just as nature's laws were immutable and predictable, so were the social and economic consequences of violating those laws. The contrast between civilization and savagery fascinated Victorian Americans. And as the pace of industrialization and urbanization increased—especially given the simultaneous subjugation of the nation's last "savages," the Indians of the Great Plains—the contrast became even starker. Since civilization required an active process to sustain, human societies tended to regress to more primitive institutional forms. Evolution did not ensure the continued success of an "advanced" society any more than it ensured the continued dominance of one species of animal over its competitors. Once deforestation passed a certain critical point, the process of decay was irreversible, much as a fatal human disease. Most humans and wild animals, subjected to extremes of heat and cold, drought and flood, would flee the ravished land. Those remaining, deprived of wood needed to build civilized communities, would revert to barbarism. Poverty would replace plenty; the "survivors" would become nomads, slaves of a pastoral economy. The religious overtones to that grim view of the future are obvious: The American forests were pictured as a latter-day Garden of Eden. Just as human beings had paid a stern price for neglecting their earlier compact with God, careless stewardship of His gifts promised divine retribution.[23]

The authors of those jeremiads thought that history provided abundant precedents to confirm their dire predictions. The high priest of forests and natural law was Marsh, whose epochal *Man and Nature; or, Physical Geography as Modified by Human Action* was published originally in 1864. An immediate success, the book was reprinted in 1865, 1867, 1869, and 1871, and a second edition appeared in 1874. Many of the articles cited in this chapter were directly or indirectly inspired by Marsh's monumental work. Late in his life Sargent complained to Robert Underwood Johnson, a leading conservationist, that the Progressives had forgotten Marsh's contribution. "No account of the movement of forest preservation in this country," Sargent wrote in 1908, "should overlook the value of this

remarkable book. I, at least, owe my interest in forests and forest preservation to it almost entirely. The younger generation apparently know nothing about it."[24]

Marsh may not have been well-known in 1908, but historians have
"discovered" him in the last twenty years. Although he was trained as a
lawyer, the consuming passions of his life were philology and physical
geography. The master of twenty languages by the time he was thirty, he
served two terms as a congressman from Vermont (where he later held the
posts of railroad commissioner and fish commissioner), helped establish
the Smithsonian Institution in 1846 (and acted as a member of its first
board of regents), and worked as professor of English at Columbia University from 1858 to 1860. In 1861 Abraham Lincoln appointed Marsh the first
minister to the new Kingdom of Italy, a post he held for the remaining
twenty-one years of his long life. Marsh knew Europe and the Middle East
well. In the late 1840s and early 1850s, he traveled extensively in Turkey,
Egypt, and Palestine, once the sites of great civilizations. The desolation of
those countries—along with that of Italy, Greece, and North Africa—reinforced observations he had made earlier concerning deforestation in his
native Vermont and New England.[25]

Marsh's basic ideas are very familiar to students of natural resources
today, but they were revolutionary (if not entirely original) in the 1860s. He
challenged the prevailing nineteenth-century assumption that resources
were inexhaustible. He demonstrated that the use of one natural resource
often had profound effects on other resources. He showed that man was
part of nature, not independent and above it. He revealed the importance
of ecological balances in nature. He argued that—far from being chaotic—
nature had order, a built-in stability. (In that sense he reinforced Charles
Darwin, who had published *Origin of Species* in 1859.) Marsh wrote:

> Nature left undisturbed, so fashions her territory as to give it
> almost unchanging permanence of form, outline, and proportion,
> except when shattered by geologic convulsions; and in these com-
> paratively rare cases of derangement, she sets herself at once to
> repair the superficial damage, and to restore, as nearly as practica-
> ble, the former aspect of her dominion.

Marsh considered the land as the one stable force in human life. The wise
use of nature's bounty would provide man with permanent, fixed values
in a changing world, not just prevent waste. "All human institutions . . .
have their instability, their want of fixedness, not in form only, but even in
spirit," he noted. "It is time for some abatement in the restless love of
change which characterizes us, and makes us almost a nomad rather than
sedentary people."[26]

The lack of "fixedness" in human institutions had been driven home to Marsh time and again as he pondered the landscape and ruins of ancient civilizations. As minister to Italy he became convinced that the destruction of forests surrounding the Mediterranean had played a large part in the fall of the Roman Empire. Over one-half of the lands that had been part of that dominion, he noted, were

> either deserted by civilized man and surrendered to hopeless desolation, or at least greatly reduced in both productiveness and population. Vast forests have disappeared from mountain spurs and ridges; the vegetable earth accumulated beneath the trees by the decay of leaves and fallen trunks, the soil of the alpine pastures which skirted and indented the woods, and the mould of the upland fields, are washed away; . . . the entrances of navigable streams are obstructed by sandbars, and harbors, once marts of an extensive commerce, are shoaled by the deposits of the rivers at whose mouths they lie; the elevation of the beds of estuaries, and the consequently diminished velocity of the streams which flow into them, have converted thousands of leagues of shallow sea and fertile lowland into unproductive and miasmatic morasses.[27]

Both scientists and popular writers picked up the fall-of-nations theme. In his essay "American Forests," which appeared less than two years after Marsh's *Man and Nature*, Frederick Starr quoted extensively from Marsh's work and concluded: "Palestine and Syria, Egypt and Italy, France and Spain, have seen some of their most populous regions turned into forsaken wilderness, and their most fertile lands into arid, sandy deserts. The danger to our land is near at hand." Such gloomy litanies became common during the last three decades of the nineteenth century. Many thoughtful Americans would have arrived at Marsh's conclusions had *Man and Nature* never been published; the book was more a digest and synthesis than a work of original research and thought. But few books have found a more receptive audience or elicited more discussion.[28]

Popular writers found examples of the law of "desertification" all around them. In 1877 *Forest and Stream* reprinted an article from the *London Economist*, which reported that following the discovery of gold in California, Chilean peasants burned large forests in the lower Cordillera mountains to raise wheat to supply the new market. That, the journal concluded, had—in fewer than thirty years—dramatically reduced precipitation and threatened the country with "sterility." Another writer told how Turkish provinces south of the Balkan Mountains in present-day Bulgaria had enjoyed "abundant crops" and "comparative prosperity" until the

Ottoman navy exhausted local forests to build ships. Since that time, drought and famine had plagued the region.[29]

In the United States, deforestation in the Adirondack Mountains was blamed for destroying navigation on the Hudson River and threatening the economic prosperity of New York State. The deserts of the Southwest were even more instructive. Evidence of ancient civilizations suggested that the region had once been heavily forested. Deforestation had touched off the process of desertification, and the deserts of the Southwest were spreading like a malignant tumor. "In the Gila valley the improvidence of a prehistoric race has already begun to Africanize our compact continent," Oswald wrote, "and if the same agencies continue to modify the climate of the Atlantic slope, our cotton states will, in fifty years from now, be reduced to the necessity of raising their crops by the aid of irrigation. The locust will ravage the plains of the Gulf coast." Others worried that "Colorado is preparing for itself the fate of Spain." They charged that most of that state's forests had been destroyed and that the consequent reduction in stream flow now required the use of reservoirs to provide farmers with sufficient water for irrigation. In California the rapid disappearance of forests surrounding Lake Tahoe to provide shaft timbers and cordwood for silver mines in western Nevada prompted the state to create the first board of forestry in the nation. The *Sacramento Daily Union* predicted that within ten years climatic changes would render the resort area "uninhabitable" and that deforestation had already reduced the flow in Sierra Nevada streams. California's board of trade warned that destruction of the Sierra forests would turn the entire Central Valley into a desert. "It may be half a century hence," the board exclaimed, "but processes of destruction are now in operation which make this calamity only a matter of time, if they continue unchecked."[30]

The fear that deforestation would destroy the United States crested in the 1870s and 1880s. The severe Great Plains drought of the late 1880s and early 1890s discredited the idea that trees or human habitation had increased the water supply, and low farm prices during the years 1893–1897 drove many farmers off the land. In the 1890s and after, Great Plains residents became interested in irrigation and in rainmaking experiments using various chemicals, explosives, and cannons. For the most part, however, they turned to dry farming as the answer to aridity. That the opening of the plains to settlement had stimulated much of the writing about "forest influences" was reflected in the dramatic decline of public interest in the forests from 1893 to 1899. In 1897 Sargent, as editor of *Garden and Forest,* announced the demise of his journal, lamenting that "there are not persons enough in the United States interested in the subjects which have been presented . . . to make a journal of its class and character self-supporting."[31]

At about the same time, technological changes reduced the nation's dependence on wood. Railroads began treating crossties with zinc chloride and later creosote, and by the 1960s ties provided thirty-five to fifty years of service instead of the five to ten years common during the 1870s or 1880s. Once chemical treatment began, hemlock, tamarack, and red oak, in addition to the more insect-resistant white oak and cedar, could be used for ties. And not only were coal and petroleum increasingly substituted for wood as energy sources, but wood also gave way to brick, stone, cement, iron, and steel in buildings, ships, bridges, freight cars, farm implements, and even desks and filing cabinets. Per capita consumption of wood declined sharply after 1905, while the use of cement increased from 20 million barrels in 1901 to 90 million in 1913. By the second decade of the twentieth century, competition from new materials prompted lumber trade associations to launch an advertising campaign to show the benefits of wood over substitutes. With supply exceeding demand, fears of a timber famine all but disappeared, and estimates of the remaining lumber supply became much more optimistic. In 1911, following the most comprehensive survey ever made of the nation's forests, the Bureau of Corporations declared that at existing rates of use the supply of timber would last fifty-five years. That was a far cry from the bleak predictions of Schurz and Sargent in the 1870s and 1880s, and double that contained in the Census of 1900.[32]

Perhaps the best way to assess the significance of nineteenth-century attitudes toward forests and conservation is to compare post–Civil War conservationists with those who followed them in the early twentieth century. Although the postwar intellectual elite ranged from philosophers to journalists to ministers, most of its leaders were scientists (including Sargent, Hough, Fernow, and Egleston). The same was true of the Progressives, though once in power they assigned much of their work to engineers. A "multiple use," or "multiple purpose," concept of natural resource development linked the two groups. Usually that idea has been attributed to twentieth-century water-resource planners, specifically their discovery that water was one resource with many related uses, such as navigation, irrigation, and power.[33] The writing on forestation of the Gilded Age, wrong as it was in many assumptions and conclusions, did the same thing. The farmer, shipper, hunter, merchant, and banker all had as much stake in the woodlands as the lumbermen. The destruction of forests represented more than greed, waste, and poor planning: It altered stream flow, dried out the land, drove off birds and game animals, contributed to massive soil erosion, and ultimately undermined the foundations of society itself. The idea that nature operated according to clearly defined, predictable natural laws served as the intellectual foundation for the faith that the various uses of each resource could be integrated and coordinated.

A persistent moralism also connected the two groups. In his brilliant

Conservation and the Gospel of Efficiency: The Progressive Conservation Movement, 1890–1920, Samuel P. Hays places so much emphasis on science, efficiency, and federal planning that he obscures the "soft" side of early twentieth-century conservation. A prime example of Progressive moralism was the crusade for federal reclamation that culminated in the Newlands Act of 1902. Proponents of that measure saw an America gone wrong. They worried about urban crowding and poverty, strikes, a return of the depression of the 1890s, the rapid growth of cities, land monopoly, and a relative decline in the nation's rural populace. They had many immediate, practical, selfish motives for favoring federal reclamation, but they sold the policy to the public as a program to salvage the "wasted," barren lives of homeless city dwellers and to arrest a perceived decay of republican ideals and civic virtue. Here was an opportunity to convert a landless, volatile, working class into an army of yeoman farmers; property ownership would serve as a ballast to the old ways and ideals. The reclamation crusade, unlike many other Progressive conservation policies, attempted to restore a lost balance to American society, just as nineteenth-century conservationists sought to teach Americans about balances in nature.[34]

On the other hand, sharp differences separated the two groups of conservationists. A handful of conservationists raised the specter of timber famine well into the new century, but the idea that such a famine would lead to desertification or that it symbolized a fatal flaw in American society disappeared. No longer did conservationists brood about the decline of American civilization, and the jeremiad quality in earlier writings faded away.[35] The post–Civil War conservationists could better remember a more predictable agricultural society and economy. They had a harder time accepting the new industrial order than did twentieth-century conservationists, who were born later and who accepted bigness (if not monopoly) as inevitable. Then, too, those who wrote about forests after the Civil War *appear* more pessimistic than their intellectual descendants because they lacked the skills to measure or to quantify the impact of human beings on nature. Both groups of conservationists consisted of scientists, but such academic disciplines as silviculture, hydraulic engineering, and agrology did not exist in the 1860s, 1870s, and 1880s. Determining the nation's timber supply depended not just on finding reliable units of measurement; students of forestry needed also to understand the rates of growth of different species of trees and whether tree cultivation on a large scale was feasible. That knowledge, in turn, depended on understanding soils, water, and weather. The conservationist of 1910 was the legatee of great advances in science and technology.

Given the gravity of their message, why did the forest conservationists fail to attract greater public attention during the 1870s and 1880s? "It is only a short time since a large proportion of the public appeared to think that forests were useful only as supplying lumber and firewood," *Forest and Stream* editorialized in 1884, "but this ignorance has now been replaced in many minds by a more intelligent comprehension of the nature of woodlands." That comprehension was not so widespread as *Forest and Stream* suggested; in the West, it did not exist outside California and the Great Plains. In most of the trans-Mississippi region, the pioneer ethic of "cut and run" prevailed in 1890 as it had in 1860. During the early decades of the twentieth century, conservation was not a "mass movement," but it certainly received more publicity than conservation efforts in the nineteenth century. Marsh's followers never constituted a unified "movement," nor did they have clear objectives and carefully drawn policies. The Progressives embraced a "new federalism" and centralization, but post–Civil War conservationists regarded government with deep suspicion. They were unable to decide whether woodlands ought to be protected as public or as private land, or by what level of government, if any. They could not decide between two fundamental choices: whether to increase the wood supply by encouraging tree planting or to preserve the existing supply by enacting laws to protect the forests from fires and wasteful logging. And since neither Congress nor late nineteenth-century presidents solicited their advice on a large scale, they had little opportunity—let alone incentive—to translate their ideals into policies. The resulting detachment from the give and take of practical politics reinforced a natural scholarly "aloofness." What Arthur A. Ekirch, Jr., wrote about Marsh applies to many other conservationists in the last third of the nineteenth century: "More interested in ideas and research than in crusading for practical reform legislation, he was not a primitivist or extreme environmentalist but a scholarly humanist who stressed the idea of a proper balance between the forces of man and nature."[36] The scientists and humanists who wrote about the forests had the luxury and liability of observing nature from the easy chair.

The unifying force behind forest conservation was a pessimistic view of the future. Roderick Nash and many others have distinguished between aesthetic and utilitarian conservation.[37] Each group viewed nature differently. However, a third group ought to be added: those who supported conservation, not so much out of a sense of beauty or even a desire to promote the greatest good for the greatest number, but because they feared nature's dominance over man. The post–Civil War conservation ethic extended beyond the forests. Any new synthesis of conservation in the period from 1865 to 1890 will have to look at land and water use, and at wildlife as well as woodlands, and it will have to consider attitudes toward the use of natural resources throughout the nation, not just in the

West.[38] It will have to explain why, in an age generally characterized as optimistic—an era imbued with faith in progress—a significant number of conservationists found the fall-of-nations theme so compelling. Not until the 1960s did such a somber view of the future reappear in the United States. Naive as they were, those nineteenth-century Cassandras seem surprisingly modern.

CHAPTER EIGHT

Forests and Reclamation, 1891–1911

At the turn of the twentieth century, a fragile relationship developed between the national policies of forestry and arid land reclamation. In the late 1880s, explorer scientist John Wesley Powell and many of his followers worried that the preservation of woodlands would imperil the advance of irrigation agriculture in the West. A decade later, however, the champions of reclamation joined hands with their former enemies. The alliance was, according to one prominent historian, the foundation of the Progressive conservation movement.[1] Nevertheless, the goals and policies of the Forest Service and the Reclamation Service often clashed. The two agencies rarely disagreed in public, but their differences contributed to the failure to achieve coordinated natural resource planning during the Progressive Era.

Nineteenth-century science was rooted in natural law, but it relied as much on history and experience as on empirical evidence. It was didactic, not just descriptive, and it placed human beings at the center of nature. In the last century, no work influenced scientific thinking about forests and stream flow more than George Perkins Marsh's monumental *Man and Nature,* first published in 1864 and reprinted five times by 1874. Marsh assumed that the physical world was one of systems, order, and balance. Heavily forested terrain was normal; deserts, grasslands, and brushlands were somehow abnormal—a symptom of bad health. A climate that provided precipitation all year long was also normal; an arid environment, where rain fell mostly during the winter or in heavy summer thunderstorms, was aberrant. Nature favored the mean, not the extreme—light, even rains year-round rather than cycles of drought and monsoon. The history of the ancient world, Marsh argued, demonstrated the penalty for stripping away the forests. Erosion and flooding removed the topsoil, rendering the denuded land barren and sterile. Ultimately, fish disappeared from streams, wildlife abandoned the riparian land, and water flow became capricious and unpredictable. Industry and commerce sickened and died; society regressed to a pastoral state. Carried to a certain point, the process of "desertification" was irreversible.[2]

Marsh's cyclical view of history was infectious. Deforestation and abuse of the land had undermined the civilizations of the ancient world, and he predicted that the United States would follow the same path unless a certain percentage of forested land was preserved in its natural state. As *Scientific American* editorialized a decade after the publication of *Man and Nature*:

> We are beginning to learn . . . that, so far from being incompatible with forests, permanent civilization is impossible without them, that the tree slayer's ambition to bring the whole land under tillage would result, if successful, in making tillage a waste of labor through climatic disturbances. Alternations of drought and deluge, blighting heats and blasting colds, have ever been the penalty for general forest destruction; and many a land once fertile is now a desert for this cause alone. Indeed woodlands are to climate what the balance wheel is to machinery, the great conservator and regulator, without which all other conditions are wasted.[3]

During the last decades of the nineteenth century, several assumptions about forests and stream flow became commonplace. Not all scientists believed that forests caused rainfall, but most assumed that woodlands profoundly influenced the climate *within* the woodland boundaries. The trees produced a sponge-like humus that soaked up moisture from thunderstorms and heavy rains; they broke up raindrops, permitting the soil to absorb precipitation more easily; they condensed fogs and dews, trapped snow and prevented it from melting as rapidly as in the open, and shielded the ground from the sun and from desiccating winds. Most important, forests served as natural reservoirs that released water slowly, providing a uniform flow. Forests conserved moisture and made it more usable.[4] In the far West of the 1870s and 1880s, boosters, speculators, and irrigation promoters began to publicize the apparent connection between forests and water supply. For example, in 1876 Colorado's constitutional convention insisted that irrigation would be impossible without forests to regulate the streams, and in March 1885 California's legislature created one of the nation's first state boards of forestry, empowering it "to act with a special view to the continuance of water sources that may be affected in any measure by the destruction of forests near such sources; to do any and all things within their power to encourage the preservation and planting of forests, and the consequent maintenance of the water sources of the State."[5] From 1885 to 1891 the California board repeatedly appealed to Congress to reserve the entire watershed from Lake Tahoe to the southern tip of the Sierra Nevada.[6]

Nevertheless, even as the beneficial influence of forests on stream flow became all but gospel in the West, there were many doubters in the

Washington offices of the United States Geological Survey (USGS). In 1888 during a severe drought, Congress gave the USGS, over which John Wesley Powell presided, responsibility for surveying the arid West's reservoir sites and irrigable land. Powell thought that this job would take a decade or more to complete, but many westerners considered it a brief prelude to the construction of dams by the central government.[7] From the beginning critics charged that the survey was too slow, too expensive, and too theoretical to be of immediate value either to farmers or to private water companies and potential investors. Some westerners believed that rainfall could be produced by detonating explosives on the ground or in the atmosphere. Others favored drilling wells. But the most dangerous critics, in Powell's eyes, were those who insisted that planting trees would increase rainfall, or at least store sufficient moisture to make artificial reservoirs unnecessary. The same drought that produced the Irrigation Survey gave impetus to the crusade for national forest reserves. Summer electrical storms and the absence of moisture contributed to massive fires in the late 1880s and early 1890s, and sparse ground cover increased the damage done by sheep, cattle, and horses pastured on the public lands.

In his famous 1878 report on arid lands, Powell argued that there was plenty of timber in the arid West—challenging the view of many Cassandras—and he suggested that the woods could be better protected from fire in private rather than public hands.[8] In the same report, he recommended dividing the West into grazing and irrigation districts that conformed to natural watersheds. Within those districts, local residents would exercise full control over all natural resources, including forests. The champions of national forest reserves found much to worry about in Powell's plan, which was embodied in legislation presented to Congress in 1889. Nevertheless in an October 1888 letter to the *Kansas City Times*, Powell was conciliatory. He denied that trees had any influence on precipitation, but he wanted to protect the forests from fire, conceding that they reduced both evaporation from the ground and the severity of storms, resulting in "more gentle rains."[9] Still, Powell became increasingly dismayed at the prospect of forest preserves and the potential creation of a large new bureaucracy that might compete with the USGS for funds, lock up reservoir sites, and prevent the construction of canals across forested land. Such an agency would undermine the value of Powell's work, which he expected to encourage private land and ditch companies. In the summer of 1889 he claimed that forests reduced snowpack by preventing snow from accumulating in great drifts "in the lee of rocks and cliffs and under the walls of gorges and canyons." The following spring he issued an even more scathing attack on the forests, arguing that 20 percent to 40 percent of the rain that fell in forests was lost to farmers because forest vegetation captured and used it. In the Wasatch Mountains of Utah, he noted, research had shown that denudation resulted in a "great increase in [the] volume of streams." And at a time when many conservationists wanted to create forest reserves as a limitation on grazing, Powell went so far as to argue that running sheep in the Sierra Nevada Mountains was a useful way to limit the number of trees.[10]

Relations between Powell and leading foresters cooled further in 1890. By the summer of that year, rumors abounded that the Irrigation Survey would soon be moved from the Department of Interior to the Department of Agriculture, where it would be merged with an artesian well survey being conducted on the Great Plains.[11] By the end of the year, Powell's relations with the champions of forestry hit rock bottom. Bernhard Fernow, head of the Forestry Office in the Department of Agriculture, testily recounted Powell's actions at a December 30, 1890, meeting in Secretary of the Interior John Noble's office attended by representatives from the American Forestry Association, American Association for the Advancement of Science, and Forestry Division. Those present wanted the secretary to push legislation closing to public entry important forests at the headwaters of major streams, but Powell, according to Fernow, had other ideas:

> Major Powell, the Director of the Geological Survey, asked permission to be present, which, of course, was politely granted. Before we had an opportunity to state the object of our visit, Major Powell launched into a long dissertation to show that the claim of the favorable influence of forest cover on water flow or climate was untenable, that the best thing to do for the Rocky Mountain forests was to burn them down, and he related with great gusto how he himself had started a fire that swept over a thousand square miles. He had used up our time when our chance came to speak. We consumed not more than two minutes, stating that we had not come to argue any theories, but to impress the Secretary with the fact that it was under the law his business to protect public property against the vandalism of which the Major had just accused himself.[12]

Powell had plenty of allies in the Geological Survey. For example, the survey's geographer, Henry Gannett, joined his boss in denying that forests had any influence on rainfall and in recommending that since trees released enormous quantities of water to the atmosphere through evaporation, "it is advisable to cut away as rapidly as possible all the forests especially upon the mountains, where most of the rain falls, in order that as much of the precipitation as possible may be collected in the streams. This will cause, not a decrease in the annual flow of streams, as commonly supposed, but an increase. . . . It may be added that the forests in the arid region are thus disappearing with commendable rapidity."[13] The leaders of the crusade for forest reserves must have winced as they read those words. C. S. Sargent, editor of *Garden and Forest* and after 1890 director of the Arnold Arboretum and professor of arboriculture at Harvard, initially favored the construction of water storage reservoirs by private companies under direction of the national government.[14] That changed after he learned about Powell's bill to create autonomous irrigation and grazing districts and after the Johnstown Dam collapsed in the Conemaugh Valley of Pennsylvania in the spring of 1889, killing many hundreds of people and causing enormous property damage. "It is high time," Sargent editorialized in *Garden and Forest*, "that some organized effort was made to check a movement which has been gathering force . . . until the government seems committed to the construction of enormously expensive works, which all experience has shown to be inadequate for the purpose they are intended to accomplish, and fraught with serious danger to the lives and property of thousands." To turn the deserts green, huge dams he called "reservoirs of death" would have to be erected.[15] Sargent reminded his readers that the head of the Geological Survey not only opposed the creation of forest reserves but also opposed the appointment of a special commission to survey and classify the forested lands. He described Powell's article in *Century* as "a rhapsody rather than a sustained and coherent argument."[16] "The serious reader," Sargent fumed, "finds it difficult to persuade himself that a man of science with any clear thought on a matter within the scope of his profession would attempt to give it expression in such a tumefied style."[17]

J. B. Harrison, commissioner of forests for New Hampshire and secretary of the American Forestry Association, also chastised Powell.[18] He warned President Benjamin Harrison that if the forests were stripped away, soil erosion would choke the West's rivers, dams, and farmland with silt and debris. "The Government ought not, I think, to authorize any scheme of irrigation which does not recognize the indispensableness of the mountain forests, as *natural* storage reservoirs, and as auxiliaries to any artificial system."[19] Bernhard Fernow contributed an essay to the Senate Select Committee on Irrigation's report in which he argued that "Reforestation on the plains and forest preservation on the mountains is of greater national concern than the location of irrigation reservoirs [by the Irrigation Survey]." He claimed that the West's major problem was rapid evaporation, not drought or the absence of rainfall. In lieu of irrigation he proposed a variation on dry farming: single rows of trees to reduce the winds that robbed moisture from plants and soils. Western streams carried sufficient water, but not at the right time; they lost volume rapidly in late June and July. If the supply could be extended for an additional month each summer, the need for artificial reservoirs would all but disappear.[20]

Such arguments had far less effect than those raised by critics of Powell's investigation of canal and reservoir sites. By 1890 they decided that his work would do little or nothing to aid western economic development. In 1890 the Irrigation Survey was terminated, in 1892 the geological and paleontological work of the Geological Survey was severely curtailed, and in May 1894 Powell resigned as director of the agency.[21] The death of the Irrigation Survey eliminated one of the main barriers to the creation of the first national forests, and by the end of 1892 fifteen had been established containing over 13 million acres. Most were set aside at the instigation of irrigators, real estate promoters, bankers, businessmen, and other boosters who lived in the vicinity of proposed reserves.[22] During the 1890s many westerners feared that the grazing industry would lock up the entire public domain by capturing the forests and the prime reservoir sites they contained. The friends of federal reclamation realized that if these reservoir sites were included in forest reserves closed to private capital there would be additional pressure on Congress to authorize a national dam-building program. Congress would then provide the water for nothing or at greatly reduced prices.[23] On the other hand, the 1893 depression also reduced the need for new reserves by driving down the demand for irrigated land as well as for cattle and sheep.[24]

The demise of the Irrigation Survey combined with the drought and the depression prompted a heroic effort by westerners to revive irrigation development in the absence of private capital. Consequently, the champions of irrigation, led by journalist William Ellsworth Smythe, formed a quasi-governmental institution to publicize the cause of reclamation, unify the region behind one policy, and secure necessary legislation in the state capitals and in Washington. In 1891 land speculators, representatives from railroads and farm machinery companies, politicians, and a handful of dreamy idealists, all of whom worried about the future of the region, met together in Salt Lake City at the first National Irrigation Congress.[25] Unfortunately the friends of irrigation could not agree on a policy. Some favored a federal program to construct hydraulic works and unify control over land and water (administration of water had become a responsibility of the states almost by default). Others pushed for federal construction with no change in the administration of water rights. A third group supported the cession of all or part of the public domain to the states, which they hoped would permit the states to build their own irrigation works or contract with private companies to have them built. Finally, many who lived in areas where irrigation already flourished (such as California) supported legislation to create autonomous irrigation districts with taxing authority. The resultant increase in land values would finance the hydraulic works.[26]

It was precisely the quibbling and ineffectiveness of the irrigation congresses that persuaded George H. Maxwell, a paid agent of the railroads generally credited with being the father of the Reclamation Act of 1902, to seek a larger constituency by attempting to unify East and West behind a national irrigation program that would benefit private (railroad) as well as public lands.[27] Maxwell needed all the political support he could get, so he set out to heal old wounds. In 1897—the same year President Grover Cleveland created a firestorm of controversy by setting aside the largest forested acreage yet designated as national reserves—Maxwell and Frederick H. Newell persuaded the Irrigation Congress to adopt a resolution declaring that "the perpetuation of the forests of the arid regions is essential to the maintenance of water-supply for irrigation as well as the supply of timber for industrial needs." The resolution urged the secretary of the interior to withdraw "all public lands which are of more value for their timber than for agriculture or their minerals."[28] The motto of Maxwell's National Irrigation Association, which the railroads bankrolled, became "Save the Forests, Store the Floods, Make Homes on the Land." Similarly, the slogan of the 1900 Irrigation Congress was "Save the Forests and Store the Floods." In 1901 Maxwell urged Congress to appropriate sufficient money to pay for forest patrols to protect the reserves from fire. "The forests are the source of all irrigation," he wrote. "We cannot irrigate without water. We cannot have water without forests. If we do not preserve them, we will have no irrigation."[29] Maxwell hoped the support of proponents of forest reserves throughout the country would help make irrigation a national issue.

The advantages were mutual: the American Forestry Association (AFA) had much to gain from the reclamationists. The AFA was similar to the Irrigation Congress in many ways. Both institutions popularized legislation hatched within government bureaus or scientific societies. Both applied pressure to the U.S. Congress. Both were infected with a strident idealism and both were made necessary by the weak federal bureaucracy. Both forests and dams promised to mitigate flooding and improve navigation. Therefore, the friends of forests and friends of irrigation claimed an equal right to tap the river and harbor fund. Moreover, since many engineers and hydrologists predicted that increasing public interest in scientific farming would soon make irrigation as common in the East as in the West, there was additional justification for creating forest reserves in both halves of the nation. Furthermore, the "Cleveland reserves" of 1897—created by the president without consulting western politicians and widely denounced in the West—convinced many champions of forest protection that they could not secure their objectives without offering a quid pro quo to the irrigation interests.

The marriage between the two conservation groups was announced at the AFA's July 1899 meeting in Los Angeles, in the midst of a great southern California drought reminiscent of the one that had visited the

West a decade earlier. By 1899 the depression had lifted, but fires still swept unchecked through the forests, and farmers had run out of water.[30] Present at the meeting were Abbot Kinney, Elwood Mead, George Maxwell, Frederick Haynes Newell (who later became director of the Reclamation Service), Gifford Pinchot, and many other notables in the two movements. Maxwell was appointed chair of the resolutions committee, which subsequently proclaimed the AFA's support for using the proceeds from leases on public grazing lands to pay for dams and canals. The honeymoon continued that fall at the Irrigation Congress meeting held at Missoula, Montana. At the beginning of 1902 the title of the American Forestry Association's monthly publication, *The Forester*, was changed to *Forestry and Irrigation*.[31]

Personal relationships contributed to the alliance as much as political expediency. In Washington many advocates of forest reserves and irrigation were active members of such organizations as the National Geographic Society and American Philosophical Society, as well as the National Forestry Congress and International Irrigation Congress.[32] Conservationists also formed informal groups within government that militated against bureaucratic myopia and infighting. Several of Powell's lieutenants in the USGS, including Frederick H. Newell, Arthur Powell Davis (second director of the Reclamation Service), and even Henry Gannett (chief geographer of the USGS), became friends and allies of Gifford Pinchot and his staff in the Forestry Bureau. During the Roosevelt presidency, these men often met together in the "Great Basin Lunch Mess"—a group of department heads, mainly from Interior and Agriculture—and Pinchot and Newell were charter members of Theodore Roosevelt's "tennis cabinet." Roosevelt met Pinchot and Newell in the late 1890s, when he was governor of New York. After he became president, the two men served as his chief advisers on matters pertaining to natural resources. They cooperated in a range of activities including drafting presidential speeches, served together on the boards of scientific societies, and directed presidential commissions, including the Public Lands Commission (1903–1905) and the Inland Waterways Commission (1907–1908).[33]

Newell served as secretary of the American Forestry Association and on the organization's executive committee from 1892 to 1903. In 1895—the same year he met Gifford Pinchot—he took charge of the new Division of Hydrology in the USGS, measuring the flow of rivers in all parts of the United States. This assignment increased his interest in the relationship between forests and water flow. He became fascinated with the difference between streams like Arizona's Gila River, whose flow occurred almost entirely during a three-week period at the end of July and the beginning of August and a subsequent three-week period from mid-October through early November, and rivers in the heavily forested Pacific Northwest whose runoff peaked in July but had a fairly large volume year-round. In 1897 Newell recommended the reservation of *all* forested public lands pending a federal survey and classification of the remaining government lands, a radical position to take at the time.[34]

Strangely enough, by the end of the 1890s Henry Gannett also became a strong supporter of national forests. In 1896 he was appointed chief of the new USGS Division of Geography. In the same year he sat on the national commission that surveyed the western forests and inspired Grover Cleveland to set aside the controversial "midnight reserves" shortly before the McKinley administration took office. In 1897 the Forest Management Act reconstituted Gannett's office as the Division of Geography and Forestry and gave it the job of mapping and surveying all new reserves. The USGS was the logical agency to perform this work because of its topographical mapping and stream flow measurements, and Gannett had as much to say about the boundaries of the forest reserves as anyone in the General Land Office or Forestry Bureau. His office became an important source of information about the forested lands, and it was equally appreciated by the General Land Office and later Pinchot's Forestry Bureau in the Department of Agriculture. During the summer of 1897, Gannett and Pinchot became fast friends as they toured the new reserves together. By January 1899, through something of a miracle given his writings ten years earlier, Gannett was listed as a director of the American Forestry Association. "Henry and I had taken to each other from the first day the work of the National Forest Commission threw us together," Pinchot noted in his autobiography. "He was a man of decided opinions and strong antagonisms, brusque in manner but with a golden heart. He knew more geography than I did, I knew more Forestry than he did, and so we worked together like Damon and Pythias, if those worthies ever did any work. . . . Gannett was . . . a vigorous, forthright, competent man of wide knowledge and varied experience."[35]

The symbiotic relationship between forest preservation and reclamation continued for several years after passage of the 1902 legislation dedicating proceeds from public land sales to the construction of dams and canals in the arid West.[36] "The recent passage by Congress of the bill inaugurating an irrigation policy," the General Land Office commissioner observed in his 1902 report, "may, in its effect, be regarded as amounting, indirectly, to legislation broadening our national forestry work, since to insure effective operation of that law necessitates the forest growth upon all watersheds throughout the public domain. . . . [B]y ringing into existence a national irrigation system a pronounced impetus has been given to the closely related movement of forestry."[37] Gifford Pinchot concluded that following passage of the national irrigation law, "the public opinion of the West has become unanimous in favor of forest preservation for the protection of the water supply, and practically so for the perpetuation of the supply of timber."[38]

Pinchot and Newell were both treading on new legal ground. In the West—particularly the Rocky Mountain West—there were persistent complaints that the national forests and reclamation projects were unconstitutional. The federal government had an undisputed right to protect and improve existing *public* lands, but neither forest preservation nor reclamation could proceed unless the government also purchased *private* land and water rights. Forests and potential reclamation projects were mottled with mines, towns, homesteads, sawmills, and other businesses. If Congress had the power to take private holdings at will, the ultimate step might be federal acquisition of all land in a state.

Officials in the Forestry and Reclamation services understandably had many common interests.[39] The Reclamation Service reserved 40 million acres of land in the West, much of it adjoining national forests.[40] At the beginning of 1906, C. J. Blanchard, the Reclamation Service's chief statistician and publicist, noted proudly: "Like Jack Sprat and his wife, they [the Forestry Service and Reclamation Service] have proceeded to lick the platter [the public domain] clean; but they have been well-behaved children and have not quarreled over their portions. The forestry infant has shown an exceeding fondness for mountain tops, steepsided hills, old pine barrens, and high altitudes generally, while the Reclamation Service has selected the valleys and mesas."[41] Nevertheless, in the years after 1902 the Reclamation Service depended far more on the Forest Service than vice versa. The agency that controlled the headwaters of the West's streams, and its remaining reservoir sites, could dictate the pace of agricultural development in the West—for example, by blocking speculative water claims. While reclamation officials withdrew millions of acres of arable land, they had no authority to reserve land exclusively for watershed or stream flow protection. That was the job of the General Land Office and, after 1905, the Forest Service. As the director of the Reclamation Service put it, "In general, it may be stated that the officers of the Reclamation Service believe it to be good public policy to keep within forest reserves as much of the catchment area of various streams as may properly be included without detriment to other interests . . . by careful control of the forest reserves, particularly in the matter of grazing." Newell recognized that in many parts of the West grazing and farming went hand in hand, but he hoped that sheep would be excluded from the forests and that, in awarding grazing permits, the Forest Service would favor new settlers over established stockmen. The primary object of federal reclamation, after all, was making homes for small farmers, not securing the greatest income from the land or providing for its most "efficient" use.[42]

Reclamation Service officials believed that the forests were more valuable as regulators of stream flow, particularly in the late summer, than as sources of grass or lumber.[43] Initially, there was close cooperation between the two agencies. In 1903, when the 60 million acres of forest reserves were still under the control of the General Land Office, Pinchot asked Newell to pressure the GLO to withdraw additional land prior to its transfer to the Department of Agriculture: "Why would it not be a good plan for you to send instructions to all your chiefs of parties or state bosses to send you every case where the watershed of a stream or reservoir should be reserved for its protection? . . . In that way we ought to get a large amount of the most valuable country, and that with very little opposition. It will not matter at all whether or not these areas are wooded now, because if you say they are needed that will settle it."[44] The Forest Service also promised to measure stream flow on the reserves, provide a supply of timber for use on government water projects, and reforest denuded land adjoining reservoir sites and canal lines.[45]

The 1905 law transferring the forest reserves to Agriculture pledged all revenue from the forests to the Forest Service, rather than to the general treasury. At the time, Pinchot hoped that the Forest Service would eventually secure control of the 300 million to 400 million acres of western grazing land outside the reserves and use that land as an additional source of income. As historian Samuel Hays has pointed out, Pinchot hoped to consolidate many other features of the conservation program under his leadership, including administration of the national parks. These plans must have worried Newell, who like Pinchot was always looking for new sources of revenue.[46] For example, when the return from public land sales proved inadequate to construct the first irrigation projects, Newell informed one of his engineers that, "possibly the Reclamation Fund may be increased by the proceeds, say, of sale of timber or leasing of grazing lands."[47] Nevertheless, Pinchot refused to relinquish any source of income, and no bureau grew faster than the Bureau of Forestry. Its staff expanded from 11 in 1898 to 821 at the time of transfer in 1905. Even before the transfer the division conducted field work in twenty-seven states and territories, and it indirectly managed over 900,000 acres of private forests.[48]

The Forest Service's grazing policy tested its relationship with the Reclamation Service. Ironically, the General Land Office took watershed protection more seriously than Pinchot. From 1891 to 1898 the secretary of the interior and the GLO consistently opposed opening the new forest reserves to grazing. Even when Congress forced them to do so in 1898, they generally restricted the privilege of running stock to those who lived in or near the reserves.[49] Pinchot, however, had different priorities. There was no assurance in 1898 or 1900 that the reserves would be permanent. Whether they survived depended in large part on how much political support could be mustered in the West, and in many parts of the region stock interests had far more power than farm groups. Some reserves were created in response to appeals from cattlemen, even though Pinchot recognized that catering to the stock growers would provoke bitter complaints from farmers.[50] Large stockmen hoped that the Forest Service could maintain and improve the range at the same time it limited access. Small operations were unprofitable and inefficient, they contended, and the cattle of small grazers—which came from inferior breeding stock—reduced the overall quality of herds.

In April 1900 Pinchot informed Commissioner of the General Land Office Binger Hermann that the grazing issue was the most important aspect of administering the national forests. "Upon it, more than upon any other," he fretted, "depends the support of the forest reserve policy by the people of the West."[51] In 1899 the General Land Office closed all reserves to sheep and banned out-of-state cattle herds.[52] Arizona sheep growers sent a delegation to Washington, D.C., to complain. One protester was Albert M. Potter, secretary of the eastern division of the Arizona Wool Growers Association. Potter so impressed Pinchot that the forester asked him to create a grazing office in the Department of Agriculture, which was done in October 1901. Potter subsequently became one of Pinchot's chief advisers. He convinced the chief forester that general grazing rules could not be applied throughout the West. To be successful, all regulations had to be tailored to local conditions and acceptable to local grazing associations. After 1905 many of these organizations formed advisory boards to negotiate with the Forest Service and determine how many animals would be permitted within each reserve each year and under what conditions. "Livestock associations often performed the role of 'company unions' for the Forest Service," historian William Rowley has written, "by supporting its policies and complying with regulations in return for concessions allowing certain stockmen to purchase and absorb smaller allotments."[53] Through Potter, Pinchot won the support of many livestock barons, including J. B. Killian of Colorado and Dwight B. Heard of Arizona. In the words of historian James L. Penick, "Pinchot shamelessly courted the leading grazing interests."[54] By doing so he won better compliance with Forest Service regulations and cut the costs of administering grazing permits, all the while insuring the permanence of the national forests. The Forest Service became an ally of the status quo as prescriptive range rights, which were frequently older than the national forests, were transformed into renewable annual grazing rights. By the 1920s these gave way to ten-year contracts with a value of their own.

While the Forest Service made nominal concessions to small groups of farmers and grazers—by reducing fees to new settlers and by opening the reserves to agricultural settlement—in many places the large livestock associations quickly won the upper hand.[55] Despite Pinchot's interest in balancing different uses of the forests, grazing became the paramount use.[56] In 1906 the Forest Service began charging stockmen a modest fee to use the reserves, a fee considerably lower than that charged on private lands or Indian reservations. "The income from the reserves is as yet but a small fraction of what may be expected as they approach full utilization," the secretary of agriculture observed in 1906. The secretary looked forward to the time the Forest Service would be self-supporting; the Service also charged for reservoir and power site permits, and for the right to build canals across the public lands.[57] The conflict over grazing came to a head in 1908. By that time the Forest Service controlled about 150 million acres of national forest, and little additional land seemed likely soon to be added to the reserves. The creation of new reserves took second place to the perpetuation and maintenance of those already established. Therefore, the political support of reclamationists, which at one time had been critical, waned in importance. Moreover, while in 1902 boosters had expected federal reclamation to reclaim between 60 million and 100 million acres, the projects launched in the first decade of the twentieth century watered no more than a few million acres. Once it became clear that the national irrigation program would be very limited, grazing took on renewed importance and watershed protection seemed less critical.

In 1907 Pinchot stocked the national forests "up to the extreme limit of the carrying power of the range."[58] Unfortunately the winter of 1907–1908 was very dry, and owing to the lack of moisture Forest Service officials allowed sheep to graze in high mountain pastures usually kept off-limits. To compound the problem, permits were assigned largely by chronology. In most of the West, established cattle and sheep growers held grazing rights superior to new settlers on government irrigation projects. These settlers, however, needed supplemental income to tide them over the hard years when crops returned little or no revenue. Reclamation officials also feared that if farmers could not gain access to the national forests, they might not take up land under government irrigation projects.[59]

An even more immediate threat came from soil erosion and siltation.[60] In February 1908, in response to a request from the Reclamation Service, Secretary of the Interior James Garfield warned Secretary of Agriculture James Wilson about the damage done by sheep grazing. "I have the honor to request that as far and as rapidly as may be practicable, sheep be excluded from watersheds of streams now or immediately to be used for irrigation, and that as to other watersheds held for future irrigation projects, sheep grazing be carefully restricted." Wilson responded that the 1908 grazing contracts had already been negotiated and could not be changed. Besides, the livestock industry was as important as agriculture. Republican tariff policies, Wilson reminded Garfield, encouraged the sheep industry: "In the past few years the policies of the present National Administration have resulted in an enormous increase in the number of sheep in the United States, as well as in almost doubling their per capita value and the value of the wool product. It would be most unfortunate if after thus giving an industry care and support, it should be curtailed by restrictive measures except when such measures are clearly necessary for the proper protection of other and larger agricultural interests." Wilson also noted that the market for products of irrigated lands depended directly on the health of the grazing industry.[61]

In the summer and fall of 1908 Newell, Pinchot, officials of the two services, and stockmen met several times to discuss the grazing question. The Reclamation Service faced strong pressure from water users on several of its projects. For example, farmers on the Salt River Water Project in Arizona called for a complete cessation of grazing in the Tonto and Verde national forests which, they claimed, had been created solely to protect the watersheds of Salt River tributaries.[62] The secretary of agriculture responded that the cost of maintaining land solely for watershed protection was prohibitive and, he noted, the inclusion of so much unforested land within southwestern national forests opened the Forest Service to severe criticism "not wholly neutralized by the strong support given by the water users of the Salt River Valley." In 1910 the secretary of agriculture and secretary of the interior nominally agreed that even land covered with brush or other scrub vegetation should be retained in national forests if it protected rivers "important to irrigation or to the water supply of any city, town, or community." Nevertheless, the controversy over grazing rights continued.[63] Many other changes in the relationship between the Forest Service and Reclamation Service occurred in 1907 and 1908. For example, by that time Pinchot recognized the potential of the vast number of power sites within national forests, and some reclamation officials feared that since hydroelectric dams required a year-round flow to drive turbines, the erection of these structures would reduce the supply of water available for irrigation during the growing season. It was not clear which side the Forest Service would take when the needs of urban power users and farmers clashed.

Ironically, at a time when public interest in watershed protection was on the wane in the West, the Forest Service put the timeworn forest and stream flow arguments to new use in the East. Even before administrative control of the western forest reserves passed from Interior to Agriculture, Pinchot had hoped to create national forests in the humid half of the nation, where the public domain had long since disappeared. In 1907 extensive flooding in the Ohio Valley aided Pinchot's campaign. Pinchot attributed the devastation to deforestation, and he predicted that floods "will continue to grow in volume and damage until the reforestation of the head water."[64] The East was also subject to wide fluctuations in stream flow, and the damage to property caused by too much water was at least as severe as that caused by too little in the West. The Forest Service was particularly interested in the Appalachian and White mountains, where it wanted to protect and restore the watersheds of the Potomac, James, Roanoke, Yadkin, Catawba, Broad, Saluda, Savannah, Chattahoochee, Coosa, Tennessee, New, Cumberland, Kentucky, and Monongahela rivers. Money spent on reclaiming arid private lands in the West was offered as one justification for creating new national forests in the East.[65] Foresters insisted that flood control and navigation improvement were their main motives for adding private lands to the national forests, but the future of hydroelectric power was equally important.

Historians of forestry in the United States have long recognized that the navigability argument was a subterfuge to dodge the constitutional issue of whether the federal government had the authority to acquire private lands to control floods. The Constitution said nothing about flood control, but it did grant the central government power to facilitate commerce. The Weeks Act, passed in 1911, gave the Forest Service the right to cooperate with any state or group of states to protect the watersheds of navigable streams, and it authorized the appointment of a special commission to determine which watershed lands ought to be acquired. The new law appropriated $1 million for the first year and $2 million for each of the following five years to fund the program. All purchases had to be approved by the legislature of the state in which the land was located.

The land secured by the federal government under this legislation grew from 2 million acres in 1920 to a total of 20 million acres in 1961. In the House of Representatives, states west of the Mississippi River cast nineteen votes in favor of the Weeks bill and fifty-six against it; only one yes vote came from the far West.[66] The adoption of the Weeks bill was a mixed blessing; debate over the legislation rekindled controversy about forests and stream flow that had all but disappeared during Theodore Roosevelt's first term.[67] In 1908 Hiram Martin Chittenden, an Army Corps of Engineers officer, denied that forests had a significant effect on stream flow. In congressional testimony, Pinchot poured water on a photograph and a blotter to show the difference between denuded and forested land, but that experiment, according to Chittenden, constituted theatrics rather than science. Any correlation, the army officer insisted, was an article of faith, not a scientific hypothesis.[68] He had seen extensive flooding in Yellowstone National Park, a fully forested region that had never been logged. Flooding was caused by heavy rainfall, not fires or lumbering, and siltation resulted more from riverbank erosion that from deforestation (particularly on the upper reaches of the Missouri River, which flowed through flat, unforested, very dry land).[69] Chittenden was not alone. Henry Gannett, ever the skeptic, continued to support the creation of national forests but questioned whether they had much influence on the nation's water supply. "In view of the agitation for the protection of our forests which has been going on for at least a generation, and which has reached such intensity that it has become with many persons almost a religion," he noted in a USGS annual report, "it is strange that there should be practically no knowledge to serve as a basis for such a cult."[70] And in 1908 Bernhard Fernow, who often fell victim to rash statements,[71] came close to admitting that Powell had been right:

> Local conditions vary the forest influence to such a degree, that instead of the forest cover being beneficial it may under some conditions even become detrimental, or at least nugatory, as regards regulation of water flow. To tell the truth, while we know much of the general philosophy of the influence of the forest cover on water flow, we are not so fully informed as to details of this influence as we might wish. . . . [E]ven today we have not very far advanced in the exact knowledge and must still remain doubtful as to the precise function of the forest, and all the general assertions that are found in literature on forest influences, except perhaps those on soil erosion, need more careful investigations.[72]

In January 1910 Gifford Pinchot was fired, and in the following months the American Forestry Association changed the name of its official publication from *Forestry and Irrigation* to *Conservation* to *American Forestry*. The journal had come full circle. Moreover, the most prominent irrigation monthly, *Irrigation Age*, strongly challenged the notion that forests benefited arid land reclamation.[73] Federal reclamation came under heavy fire, and Frederick Haynes Newell left the Reclamation Service in 1915. With both Pinchot and Newell gone, the network of personal relationships dissolved, and the promise of unified natural resource planning disappeared with it.

For too many years historians have focused on the conflicts between the proponents and opponents of conservation rather than conflicts among the champions of conservation. A recent survey of forest history remarked:

> Beginning in 1906, W J McGee, Pinchot, Roosevelt, and others sought to replace the existing fragmented approach of several agencies by bringing unified planning to entire watersheds. Their claims for the necessity of such action rested on inadequate studies of the effect of deforestation on stream flow. The Army's Corps of Engineers, in charge of flood control, saw its vested interests threatened. Led by Hiram Martin Chittenden, it counterattacked, pointing out the dearth of thorough studies and the unsubstanti-

ated claims that its opponents were making in the name of science. For better or for worse, the corps won, thereby delaying the implementation of integrated timber/watershed management.[74]

There are several flaws in this interpretation. It erroneously suggests that the primary concern of Pinchot, McGee, and Roosevelt was "unified planning," and it implies that the opponents of river basin planning simply engaged in politics as usual (the protection of "vested interests"). The lessons of "science," however, were neither as clear nor as disinterested as Pinchot and Newell claimed. Each man held ideas that were inconsistent, and their view of nature was tinctured by a moralism and self-righteousness that few scientists today would consider consistent with the "scientific method." Progressive Era science was long on theory and short on verification. Powell rejected the idea that forests were natural reservoirs, but on at least one occasion he suggested that irrigation contributed to the spread of cedar, piñon, and pine forests by increasing the ambient humidity.[75] On another occasion he maintained that water from forests carried natural fertilizers that in and of themselves "will be full compensation for the cost of the process [of irrigation]."[76]

Similarly, although Gifford Pinchot often criticized the American Forestry Association for being the haven of "tree cranks," he repeatedly predicted that in twenty to twenty-five years the United States would experience a severe timber famine that would drive up the price of homes, mining, railroads, and even food. He preached this jeremiad long after the message had been discredited by most foresters. He did so for the same reason that he attributed flooding to deforestation: it was easier to mold public opinion through the use of fear rather than truth.[77] Indeed, in the Progressive Era, science was used as often to impose order or discipline on society, or to reform the structure of government, as to describe processes of nature. Science was an extension of politics. Then as now ideas were political weapons, and no one had a keener political sense than Gifford Pinchot and Frederick Haynes Newell.

Historians have long recognized that politics count for more than science in the formulation of public policy; that bureaucratic loyalties and social networks motivate policymakers as much as shared ideals; and that "government" in the opening decades of this century was an interlocking set of both public and private institutions. These institutions included the American Forestry Association, National Geographic Society, Yale University, Massachusetts Institute of Technology, the United States Geological Survey, and the Forest Service. Nevertheless, historians of natural resources have treated "conservation" as a far more coherent "movement" than it really was. Once conservation history was an extended morality play replete with heroes and villains—such as Pinchot and Richard

Ballinger—and with altruism and greed. In recent decades historians have looked more closely at the political, intellectual, and institutional context of natural resource policies. As a result many leaders in the conservation movement, including Frederick H. Newell and Gifford Pinchot, have lost their halos. But we have a long way to go before we understand the conflicts among the conservationists and how resource agencies assumed the "personalities" they exhibited.

PART FOUR
Federal Reclamation

The last two chapters in this volume—"Irrigation, Water Rights, and the Betrayal of Indian Allotment" and "Reclamation and Social Engineering in the Progressive Era"—examine federal water policy in the early twentieth century. Two bureaus hoped to use irrigation to transform the American West—the Indian Irrigation Service and the Bureau of Reclamation. During the first three decades of the twentieth century, the history of the two agencies became closely entwined.

As early as 1871, General William Tecumseh Sherman observed that turning the Indians of the Southwest into farmers would solve many problems. In some years, Congress did not provide sufficient money to feed them, and something had to be done to prevent the Apaches from raiding white settlements and from wandering off their reservation in search of forage for stock. The Indian Office's goal of making the Indians self-sufficient was widely perceived as good for the taxpayers as well as good for the Indians; the cost of providing rations and other supplies would be reduced or eliminated. "It has been asserted that with a proper system of irrigation on the Navajo Reservation adjacent to the San Juan River," the Commissioner of Indian Affairs observed in 1902, "two-thirds of the families occupying that reservation could make homes and become self-supporting."[1]

Above all, the construction of dams and irrigation ditches provided Indians with valuable training in manual labor and in managing time—along with a discretionary income that had the potential to teach the virtues of thrift. In the 1870s and 1880s, most reservation Indians were too far removed from white settlements to find outside employment. Work on reservation irrigation projects taught valuable skills, such as carpentry and masonry, and many agents reported that the Indians took pride in building canals because they could see direct benefits to their community as well as to themselves. Over one-third of the cost of the Zuni dam at Blackrock, New Mexico, begun in 1903 and completed in 1908, was paid in wages to Indians. As the commissioner of Indian affairs noted in 1906, "The lesson taught by the experiment with Indian labor at this dam is unquestionably that if the Indian can be weaned from his habits of irregularity of days and hours, induced to postpone or rearrange his religious festivities so that they shall not interfere with the demands of his employment, and taught the white man's idea of laying something aside for to-morrow instead of spending all to-day, he can be made into a very valuable industrial factor in our frontier country." In fiscal year 1910, more than 10 percent of the Indian Office's appropriation went to Indians as wages.[2]

To be sure, not all Indians supported the irrigation policy. Although Indian Service officials argued that idle Indian land was more likely to fall into white hands than prosperous farms, some tribes feared *any* policy that would drive up the value of their land and make it more attractive to whites. To these Indians, opposition to irrigation became a patriotic duty. Others suspected that officials in the Indian Office were too optimistic and that no amount of irrigation would turn their sterile land into productive farms. They also feared that the commitment to irrigation would result in less federal aid, especially to those Indians who raised livestock.[3]

Congress made the first appropriation for Indian irrigation in 1867, but annual expenditures did not begin until the 1890s, as part of the new allotment policy instituted by the Dawes Act (1887). The Indian Office assumed that irrigation would pay for itself. Providing water to Indian farms would increase the value of the "surplus" land left over after allotment, creating a fund to pay for improvements. In 1890, a special commission promised the Crow Tribe in Montana that the federal government would spend $200,000 to bring water to land adjoining the Big Horn and Little Big Horn rivers if the Indians accepted a smaller reservation. "Plainly, then," the commission concluded, "if it is the object of the Government to make the Crows self-supporting, one of the first steps to be taken is to make the land alloted to them productive by means of a thorough system of irrigation." Irrigation was not just desirable, it was a necessity. Without it, allotment on the arid and barren Crow reserve could not be justified and the Indians would oppose it. Work on the main canal began in 1892, and by 1896, 100 miles of main ditch had been constructed, capable of serving about 25,000 acres.[4]

Historians have ignored the close relationship between federal water policies and the allotment of Indian land; the Dawes Act (1887) has been studied largely in isolation.[5] Dividing up the reservations was designed to replace stock-raising with farming, common land with private land, and the tribe with the nuclear family. In 1908, in a very ambiguous ruling, the U.S. Supreme Court decided that Native Americans had the right to sufficient water to make their reservations agriculturally productive, whether or not they used the water at the time of the ruling. The court did not set a limit on the reserved supply, nor did it say whether its decision applied to *all* reservations. Nevertheless, its intent was clear. Since Congress wanted the Indians to become farmers, and since most of the reservations were arid or semiarid, the transformation could be accomplished only through irrigation. Since the process might take years, the court intended to set aside sufficient water to make that possible. In the absence of water, most reservations would be limited to raising livestock, an occupation that did not instill the love of private property, or promote self-sufficiency and independence.[6]

The Indian Irrigation Service enjoyed modest success in the 1890s, but that ended after Congress passed the Reclamation Act in 1902. Reclamation Service officials quickly recognized that the Indian reservations contained a great deal of land that could be purchased or leased by white farmers and that the proceeds from surplus land sales could be used to pay for reclaiming land owned by whites as well as Indians. In 1907, the Reclamation Service took over the construction of the largest irrigation projects on Indian reservations or former reservations—with the complicity, if not full support, of the Indian Office. Officials in the Bureau of Indian Affairs hoped that white farmers would serve as models to would-be Indian irrigators. Therefore, they encouraged whites to take up land on the former reservations.

Had the Reclamation Bureau intended only to take over the construction work of the Indian Irrigation Office, the Indians might have profited from the Reclamation Service's able engineering staff; it made little sense to have two government agencies doing the same work. But the Reclamation Service feared any special category of Indian water rights. Indeed, it opposed *any* water right that could not be quantified. For example, in those western states that recognized riparian rights as well as prior appropriation, riparian rights were regarded as a major obstacle to federal reclamation because they prevented the government from determining the West's surplus water—the amount available for future use. The creation of yet another set of open-ended water rights would add strength to the riparian doctrine, which the U.S. Justice Department had challenged in *Kansas v. Colorado.*[7]

The Reclamation Bureau had a large legal staff, and it convinced the Justice Department that any attempt to adjudicate Indian rights would destroy the irrigation program in its infancy, a program that Theodore Roosevelt was particularly fond of. Moreover, any policy that allowed Indians to reserve large quantities of water for future use would so anger white settlers that it might result in renewed violence against the Indians. The Indian Office concluded that Winters's rights were unenforceable and that it should apply for water under state law, like other users, and try to "reserve" an adequate water supply by encouraging whites to lease irrigable Indian land.[8] When the Indians were ready to farm, the leases could be canceled. Moreover, during World War I, officials in the Bureau of Indian Affairs considered it a patriotic duty to aid the war effort by increasing production on Indian land. By the 1920s, the Indian irrigation projects served far more whites than Indians—often at the expense of the Indians.

In a larger sense, these two chapters demonstrate that neither the Bureau of Indian Affairs nor the Reclamation Bureau had any clear vision of the future—or any ability to carry out such a vision—which was obvious in the administration of the Reclamation Act. The Reclamation Act had been sold to the public as a moral reform that would populate the West by draining off the East's surplus population, defusing urban tensions that had become starkly visible during the dark years of the 1890s. Once in power, however, neither the director of the Reclamation Service, F. H. Newell, nor his second-in-command and successor as director, A. P. Davis, exhibited much interest in social reform. For example, settlers asked the Reclamation Service to use proceeds from the sale of town lots within government projects to build schools, parks, and modern sanitation and electric systems. Reclamation Service officials refused; they, like most members of Congress, opposed social engineering. Government "paternalism," it was feared, would undermine self-discipline, personal responsibility, and the work ethic. Therefore, farmers designed their own communities, and project towns turned out to be as dull and drab as most of the nineteenth-century settlements they mimicked. Without a fight, the Reclamation Bureau forfeited its best chance to use irrigation to remake rural society.

The Reclamation Bureau never decided whether its basic goal was to serve existing farms or create new ones; whether it should build a new society or simply furnish established farmers with dams, canals, and cheap land; or whether its basic goal was to develop the rural West or the region as a whole. Two of the men most responsible for promoting federal reclamation in the years before 1902—William Ellsworth Smythe and George Maxwell—expressed deep disappointment and frustration at the direction federal reclamation took in the years after 1902. For both, federal reclamation was a partial solution, at best.

The federal reclamation program started from two faulty premises: that a sharp line divided rural and urban America and that a substantial number of Americans preferred country life to city life. Smythe and Maxwell, however, assumed that urban America was here to stay and that something had to be done to allow the factory worker to feed his family and supplement his income. The answer was Smythe's "Little Lander" homesteads and Maxwell's "Homecroft" scheme. These called for the creation of belts of surburban farms of a few acres or less where women and children could cultivate the soil while the head of the household worked in a nearby city. Everyone would benefit from these garden homes. Factory owners could pay lower wages; the families would be largely insulated from economic slumps and downturns; they would benefit from hard, clean work in the open air; and sales of chickens, eggs, and produce would spell the difference between subsistence and a comfortable living.

Although federal reclamation was restricted to the far West, Smythe and Maxwell considered irrigation an instrument of social reform that promised greater benefits in the densely populated East than in the sparsely populated West. It produced larger crop yields per acre, allowed farmers to raise plants that could not be grown without the scientific application of water, and banished the fear of drought. Smythe and Maxwell found irrigation an immensely attractive way to manipulate nature. Yet their dream of blending rural and urban America failed. They were unable to raise the capital needed to move a substantial number of workers to the "suburbs," and while garden homes received considerable attention in the press, they threatened the efforts of labor unions to raise wages and improve urban living conditions. After World War I, the problem of agricultural overproduction reappeared and the dream of using irrigation to transform American society faded.

CHAPTER NINE

Irrigation, Water Rights, and the Betrayal of Indian Allotment

In June 1970, Alvin Josephy, Jr., published a searing article for the new conservation section of *American Heritage* magazine. The essay, "Here in Nevada a Terrible Crime," was a tract for the times. Pyramid Lake, the second largest desert lake in the United States and one of the nation's natural wonders, was drying up. Non-Indian farmers had systematically diverted more than half of the Truckee River, the lake's major source of water, into the Truckee-Carson Irrigation Project sixty miles east of Reno. Unlike nearby Lake Tahoe, a sacrifice to the gods of gambling and tourism, Pyramid Lake was seldom visited. Nestled among stark, austere, forbidding mountains, it offered solitude and contemplation.

The story would have been sad enough if nature had been the only victim. The declining water level threatened to create a land bridge to Anaho Island, a 750-acre National Wildlife Refuge, exposing the largest colony of white pelicans in North America to a host of hungry predators. But the lake was also the heart of a Paiute Indian reservation, and in 1967 almost 70 percent of the reservation's residents were unemployed and more than half its families earned less than $2,000 a year.

The poverty of the Indians, Josephy emphasized, did not result from laziness or inadequate resources, nor were the Paiutes simply human relics or prisoners of an outmoded culture. They had been betrayed by the Department of Interior, the trustee and guardian of their patrimony. For decades the department had supported the interests of the project farmers who cultivated land once part of the first irrigation project constructed under the Reclamation Act of 1902. Meanwhile, the lake had declined eighty feet since the beginning of the century. As a consequence, the cutthroat trout—fish that once flourished in the lake, spawned in the Truckee River, and served as a major source of tribal income—had disappeared. When representatives of California and Nevada sat down to divide up the Truckee River's "surplus" water in 1955—with the explicit consent of Congress and the acquiescence of the Department of Interior—the Paiutes were not offered a seat on the interstate commission. Indian rights and needs played little part in the negotiations.[1]

The Paiute tragedy was a classic example of the misuse of Indian natural resources. Public disclosure of that poignant story coincided with the "rediscovery" of special water rights originally promised to American Indians by the United States Supreme Court in the 1908 Winters case.[2] That decision was largely ignored or forgotten until 1963, when the high Court suggested that reservation Indians held open-ended or elastic rights to sufficient water to develop their reservations—a right not restricted to existing uses or even to the development of maximum agricultural potential.[3]

In the 1960s and 1970s, water rights received increasing attention from politicians, lawyers, writers, and even a few academics.[4] But, with the exception of land issues, few historians looked at the use of Indian natural resources.[5] This chapter explores how irrigation changed from being the handmaiden of the campaign to "civilize" the Indians into one of its greatest enemies in the period from 1891 to the 1920s. It also explains how Indian water rights became captive to experiments in federal reclamation, thereby contributing to the failure of allotment.[6]

In the American Southwest, Indians practiced irrigation long before the advent of reservations or the establishment of the national arid-lands reclamation program in 1902. Eight-hundred years ago Hohokam Indians watered about 100,000 acres in the area of present-day Phoenix using an elaborate 135-mile network of canals, many carved through tough volcanic outcroppings and lined with clay to prevent seepage. Other irrigators, including the Subaipuris and Pimas, succeeded the Hohokam civilization, which vanished around 1400.[7]

Nevertheless, irrigation did not become an important part of national Indian policy until after the adoption of the Dawes General Allotment Act in 1887. Thereafter, one measure of the absorption of the dominant culture was how intensively the members of particular tribes used the land. Irrigation promised the same benefits to whites and Indians—smaller and more compact farms, immunity from drought, higher value crops, and larger yields. It also permitted the cultivation of less fertile soil.[8]

Congress made the first federal appropriation ($76,000) for Indian irrigation in 1867 to help concentrate natives from the lower Colorado River on a reservation in Arizona. That water system was abandoned in 1876,[9] and regular appropriations for irrigation did not begin until the early 1890s.[10] In July 1890, the Indian Office recommended an irrigation survey of Navajo land to prevent herdsmen from leaving the reservation; about 9,000 Indians had abandoned their sanctuary in search of water and pasture. Civil war threatened as whites and Indians competed for a scarce resource. The War Department completed its hydrologic investigation in 1892, and Congress voted $40,000 to begin work on the project.[11] At about the same time, Congress set aside $200,000 from money due the Crow Indians—in payment for the sale of part of their reservation—to construct "irrigating appliances for the lands retained by them." By 1896, $257,599 had been spent on the Crow water system, most of it in wage payments to Indian laborers. The Indian Bureau also began new works on the Fort Peck, Fort Hall, and Blackfeet reservations. It spent additional money to repair primitive canals on the Pima, Yakima, Pyramid Lake, and Walker River reservations and to sink test artesian wells on the Rosebud, Standing Rock, and Pine Ridge reservations in South Dakota.[12]

Agents and superintendents frequently praised the industry, skill, and dedication of native workers, but for a variety of reasons most Indians did not appreciate the value of irrigation. Its potential benefits remained obscure to people accustomed to hunting or stock-raising, and with good reason. The agent in charge of irrigation on the Navajo Reservation described its residents as "quick, shrewd, and intelligent," but noted that they opposed cultivating their parched and barren land for fear that the improvements would attract covetous whites and rival tribes. "Success" had its price.[13]

Irrigation offered substantial incidental benefits. Because most reservations were remote and isolated, Indians had little opportunity to work at manual labor—even though agents and superintendents encouraged them to look for jobs on non-Indian farms, irrigation projects, and railroad construction gangs. The Indian service was convinced that its charges would learn thrift only through work and that annuities and payments for surplus land would be squandered unless native people understood the value of money. By setting aside part of the proceeds from reservation land sales to pay for irrigation, and then returning most of that money to the Indians in the form of wages, the Indian Office could undermine what one commissioner called "the racial prejudice against common manual labor." Working for wages would promote habits of regularity, industry, and thrift, the bureau believed; it would also encourage independence and individualism by teaching a wide variety of vocational skills, including carpentry and masonry.

Many officials went even further; they believed that successful family farming was *impossible* without training in manual labor. The value of irrigation as a way to raise more valuable crops became secondary. For example, in 1900 Congress appropriated $30,000 to construct new canals on the Pima Reservation, even though the absence of a storage dam on the Gila River meant there was no water to fill the ditches. "While the ditches may not be of use," the commissioner commented, "it is certainly wise to require Indians to perform labor in return for the appropriation, as otherwise they might be led to abandon their former habits of industry and become pauperized."[14] Floods and thunderstorms frequently washed out the flimsy canals and headgates constructed by the Indian Office's unskilled work force, but the commissioner justified hydraulic projects as essential to character building.[15]

Officials in the Indian service understood the value of larger, more efficient, and dependable works. But they worried about losing authority over irrigation to the War Department or the U.S. Geological Survey, both agencies well-staffed with hydraulic engineers. During the drought of the late 1880s and early 1890s, and the long economic depression that followed, many westerners demanded that the nation launch a massive arid-land reclamation program. That raised the possibility that rival agencies might use Indian irrigation as the stepping-stone to a larger national reclamation program. The commissioner repeatedly appealed to Congress for money to hire skilled engineers. However, the first "superintendent of irrigation," appointed in 1898, was not much of an engineer—although he had been a loyal employee of the Indian service and had supervised construction of the Crow Reservation works beginning in 1891.

Regular appropriations for Indian irrigation and funds charged against annuities dramatically increased in the twentieth century—$30,000 in 1892, $100,000 in 1902, $200,000 in 1909, and $325,000 in 1913. By 1914 the reservations had been divided into five districts, each under a supervising engineer directed from Washington. However, the Indian Bureau never enjoyed an adequate engineering staff, and its canals and ditches rarely matched the quality of the Reclamation Service structures built after 1902. Because heavy construction work on Indian projects was contracted to many different private engineering firms, the works lacked coordination and standardization of design.[16]

The Indian projects served a substantial amount of land. In 1910 their ditches covered nearly half the land that could be watered within Reclamation Service projects. At the end of World War I, a period that witnessed a boom in land and crop prices, the Indian commissioner proclaimed that Indians had responded "nobly to the call for greater production and materially increased the acreage cultivated and the yield per acre." The amount of irrigated land more than doubled between 1914 and 1919, and in the latter year the total value of crops produced on Idaho's Fort Hall Reservation exceeded the entire cost of the irrigation system.[17]

Unfortunately, rosy statistics masked a grim struggle between the Indian Office and the Reclamation Service for control over Indian land and water. That conflict began in 1902, fed by the reluctance of the supremely confident officers of the Reclamation Service to share their mission with any other agency. Shortages of irrigable public land and water, and inadequate revenue to construct the twenty-four Reclamation Service projects authorized by the end of 1906, compounded the difficulties. In the years after 1904 the new agency invaded many reservations. In California and

Nevada, the service drew the boundaries of its Lower Colorado Project to include the most fertile, accessible land within the Yuma Reservation, where several hundred Yuma Indians clung to a precarious existence wrested from the alluvial soil adjoining the Colorado. In 1904, Congress gave the Reclamation Service the right to "reclaim, utilize, and dispose of any lands" within the reservation as long as each Indian received an irrigated farm. The government sold nearly half the reservation land (6,500 acres) to non-Indian settlers. Proceeds from those sales were credited to the Indians, less the cost of irrigation works. Farms owned by whites within the reservation averaged about forty acres, four to eight times larger than the plots assigned to the Indians.[18]

Subsequently, the policy folowed on the Yuma Project was extended to other reservations. For example, in the Carson Sink Valley, heart of the proposed Truckee-Carson project, 196 Nevada Paiutes held about 30,000 acres of alloted land. In the summer of 1906, however, the secretary of the interior canceled those allotments in exchange for ten-acre irrigated plots. In all, the Indians gave up 26,720 acres. The commissioner of Indian affairs commented bitterly:

> The newspapers of Nevada are even urging white settlers to go upon the lands [before the Indians have left], take their choice, build homes, and make improvements, assuring them that the Reclamation Service will supply them with water and the Indian Bureau must give way.[19]

In any contest between whites and Indians, political expediency, if nothing else, dictated that the Reclamation Service support white farmers. The 1902 act, after all, had been written for those homesteaders.

The Reclamation Service proposed many laws relating to specific reservations. In 1904 it extended its influence to the Yuma Reservation, the Pyramid Lake Reservation in Nevada, and the Crow Reservation in Montana.[20] Two years later the Reclamation Act reached the Yakima Reservation.[21] In 1906, the Reclamation Service proposed taking over the largest Indian Bureau water projects, and an interagency agreement was adopted in the following year. All money earmarked for construction work by the Indian Office was transferred to Reclamation Service accounts, and the latter agency assumed *direct* responsibility for projects on the Blackfeet, Fort Peck, Flathead, and Pima reservations. Because water was scarce in the arid West, federal reclamation policies had a profound effect on many other western reservations.[22]

The Indian Office gave way to political pressure for several reasons. First, Commissioner Francis E. Leupp and his successor, Robert G. Valentine, supported the Roosevelt administration's conservation policies, including federal reclamation. A coordinated irrigation program would prevent duplication of effort and promote the most efficient use of natural resources. The Reclamation Service, experts claimed, could do a much better job of building and maintaining large hydraulic works than the Indian Bureau. Leupp and Valentine also knew that reclaiming the arid West took precedence over Indian affairs—with both the secretary of the interior and President Roosevelt. Had the Indian Office tried to block the institutional imperialism of the Reclamation Service, it would have placed itself in the position of resisting one of the administration's most popular programs. The service was expected to reclaim as many as 50 million acres—an area half the size of California. As the national irrigation program developed, therefore, the Indian Office would not be able to escape the burgeoning power and influence of the service; better to form a pragmatic alliance at the outset.

In addition, Leupp considered competition between whites and Indians part of a "conditioning process." In his 1905 report he observed:

Perhaps in the course of merging this hardly used race into our body politic many individuals, unable to keep up the pace, may fall by the wayside and be trodden underfoot. Deeply as we deplore this possibility, we must not let it blind us to our duty to the race as a whole. It is one of the cruel incidents of all civilization in large masses that some, perhaps a multitude, of its subjects will be lost in the process.[23]

A good many Americans had called for a final answer to "the Indian question." Leupp shared their view that only the fit should survive.

Nevertheless, persistent water shortages in the West ensured that the two agencies would come into conflict sooner or later. The stage had been set even before the Reclamation Service was established. The droughts of the 1880s and early 1890s, coupled with increasing upstream diversions by non-Indian farmers, dramatically reduced Indian water supplies. White appropriators on the Blackfoot River, which ran through Idaho's Fort Hall Reservation, forced the local Indian agent to recommend hiring a private company (the Idaho Canal Company) to provide supplemental water to the reservation from the Snake River. Although the latter stream was over-appropriated, the water company held an old claim.[24]

In the Southwest, diversions from the Gila River dried up the Pima Reservation's water supply. Because the Pima were an agricultural people and held some of the earliest rights to the river, the Indian Office considered the possibility of a suit. However, above the Pima diversion, more than 900 whites, some as far as 200 miles from the reservation, used water from the stream. The agency superintendent predicted that it would take a long time to secure a comprehensive decree allocating the stream's water, that it would cost $20,000 to $30,000, and that a decree probably would be unenforceable. Despite many different hydrographic studies and congressional approval of a major storage reservoir, the problem persisted at least as late as 1920.[25] Similar shortages due to the violation of well-established Indian water rights occurred on the Yakima and Fort Belknap reserves.

The Reclamation Service insisted that the two basic measures of water rights were priority—"first in time, first in right"—and beneficial use, the requirement that claims could be perfected only by applying water to the soil. The first director of the service, Frederick H. Newell, warned in 1902 that the Indian Office could not reserve water in anticipation of future needs; what was not put to use within a reasonable period, he said, would be lost. Although the Bureau of Indian Affairs often claimed that it did not have to observe state water laws, it religiously filed claims and willingly subjected Indian rights to state codes.[26]

During the Roosevelt and Taft administrations the Indian Office deferred to the Reclamation Service, hoping thereby to increase the Indian water supply through the storage of surplus floodwater rather than by laying claim to an already fully appropriated stream flow.[27] Nevertheless, by the end of the Roosevelt administration—as the government opened its irrigation projects outside the reservations to white settlers—Francis Leupp began to recognize the irreconcilable conflict between federal reclamation and Indian rights.[28]

Initially, the Department of Justice and the courts supported Leupp. Norris Hundley has written two meticulous, carefully reasoned, and well-documented essays discussing the famous case of *Winters v. United States* and its aftermath.[29] The Fort Belknap Reservation in Montana had been set apart, in the words of the 1888 treaty that created it, "for the permanent home and abiding place of the Gros Ventre and Assiniboine bands or tribes." On no part of the reservation could crops be raised without irrigation, and in 1898 the Indians watered 30,000 acres. Beginning in 1900, white farmers upstream from the reservation diverted increasing amounts of water from the Milk River, and in the spring of 1905 the stream dried up before it reached Indian pasture and farmland.[30]

At first the reservation agent urged the Indian Office in Washington to press suit to uphold *appropriative* rights, on the grounds that a former agent had filed for 10,000 miner's inches of water in 1898, a claim senior to most others on that stretch of the river. The Justice Department asked Carl Rasch, U.S. attorney for the District of Montana, to intervene on behalf of the Indians. Rasch decided that relying solely on prior appropriation was a risky strategy because the agent who filed on water had done so in his own name, rather than on behalf of the United States or individual water users within the reservation. There was always danger, moreover, that older non-Indian claims might surface. Therefore, Rasch broadened the government's case to argue that the *entire* flow of the Milk River had been reserved for the Indians. When the case finally reached the U.S. Supreme Court in 1908, the tribunal upheld the petitioners, arguing that the Indians and the federal government had set aside the water for both existing and future needs.

The purpose of reservations, the Court reasoned, was to make the Indians a pastoral people and to destroy a nomadic lifestyle. Because the lands set aside were worthless without irrigation, the Indians would not have signed the treaty creating the reservation unless they had assumed that the water remained with the land. The absence of any reference to water rights in the treaty spoke volumes to white lawyers, but the Supreme Court ruled that it was bound to interpret the document the way the Indians had understood it. (Treaties explained to Indians through interpreters could not be construed with the same degree of precision as contracts between whites.) The Court concluded that the water had been reserved by both the Indians and the federal government. "The evidence suggests," Hundley concludes, "that the Winters court intended for the Fort Belknap Indians to have all the water from the Milk River that they could put to reasonable use." Many questions were left in the wake of the Winters decision: Was the implied reservation of water limited to the needs of the Indians at the time the reservation was created? Or was it an "indefinitely expandable mortgage" held by the United States on behalf of the Indians? Moreover, could Indian rights be leased or sold to whites?[31]

Hundley does not discuss the reaction of the Reclamation Service to the case or the intense infighting that took place within the Interior Department. As the Justice Department's argument took shape in the last half of 1905, officials in the Reclamation Service carried their case directly to Theodore Roosevelt. The opening shot in the battle between the Reclamation Service and the Justice Department was a memo dated December 8, 1905, drafted by Reclamation's chief legal officer. That document charged that the Justice Department's attempt "to obtain for the Indians rights greater than could be claimed by any white man" threatened the "broad general principles of policy necessary for the development of the entire arid region." By claiming that the Indians held a species of riparian rights, the memo contended, Justice had undermined one of its major arguments in the pending case of *Kansas v. Colorado.*[32]

In the latter case, the state of Kansas was trying to block upstream diversions on the Arkansas River in Colorado. Kansas claimed traditional riparian rights to the entire uninterrupted flow of the stream. Government engineers believed that formal recognition of the primacy of riparian rights in downstream states would prevent the nation from impounding water at the headwaters of interstate streams. And because riparian rights were indefinite by nature—and impossible to quantify—their recognition would also prevent the federal government from determining the surplus water in a stream or from seeking an adjudication of water rights to quiet titles prior to the construction of new irrigation projects.[33]

Theodore Roosevelt asked the attorney general to respond to the Reclamation Service memo. The nation's chief legal officer replied:

> I am of the opinion that it was necessary and proper for the Government, in defending Indian rights within the comparatively narrow field of reservation lands, to invoke the doctrine of riparian rights, although elsewhere the Government is recognizing recent ramifications of that doctrine.

The Indian case was exceptional, "and their rights antedate modern evolution in the law of waters." The Bureau of Indian Affairs, the attorney general explained, had a solemn responsibility to protect Indian resources. He denied that there was any inconsistency between the Winters case and *Kansas v. Colorado*. Variations in state water laws were bound to dictate different strategies and arguments in different federal courts. Nevertheless, he concluded his letter of December 18, 1905, on a prudent note:

> [If] everything else must give way to the great irrigation work in which the Government is now engaged, further contention on the basis of riparian rights may well cease; and yet I believe that wherever that doctrine can be successfully invoked in behalf of the Indians, especially under their treaties, this should be done.[34]

Secretary of Interior Ethan Allen Hitchcock also issued a report on the Winters case. Because he supervised both the Indian Office and the Reclamation Service, one could expect his memorandum to be ambiguous. On one hand, he claimed that the riparian doctrine was gradually giving way in the West to the doctrine of prior appropriation. The government should do everything possible, he maintained, to extinguish riparian rights:

> Should the Supreme Court approve of the doctrine [of Indian water rights] which now seems to prevail in Montana and Washington, and the same be strictly enforced throughout the arid region, the policy of the Government as indicated in the Reclamation Act would be defeated and the development of the entire arid West be materially retarded, if not entirely destroyed.

Nevertheless, Hitchcock also argued that the treaty creating the Fort Belknap reservation had reserved sufficient water "to insure to the Indian [the] means to irrigate their farms." That interpretation, contended the attorney general, was "in accord with the rules which the supreme court has repeatedly laid down in arriving at the true sense of treaties with the Indians." He confirmed that when the Indians accepted the reservation in 1888, they had "reserved the right to the use of the waters of Milk River, at least to an extent reasonably necessary to irrigate their lands." Although Hitchcock upheld the Indian right, he did not define carefully its origin or extent.[35]

In the half-dozen years following the Winters decision, Commissioner of Indian Affairs F. E. Leupp pushed Hitchcock to adjudicate Indian water rights "on every reservation where a conflict has arisen between white settlers and the Indians," but the Indian Office failed to settle on a consistent course to protect Indian rights.[36] In most cases, it filed for water just as the Reclamation Service did for white farmers, and in 1911 Commissioner Valentine gratefully reported that state authorities "frequently cooperate."[37]

Occasionally, native voices could be heard above the legal debate, but the Justice Department remained mute and the Supreme Court made no further comment on Indian water rights until 1939.[38] Congress might still have come to the aid of the Indians, but it, too, favored the Reclamation Service. In 1912, for instance, the chairman of the House Committee on Indian Affairs introduced a resolution to adjudicate the water rights of the Pima and Yakima Indians, but the secretary of the interior demurred and the House acquiesced.[39]

Nevertheless, a significant congressional protest against the narrow definition of Indian water rights erupted in 1913–1914. It was prompted in large part by the change in administrations that brought Franklin K. Lane to Washington as secretary of the interior and Cato Sells as commissioner of Indian affairs. Soon after they took office, Congress—at the urging of the Indian Office—formed a joint committee to study the Yakima River conflict. And when Wyoming's state engineer refused to grant water to Shoshone Indians on the Wind River Reservation without evidence of use, Lane asked Congress for legislation to "provide for confirmation and protection of the prior reserved rights [Winters doctrine rights] for such [reservation] lands."[40]

The Senate Indian Committee followed the initiatives of Lane and Sells. When the annual Indian appropriations bill came up for routine discussion before the full Senate in June, several members of the committee— Senators Joseph Robinson (Arkansas), Carroll Page (Vermont), Joseph Lane (Oregon), and Henry Ashurst (Arizona)—were ready. The usual pro forma discussion on the floor turned into a week-long debate as the senators tried to win approval for a series of amendments drafted in the Indian Office.[41] Senator Lane offered an amendment requiring the federal government to reserve "so much water as may be necessary" for domestic use, stock watering, and irrigation on the Fort Hall Reservation. Failure by the

Indians to put water to use within the period stipulated under state law—five years in many western states—would not affect the amount of water set apart for reservation use, according to the amendment. Lane's amendment, and one pertaining to the Fort Belknap Reservation, lost on points of order. Senator Robinson sought to limit federal irrigation expenditures on Montana reservations to one-third of the appropriation unless the *state* adopted legislation to guarantee that Indian water rights would be held in trust as long as necessary *and* date from the time of filing rather than from the date of actual use. His amendment was rejected on a voice vote.[42]

Members of the committee repeatedly warned that no further appropriations should be made for Indian irrigation until the law ensured that Indians would enjoy some of the benefits. On the Flathead Reservation in Montana surplus land sold to whites for $4 to $7 an acre commanded $100 to $500 an acre when irrigated; that, the Senate committee argued, constituted a major federal subsidy to white farmers.[43] None of the "unearned increment" benefited native people, although some of the land they retained appreciated in value. (The Indians did not profit from land speculation because most of their allotments, while theoretically irrigable, were beyond the reach of government canals.) They also encountered discrimination in the delivery of water. Often their ditches received no water until July, when swollen mountain streams carried the greatest volume. As the number of non-Indian farmers on Indian reservations increased, the volume of water provided to Indians decreased.

Worst of all, the Indians subsidized federal reclamation through both sales of "surplus" land and the substantial mortgage placed on the land they retained. They had no say in how the proceeds from land sales would be spent, even though the irrigation works they paid for served mainly white farmers. Non-Indian farmers who took up land within the $6 million Flathead project did paid a pro rata share of the cost of building the irrigation works. But they had twenty years to pay, *without interest*. That constituted yet another subsidy.[44] If the project was successful, the Indians *might* get back the money they had loaned to Reclamation's "revolving fund." But because they had no voice in how their money was spent, that revenue could be lavished on project additions from which the Indians received no return at all. And if the project failed, they had no assurance that the government would make good on the debt of white farmers. In any case, the Indians received nothing for providing the capital to get many government irrigation projects started.

To complicate matters, on the Flathead and other Indian projects it supervised, the Reclamation Service made the reimbursement of operation and maintenance costs—as opposed to construction costs—a cumulative lien on the irrigable Indian land. If an aspiring Indian farmer waited five or ten years to irrigate his land, then he had to pay that substantial debt before receiving any water—*if* he still had the legal right to water. Meanwhile, there was no money to fence or level land, buy plows, seed, and cattle, raise a barn, or build a home. Members of the Committee on Indian Affairs urged that individual farmers pay for the reclamation of Indian land as white farmers paid for Reclamation Bureau projects; the money should not be taken from tribal funds. In this way, the committee believed, the Indians could use the revenue from land sales as a nest egg. If federal Indian policies were designed to promote personal initiative and responsibility instead of tribal collectivism, should not each Indian farmer make his own contracts and pay his own debts? "The system is wrong," Senator Robinson concluded. "You would not get a white man standing in the place of these Indians to go into a scheme of this sort as long as time runs." Oregon's Senator Lane was even more critical, charging that the Indians had been

> pressed into it [the Flathead project] by their guardians, and their land is being held for all of it, while they receive but a fraction of the benefit. It is a great wrong that is being perpetrated on them. . . . It is wicked.[45]

The "wicked" nature of reservation reclamation policies was all the more obvious because the motives of the Reclamation Service were so transparent. Senator Myers of Montana candidly explained why Indian money was needed to build the Flathead project:

> It is because the demand on the reclamation fund for [white] projects now under way is so very great and so pressing that the Reclamation Service claims that it has need for all the money in the reclamation fund and more for projects already started and now under headway. . . . It would be hard to get the Government to put this under the expenditures of the Reclamation Service, when the Reclamation Service is already hard pressed for funds.[46]

The Service had overestimated the money it would receive from the sale of non-Indian lands in the West and the amount that project farmers would return to the revolving fund.

Here was a dilemma. A thorough survey of Indian water rights might take years to complete. Meanwhile, all reservation rights would be under a cloud. White settlers would not buy native land, and residents on reservation projects, Indian as well as white, would be unable to make their payments or borrow money to improve their farms. Myers concluded:

> If you halt this work you do the greatest possible injustice to the Indian, because the Indian has got to get his money back out of

the sale of land to the white man; and if the white man does not get water on his land, he can not make his payments. Therefore if you halt this work, the Indian will be the chief sufferer.[47]

The Senate debate was significant both for its theoretical discussion of the Winters doctrine and its exposure of conditions on Indian irrigation projects. Senator Robinson's careful, perceptive analysis, and the comments of other members of the Indian committee demonstrate that the defenders of Indian rights understood the doctrine almost as well as the lawyers who dusted it off in the 1960s and 1970s—after it had been neglected for so many decades.[48]

Critics of the Winters decision also fully grasped what was at stake. Western senators and congressmen, recognizing the threat to the Reclamation Service and non-Indian farmers, insisted that native people could acquire water only by prior appropriation. Though they dismissed the Winters case as bad law, they considered it worrisome enough to offer ingenious—and sometimes plausible if facile—arguments to explain that the Supreme Court had not meant what it seemed to mean. Senator Thomas considered the case an aberration because it ran counter to a long series of court decisions that upheld the principle that water rights depended on beneficial use. Senator Works of California, a lawyer who specialized in water rights, expressed sympathy for the Indians but insisted that the case had limited application; the courts, he said, had considered only the rights of Fort Belknap Indians, and Montana was still a territory when the reservation was established in 1888. Although the Constitution gave the federal government authority over the resources of the territories, Works reasoned, when Montana achieved statehood in 1889, sovereignty over all surplus property not specifically retained by the nation remained with the state. Whether the state of Montana had any obligation to honor a contract made with Indians before statehood was a live question, but the California senator was confident that federal treaties and executive orders could not confer special rights on Indians *after* a state had entered the union.[49]

Senator Myers added that the Winters doctrine applied only to reservation Indians. Once the reservation had been allotted, all special rights lapsed. Shafroth of Colorado maintained that the Winters court meant only to reserve water in use at the time the treaty was ratified. In effect, the decision simply attached specific grants to parcels of irrigated land; it did not create a new category of rights. That was something of a guarantee, because Indians could not lose water through disuse. Nevertheless, they could not claim more than they used at the time they accepted reservation life.[50]

A special commission of reservation superintendents appointed to survey conditions on the reservations reaffirmed the recommendations of

the Indian committee.[51] That group called for direct federal appropriations for Indian water projects rather than advances from land sales. It also
recommended the attachment of irrigation charges to specific parcels of
land and urged the rapid completion of the Indian projects so that payments by white farmers would be returned to the Indians as rapidly as
possible. Finally, recognizing the lack of cooperation between the Reclamation Service and Indian Office, the commission suggested that no further
reclamation work be permitted on the reservations without the approval
of the commissioner of Indian affairs. Congress responded by shifting
water charges away from tribal lands to individual irrigable allotments.[52]
But the Reclamation Service remained firmly in command. The Indian
commissioner observed in 1915 that "the conditions under which the
cooperative irrigation works on these reservations [Flathead, Fort Peck,
and Blackfeet] has been done in the past is not for their [the Indians] best
interest, and . . . its continuance would be a great injustice."[53]

The agricultural boom during the First World War obscured and exac-
erbated the native water rights issue.[54] During the war Indian people
were all but forgotten in the quest to open new acreage to the plow and to
provide food for the allies. On the Blackfeet Reservation the number of
irrigated farms increased from 18 in 1915 to 328 in 1919. Although Indians
worked nearly 90 percent of the farms in 1915, by the end of the war white
tenants held more than 70 percent.[55]

Crop prices and real estate values plunged during the 1920s. As more
and more white farmers defaulted on their irrigation payments, they sav-
agely criticized the Reclamation Bureau. Discredited and unpopular in
most parts of the West, in 1924 the once-pampered child of the Roosevelt
administration relinquished control over most of its non-Indian projects to
the farmers and returned the reservation waterworks to the Indian Office.

During the 1920s Congress appropriated very little for Indian irrigation, and by the end of the decade conditions on the reservations appeared
more hopeless than ever. The allotment policy had clearly failed. As part of
a survey of the reservations, the Senate Committee on Indian Affairs published a remarkable report written by two engineers in the Agriculture
Department, Porter Preston and Charles Engle. Their lengthy study represented the most thorough investigation of Indian irrigation agriculture
compiled to that date. It exposed the shortsightedness of the irrigation program.[56]

According to Preston and Engle there were 150 irrigation projects on
the reservations in 1927, ranging in size from a few acres to the Yakima
Reservation's 89,000 acres under ditch. Nearly 700,000 acres had been provided with irrigation within allotted and unallotted reservations at a cost
of $27 million and an additional expense of $9 million for operation and
maintenance. About 30 percent of this land belonged to white farmers.

While Indians watered only about 16 percent of their irrigable land, whites cultivated two-thirds. The most unfavorable conditions prevailed on projects constructed by the Reclamation Service. On the Wapato project in the Yakima Reservation, only 6 percent of Indian allotments were actually irrigated by their owners; on the Blackfeet and Flathead reservations the figure was roughly 1 percent. In fact, 40 percent of all the land irrigated by Indians in the West was located within the Uintah Reservation in Utah and the Gila River Pima Reservation in Arizona.

As dreary as those statistics seem, actual conditions were worse. Most Indians who used irrigation, the Agriculture department engineers said, simply flooded pasture land to stimulate the growth of native grasses for livestock; Indian crops, therefore, returned only about half the per-acre income of white farmers. The report concluded:

[M]any of the so-called Indian irrigation projects are in reality white projects. . . . The continual decrease in the acreage farmed by Indians is the inevitable result of the allotment system.[57]

The practice of leasing allotments began in 1891 and grew dramatically in the twentieth century as irrigation made Indian lands far more attractive. Often native people—young and old—were incapable of cultivating their land; on many reservations irrigated allotments were too large for a "head of household" to manage. If Indians could not use the land, it might as well be used by whites. BIA officials were reluctant to discourage leasing. They believed that native people had to learn to make choices and take responsibility for their acts. Leasing served several useful purposes, the bureau believed. Whites provided Indians with an object lesson in how to farm. By encouraging non-Indians to take up reservation land, Indians could model themselves after successful white farmers imbued with the ethic of industry and thrift. Equally important, leases provided cash for farm equipment, livestock, and other agricultural needs. Finally, leasing irrigated allotments insured that there would be water to farm that land if and when the allottee decided to take over cultivation himself.[58]

The Indian Office occasionally grumbled about renting native land to whites, as in 1914 when the commissioner called the policy "a poor one at best." But in the end the bureau did more to encourage than discourage the practice.[59] Although Preston and Engle recognized the risk, they recommended that Indians lease as much land as possible "in order to protect the water rights, and to derive some income from which to pay irrigation charges."[60]

Federal reclamation was launched in 1902 as a bold experiment in social engineering as well as a practical program to reclaim desert land.[61] Much was expected and promised. Had the Newlands Act never been passed, irrigation still would have increased dramatically during the first two decades of the twentieth century, and it would have threatened the water supply available to Indians. As it turned out, federal reclamation irrigated only a small fraction of western land by 1920; state-sponsored irrigation districts served a much greater area. Nevertheless, the enormous influence of the Reclamation Service within the executive branch, particularly Interior, forced the Indian Office and Justice Department to relax their trusteeship over Indian natural resources.

Beginning with Franklin K. Lane, most secretaries of interior were westerners highly responsive to political pressure, and state control over water was a sacred cow in the arid states. The Reclamation Service had far greater technical expertise than the Bureau of Indian Affairs, and Norris Hundley observes that the secretaries "usually decided not to alienate the non-Indian voters and congressmen."[62] The executive officer most responsible for protecting Indian rights became caught in a conflict of interest of tragic proportions.

Many historians have argued that the desire to force Indians to become farmers was shortsighted, impractical, and self-defeating. Perhaps so, although one recent study by an economist suggests that many tribes made progress as farmers before the allotment policy took hold.[63] What is beyond debate is that irrigation offered new opportunities to exploit Indian natural resources. By the 1920s the Indian irrigation policy had reached a dead end. The success or failure of reclamation in the West, at least from the perspective of Congress, hinged on the ability of both Indian and non-Indian farmers to repay their debt to the nation. When those farmers defaulted, appropriations for irrigation by both the Indian Office and Reclamation Bureau dried up. Originally, the Bureau of Indian Affairs had suffered from the success of the Reclamation Service; now it suffered from its failure. The Reclamation Bureau cast a long shadow.

CHAPTER TEN

Reclamation and Social Engineering in the Progressive Era

Much has been written about the organization and policy objectives of the irrigation crusade of the 1890s, the legislative battles leading to the adoption of the Newlands Act in 1902, and the triumphs and shortcomings of federal arid land reclamation. But historians have largely ignored reclamation as a tool of social reform during the Progressive Era (1890–1920).[1] Arid land reclamation was nostalgia for a simpler rural past, the pipe dream of western visionaries and cranks, sheer political cant, and a smokescreen for land speculators and businessmen bent on lining their pockets. Yet, whatever the impracticality of this movement, whatever the element of fantasy, the passions it generated and the boldness of its objectives gave it the greatest potential of all the Progressive dreams. It sought to reclaim "worthless" lives along with worthless desert soil, and it provided an excellent opportunity for social engineering, especially in community planning. This chapter examines the intellectual foundation of the reclamation movement and the movement's effort to use irrigation to remold American institutions.

The first organized campaign to expand irrigation agriculture in the United States developed in the late 1880s and early 1890s as a result of the drought of 1889–1890 on the Great Plains, the demise of the range cattle industry, the increasing popularity of irrigation districts prompted by California's Wright Act (enacted in 1887), the five new western states that entered the union in 1889 and 1890, and by John Wesley Powell and the U.S. Geological Survey's investigation of the arid West's water supply and reservoir sites authorized by Congress in 1888. Before the middle 1890s, private land and canal companies dominated the irrigation movement. Their influence could be seen in the persistent western demand that the national government cede the arid lands to the states as a spur to private reclamation. This was essentially an economic movement, and it attracted relatively little attention in the eastern United States.

The depression of 1893—the most protracted economic slump since the 1830s—laid the foundation for a second irrigation crusade with broader objectives and a broader constituency. The depression lasted at least until 1897 and convinced many Americans that the United States was on the verge of class warfare and revolution. The West suffered particularly from the disappearance of investment capital. In 1896, the editor of *The Irrigation Age* acknowledged that the dramatic increase in irrigation agriculture which occurred from 1887 to 1892 had halted. "Before the close of 1892 capital had begun to flow freely in this direction, where it gave promise of exceptional returns from investment," he lamented. "Since that time not only have no new investments been undertaken, but many of the greater works which were unfinished have been left in such a state as to involve heavy loss and to preclude any possible profit from the amounts already expended."[2]

At the depth of the depression, William Ellsworth Smythe, editor of *The Irrigation Age* and the foremost publicist of the reclamation movement in the years from 1891 to 1895, expressed the alarm of many Americans in an essay he called "The Republic of Irrigation":

> We are in the midst of a world-wide depression that will be historic. Industries are in total or partial idleness. Millions of people who have formerly added something each Saturday night to their savings accounts are drawing to-day upon their principal. Tens of thousands are menaced by real hardship, and thousands of desperate men [Coxey's Army] are marching in the direction of the national capital to demand relief. . . . It almost seems as if there were too many people in this world—as if there were more mouths to feed than food with which to satisfy them. Whether we have reached the crisis of our social and industrial woes, or whether even more dangerous than any yet encountered are still before us, no one can tell. But it seems plain that the world demands some new field for the profitable employment of human energies, some field which will not only absorb labor, but reward it, at least, with the means of a living.[3]

The abandonment of unprofitable farms, the invention of labor-saving machinery, heavy immigration, a high birth rate, and the shortage of cheap land in the humid half of the nation were all blamed for the population pressure. George Maxwell, the irrigation movement's chief voice in the late 1890s, predicted that within a decade or two the population density of the United States would rival that of western Europe; American cities already exhibited a wide range of social and economic problems once believed to be endemic to the Old World.[4]

Not surprisingly, after 1893 irrigation crusaders blamed big business and the city for destroying the unity of the family, for crushing the opportunity of small businessmen, and for producing a volatile tenant class—or "landless proletariat." Most Americans still considered the family farm the foundation of a healthy economy and essential to the perpetuation of democratic institutions and civic virtue. A. P. Davis, who became second-in-command of the Reclamation Service after passage of the Newlands Act in 1902, warned that the West could no longer be used as a safety valve to relieve urban pressures, as he claimed it had in 1837 and 1857. In the fall of 1893, California's adjutant general had alerted the state militia to expect riots among the unemployed. "It will be noticed that the men against whom these warlike preparations were made were not idlers," commented Davis, "for [the adjutant general] says there would be no danger as long as there was work to be had. They were industrious American citizens, who could become dangerous only after work had been denied them, and starvation gnawed at their vitals. They were men who loved law and order, but perhaps loved an emaciated wife or hunger-pinched child more than enthroned power. . . . So severe a test has never before been applied to the institutions of any country."[5]

The ideologues of irrigation noted that 90 percent of the American population lived east of the Missouri River, so the future of American institutions depended on moving surplus people to surplus land. This was no easy task, given the cost of moving west, the trauma of leaving familiar surroundings, and the prevailing eastern view of the "Wild West" as a wilderness inhabited by cowboys, miners, prostitutes, savage Indians, and lonely stockmen, with only scattered oases of civilization. Nevertheless, irrigation promoters believed that economic discontent would overcome these barriers to settlement.

Irrigation's popularity derived from the fact that it offered something to everyone, east and west. It promised land for the landless, the redistribution of surplus workers, new markets for eastern manufacturers and railroads, the shoring up of cherished American values, and even a laboratory for the construction of model rural communities.[6] In William Ellsworth Smythe's *Conquest of Arid America*, irrigation became a coherent, optimistic philosophy that bordered on religion. Settlement of the arid West became providential, the culmination of American history.[7]

Smythe echoed Frederick Jackson Turner's claim that the West had passed through distinct stages of development. The hunter and trapper had given way to the cowboy and "rude miner," and irrigation would force the "land boomer" and "speculative farmer" to give way to cooperative communities based on intensive farming. While useful to earlier generations the rugged individualism which helped build the nation was an anachronism. Smythe hated monopoly but thought that the forms of "association and organization" suggested by large corporations and labor unions could be put to good use in the arid West. Irrigation encouraged a strong sense of community because few individuals could afford to pay for their own dams and canals, and a common water system demanded some form of community control. Moreover, the cohesiveness of irrigation communities would allow settlers to experiment with common banking, marketing, and manufacturing institutions. The high cost of land in irrigated communities worked against monopoly, and intensive agriculture allowed families to earn a good living on five- to twenty-acre farms. The denser population would escape the isolation and loneliness of rural families living on quarter sections in Kansas or Nebraska; it would enjoy a wide range of social amenities—from mail delivery to performing arts groups—not available to most farm families.[8]

Much as he respected his heritage, Smythe did not simply want to return to the New England villages of his ancestors; like most spokesmen for the irrigation movement, he looked forward as well as backward. He envisioned a decentralized economy and society characterized by self-sufficient communities relatively immune to economic cycles. Those communities would be carefully planned, and economic institutions—such as processing and marketing cooperatives—would be as democratic as the political institutions. Irrigation was the foundation, but it could not work the transformation alone. It would be assisted by cheap hydroelectric power produced by water stored for irrigation. The electricity would permit farmers to pump underground water to supplement scanty and often irregular surface water sources. It would also revive the cottage industries of an earlier age, curbing the migration of those who left the farm in search of city jobs. Electricity would bring the benefits of urban life to the country and permit people in the arid West to live in villages rather than in sprawling cities. "The great cities of the western valleys will not be cities in the old sense," Smythe maintained, "but a long series of beautiful villages, connected by lines of electric motors, which will move their products and people from place to place." Businessmen would commute from offices in "the city" to small irrigated farms. The telephone would also help soften the demarcation line between "rural" and "urban."[9]

The irrigation crusade lost much of its momentum in the middle 1890s, and the silver issue took center stage in the West. Landless easterners usually lacked the $1,000 to $2,000 required to move west and set up an irrigated farm. They also lacked the knowledge of how to cultivate desert land. So Smythe pinned his hopes on irrigation colonies devoted to the "small man." In the early months of 1895, he held mass meetings in Boston and Chicago, urging the formation of "colonial clubs" to establish irrigation communities based on Colorado's successful Greeley Colony.[10] In March, Smythe formed the Plymouth Society and found forty midwestern families—settlers drawn from "urban business and professional life"— willing to work 5,000 acres he had selected in Idaho's Payette Valley. The

New Plymouth Colony offered 20-acre homesteads for $400. Each resident was expected to buy stock in the town of "Home Acres" at the rate of $10 for each acre of land he owned. The land was served by a network of canals built by a bankrupt ditch company, and Smythe hoped the colony would demonstrate that "there is an industrial system in Arid America which enables every family to obtain a generous living, regardless of panics, drouth, and political misfortunes, and guarantees this living for an indefinite period." The village, inspired by the New England town and Mormon communities, was laid out in a circle with one-acre town lots adjoining the farms. Smythe hoped to build a hotel, streets, schools, a community hall, creamery, cannery, power plant, and other common industries. Unfortunately, the community plan won little support from the settlers. The colonists practiced diversified agriculture and formed cooperative ice and fruit curing plants, but most lived on their farms rather than in the village. The town survived, but not as the model community Smythe had envisaged.[11]

Like many other late nineteenth-century reformers, Smythe identified more closely with the urban middle class than with the poor. Most of his colonists came from Chicago and paid their own way. So the Plymouth Colony provided economic opportunity, but not for the unemployed or the social "misfit." Nevertheless, at the same time Smythe was drumming up support for his colony in Idaho, the model irrigation community idea won the support of General Frederick Booth-Tucker of the Salvation Army. In an address in New York City, Tucker claimed that the cost of hospitals, poor relief, prisons and other institutions of social control cost far more than providing homes in the arid West. "Why should you not spend money to . . . defend your Government, your society, against your expensive paupers and criminals?" he asked. The "pivot of true social reform" turned on the preservation or restoration of the family: "We must show the poor man how he can afford to get married . . . and become a home owner."[12]

By 1877, the Salvation Army had raised enough money to establish three colonies of 20-acre irrigated farms in California, Colorado, and Ohio. But private contributions never matched expectations. Even though benefactors offered the organization 70,000 acres free, it could not raise the $750,000 needed to place 2,000 urban poor on this land. By 1904, the Army had spent $300,000, but only 530 people resided within the colonies and they cultivated only 3,000 acres. Tucker bitterly noted that while $50 to $100 million was spent on poor relief in the United States each year, the nation had not followed the lead of British India where $125 million had been spent on irrigation works in the previous nine years, providing homes for 800,000 people on "once arid and abandoned lands."[13]

The irrigation movement of the 1890s won relatively little organized support in the East. But it did publicize the value of irrigation nationwide

and provided an intellectual justification for the national reclamation program adopted in the twentieth century. George Maxwell, the irrigation
crusade's chief spokesman from 1898 to 1902, sold federal reclamation to
eastern labor unions, boards of trade, chambers of commerce, trade associations, and civic federations, as well as to the public at large. He promised
jobs to those who built the canals, new markets to manufacturers, and
more freight traffic to the railroads—in short, something for everyone. The
preservation of American institutions by creating new homes served as a
powerful cement to hold the different groups which comprised the irrigation crusade together, just as it served as a convenient "cover" for economic self-interest.[14]

The homemaking ideal and the lingering fear of domestic turmoil left
over from the "terrible nineties" helped push the Newlands Act through
Congress in 1902. They also explain why many congressmen and senators
expected that federal reclamation would encompass far more than the construction of dams and canals. The arid West's value as a safety valve was
the most common theme in congressional speeches favoring the Newlands
Act. Newlands himself warned that "the evils of land monopoly . . . produced the great French revolution, . . . caused the revolt against church
monopoly in South America," and more recently led to the "outbreak of
the Filipinos against Spanish authority." Senator Thomas M. Patterson of
Colorado claimed that the addition of each new state was "better than a
standing army." Those who feared the rising tide of "new immigration"
touted the West as a place to isolate the contagion of dangerous ideas as
well as a classroom to teach the virtues of American institutions. Representative Wesley L. Jones of Washington declared that "the home is the [basic]
unit of our Government." Give the landless and unemployed easterner a
desert home and "the seed of anarchy and lawlessness will shrink and die,
while love for family and country will well up in the heart and grow
stronger and stronger from day to day." Federal reclamation also held out
the prospect of checking the migration to the cities from worn-out, unprofitable farms in the East and South. Representative Oscar Underwood of
Alabama noted that "the farm boys in the East want farms of their own. It
gives them a place where they can go and build homes without being
driven into the already crowded cities to seek employment."[15]

In 1902, federal reclamation won support in every part of the country, and the Newlands Act sailed through Congress. Those who supported the measure regarded Frederick Haynes Newell as the ideal man
to implement the new program. Unlike such promoters as Smythe and
Maxwell, he had long experience as a civil engineer, having served as
head of the U.S. Geological Survey's hydrographic branch since 1890. He
was also a man of broad interests—one of the founders and the first secretary of the National Geographic Society and an early president of the

American Forestry Association. Newell's active participation in the Smithsonian Institution helped him maintain close ties to Washington's scientific community.[16]

Edwin T. Layton has shown that in the early decades of the twentieth century, the leaders of professional engineering societies asked their followers to become more than agents and arbiters of technological change and material progress. They believed that human society followed laws as predictable as those which governed the universe or natural world, and that engineers, as "logical thinkers" trained to weigh evidence carefully and without bias, could solve a wide range of social and economic problems.[17] Newell called the new century the "age of the engineer," urged engineers to study "the human machine," and noted with satisfaction that "modern education" was devoted to uncovering the laws of society and "applying these to the material welfare of all mankind." "Among all the various occupations there is none more capable of leading in service to mankind and in realizing higher ideals than engineering," Newell declared in 1915. "The engineer should be a man of vision—a missionary of light and progress. His life is devoted to careful, impartial measurement and weighing of facts."[18]

With Newell at the helm, many champions of federal reclamation expected the new program to be a bold social experiment. For example, in 1906 Francis G. Newlands predicted:

Doubtless in the near future the Reclamation Service, in laying out the public lands under the various projects, will provide for well-planned towns, in which the owners of the adjoining farms will gather for social, educational, and religious purposes. Intensive cultivation, which irrigation facilitates, will so promote small holdings as to enable the residents of these towns to be within easy reach of their farms. Reservations will be made for schools, libraries, churches, and public squares. Water, sewerage, and electric-light systems will be planned and provided and thus farm life will lose much of its unattractiveness and isolation. Our frontier towns will not be, as heretofore, accidental growths, devoid of comfort and attractiveness. Collectivism will be employed with great economic advantage in comprehensive plans covering town development, sanitation, and architecture and ending in the individualized home near the outlying farm, associated with all the advantages of religious, educational, and social life.

In 1905 the chairman of the Rural Settlement Section of the National Irrigation Congress noted that the nation had an "opportunity to start rural life on a plane never before known . . . by bringing settlers together into communities with social advantages, proper sanitation conditions, and better educational facilities than have ever been known outside the cities."[19]

Initially, the Reclamation Service seemed eager to build model communities. On April 16, 1906, the Town-Site Act became law, allowing the Service to sell towns and cities the surplus power and water produced by its irrigation systems. The law required that publicly owned utilities receive preference. Newell believed that Congress intended "to encourage the concentration of irrigators . . . in numerous small villages," and that the law would enable settlers "to enjoy material and social advantages incident to village residence, combined with [the] health and freedom of rural life." Soon thereafter, the Reclamation Service adopted a model town plan which was highly innovative for its time. Midwestern communities were depressingly similar, with standard-sized lots, square blocks, and streets running north to south and east to west. A park and business district were usually at the center of town. However, the Reclamation Service's plan had eight broad avenues converging at the center of town; four ran diagonally and four in the traditional fashion, so the streets radiated out from the center like spokes from the hub of a wheel. Perhaps to emphasize the town's new priorities, a school rather than business district dominated the community. Another major difference from the traditional midwestern town was that lots varied in size from 36 feet to 140 feet in the business district just east of the school to 325 feet by 610 feet on the edge of town. The larger lots were designed to permit those who worked at full-time jobs in town to own small garden farms large enough to feed their family and return some revenue. The entire town was a compact one-half-mile square.[20]

Unfortunately, the Town-Site Act did not permit the Reclamation Service to use proceeds from sales of town lots to pay for civic improvements, and several subsequent efforts to turn the law in that direction failed. For example, on March 13, 1912, a South Dakota congressman proposed legislation to permit the service to use 50 percent of town-lot revenue for the "construction of school houses, water and sewer systems and other municipal improvements," such as planting trees as windbreaks. However, the legislation made no provision for transferring control over completed utility systems from the government to the community, and because the repayment of project construction costs by farmers had lagged, Congress insisted that the money from lot sales be used to replenish the revolving fund, along with revenue from power sales.[21]

Railroads and land companies often laid out towns with paved streets and other improvements, so the Reclamation Service was at a competitive disadvantage when it attempted to lure settlers onto its irrigation projects. Aside from Congress's reluctance to provide money to build towns, the service faced many other obstacles to community planning. Most government projects were a mixture of public and private land already served by small towns, and while the service routinely withdrew from entry all public land within a potential project, land speculators and bona fide settlers often jumped the gun and grabbed the best town sites. Moreover, the farmers themselves tended to be more imitative than innovative. C. J. Blanchard, chief statistician for the service, noted: "There is need also on each of these projects for an expert in landscape gardening and farm building architecture. It is most discouraging to see so many of our farmers from the middle West and far East erecting in the desert the same old fashioned, unsanitary, and inconvenient farm houses and out buildings." The appreciation of land values would have offset the cost of civic improvements, but most farmers were reluctant to add to their debts.[22]

In 1912, Frank A. Waugh, a prominent member of the American Civic Association and professor of landscape gardening at Massachusetts Agricultural College, complained to Blanchard that Reclamation Service officials had no knowledge of the model rural towns being designed in England and Germany. The government towns, Waugh declared, were "merely repeating the thoroughly bad types of planning which heretofore prevailed in the prairie states." When Secretary of the Interior Walter Fisher pleaded that his department had no money to hire community planners, Horace McFarland, president of the American Civic Association, offered the services of Waugh and four other members of the federation "as a service through the American Civic Association to the American people." The panel made a formal report to the Service, but its recommendations were ignored. At the time, most of the original projects had already opened and only one town—Bard on the Yuma Project in Arizona—was being laid out. By 1913 or 1914, interest in community planning was all but gone.[23]

Here was a lost opportunity. That the U.S. Reclamation Service never put its community plan into use, that it never went beyond building dams and canals, was as much due to the personality and philosophy of Frederick Haynes Newell as to the barriers to community building mentioned above. In 1910, Newell proudly reported that the great object of the Reclamation Act was "being reached" and that 10,000 families had been settled on government projects and adjoining towns (at the staggering cost of $60 million). He took pride in reclaiming wasted lives. In 1912 he told a group of federal irrigation project managers:

It is the object of this work to take the man who is working on the streets, who has his family in a boarding house, who has no interest whatever in public affairs, and put him on a 40 acre or 20 acre irrigated farm unit and tell him "That is yours; if you live on it and cultivate the soil and pay for the water." Such a man is thereby transformed politically and socially from a man, almost a danger to the community, to a citizen of the type that forms the foundations of strong, intelligent democracy. That is the excuse for Uncle Sam putting money into reclamation.

In 1918, the American Geographical Society awarded Newell its Cullum Gold Medal. One side of the medallion bore the inscription: "He carried water from a mountain wilderness to turn the waste places of the desert into homes for freedom."[24]

The award was ironic. Newell worried more about creating successful farms than about shoring up the foundations of the republic—and the two objectives often clashed. Federal reclamation did not follow a coherent philosophy. Congress never specified where, and from what social classes, the service should "recruit" its settlers, nor did it give Newell and his lieutenants authority to screen them. The question of whether the government should direct its effort at the urban proletariat, small businessmen "crushed" by gigantic corporations, or poor eastern, southern, and midwestern farmers, was left unresolved. Reclamation had been sold to the nation as a way to provide homes and defuse urban tensions, but Congress did not provide money to help the homeless move west, nor did it provide teachers to instruct government settlers in the art of irrigation agriculture. The question of how much the government should intervene in the lives of project residents was vital. Should the government simply provide the means to allow settlers to achieve economic independence, or should it work to promote and inculcate values and ideals? Should it allow farmers to build their own communities, repeating the mistakes of the past, or should the farmers be considered part of a social experiment?

Newell and other Reclamation Service officials were torn between restoring or preserving traditional values and promoting such twentieth-century values as cooperation, planning, and efficiency. They were caught between a deep respect for an older America and the faith that engineers could produce an entirely new social order. Time and again, Newell bowed to the ethics of personal responsibility, individualism, and independence in his administration of the federal reclamation program; he despised government paternalism. In a 1913 letter to his close friend, Gifford Pinchot, he commented on a trip to Canada:

I have just made a visit to Canada and have gone over the large irrigation systems in Southern Alberta where the C.P.R. [Canadian Pacific Railroad] Co. and Government have united in doing everything possible for the irrigator. The result has been a great development of the country in one sense, accompanied by more or less demoralization of the farmers as they have come to expect everything done for them. . . . I am fully in accord with the belief that any interference by the Government or by large corporations, like the C.P.R., will be mischievous in stagnating the efforts of the farmers. This is true also of our Reclamation Service Projects. On the whole, we have done too much in taking the initiative and in trying to expedite development.[25]

Nineteenth-century land and water companies built main canals but left the construction of distribution and drainage ditches to the farmers themselves. Newell thought that most twentieth-century farmers were lazy compared to their nineteenth-century counterparts. "It was found that the construction of the reservoirs and main-line canals [by the U.S. government] was not followed by the expected cooperation on the part of the settlers," he wrote in 1912, "and that to enable the lands to be cultivated it would be necessary to provide a complete system by which the water is taken to the vicinity of each farm." Not only that, but farmers expected the Reclamation Service to build bridges, roads, and other improvements. In 1916, the year after Newell was fired as director of the Reclamation Service, he described most irrigation farmers as "inexperienced" or "adventurers" who expected "easier things." These were men who had "never made a success elsewhere; [they] attribute their failure to make good under the new conditions not to their own inability, but largely to the faults of the country or system." As complaints about management of the irrigation projects—from both farmers and critics in Congress—poured into Washington in the decade from 1905 to 1915, Newell became more and more defensive. He resisted the requests of government farmers to extend their repayment schedule from ten to twenty years or more and opposed low-interest loans and all other forms of federal aid.[26]

Newell's reluctance to provide more assistance to the desert homemakers won censure from William Smythe, George Maxwell, and Elwood Mead, the most prominent leaders of the reclamation movement in 1902. Mead, as head of the Office of Irrigation Investigations in the U.S. Department of Agriculture, had been Newell's chief rival for leadership of the federal reclamation program. In 1907 he became director of the Australian province of Victoria's State Rivers and Water Supply Commission. Victoria gave farmers fifty years to repay the cost of government irrigation works, rather than the ten years provided for repayment in the United States. The Victorian government also built homes for settlers and allowed them fifteen years to repay that cost; loaned money for stock and farm equipment at 5 percent interest; graded and seeded ten acres on each homestead; and provided expert farming advice free. Mead proclaimed that the United States was "far behind the England of Lloyd George or the Australia of Andrew Fisher in social and industrial laws."[27]

William Smythe shared Mead's conclusion that federal reclamation had lost sight of the people it had been created to serve. He called for "scientific colonization," pointing to New Zealand as a model. New Zealand's government had purchased large estates and leased small plots to farmers for 999 years to prevent a recurrence of land monopoly. The state provided roads, bridges, and finished villages as well as irrigation works. Each year, the settlers repaid 5 percent of the cost of their land and improvements. In 1905, Newell's policies prompted Smythe to give an address before the National Irrigation Congress entitled "The Unfinished Task." Smythe asked: "What are we doing for that class of homeseekers—always a large element in every American movement of population—who are without sufficient means to come here [move West], get a foothold in the reclaimed desert, and await the slow return? Nothing—worse than nothing." Like Mead, he urged the government to help farmers get started and endure the wait before their farms could turn a profit. In 1909, on 550 acres south of San Diego, he launched a "Little Landers" scheme which he hoped would ultimately "reclaim the social and economic wastes of American city and town" by providing urban workers with one-acre homesteads on the fringes of major American cities. In effect, the Little Landers returned to the land without giving up the city. For $300, each colonist received a town lot, farm, and a share in utility and marketing cooperatives. Unfortunately, most of the thirty families settled at San Ysidro during the first year consisted of middle-aged or elderly couples who could not support themselves on their tiny truck farms. By 1916, Smythe had established four additional colonies adjoining other California cities, but none proved successful. As in the New Plymouth colony, most settlers showed little enthusiasm for model irrigation communities.[28]

George Maxwell retained the fear of social upheaval which helped make reclamation a national issue in 1901 and 1902, and, like Smythe, joined the "back to the land" movement. He described the slums and tenements of eastern cities as "social dynamite, certain to explode sooner or later." Most residents of New York's East Side, he noted, were socialists or anarchists who carried bitter class hatreds from Poland, Hungary, Italy, and other European countries. Maxwell thought that late-nineteenth-century back-to-the-land movements had failed because they drew too sharp a line between city and country. By 1904, he settled on the "homecroft" as a solution to urban overcrowding and unemployment. He estimated that urban workers used 43 percent of their wages for food and another 18 percent for rent. Families with one-acre homes on the outskirts of large cities could produce their own food and sharply reduce their cost of living. They could live on lower wages, enjoy the benefits of home ownership, and improve their health. "You are developing racehorses and fat cattle and fine hogs and all kinds of domestic animals," Maxwell observed to a group of manufacturers, "and how much attention are you giving to improving the human machine in your factories in health, strength and physique?" Industrialists would benefit from homecrofts because they could pay workers less and sell their goods cheaper, especially in foreign markets.[29]

Always the promoter, Maxwell used a new magazine, *Maxwell's Talisman*, to publicize the homecroft idea. Early issues prominently displayed Maxwell's creed: "We believe that the patriotic Slogan of the whole People of this Nation should be 'Every Child in a Garden—Every Mother in a Homecroft—and Individual Industrial Independence for Every Worker in a Home of his Own on the Land,' and that until he owns such a Home, the concentrated purpose and chief inspiration to labor in the life of every wage worker should be his determination to 'Get an Acre and Live on it.'" Maxwell's immediate objectives included adding gardening to the public school curriculum, creating homecroft schools, promoting the New Zealand system of land settlement, exempting all improvements on homecrofts from taxation, and increasing the land available for homes in the East through a federal program to prevent floods and reclaim swampland. He continued to support federal arid land reclamation, encouraging Congress to dip into the general treasury to pay for projects (subject to repayment by settlers)—but not with the enthusiasm of 1902 or 1903.[30]

The homecroft idea built on the principle that irrigation could be used with as much profit in humid as in arid regions; without it, 1-acre homesteads would have been infeasible.[31] Maxwell established his first homecroft in Watertown, Massachusetts, where he bought 50 acres of land and sold it on time for little more than what factory workers paid in rent. Prominent Watertown residents contributed land for children's garden plots; classes in "scientific gardening" met twice a week after school, on Saturday mornings, and continuously during the summer vacation. Maxwell also established a homecroft colony in Arizona's Salt River Valley, where in 1902 he had pushed for the construction of one of the first federal reclamation projects. There he bought 160 acres, leveled it, planted palm and olive trees, constructed a network of irrigation ditches, and dug underground wells so that settlers would never run short of water. He divided the land into 5-acre lots and sold only to those experienced at truck gardening and poultry raising, expecting this colony to be "a demonstration and working model for the subdivision of land now held in large tracts near every town or village into small Garden Homes." In 1909, he promised to settle 10,000 families in the Salt River Valley within five years by persuading prominent residents of Mesa, Arizona, to take stock in his Homecroft Company— presumably on the expectation of rising real estate prices.[32]

Money was Maxwell's biggest problem. Consequently, in late 1906 he proposed a national homecroft bill to create a government postal savings bank. The bank would issue government bonds, called "Homecroft Certificates," using the savings as collateral. The bill provided for a Home-croft Bureau and empowered the secretary of the interior to buy large tracts of land on the outskirts of American cities. The bureau would be responsible for clearing, fencing, and leveling the land in preparation for irrigation and for planting trees, building streets and sewers, and stringing power lines. Settlers would have twenty years to repay the cost of their homes at 4 percent interest. Maxwell's continuing interest in the Progressive conservation movement was clear in that the bill required that 10 percent of the bond issue be used to purchase land for inclusion in national forests and for replanting cutover land. Apparently, he also expected some of the money to be used for swamp and arid land reclamation. Passage of the bill, he promised, would produce a "Trinity of National Service—the Forestry Service, the Reclamation Service, and the Homecroft Service." By 1907, however, Maxwell was a political outsider, no longer a prominent member of the Progressive conservation "club." His scheme won no support in Congress.[33]

As Paul Conkin and others have shown, the back-to-the-land crusade manifested itself in many different ways during the Progressive Era, ranging from the city gardens movement to the soldier resettlement plans introduced during and after World War I to Elwood Mead's model farm program in California during the 1920s.[34] Historians have largely neglected the part irrigation played in that crusade. The motives of those who supported arid land reclamation were diverse. Some reacted to the urbanization, institutional centralization, impersonality, and class conflict attendant on the rise of industrial America by trying to re-create an America of small villages in the desert. Others saw reclamation as a tool to create an entirely new cooperative society and hoped irrigation would aid in community planning. Still others sought relief from a wide range of immediate social and economic problems.

Arid land reclamation encouraged planned social development and in some ways anticipated such New Deal programs as the Tennessee Valley Authority and Resettlement Administration. It rested on the assumption that irrigation could help redistribute the nation's "surplus" population as well as reform—or at least revive—its basic values and institutions. Had overcrowded cities been the only problem, reformers could have pushed the reclamation of marsh, swamp, or logged-over land in the South. Instead, they pointed to a sectional imbalance and demanded the opening of fresh lands in the West. Federal reclamation did little to promote this demographic revolution, or even to fortify American institutions and values. The Bureau of Reclamation's latest historian has declared that "the 1902 Reclamation Act was a significant break with nineteenth-century laissez-faire land policies that stressed individualism and self-sufficiency."[35] Yet the bureau provided little aid to settlers and spent little time planning the communities in which they would live. The Newlands Act initially promised government farmers a ten-year interest-free loan against the cost of their irrigation works, but the farmers themselves had to pay all the additional costs of creating farms. The promise of federal reclamation was never fulfilled, and the government's irrigation projects were settled in the same chaotic, unsupervised fashion as private irrigation projects in the nineteenth century. Through no fault of the Reclamation Bureau, from 1910 to 1930 urban growth consistently surpassed rural growth. For example, from 1910 to 1920, the nation's farms increased by only 1.4 percent in number. But the nation could take no pride in the fact that by 1927 more than one-third of all farmers on government irrigation projects were tenants.[36]

By the 1930s, the dream of using irrigation as a tool of social reform had all but disappeared. In the 1920s, depressed farm prices made rural life less attractive, and by the end of that decade most Americans had accepted, if only grudgingly, the dominance of the city in American life. Ironically, when Americans moved West—especially during and after World War II—they usually settled in the region's burgeoning cities such as Los Angeles, San Francisco, Portland, or Seattle. The future of irrigation would be as the ally of large-scale, corporate agriculture rather than the family farm. Far from being a revolutionary tool for social change, irrigation became, and remained, the servant of "agribusiness" and the status quo.

AFTERWORD

Political historians of the Progressive and New Deal eras have emphasized the differences between the two periods more than the similarities and continuities. If, as historian James L. Penick, Jr., has claimed, the progressives were "moving toward the concept of a professional governing class" and were devoted to "the bourgeois ideal of disinterested bureaucracy, with its commitment to a sharp division between the objective and the subjective, the public and the private, the personal and the impersonal," once in power progressive conservationists behaved much like nineteenth-century politicians. The most important characteristic of conservation in the Progressive Era was not the emergence of bureaucracy or a professional civil service. It was the attempt by men like Frederick H. Newell and Gifford Pinchot to enlist "the public," or at least middle-class professionals, in their causes. Each agency staked its future on developing elaborate ties to constituencies outside government. Science was employed as a political weapon—to win the largest constituency.[1] Forest Service publications increased from three in 1901 to sixty-one in 1907, and they were more concerned with promoting bureau policies than with teaching the public about trees, water, and wildlife. The Forest Service's mailing list of over 800,000 civic and commercial organizations, newspaper editors, and politicians allowed it to apply pressure to congressional committees in the interest of particular pieces of legislation.[2]

The emergence of "iron triangles" was as notable a structural change in government as "bureaucratization" and the professionalization of forestry and hydrology.[3] The success of the new agencies came not because they were organized differently from nineteenth-century bureaus or because they practiced a new style of politics but because they were run by better salesmen—salesmen who knew how to target particular urban "markets." Penick has remarked that "Pinchot's power rested on the methods of the modern promoter who understood how to take advantage of the greater concentration of population and the advanced techniques of mass communication, rather than on the calculated restraint of the scientist in his laboratory."[4]

Pinchot and Newell's attempts to focus public opinion on conservation reflected the weakness, not the strength, of bureaucracy. The constraints on the emergence of a "bureaucratic state" have been remarkably effective and remarkably persistent.[5] True, the nation was bound together in 1940 as it had not been in 1900, and the power of localistic political parties and the courts had weakened. So had the states' rights arguments of westerners and southerners. One great barrier to federal conservation in the Progressive Era was the western bloc in the U.S. Senate that resisted, with considerable success, the expansion of federal authority over natural resources. In the early 1930s, states' rights all but disappeared, in part because westerners desperately needed federal aid but in part because the New Deal gave western states far greater influence over conservation policies than they had enjoyed in the Progressive Era.[6] Although they accepted professionalization and the need for administrative efficiency, many friends of the New Deal were far from convinced that the nation needed a bureaucratic state. The United States lacked a national university to teach potential civil servants about government and the law as well as turn them into experts in particular fields. It also lacked a Congress, judges, and political parties willing to tolerate independent bureaucracies. Although the New Deal created many new institutions, resistance to the growth of bureaucracy came from many quarters. As Arthur Schlesinger has observed, from the beginning of the New Deal those social planners "who thought in terms of an organic economy and managed society" were challenged by the "neo-Brandeisians, who thought in terms of the decentralization of decision and the revitalization of choice."[7]

Ellis Hawley has argued that the the New Deal did little to alter the nature of the American state because there were powerful alternatives to bureaucratization. These included the view that the New Deal governmental apparatus was temporary, designed to meet the needs of the economic crisis but not to persist beyond that crisis; the tarnished, but not altogether discredited, vision of a "business commonwealth"; a "populist commonwealth" that would return power to local communities and interest groups; and a "broker state" that would encourage Congress rather than government bureaucrats to mediate and choose between deserving private interest groups. "What the New Deal really had at hand, then," Hawley concludes, "was not only a set of prescriptions for giving America an administrative state, but also formulations for using government in ways that were supposed to allow us to continue without such a state. And in practice, much of the New Deal state grew out of efforts to apply these formulas. . . . The state that emerged had a 'hollow core' where the state managers were supposed to be." Hawley does not discuss conservation legislation, but his analysis reminds us that the power and size of the central government can grow even in a society hostile to bureaucracy and bureaucratic ideals. Much New Deal conservation legislation was consciously antibureaucratic.[8]

Conservation policies changed dramatically from the Progressive Era to the New Deal. Although the ideal of the family farm and the importance of improving inland waterways faded, other policies that dated to the opening decades of the twentieth century, such as multiple-use water planning and sustained yield forestry, came into their own in the 1930s, and new policies such as soil conservation and outdoor recreation became a part of conservation for the first time. By 1940, the public domain was gone, and the West was on the verge of an economic "takeoff" fueled by cheap water and power from government dams. Moreover, a revolution was under way because a handful of government officials had come to view parks and wilderness areas as ecosystems rather than isolated natural curiosities and examples of spectacular scenery. Nature was developing a character independent of human beings and within a few decades would, according to many environmentalists, enjoy rights of its own. And because many conservation policies of the 1930s were thinly veiled relief measures, far more Americans participated in conservation during that decade than in any previous era; the charge that conservation was "elitist" was heard less and less often.

In the late nineteenth century, public policy in the United States was limited by the American obsession with economic growth, economic liberty, limited government, and localism. The absence of a monarchical class, a hereditary aristocracy, an established church, and a military caste or elite made bureaucratization all but impossible. So did the nation's multiplicity of ethnic and religious groups and the deep sectional differences that separated East, South, and West. At all levels American government was defined by the absence of restraint rather than an ability to plan or to lead. Many Americans developed a healthy fear of both private and public power. But since the private corporation was chartered by government, venal and irresponsible public officials could do even more economic damage than venal and irresponsible businessmen. In any case, nineteenth-century public policy did a good job of privatizing control over natural resources but a poor job of defining common interests in those resources.

The twentieth century gave birth to the "regulatory state." National forests and parks were created, administrative control over water was established, and the ethic of "wise use" was instituted. The emergence of a concept of "common," inalienable public land was no small accomplishment. But many conservation policies reflected a changing economy more than changes in the structure of government or in basic American values. The federal and state governments became more active as economic horizons seemed to shrink, but there is no clear break in public policy between the mid-nineteenth and early twentieth centuries. Looked at closely, there is remarkable continuity.

In many cases—though certainly not all—large corporations found the reservation policy good for business because it restricted access by small operators in the name of conservation. This was particularly true in grazing, timber, and water policies. Nor did those who managed the national conservation program favor a substantial alteration in the status quo. Federal reclamation failed in large part because Frederick Haynes Newell, the first director of the Reclamation Service, was wedded to a nineteenth-century view of government and agriculture. He deeply feared government "paternalism." In effect, he saw federal reclamation as a way to equalize conditions between the Far West and Midwest: the government should provide the missing water but no more. Gifford Pinchot took a bolder view of state power, but his bureau could succeed only if it built up a constituency of resource users and did not simply rely on middle-class reformers. It was far from revolutionary.

It is high time that historians take a fresh look at public policy and natural resources in the nineteenth and twentieth centuries. We are much in need of new categories to replace such timeworn labels as "progressive," "reformer," "aesthetic conservationist," "utilitarian conservationist," and even "conservationist." These terms do not capture the complexity of natural resource policies and politics. Too many environmental historians have looked at the past as a morality play in which the champions of the "public good" battled against the "plunderers of nature." On reexamination, we should not be surprised or dismayed to find that many heroes of the past were far more complicated, and interesting, than they wanted us to believe.

NOTES

PART ONE: WATER LAW

1. On the revolution in water law in the East, see Theodore Steinberg, *Nature Incorporated: Industrialization and the Waters of New England* (New York, 1991), and Morton Horwitz, *The Transformation of American Law, 1780–1860* (Cambridge, Mass., 1977), 31, 34, 253–54.

2. See, for example, Charles F. Wilkinson, *Crossing the Next Meridian: Land, Water, and the Future of the West* (Washington, D.C., 1992), 260–71, and Wilkinson, *The Eagle Bird: Mapping a New West* (New York, 1992), 53–54.

3. Walter Prescott Webb, *The Great Plains* (Boston, 1931); C. S. Kinney, *A Treatise on the Law of Irrigation and Water Rights and the Arid Region Doctrine of Appropriation of Waters*, 4 vols. (San Francisco, 1912).

4. Legal scholars continue to argue that miners were unanimous in their support of prior appropriation from the beginning, that it was adopted wholesale. As the eminent legal scholar Charles F. Wilkinson says, "The mining camps had no use for a riparian law" (see *The Eagle Bird*, 46).

5. Donald J. Pisani, *To Reclaim a Divided West: Water, Law, and Public Policy, 1848–1902* (Albuquerque, 1992), 11–32.

6. Donald J. Pisani, *From the Family Farm to Agribusiness: The Irrigation Crusade in California and the West, 1850–1931* (Berkeley, 1984), 102–28, 154–90.

7. Ibid., 191–282.

8. As quoted in ibid., 252.

9. Pisani, *To Reclaim a Divided West*, 52–64.

10. Donald Worster, *Rivers of Empire: Water, Aridity, and the Growth of the American West* (New York, 1985), 332–33.

11. Pisani, *To Reclaim a Divided West*, 127–68.

CHAPTER 1. ENTERPRISE AND EQUITY

1. Walter Prescott Webb, *The Great Plains* (Boston, 1931), 431–52.

2. Several recent books deserve particular mention. Robert G. Dunbar's concise, lucid volume *Forging New Rights in Western Waters* (Lincoln, 1983), is the only survey of western water law and has the great virtue of discussing twentieth- as well as nineteenth-century laws, and underground as well as surface water. It is a well-researched synthesis based on decades of work in western water law. (For a summary statement see Dunbar's "The Adaptability of Water Law to the Aridity of the West," *Journal of the West* 24 [January 1985]: 57–65.) Five chapters in my *From the Family Farm to Agribusiness: The Irrigation Crusade in California and the West,*

1850–1931 (Berkeley, 1984), 30 –53 and 129 –282, treat the evolution of court and legislative water law in nineteenth-century California. Although Michael C. Meyer's *Water in the Hispanic Southwest: A Social and Legal History, 1550 –1850* (Tucson, 1984) does not discuss law in the American Southwest either before or after 1850, its thorough analysis of the nature of Spanish water law makes it required reading. Also see John D. W. Guice, *The Rocky Mountain Bench: The Territorial Supreme Courts of Colorado, Montana, and Wyoming, 1861–1890* (New Haven, 1972); Gordon Morris Bakken, *The Development of Law on the Rocky Mountain Frontier: Civil Law and Society, 1850 –1912* (Westport, Conn., 1983); Arthur Maass and Raymond L. Anderson, . . . *and the Desert Shall Rejoice: Conflict, Growth, and Justice in Arid Environments* (Cambridge, Mass., 1978), 224–31; Norris Hundley, Jr., *Water and the West: The Colorado River Compact and the Politics of Water in the American West* (Berkeley, 1975), 66 –73; Gordon R. Miller, "Shaping California Water Law, 1781 –1928," *Southern California Quarterly* 55 (Spring 1973): 9– 42; Douglas R. Littlefield, "Water Rights During the California Gold Rush: Conflicts over Economic Points of View," *Western Historical Quarterly* 14 (October 1983): 415–34; and M. Catherine Miller, "Riparian Rights and the Control of Water in California, 1879 –1928: The Relationship Between an Agricultural Enterprise and Legal Change," *Agricultural History* 59 (January 1985): 1–24.

3. In the arid West prior appropriation conferred on the first claimant to a stream an exclusive right to use water. The water could be used on any land, any distance from the water source. The amount was unlimited, save for the legal requirement that it be put to a "beneficial use." The first user enjoyed the only absolute grant. All other rights depended on the extent and priority of previous claims. In most states appropriative water rights were and are regarded as a species of property that can be sold in whole or in part.

4. Riparian rights were part of the title to land adjoining a stream. They did not exist independent of the land, nor were they absolute. In these two ways they differed markedly from appropriative rights. In theory, this system only served those whose land bordered a stream. A riparian user could divert water for any useful purpose, and the amount could vary from day to day, month to month, or year to year. Lack of use had no effect on the right. Except for the water they used for domestic needs and stock, riparian claimants could not substantially reduce the flow of a stream if downstream neighbors objected. In other words, riparian rights were "correlative," definable only as they related to other riparian claims.

5. James Willard Hurst, *Law and Markets in United States History: Different Modes of Bargaining Among Interests* (Madison, 1982); *The Growth of American Law: The Law Makers* (Boston, 1950), 4; *Law and Economic Growth: The Legal History of the Lumber Industry in Wisconsin, 1836 –1915* (Cambridge, Mass., 1964), 171–72; *Law and Social Order in the United States* (Ithaca, 1977), 23, 106; "The Release of Energy," in Lawrence M. Friedman and Harry N. Scheiber, eds., *American Law and the Constitutional Order: Historical Perspectives* (Cambridge, Mass., 1978), 109–20, esp. 111, 112, and 114. See also Harry N. Scheiber, "At the Borderland of Law and Economic History: The Contributions of Willard Hurst," *American Historical Review* 75 (February 1970): 744–56; David H. Flaherty, "An Approach to Legal History: Willard Hurst as Legal Historian," *American Journal of Legal History* 14 (July 1970): 222 –34; Earl Finbar Murphy, "The Jurisprudence of Legal History: Willard Hurst as a Legal Historian," *New York University Law Review* 39 (November 1964): 900 –943; Robert W.

Gordon, "J. Willard Hurst and the Common Law Tradition in American Legal Historiography," *Law and Society Review* 10 (Fall 1975): 9–56; and Stephen Diamond, "Legal Realism and Historical Method: J. Willard Hurst and American Legal History," *Michigan Law Review* 77 (January–March 1979): 784–94.

6. Much of Harry Scheiber's excellent work has focused on eminent-domain law. As a sample, see his "Property Law, Expropriation, and Resource Allocation by Government, 1789–1910," in Friedman and Scheiber, *American Law and the Constitutional Order*, 132–41; "The Road to Munn: Eminent Domain and the Concept of Public Purpose in the State Courts," *Perspectives in American History* 5 (1971): 329–402; "Federalism and the American Economic Order, 1789–1910," *Law and Society Review* 10 (Fall 1975): 57–118; and "Public Rights and the Rule of Law in American Legal History," *California Law Review* 72 (March 1984): 217–51.

7. Morton J. Horwitz, *The Transformation of American Law, 1780–1860* (Cambridge, Mass., 1977), 34.

8. Ibid., 253–54. Also see Horwitz's "The Transformation in the Conception of Property in American Law," in Friedman and Scheiber, *American Law and the Constitutional Order*, 148, and his "The Emergence of an Instrumental Conception of American Law, 1780–1820," in *Perspectives in American History* 5 (1971): 287–326.

9. Justice Shaw's quote is as printed in Horwitz, *The Transformation of American Law*, 41. Horwitz discusses the emergence of prior appropriation on pp. 34–42. He states that "[b]y mid-century it had outlived its usefulness and . . . was discarded" (p. 42), though he does not explain why it died out. Although not as concerned with changes in water rights, readers should also see William E. Nelson, *Americanization of the Common Law: The Impact of Legal Change on Massachusetts Society, 1760–1830* (Cambridge, Mass., 1975); Leonard W. Levy, *The Law of the Commonwealth and Chief Justice Shaw* (Cambridge, Mass., 1957); and G. Edward White, *The American Judicial Tradition: Profiles of Leading American Judges* (New York, 1976), 42–43, 56, and 61. White notes that not all judges were as willing to use the power of the state to stimulate economic activity as Shaw and the Massachusetts court. Jurists such as Joseph Story and James Kent took a much more traditional view of the sanctity of private property.

10. Webb, *The Great Plains*, 432; Miller, "Shaping California Water Law, 1781–1928," 23, 34; Dunbar, "The Adaptability of Water Law to the Aridity of the West," 57. Harry Scheiber and Charles W. McCurdy have observed, in "Eminent-Domain Law and Western Agriculture, 1849–1900," *Agricultural History* 49 (January 1975): 113, that this narrow view has not been restricted to water law. "What both the romantic and pessimistic versions of early Far Western legal development have in common," the two men wrote, "is their emphasis on the alleged novelty and innovativeness that marked the early history of resource laws."

11. *Bear River and Auburn Water and Mining Co. v. New York Mining Co.*, 8 Cal. 327, 332 (1857); *Yunker v. Nichols*, 1 Colo. 551 (1872); *Boquillas Land & Cattle Co. v. Curtis*, 11 Ariz. 128, 140 (1907).

12. *Crandall v. Woods*, 8 Cal. 136 (1857); *Bear River and Auburn Water and Mining Co. v. New York Mining Co.*, 8 Cal. 327, 333 (1857).

13. Dunbar, "The Adaptability of Water Law to the Aridity of the West," 57; Gordon Morris Bakken, "The Influence of the West on the Development of Law," *Journal of the West* 24 (January 1985): 67. Contemporary scholars have inherited this

view of the rigidity of the common law from C. S. Kinney, the dean of western water lawyers, via Webb. They have absorbed without question the opinions and judgments of early twentieth-century scholars of water law, including Samuel Wiel, L. Ward Bannister, and, particularly, C. S. Kinney. See Clesson S. Kinney, *A Treatise on the Law of Irrigation and Water Rights and the Arid Region Doctrine of Appropriation of Waters*, 4 vols. (San Francisco, 1912), 1:871, 1011, and 1015, and Webb, *The Great Plains*, 448.

14. For example, see *Yunker v. Nichols*, 1 Colo. 551, 553 (1872); *Coffin v. Left Hand Ditch Company*, 6 Colo. 443, 446 (1882); *Drake v. Earhart*, 2 Ida. 750, 753 (1890); and *Stowell v. Johnson*, 7 Utah 215 (1891). Also see *Reno Smelting Works v. Stevenson*, 20 Nev. 269, 281–82 (1899); *Farm Investment Co. v. Carpenter*, 9 Wyo. 110, 136 (1900); and Dunbar, *Forging New Rights in Western Waters*, 78–82.

15. *Fitzgerald v. Urton*, 5 Cal. 308, 309 (1855); *Bear River and Auburn Water and Mining Co. v. New York Mining Co.*, 8 Cal. 327, 334 (1857).

16. Charles N. McCurdy, "Stephen J. Field and Public Land Law Development in California, 1850–1866: A Case Study of Judicial Resource Allocation in Nineteenth Century America," *Law and Society Review* 10 (Fall 1975): 256.

17. *Boggs v. Merced Mining Co.*, 14 Cal. 279, 377 (1859); *Lux v. Haggin*, 69 Cal. 255, 4 Pac. Rep. 919, 923 (1884); *Thorp v. Freed*, 1 Mont. 651, 669 (1872). Also see *Irwin v. Phillips*, 5 Cal. 140 (1855); *Moore v. Smaw*, 17 Cal. 199 (1861); and *Drake v. Earhart*, 2 Ida. 750, 764 (1890).

18. *U.S. Statutes at Large*, 14:253; 16:218; 19:377. For a discussion of the motives behind the 1866 law see Justice Stephen J. Field's reasoning in *Basey v. Gallagher*, U.S. 670, at 683–84 (1874).

19. Katharine Coman, "Some Unsettled Problems of Irrigation," *American Economic Review* 1 (March 1911): 4; Webb, *The Great Plains*, 448; Carey McWilliams, *Factories in the Field: The Story of Migratory Farm Labor in California* (Santa Barbara, 1971); Wallace Stegner, *Beyond the Hundredth Meridian: John Wesley Powell and the Second Opening of the West* (Boston, 1953), 226.

20. John Wesley Powell, "Report on the Lands of the Arid Region of the United States, with a More Detailed Account of the Lands of Utah," 45th Cong., 2d sess., House Executive Documents, no. 73, serial 1805 (Washington, D.C., 1878), 41. The quote is from Howard R. Lamar, *Dakota Territory, 1861–1889: A Study of Frontier Politics* (New Haven, 1956), 279. Also see Lewis F. Crawford, *History of North Dakota* (Chicago, 1931), 327, 342. For additional criticism of prior appropriation and water monopoly by scientists and federal officials see George Perkins Marsh, "Irrigation: Its Evils, the Remedies, and the Compensations," 43rd Cong., 1st sess., Senate Miscellaneous Document, no. 55, serial 1854 (Washington, D.C., 1874), 16–19; the testimony of Powell's chief lieutenant on the Irrigation Survey, C. E. Dutton, in "Ceding the Arid Lands to the States and Territories," 51st Cong., 2d sess., House of Representatives, no. 3767, serial 2888 (Washington, D.C., 1891), 169, 170, 185, 186; Elwood Mead, head of the Office of Irrigation Investigations in the U.S. Department of Agriculture, in his *Irrigation Institutions: A Discussion of the Economic and Legal Questions Created by Growth of Irrigated Agriculture in the West* (New York, 1903), 207; and University of Wisconsin economist and adviser to the Department of Agriculture Richard T. Ely to R. P. Teele, July 27, 1903, in "Correspondence of R. P. Teele, 1904–1909" Record Group 8, Records of the Bureau of

Agricultural Engineering, Office of Irrigation Investigations, Federal Records Center, Suitland, Maryland.

21. The Kern County Land and Water Company is discussed in Pisani, *From the Family Farm to Agribusiness*, 191–249. The quote is from William Hammond Hall to Elwood Mead, October 4, 1889, in "Elwood Mead, Territorial & State Engineer: Incoming Correspondence from Federal Government Officials, 1888–1890," Wyoming State Archives, Cheyenne. Also see Hall to J. DeBarth Shorb, August 21, 1886, in Incoming Business Correspondence, Shorb Collection, the Huntington Library, San Marino, California.

22. The quotes are from Bakken, *The Development of Law on the Rocky Mountain Frontier*, 71, and Frank J. Trelease, "Uneasy Federalism—State Water Laws and National Water Uses," *Washington Law Review* 55 (November 1980): 752–53.

23. Pisani, *From the Family Farm to Agribusiness*, 339–40; Mead, *Irrigation Institutions*, 277.

24. Dunbar, *Forging New Rights in Western Waters*, 101; Samuel Fortier, "The Agricultural Side of Irrigation," *Official Proceedings of the Eighteenth National Irrigation Congress Held at Pueblo, Colorado, September 26–30, 1910* (Pueblo, n.d.), 335.

25. John Norton Pomeroy, *A Treatise on the Law of Water Rights* (St. Paul, 1893), 328–29.

26. James Wilson, untitled speech, *The Official Proceedings of the Eleventh National Irrigation Congress Held at Ogden, Utah, September 15–18, 1903* (Ogden, 1904), 164.

27. For example, J. A. Alexander, in his *The Life of George Chaffey* (Melbourne, 1928), 35, called riparianism "a serious obstacle to the development of irrigation in the West," and in his survey of water resource development in California, *Aqueduct Empire: A Guide to Water in California, Its Turbulent History and Its Management Today* (Glendale, 1968), 409, Erwin Cooper charged that such rights were a "potential death sentence" on all other water claims. In a revised edition of his 1942 classic, *Our Landed Heritage: The Public Domain, 1776–1970* (Lincoln, 1976), 329, Roy M. Robbins declared that "[t]he heterogeneous [nineteenth century] medley of riparian laws and customs had led to chaos."

28. Dunbar, *Forging New Rights in Western Waters*, 68. Also see Gordon R. Miller, "Shaping California Water Law, 1781–1928," 11, 23.

29. *Eddy v. Simpson*, 3 Cal. 249, 252 (1853); *Hill v. Newman*, 5 Cal. 446 (1855); *Conger v. Weaver*, 6 Cal. 55 (1856); *Hoffman v. Stone*, 7 Cal. 46, 48 (1857), *Hill v. Smith*, 27 Cal. 432 (1865).

30. *Union Mill and Mining Co. v. Ferris*, 2 Saw. 176, 195 (1871); *Vansickle v. Haines*, 7 Nev. 249, 286 (1872); *Drake v. Earhart*, 2 Ida. 750, 763–64 (1890); *Crawford v. Hathaway*, 67 Neb. 365 (1903); Pomeroy, *A Treatise on the Law of Water Rights*, 346–47.

31. Bakken, *The Development of Law on the Rocky Mountain Frontier*, 36–39. In 1880, in *Monroe v. Ivri*, 2 Utah 535, the court proclaimed that land and water were open to appropriation by all. Subsequently, the Utah legislature adopted an appropriation statute, but it was invalidated by the territorial supreme court. Appropriation was not formally recognized until after statehood, in 1897.

32. Dunbar, *Forging New Rights in Western Waters*, 82; Joseph F. Smith to

William E. Smythe, December 14, 1901, Record Group 8, Records of the Bureau of Agricultural Engineering, Office of Irrigation Investigations, General Correspondence, 1898–1912, box 1, General Correspondence, 1898–December 31, 1902, Federal Records Center, Suitland, Maryland.

33. *General Laws, Joint Resolutions, Memorials, and Private Acts, Passed at the First Session of the Legislative Assembly of the Territory of Colorado* (Denver, 1861), 67–69. The law made an exception for irrigators on Hardscrabble Creek, a tributary of the Arkansas River, by promising each of them enough water to serve 160 acres. However, even in this case it upheld riparian principles. In dry years, "the occupant nearest the source of said stream shall be first supplied."

34. *General Laws, Joint Resolutions, Memorials, and Private Acts, Passed at the Second Session of the Legislative Assembly of the Territory of Colorado* (Denver, 1862), 48.

35. *General Laws, Joint Resolutions, Memorials, and Private Acts, Passed at the Third Session of the Legislative Assembly of the Territory of Colorado* (Denver, 1864), 58. Also see Dunbar, *Forging New Rights in Western Waters*, 75–76. Dunbar does not consider the statutes passed by Montana, Wyoming, and Idaho.

36. Irrigators made the choice themselves when not served by private companies. *Acts, Resolutions and Memorials, of the Territory of Montana, Passed by the First Legislative Assembly* (Virginia City, Mont., 1866), 367–69; *The Compiled Laws of Wyoming* (Cheyenne, 1876), 377–79; *General Laws of the Territory of Idaho Including the Code of Civil Procedure, Passed at the Eleventh Session of the Territorial Legislature* (Boise City, 1881), 273–75. Justice Wade's quote is from his dissent in *Thorp v. Freed*, 1 Mont. 651, at 656 and 668 (1872). On the Montana law also see *Smith v. Denniff*, 24 Mont. 20, 22–23 (1900). *Basey v. Gallagher*, 87 U.S. 670, 675 (1874), reprinted an 1870 Montana law that extended the privilege of diversion to anyone who owned "agricultural lands within the limits of this Territory."

37. A Mexican riparian grant carried the right to use water for domestic needs but nothing more. Under both Spain and Mexico, water was assumed to be a resource separate from the land, though ultimate ownership remained with the state.

38. Meyer, *Water in the Hispanic Southwest*, 161, 163; Betty Eakle Dobkins, *The Spanish Element in Texas Water Law* (Austin, 1959), 143; Thomas F. Glick, *The Old World Background of the Irrigation System of San Antonio, Texas* (El Paso, 1972); Edwin P. Arneson, "Early Irrigation in Texas," *Southwestern Historical Quarterly* 25 (October 1921): 121–30; Kinney, *A Treatise on the Law of Irrigation and Water Rights*, 1:989–96; Webb, *The Great Plains*, 441.

39. *California Statutes* (1854), 76. For a full discussion of the 1854 law and its amendments see Pisani, *From the Family Farm to Agribusiness*, 39–45.

40. *California Statutes* (1859), 217; (1862), 235 and 540; (1864), 87 and 375; (1866), 609 and 777.

41. *California Statutes* (1866), 313–14; (1868), 113; (1876), 547. The legislature formally recognized prior appropriation in 1872, when it first specified procedures for posting and filing water claims. The spread of riparian rights and perhaps even the exclusive "pueblo rights" to water enjoyed by such cities as Los Angeles and San Diego also helped undermine the 1854 law.

42. Howard R. Lamar, *The Far Southwest, 1846–1912: A Territorial History* (New Haven, 1966), 91.

43. *General Laws of New Mexico* (Albany, N.Y., 1880), 13–23. Also see Wells

Hutchins, "The Community Acequia: Its Origin and Development," *Southwestern Historical Quarterly* 31 (January 1928): 261–84, and Bakken, *The Development of Law on the Rocky Mountain Frontier,* 34.

44. Arizona's first territorial legislature met in 1864 and borrowed most of its irrigation law from New Mexico. Section 25 declared that "[t]he regulations of acequias, which have been worked according to the laws and customs of Sonora and the usages of the people of Arizona, shall remain as they were made and used up to this day." The lawmakers also promised that "rights in acequias or irrigation canals heretofore established shall not be disturbed." Nominally, these provisions protected the Santa Cruz Valley's community ditch system, which served the territory's largest block of farmland. However, the law also reflected the preeminence of mining. It repeatedly emphasized that in case of conflicts over water, farmers had to give way. The law was inconsistent. While it sanctioned the traditional water systems, Section 17 specified that in dry times, the water supply of farmers would not be cut back equally—as in California, Texas, or New Mexico's communal systems—but "according to the dates of their respective titles or their occupation of the lands either by themselves or their grantors. The oldest titles shall have precedence always." Prior appropriation was grafted onto a completely antagonistic system. See *The Howell Code Adopted by the First Legislative Assembly of the Territory of Arizona* (Prescott, 1865), 422–26, and R. H. Forbes, "Irrigation in Arizona," U.S.D.A. Office of Experiment Stations, *Bulletin No. 235* (Washington D.C., 1911), 57.

45. Spanish and Mexican principles of water use were not restricted to the Southwest. The Colorado legislature initially recognized and accepted irrigation as practiced in the Rio Grande's San Luis Valley. By limiting the law to Costilla and Conejos counties, the lawmakers were able to grant farmers the first claim on water during the growing season even though mining was the territory's dominant economic activity. See *General Laws, Joint Resolutions, Memorials, and Private Acts, Passed at the Fifth Session of the Legislative Assembly of the Territory of Colorado* (Central City, Colo., 1866), 61–64.

46. Dobkins, *The Spanish Element in Texas Water Law,* 136–39; Will Wilson, "A Reappraisal of Motl v. Boyd," *Proceedings, Water Law Conference June 17–18, 1955* (Austin, 1955), 38–43; A. A. White, "The Flow and Underflow of Motl v. Boyd," ibid., 44–60.

47. Dunbar's *Forging New Rights in Western Waters,* 99–132, provides a good overview of the new administrative systems, but does not devote enough attention to the implications of these reforms.

48. Moses Lasky, "From Prior Appropriation to Economic Distribution of Water by the State—Via Irrigation Administration," *Rocky Mountain Law Review* 1 (April 1929): 171; Bakken, *The Development of Law on the Rocky Mountain Frontier,* 32. Dunbar acknowledges in his 1985 essay that increasing state control over water "did not displace the appropriative right, but rather subjected it to government control. The content remains, the freedom to appropriate without anybody's leave is gone" ("The Adaptability of Water Law to the Aridity of the West," 62).

49. *Proceedings of the Constitutional Convention of Colorado, 1875 and 1876* (Denver, 1906), 44, 374.

50. Dunbar, *Forging New Rights in Western Waters,* 209, 217.

51. See Dunbar's chapter "The Appropriation Right and Its Critics," in ibid., 209–17, especially 214–16.

52. "National Water Resources," 87th Cong., 1st sess., Senate Reports, no. 29 (Washington, D.C., 1961), 54.

53. *Lexington & Ohio Rail Road v. Applegate,* 8 Dana 289, 309 (1839).

54. The courts did not simply bend to the needs of the dominant industry or economic activity. For example, Harry Scheiber has shown, in "Public Rights and the Rule of Law in American Legal History," that California courts often gave agriculture preference over the "modern sector." Similarly, the law often favored small businesses over corporate capital (pp. 240, 251).

55. Guice, *The Rocky Mountain Bench,* 113.

56. *Los Angeles Times,* July 28, 1902, 8. Also see Frederick Haynes Newell's *Irrigation in the United States* (New York, 1902), 291–92.

CHAPTER 2. THE ORIGINS OF WESTERN WATER LAW

1. On the historiography of nineteenth-century western water law see Donald J. Pisani, "Enterprise and Equity: A Critique of Western Water Law in the Nineteenth Century," *Western Historical Quarterly* 18 (January 1987): 15–37. For a small sample of the historical literature on the origins of water law in California during the 1850s, see Douglas R. Littlefield, "Water Rights During the California Gold Rush: Conflicts over Economic Points of View," *Western Historical Quarterly* 14 (October 1983): 415–34; Gordon R. Miller, "Shaping California Water Law, 1781–1928," *Southern California Quarterly* 55 (Spring 1973): 9–42; and Pisani, "The Crucible of Western Water Law," in *From the Family Farm to Agribusiness: The Irrigation Crusade in California the West, 1850–1931* (Berkeley, 1984), 30–53. I have relied heavily on Littlefield's provocative article. It traces three leading water cases in Nevada and El Dorado counties from miners' arbitration committees to the supreme court. Littlefield was the first professional historian to show that inconsistencies in California water law developed largely from variations in local mining conditions.

The common law doctrine of riparian rights, which prevailed throughout the humid eastern half of the nation in 1850, restricted water use to those who owned land adjoining streams. ("Riparian" is derived from the Latin word for "riverbank.") At that time, the law did not regard water as a species of property apart from the land. In theory, each riparian owner had the right to an uninterrupted flow of water, undiminished in quantity or quality. (In practice, legislatures and courts often permitted diversions for the purpose of powering mills and factories or to fill transportation canals, but only if landowners were compensated for damages.) Riparian rights had no independent existence; they could be defined only in relation to each other. They were based on geography and reflected traditional uses of water in a water-rich environment. A second system of water law, prior appropriation, originated in California. By granting the first person or group that tapped a stream an absolute right not just to use water but to sell it and transport it, prior appropriation relied on time, rather than place, to allocate this resource.

2. Herbert O. Lang, *A History of Tuolumne County California* (San Francisco, 1882), 99–100; *Daily Alta California* (San Francisco), May 14, 1850; *Weekly Columbian* (Columbia, Calif.), November 8, 1856.

3. *Stockton Times* (Stockton, Calif.), April 13, 1850. Also see the *Stockton Journal*, March 15, 1851.

4. *Daily Alta California*, August 4, 1852.

5. *Columbia Gazette* (Columbia, Calif.), October 30, 1852. The *Gazette* invariably portrayed the water company as a public benefactor—as local newspapers later depicted early railroads—pointing out that large-scale mining could not exist without it. See particularly the issues of February 19, April 9, and June 25, 1853. Also see William R. Kenny, "History of the Sonora Mining Region of California, 1848–1860" (Ph.D. diss., University of California, Berkeley, 1955), 298–305.

6. Lang, *History of Tuolumne County California*, 127–28; *Daily Alta California*, November 23, 1852.

7. Kenny, "History of the Sonora Mining Region of California, 1848–1860," 301; *Daily Alta California*, September 16, November 29, and December 1, 1852.

8. *Daily Alta California*, February 11 and April 29, 1853; *Columbia Gazette*, January 22, February 12, April 9 and 23, and October 29, 1853.

9. *Daily Alta California*, August 2, 1853; *Columbia Gazette*, April 1 and 29, 1854. The daily income of miners averaged about twenty dollars in 1848 but declined to ten dollars in 1850, five dollars in 1853, and three dollars in the late 1850s; Philip Ross May, *Origins of Hydraulic Mining in California* (Oakland, Calif., 1970), 25.

10. The Tuolumne Hydraulic Company's enormously expensive system headed at the Tuolumne River at five thousand feet, where a dam impounded the water. The system had been costly to build because the country between the river and the mining camps it served—Sonora, Camp Seco, Yorktown, Poverty Hill, Chinese Camp, Chile Camp, Sullivan's Creek, and Montezuma Flats—was extremely rugged, requiring extensive, heavy flumes and the excavation of ditches in solid rock. The Tuolumne County Water Company had been wise to tap the much more accessible Stanislaus River. The *Daily Alta California* of October 8, 1855, reported that the Tuolumne Hydraulic Company's fifty-mile canal cost $300,000 to build, about the same amount that had been spent on the Tuolumne County Water Company's works. The *San Francisco Daily Herald*, January 28, 1956, estimated that as of that date more than $2.5 million had been invested in Tuolumne County hydraulic works.

11. *Daily Alta California*, July 14 and December 8, 1853, January 1, 1854.

12. *Daily Alta California*, March 17 (quote), 27, and 28, 1855. Strikes against private water companies were very common during the middle 1850s. See, for example, the *Weekly San Joaquin Republican* (Stockton, Calif.), December 1, 1855, and March 29, 1856, which recounted conflicts near Nevada City and in the Chile District of Mariposa County.

13. *Columbia Gazette*, October 7, 1854; *Weekly Columbian*, November 22, 1856.

14. *Columbia Gazette*, October 14, 1854; *Tuolumne Courier* (Columbia, Calif.), November 13 and December 4, 1858; Lang, *History of Tuolumne County, California*, 162–78; Edna Bryan Buckbee, *The Saga of Old Tuolumne* (New York, 1935), 265–81; John Heckendorn and W. A. Wilson, *Miners & Business Men's Directory for the Year Commencing January 1st, 1856* (Columbia, Calif., 1856), 25; Tyrrell Martinez and

Frank J. Drummond, "The Early Mining Laws of Tuolumne and Calaveras Counties," undated typescript at Bancroft Library, University of California, Berkeley, 24.

15. *Weekly San Joaquin Republican,* April 12, 1856; Kenny, "History of the Sonora Mining Region of California, 1848–1860," 426.

16. *Weekly Columbian,* December 13, 1856 (quote), March 28 and April 4, 1857; *Weekly San Joaquin Republican,* July 25, 1857; *Sacramento Daily Union,* March 17, 1858.

17. William H. Hutchinson, "An Early-Day Memory," *Overland Monthly* 22 (September 1893): 259–60; *Daily Alta California,* December 3, 1858.

18. Kenny, "History of the Sonora Mining Region of California, 1848–1860," 440. The *Daily Alta California,* October 19, 1859, reported that the exodus to the Fraser River country alone had reduced the assessed value of property in Tuolumne County by 10 percent.

19. *Tuolumne Courier,* May 7, 1859, October 13 and 27, 1860.

20. *Columbia Weekly News,* February 24, May 26, and August 18, 1859; *Columbia Times* (Columbia, Calif.), February 2 and 9, July 5, 14, and 25, September 13 and 27, October 11 and 18, November 22 and 29, 1860; March 21, 1861. The quotes are from the issues of July 5 and October 18. Also see Kenny, "History of the Sonora Mining Region of California, 1848–1860," 449–50.

21. *Sacramento Daily Union,* November 14, 1861; *Daily Alta California,* December 20, 1862. The *Alta* estimated that this system had cost nearly $4 million to construct. No more than one-quarter to one-third of that amount had been invested by the Tuolumne County Water Company.

22. The quote is from John Carr, *Pioneer Days in California* (Eureka, Calif., 1891), 142. Also see Isaac Cox, *Annals of Trinity County* (San Francisco, 1858), 53, and James W. Bartlett, *Trinity County California* (Sacramento, 1926), 13. Miners throughout California joined together to turn rivers from their courses during the early 1850s. For example, the *Daily Alta California,* July 30, 1851, reported that dams were being erected on the north, south, and middle forks of the American River and that miners working the beds of those streams averaged $200 a day per person. Along the middle fork, the entire stream had been turned out of its bed for miles.

23. Cox, *Annals of Trinity County,* 157. Claim sizes varied from camp to camp and district to district. Some districts provided larger claims to miners who constructed ditches. For example, one of the first miners to arrive at Yankee Jim's in Placer County in 1850 recounted that he was chased from his claim by a ditch owner who said: "Stranger, do you see that ar ditch up thar? The law here is that a man claims everything below his mining ditch. That ditch belongs to me, and you had better git from here, or I'll call a meetin' of the miners" (*Evening Bulletin* [San Francisco], March 1, 1859).

24. Cox, *Annals of Trinity County,* 191–93.

25. Helen Loomis, "Search for William Ware," *Trinity, 1983: Official Yearbook, Trinity County Historical Society* (Weaverville, Calif., 1983), 23–24; *Shasta Courier* (Shasta, Calif.), May 14, 1853.

26. Isaac Cox, who published the first Trinity County history in 1858, noted that the Ware and Howe races carried sufficient water to serve twenty-four long toms while the fourteen races downstream, which were collectively over twice as long as the Ware and Howe systems, had a capacity to serve 190 toms. See Cox, *Annals of Trinity County,* 158–60.

27. Carr, *Pioneer Days in California*, 254–62 (the quote is from 261); Cox, *Annals of Trinity County*, 159–60, 191–93.

28. *Shasta Courier*, June 11, 1853; "Mining Laws," in *Tenth Census of the United States* (Washington, D.C., 1885), 14:278–79; Charles J. Hughes, "The Evolution of Mining Law," in *Report of the Twenty-Fourth Annual Meeting of the American Bar Association Held at Denver, Colorado, August 21, 22, and 23, 1901* (Philadelphia, 1901), 332–34.

29. *Shasta Courier*, June 25, 1853.

30. Hughes, "The Evolution of Mining Law," 333; John F. Davis, *Historical Sketch of the Mining Law in California* (Los Angeles, 1902), 31–32.

31. *Democratic State Journal* (Sacramento), December 10, 1853; *Shasta Courier*, January 14, 1854.

32. Bartlett, *Trinity County California*, 12; *Daily Alta California*, December 23, 1859. On May 26, 1857, the *Alta* reported that Trinity County contained the largest number of mining ditches of any California county—120 of the state's total of 325. All were relatively small and technologically unsophisticated, no match for the elaborate water systems in Nevada or El Dorado counties.

33. The quotes from Judge McCorkle's decision in *Davis v. Ware*, decided on April 21, 1854, are as reprinted in Oscar T. Shuck, "Our First Water Rights Decision," in *History of the Bench and Bar of California* (Los Angeles, 1901), 362.

34. Cox, *Annals of Trinity County*, 192. Cox also noted that when he finished his book during the summer of 1858, the miners were "in a full blaze of litigation," which he promised would do nothing but enrich lawyers and check "all desire in [the] future on the part of such as might otherwise feel inducement to invest money and labor in works for public good, to do so" (p. 160).

35. Thomas M. Marshall, "The Miner's Laws of Colorado," *American Historical Review* 25 (April 1920): 431; Charles H. Shinn, *Lands Laws of Mining Districts* (Baltimore, 1884), 57–58.

36. Shinn, *Land Laws of Mining Districts*, 61; Shinn, *Mining Camps: A Study in American Frontier Government* (New York, 1885), 256.

CHAPTER 3. STATE VS. NATION

1. *Federal Power Commission v. Oregon et al.*, 349 U.S. 435 (1955).

2. Ibid., 349 U.S. 457.

3. *Arizona V. California et al.*, 373 U. S. 546 (1963). On this case, see Norris Hundley, Jr., "Clio Nods: *Arizona v. California* and the Boulder Canyon Act—A Reassessment," *Western Historical Quarterly* 3 (1972): 17–51.

4. For a small sampling of legal literature on the federal reserved rights doctrine, see Eva H. Morreale, "Federal-State Conflicts over Western Waters—A Decade of Attempted 'Clarifying Legislation,'" *Rutgers Law Review* 20 (1966): 435–526; Frank J. Trelease, "Water Resources in the Public Lands: PLLRC's [Public Land Law Review Commission's] Solution to the Reservation Doctrine," *Land and Water Review* 6 (1970): 98–107; David R. Warner, "Federal Reserved Water Rights and Their Relationship to Appropriative Rights in the Western States," *Rocky*

Mountain Mineral Law Institute Proceedings (1970): 339– 420; Charles E. Corker, "Federal-State Relations in Water Rights Adjudications," ibid. (1972), 479 –603; and Raphael J. Moses, "The Federal Reserved Rights Doctrine—From 1866 Through Eagle County," *Natural Resources Lawyer* 8 (1975): 221–35.

5. The best survey of federal reclamation is Paul Wallace Gates, *History of Public Land Law Development* (Washington, D.C., 1968), 635–98. Also see Michael E. Robinson, *Water for the West: The Bureau of Reclamation, 1902–1977* (Chicago, 1979), and William E. Warne, *The Bureau of Reclamation* (New York, 1972).

6. *U.S. Statutes at Large*, 14:253; 16218; 19:377.

7. See the *Colorado Constitution* (1876), Art. 16, sec. 5, and the *Wyoming Constitution* (1891), Art 8, sec. 1. Neither state has rescinded its claim to ownership and both have argued that congressional ratification of their constitutions implied de facto recognition of state sovereignty over water.

8. See the following U.S. Department of Agriculture, Office of Experiment Stations bulletins written by Mead and his lieutenants: "Water Rights on the Missouri River and Its Tributaries," *Bulletin No. 58* (1899); "Water-Right Problems of the Bear River," *Bulletin No. 70* (1899); and "Abstract of Laws for Acquiring Titles to Water from the Missouri River and Its Tributaries, with the Legal Forms in Use," *Bulletin No. 60* (1899). Mead's most famous report discussed the outdated water laws of California: "Report of Irrigation Investigations in California," *Bulletin No. 100* (1901).

9. James R. Kluger, "Elwood Mead: Irrigation Engineer and Social Planner" (Ph.D. diss., University of Arizona, 1970), 23–31. See also Lawrence B. Lee, "Elwood Mead and the Beginnings of National Reclamation" (typescript in possession of the author), and Paul K. Conkin, "The Vision of Elwood Mead," *Agriculture History* 34 (1960): 88 –97.

10. Francis E. Warren to Theodore Roosevelt, October 29, 1901, Records of the Bureau of Agricultural Engineering, Irrigation Investigations Division, General Correspondence, 1898–1902, Record Group 8, National Archives, Suitland, Maryland. See also Fred Bond to Warren, October 26, 1901; William Ellsworth Smythe to Elwood Mead, October 28, 1901; Warren to Mead, October 29, 1901; and Bond to Mead, December 3, 1901, ibid.

11. William Ellsworth Smythe, "State and National Irrigation Policies," *Land of Sunshine* 15 (July 1901): 65–72, and "20th Century West," ibid. (November 1901): 377–82; Hiram Martin Chittenden, "Government Construction of Reservoirs in Arid Regions," *North America Review* 174 (February 1902), 245–58.

12. Elwood Mead, "Memorandum Regarding Section 8 of the Irrigation bill" (undated, but probably April 1902), Elwood Mead file (1902), Benjamin Ide Wheeler Correspondence, University of California Archives, Berkeley; Mead, "Problems of Irrigation Legislation," *Forum* 32 (January 1902): 580 – 81.

13. *Cong. Rec.*, 57 Cong., 2 sess. (June 13, 1902), 6766; *U.S. Statutes at Large*, 32:388.

14. *Salt Lake City Tribune*, July 28, 1902.

15. The water laws considered by western legislatures in 1903 are discussed in *Forestry and Irrigation* 9 (March 1903): 111–12; 10 (April 1903): 167–69.

16. Francis G. Newlands to F. H. Newell, February 6, 1903, Newell Collection, Hebard Library, University of Wyoming; L. H. Taylor to Newell, Jan. 27, 1903,

Records of the U.S. Reclamation Bureau, file 110-E8, Legislation: Correspondence re Irrigation Laws, Water Codes, etc., in Nevada, Record Group 115, National Archives, Washington, D.C.; A. E. Chandler, "The Irrigation Laws of Nevada," and F. G. Newlands, "State-Cooperation in National Irrigation," both in *Official Proceedings of the Eleventh International Irrigation Congress, 1903* (Ogden, Utah, 1904), 142–50, 411–13; *Nevada State Journal* (Reno), June 19, 1904.

17. For a brief sketch of Morris Bien's early career, see *Forestry and Irrigation* 2 (February 1905), 59. See also his typescript "Autobiography," Morris Bien Collection, Western Heritage Library, University of Wyoming.

18. For the Bien code, see his undated "Memorandum of Principles to Be Incorporated in State Irrigation Laws," and his memorandum dated March 15, 1905, file 110-E8, Legislation: Correspondence re Irrigation Laws, Water Codes, etc., in Nevada RG 115. See also his typescript "Autobiography," 17–18, Morris Bien Collection, University of Wyoming; his "Proposed State Code of Water Laws," in U.S. Geological Survey, *Water Supply and Irrigation Paper #146* (Washington, D.C., 1905), 29–34; his address to the 1904 irrigation congress, *Official Proceedings of the Twelfth International Irrigation Congress* (Galveston, Texas, 1905), 169–89; and his speech to the 1905 congress, *Official Proceedings of the Thirteenth International Irrigation Congress* (Portland, 1905), 158–64.

19. The Reclamation Service submitted the Bien code to lawyers, engineers, and politicians throughout the West, asking for comments and suggestions. See file 110-E8, Legislation: Correspondence re Irrigation Laws, Water Codes, etc., in Nevada RG 115, especially L. G. Carpenter to Bien, October 27, 1904; John G. North to Bien, January 9, 1905; Lucien Shaw to Bien, January 13, 1905; and W. M. Wooldridge to F. H. Newell, January 9, 1905.

20. *Portland Oregonian*, February 12 and 19, 1905.

21. *U.S. Statutes at Large*, 30:36.

22. *Howell v. Johnson*, 89 Fed. Rep. 559 (1898); see also *Benton v. Johncox*, 17 Wash. 277 (1897), and *Cruse v. McCauley*, 96 Fed. Rep. 369 (1899).

23. *United States v. Rio Grande Dam and Irrigation Company*, 174 U.S. 690 (1899). For a good survey of the events leading up to the Rio Grande case, see Ira G. Clark, "The Elephant Butte Controversy: A Chapter in the Emergence of Federal Water Law," *Journal of American History* 61 (1975): 1006–33.

24. *U.S. Statutes at Large*, 29:377.

25. The Bien quotations are from his "Informal Statement Concerning the Right of Appropriation of Water and Riparian Rights in the Arid Region" (1906) in file 762, Legal Discussions—General, RG 115. See also his earlier "Memorandum Concerning the Origins of the Right of Appropriation of the Waters of the Public Domain" (February 6, 1904), ibid.; "Relation of Federal and State Laws to Irrigation," in *Official Proceedings of the Eleventh International Irrigation Congress, 1903* (Ogden, Utah, 1904), 397–402; and his paper bearing the same title in U.S. Geological Survey, *Water Supply and Irrigation Paper #93* (Washington, D.C., 1904), 232–37.

26. F. H. Newell to T. A. Noble, April 13, 1904, file 110-E16, Legislation: Irrigation Law, Water Codes, etc., Washington through 1910, RG 115.

27. *Kansas v. Colorado*, 206 U.S. 46 (1907).

28. Ibid.; see also the *Annual Report of the Attorney General of the United States, 1907* (Washington, D.C., 1907), 16.

29. "Statement of Frank L. Campbell, Assistant Attorney-General for the Interior Department in Response to the Request of the Solicitor General in Regard to the Attitude of the Government [in *Kansas v. Colorado*]," in file 762, Legal Discussions—*Kansas v. Colorado*, RG 115.

30. *Winters v. The United States*, 207 U.S. 564 (1908). This case was argued before the Supreme Court on October 24, 1907, and decided on January 6, 1908. For a discussion of this complicated case and its aftermath, see Norris Hundley, "The Dark and Bloody Ground of Indian Water Rights: Confusion Elevated to Principle," *Western Historical Quarterly* 9 (1978): 455–83, and Hundley, "The 'Winters' Decision and Indian Water Rights: A Mystery Reexamined," ibid., 13 (1982): 17–42.

31. U.S. Attorney General William H. Moody described the background to the Winters case in his letter to Theodore Roosevelt, December 18, 1905, in file 752, Legal Discussions—General, RG 115. He also forwarded an undated memorandum, apparently prepared by the solicitor general, entitled "Memorandum Relative to Cases Involving Water Rights of Indians in Montana and Washington," contained in the same file.

32. Morris Bien, "Memorandum: Conflicting Attitude [of] Justice Dept. on Irrigation Matters," December 8, 1905, and "Attitude of the Department of Justice in Irrigation Matters," December 20, 1905, in file 762, Legal Discussions—General, RG 115.

33. *Annual Report of the Attorney General of the United States, 1907* (Washington, D.C., 1907), 16; Morris Bien to F. H. Newell, May 19, 1907, file 665, Correspondence and Briefs re Suit of Kansas vs. Colorado, RG 115; A. E. Chandler to Newell, June 7, 1907, file 762.1, General Legal Discussion—Constitutionality of Reclamation Act, ibid.; Chandler to Bien, October 12, 1909, ibid.; and B. E. Stoutmeyer, "Brief on Constitutionality of Reclamation Act and Case of Kansas v. Colorado" (September 1908), ibid.

34. The Reclamation Service dusted off the reserved rights doctrine in *Wyoming v. Colorado*, 259 U.S. 419 (1922) with no greater success. See file 132.2, General—Correspondence re Wyoming vs. Colorado, Laramie River thru 1929, RG 115.

35. *Third Annual Report of the Reclamation Service, 1903–1904* (Washington, D.C., 1905), 53–54; map of reserved lands facing p. 30 in *Fourth Annual Report of the Reclamation Service, 1904–1905* (Washington, D.C., 1906); *Official Proceedings of the Thirteenth International Irrigation Congress* (Portland, 1905), 210; *Official Proceedings of the Sixteenth International Irrigation Congress* (Albuquerque, 1908), 136–52 and 270–73; *Official Proceedings of the Eighteenth International Irrigation Congress* (Pueblo, Colo., 1910), 305–15. For other examples of conflict between the Reclamation Service and private water users, see *Irrigation Age* 20 (April 1905): 168–70, 20 (May 1905): 239–40, and 21 (April 1906): 169; and *Forestry and Irrigation* 10 (May 1904): 223–24.

36. *Annual Report of the Attorney General of the United States, 1926* (Washington, D.C., 1926), 85; see also the attorney general's reports for 1910, 29; 1911, 32 and 41–42; 1914, 38–39; 1917, 45; 1918, 95; 1919, 113–15; and 1921, 86.

37. John F. Truesdell to J. F. Richardson, May 15 and 29, 1918, file: Truckee River—Water Right Adjudication, 1918, Truckee-Carson Irrigation District Archives, Fallon, Nevada.

38. *Churchill County Standard* (Fallon, Nev.), February 24, 1926; *Reno Evening*

Gazette, March 2, 1926. The Colorado District Court made a ruling similar to the Nevada decrees. See Ethelbert Ward, special assistant to the attorney general of the United States, "Memorandum: Federal Irrigation Water Rights," January 22, 1930, Wells Hutchins Collection, item 588, Water Resources Archives, University of California, Berkeley. Ward represented the Reclamation Bureau and his memo is a good later statement of the Bureau's position on federal water rights.

PART TWO: LAND

1. Cadwallader Colden's remarks are as reprinted in Edith M. Fox, *Land Speculation in Mohawk County* (Ithaca: Cornell University Press, 1949), 43.

2. As quoted in Alan Taylor, *Liberty Men and Great Proprietors: The Revolutionary Settlement on the Maine Frontier, 1760–1820* (Chapel Hill, 1990), 181.

3. Henry W. Tatter, *The Preferential Treatment of the Actual Settler in the Primary Disposition of the Vacant Lands in the United States to 1841* (New York, 1979).

4. Allan G. Bogue, "The Iowa Claim Clubs: Symbol and Substance," *Mississippi Valley Historical Review* 45 (September 1958): 231–53.

5. Paul Wallace Gates's essays on California land have been collected in *Land and Law in California* (Ames, Iowa, 1991). His most important work on possessory rights is "Tenants of the Log Cabin," *Mississippi Valley Historical Review* 49 (June 1962): 3–31.

6. Donald J. Pisani, *From the Family Farm to Agribusiness: The Irrigation Crusade in California and the West, 1850–1931* (Berkeley, 1984), 78–128.

7. I survey the events leading up to passage of the Reclamation Act of 1902 in *To Reclaim a Divided West: Water, Law, and Public Policy, 1848–1902* (Albuquerque, 1992), 273–325.

8. The commutation clause of the Homestead Act permitted original entrants to "commute" claims into preemption entries for $1.25 an acre after six months of residence. This provision was designed to allow farmers to pay for improvements by borrowing against the value of their land—which otherwise could not be done until a final patent had been secured, five years from the original filing. In practice, it was used by cattle, mining, timber, and land companies to secure huge holdings by purchasing the titles of unsuccessful farmers.

CHAPTER 4. SQUATTER LAW IN CALIFORNIA

1. There is no full-scale study of the Sacramento squatter riots, and historians have largely ignored the squatter perspective. For brief descriptions, see Joseph Ellison, *California and the Nation, 1850–1869: A Study of the Relations of a Frontier Community with the Federal Government* (Berkeley, 1927), 10–11, and W. W. Robinson, *Land in California: The Story of Mission Lands, Ranchos, Squatters, Mining Claims, Railroad Grants, Land Scrip, Homesteads* (Berkeley, 1948), 114–16. For the views of participants on each side, see Charles Robinson (one of the squatter leaders), *The Kansas Conflict* (New York, 1892), 36–65, and J. D. B. Stillman (leader of the posse

sent to capture Robinson), *Seeking the Golden Fleece: A Record of Pioneer Life in California* (San Francisco, 1877), 168–79.

2. The best biographies of Sutter are James Peter Zollinger, *Sutter: The Man and His Empire* (New York, 1939); Richard Dillon, *Fool's Gold: The Decline and Fall of Captain John Sutter of California* (New York, 1967); and Julian Dana, *Sutter of California* (New York, 1934).

3. In a letter to J. A. Crittenden dated February 2, 1858, Sutter admitted that during the Gold Rush he had been "unfitted for business." See John Sutter Papers, box 2, Bancroft Library, University of California, Berkeley (hereafter Bancroft Library).

4. Dillon, *Fool's Gold*, 268, 298, 305–6; Zollinger, *Sutter*, 263–64, 268, 271–72, 275; T. J. Schoonover, *The Life and Times of John A. Sutter* (Sacramento, 1907), 189, 218; Peter H. Burnett, *An Old California Pioneer* (Oakland, 1946), 171–72, 178.

5. Helen S. Giffen, ed., *The Diaries of Peter Decker: Overland to California in 1849 and Life in the Mines, 1850–1851* (Georgetown, Calif., 1966), 155; Erwin G. Gudde, *Sutter's Own Story: The Life of General John Augustus Sutter and the History of New Helvetia in the Sacramento Valley* (New York, 1936), 218–19; Dillon, *Fool's Gold*, 312–13. One of Sutter's business associates recounted an episode in which Sutter knowingly sold land that had already passed out of his hands. See Marguerite Eyer Wilbur, ed. and trans., *A Pioneer at Sutter's Fort, 1846–1850: The Adventures of Heinrich Lienhard* (Los Angeles, 1941), 249.

6. Joseph McGowan, *History of the Sacramento Valley* (New York, 1961), 1:114–15; William Prince to Charlotte Prince, November 6, 1849, and August 6, 1850, William Prince Letters, Bancroft Library.

7. *Alta California* (San Francisco), January 11, 1849.

8. John Sutter to Bennett Riley, December 11, 1849, John Sutter Papers, box 1, Bancroft Library; Zollinger, *Sutter*, 283; Burnett, *Old California Pioneer*, 175–76.

9. *Daily Alta California*, May 24, 1850.

10. *Placer Times* (Sacramento), December 15, 1849, June 7, 1850; Robinson, *Kansas Conflict*, 46. The squatter proclamation is reprinted in Schoonover, *Life and Times*, 194–96.

11. Walton Bean, *California: An Interpretive History* (New York, 1973), 260.

12. Three days after the main squatter "riot," the *Sacramento Transcript* of August 19, 1850, editorialized: "The remote evils resulting from such an excitement as we have passed through are much to be deplored, and should be avoided if it is within the range of possibility. The utter stagnation of all business, the cessation of works of public improvement, the stop placed upon private works of enterprise, the forgetfulness of the thousand and one subjects which should demand the attention of the public, these all call upon us to allay the excitement . . . and to resume our former condition of quiet." In November, William Prince reported that "[u]ntil the Riot of August last there was no difficulty in selling Goods. . . . The riot stopped the sale of property [town lots] and greatly reduced the price, & made money scarce, & it is very scarce now among all property holders." Prince's profits went from $500 a day in June to $40–$50 in late August. See Prince to Charlotte Prince, November 11, 1850, William Prince Letters, Bancroft Library, as well as his letters of November 17 and October 14. The great fear of merchants, of course, was that during Sacramento's time of troubles, Sutterville, Stockton, and other rival

communities would capture trade and potential settlers. To compound the city's problems cholera appeared—a fact the San Francisco papers eagerly publicized.

13. Hubert Howe Bancroft, *California Inter Pocula: A Review of Some Classical Abnormalities* (San Francisco, 1888), discusses the contests over land on pp. 396–412. The quotes are from pp. 397–98, 402, 407–8. Also see Bancroft's discussion of the land commission created in 1851 to sort out Mexican land titles in *History of California, 1848–1859* (San Francisco, 1888), 529–81. For Josiah Royce's views, see his *California: From the Conquest in 1846 to the Second Vigilance Committee in San Francisco, A Study of American Character* (Boston, 1886), 467, 469, 489–90, 499.

14. Paul W. Gates's brilliant essays, written from the late 1950s to the early 1970s, are the place to start any study of land in California. They have been collected in *Land and Law in California: Essays on Land Policies* (Ames, Iowa, 1991). Gates's perspective had limitations, however. In his mind, frontier land conflicts generally pitted rapacious capitalists against democratic pioneers, "haves" against "have-nots," vested rights against possessory rights, and "speculators" against actual settlers. Courts, and to a lesser extent legislatures, defended the status quo and shored up the established order. He minimized the strong support for "settler rights" exhibited by California jurists and the state legislature during the early 1850s.

15. Zollinger, *Sutter*, 300, 305, 317.

16. Schoonover, *Life and Times*, 210–11.

17. Mary Floyd Williams, *History of the San Francisco Committee of Vigilance of 1851* (Berkeley, 1921), 540; John Caughey, *California: A Remarkable State's Life History* (Englewood Cliffs, N.J., 1970), 246–47; Roy Robbins, *Our Landed Heritage: The Public Domain, 1776–1970* (Lincoln, 1976), 193.

18. John Phillip Reid, *Law for the Elephant: Property and Social Behavior on the Oregon Trail* (San Marino, Calif., 1980); Allan G. Bogue, "The Iowa Claim Clubs: Symbol and Substance," *Mississippi Valley Historical Review* 45 (September 1958): 231–53; Donald J. Pisani, *To Reclaim a Divided West: Water, Law, and Public Policy, 1848–1902* (Albuquerque, 1992), 11–32. James Willard Hurst is the father of this "instrumentalist" view of the law. See, for example, his *Law and the Conditions of Freedom in the Nineteenth-Century United States* (Madison, 1956).

19. Charles Sellers, *The Market Revolution: Jacksonian America, 1815–1846* (New York, 1991), 238–39. Other recent syntheses of the Jacksonian period include Lawrence Frederick Kohl, *The Politics of Individualism: Parties and the American Character in the Jacksonian Era* (New York, 1989), and Harry L. Watson, *Liberty and Power: The Politics of Jacksonian America* (New York, 1990).

20. The literature on preemption and the homestead policy is vast. For a recent introduction to the subject see William F. Deverell, "To Loosen the Safety Valve: Eastern Workers and Western Lands," *Western Historical Quarterly* 19 (August 1988): 269–85. Also see the standard works on American land policy, including Paul W. Gates, *History of Public Land Law Development* (Washington, D.C., 1968); Benjamin Horace Hibbard, *A History of the Public Land Policies* (New York, 1924); Robbins, *Our Landed Heritage;* John Opie, *The Law of the Land: Two Hundred Years of American Farmland Policy* (Lincoln, 1987); and William K. Wyant, *Westward in Eden: The Public Lands and the Conservation Movement* (Berkeley, 1982).

21. Paul W. Gates, "Tenants of the Log Cabin," *Mississippi Valley Historical Review* 49 (June 1962): 6, 12–14, 28; Henry W. Tatter, *The Preferential Treatment of the*

Actual Settler in the Primary Disposition of the Vacant Lands in the United States to 1841 (New York, 1979), 312–13. Also see Stephen Aron, "Pioneers and Profiteers: Land Speculation and the Homestead Ethic in Frontier Kentucky," *Western Historical Quarterly* 23 (May 1992): 179–98.

22. *Green v. Biddle*, 8 Wheaton 11 (1823).

23. Gates, "Tenants of the Log Cabin," 17, 27–29; Tatter, *Preferential Treatment*, 331–50.

24. Leonard Pitt, *The Decline of the Californios: A Social History of the Spanish-Speaking Californians, 1846–1890* (Berkeley, 1966). Mexican law—particularly the Colonization Act of 1824 and supplemental regulations adopted in 1828—required those who requested land to provide a rough sketch of the desired parcel and to swear that it had not been claimed already. Once a local alcalde approved the award, the governor issued a *concedo*, which outlined the conditions necessary to receive a formal patent—including completion of a boundary survey, construction of a house, and continuous residence. Finally, the required documents were sent to the territorial legislature for approval. Few, if any, claims in Mexican California met all these requirements.

25. William Robert Garner, *Letters from California, 1846–1847* (Berkeley, 1970), 181.

26. As David J. Langum puts it, "Rights [under Anglo-American law] were absolute entitlements and duties [were] their stern correlatives, owed unconditionally. No matter how onesided or unfair, a contract should be enforced strictly according to its terms. Courts should not rewrite agreements. If debts were owed or damages assessed, judgment should be rendered for immediate payment in cash, with no extensions and regardless of a defendant's personal needs or ability to pay. The common law would make the world safe for contract. Furthermore, at common law rights were defined in accordance with complicated but neutral rules . . . clearly stated and preferably written down for all to see. . . . [T]he essence of Anglo-American law . . . was rugged individualism, let the chips fall where they might, and an attitude on the part of litigants and the law alike of whole hog or none. It was with these ideas in their background that the expatriates framed their concepts of how a legal system ought to operate and by which they judged the California scheme of things and found it wanting" (*Law and Community on the Mexican California Frontier: Anglo-American Expatriates and the Clash of Legal Traditions, 1821–1846* [Norman, 1987], 270–71). Also see Walter Colton, *Three Years in California* (New York, 1850), 20.

27. Gates, *Land and Law*, 3–63.

28. See, for example, Richard Griswold del Castillo, *The Treaty of Guadalupe Hidalgo: A Legacy of Conflict* (Norman, 1990), 73–74, and Pitt, *Decline of the Californios*, 85. Ironically, Griswold del Castillo points out that the United States government followed a far less lenient policy toward Hispanic grants in New Mexico, where only 15 percent of the claims filed by 1880 were approved. In 1891, Congress created a Court of Private Land Claims to rule on the remaining Mexican grants. The court met between 1891 and 1904 and, holding strictly to the requirements of Mexican law, rejected two-thirds of the applications it considered. Ultimately only 6 percent of the land claimed was patented. "Thus," Griswold del Castillo concludes in *Treaty of Guadalupe Hidalgo*, "using the Court of Private Land Claims, the U.S. government enlarged the national domain at the expense of hundreds of Hispano villages, leaving a bitter legacy that continued to fester" (p. 81).

29. *Congressional Globe*, 31st Cong., 2d sess., Senate, January 3, 1851, 158–59; January 28, 1851, 362; Appendix, 48–53.

30. Paul W. Gates, "The California Land Act of 1851," "Adjudication of Spanish-Mexican Land Claims in California," "The Frémont-Jones Scramble for California Land Claims," chaps. in *Land and Law*.

31. *Daily Alta California* (steamer edition), January 15, 1853; ibid., July 11, 1853.

32. Gates, *Land and Law*, 272–99; Donald J. Pisani, "Land Monopoly in Nineteenth-Century California," *Agricultural History* 65 (Fall 1991): 18–21. Opening unsurveyed land to preemption was unprecedented, but other options would have demonstrated far more sympathy to squatters. For example, had Congress purchased the largest Mexican claims at 1848 prices, leaving the original claimants sufficient land for a farm, it could have given each squatter 160 or 320 acres free, as the Oregon Donation Act of 1850 had done. This and similar proposals, however, violated the Treaty of Guadalupe Hidalgo. U.S. Senator William Gwin introduced an unsuccessful bill to compensate squatters on Mexican grants with eighty acres of public land elsewhere if the grant was confirmed. There were also proposals to grant free town lots to urban squatters. Bean, *California*, 157, 160–61; Gates, *History of Public Land Law Development*, 388–89; *Daily Alta California*, January 31 and March 1, 1851.

33. Pisani, "Land Monopoly," 23–24.

34. Josiah Royce attributed much of the squatter's "mind-set" to the American sense of destiny. "Providence . . . and manifest destiny were understood in those days to be on our side," he observed, "and absolutely opposed to the base Mexican. Providence, again, is known to be opposed to every form of oppression; and grabbing eleven leagues of land is a great oppression. And so the worthlessness of Mexican land-titles is evident" (see Royce, *California*, 472).

35. C. B. Macpherson, *The Political Theory of Possessive Individualism: Hobbes to Locke* (Oxford, 1962).

36. Gates, *Land and Law*, 64–93; Christian G. Fritz, *Federal Justice in California: The Court of Ogden Hoffman, 1851–1891* (Lincoln, 1991), 137, 141; Robin W. Winks, *Frederick Billings: A Life* (New York, 1991), 97; Carl B. Swisher, *History of the Supreme Court of the United States: The Taney Period, 1836–64* (New York, 1974), 778.

37. Lewis Grossman, "John C. Frémont, Mariposa, and the Collision of Mexican and American Law," *Western Legal History* 6 (Winter/Spring 1993): 17–50.

38. Paul W. Gates, "The Land Business of Thomas O. Larkin," *California Historical Quarterly* 54 (Winter 1975): 333; *Daily Alta California*, July 16, August 5, and December 23, 1853.

39. Stephen J. Field noted that many squatters chose grants whose declared boundaries enclosed more land than specified in the grant itself. They attempted to locate on the surplus, "forgetting that other immigrants might do the same thing, each claiming that what he had taken was a portion of such surplus, until the grantee was deprived of his entire property" (see *Personal Reminiscences of Early Days in California with Other Sketches* [n.p., 1880], 139).

40. *Daily Alta California*, August 16, 1850, July 22, 1853; *San Joaquin Republican* (Stockton, Calif.), January 16, 1856.

41. *Daily Alta California*, January 1, and 20, 1852.

42. Peter H. Burnett, *Recollections and Opinions of an Old Pioneer* (New York, 1880), 386, 390; Stillman, *Seeking the Golden Fleece*, 168–79; Winks, *Frederick Billings*, 72.

43. *Cal. Stats.* (1850), 203. Two years later, the legislature replaced the 1850 law with more detailed legislation that opened the public lands to all—not just to squatters who had arrived before April 1850. The new law required that the land be used for farming or grazing and raised the value of required improvements to $200. It also laid down guidelines for marking boundaries and filing claims with county recorders. This statute differed markedly from subsequent federal preemption laws by allowing claimants to leave homesteads for up to twelve months if they paid the county recorder a $15 fee; *Cal. Stats.* (1852), 158. The *Daily Alta California,* June 6, 1852, concluded that the new law was concocted "to subserve the ends of a species of puny land-sharks whose combined proceedings are as detrimental to the true interests of the State as are the gigantic operations of the over-grown capitalist."

44. *Cal. Stats.* (1850), 344.

45. "Report on Civil and Common Law," February 27, 1850, in *California Reports,* 1850, 588–89. Also see Nathaniel Bennett's preface to the same volume, and Rosamond Parma, "The History of the Adoption of the Codes of California," *Law Library Journal* 22 (January 1929): 8–21.

46. *Sunol v. Hepburn,* 1 Cal. 254 (1850).

47. *Woodworth v. Fulton,* 1 Cal. 295 (1850), 310. The court sustained this ruling in *Folsom v. Root,* 1 Cal. 374 (1851). San Francisco's leading newspaper, the *Daily Alta California,* always antagonistic to squatters, predicted that the Woodworth decision would lead to anarchy and begged the legislature to do something. On February 2, 1851, it recounted the story of a squatter who had fenced off half of Telegraph Hill. "The principle of this squatterism," the paper editorialized, "instead of procuring a lot of ground to live upon will, we fear, be made a means to extort money from the holders of property in this city, who, looking upon the recent decision of the Supreme Court, will in many cases be glad to compromise with the invaders of their property." In short, the case would force legal owners to dispose of their land for far less than its real value. On the following day, the *Alta* observed, "The community stands upon the brink of a volcano. . . . There is no time to lose." In addition to the issues of February 2 and 3, 1851, also see the *Alta* for January 18, February 6, and February 11, 1851.

48. *Cohas v. Raisin,* 3 Cal. 443 (1853).

49. *Leese and Valejo v. Clarke,* 3 Cal. 17 (1852), 26. Also see *Clarkson and Vanderslice v. Hanks,* 3 Cal. 47 (1853).

50. As Hubert Howe Bancroft, always the champion of law, order, and property, put it in *California Inter Pocula:* "The squatters of California were at first denounced by the officers of the law, who called them outlaws, murderers; but when these same office-holders desired reelection, and squatterism had become a power in the state, then candidates of every party vied with each other in grovelling prostration. From their vocabulary the term 'squatter' was stricken, and every land-robber was an honest settler" (p. 402).

51. *San Francisco Daily Herald,* January 21, 1856.

52. Royce, *California,* 423; Williams, *History of the San Francisco Committee,* 392–93; William Henry Ellison, *A Self-Governing Dominion: California, 1849–1860* (Berkeley, 1950), 233; *San Francisco Daily Herald,* June 5, 6, and 10, 1854; *California Chronicle,* June 6, 7, and 9, 1854; *Daily Alta California,* June 6, 7, and 10, 1854.

53. *Frémont v. U.S.*, 17 Howard 442 (1854), 241–54; Winks, *Frederick Billings*, 118 –19.

54. In the 1856 presidential election, Frémont carried eleven states but won only 18 percent of the popular vote in California. Winks, *Frederick Billings*, 120.

55. Grossman, "John C. Frémont," 35 –36.

56. Swisher, *History of the Supreme Court*, 746–48.

57. *U.S. v. Kingsley*, 12 Peters 476 (1838); *U.S. v. Wiggins*, 14 Peters 334 (1840); *U.S. v. Boisdorè*, 11 Howard 63 (1850).

58. *Frémont v. U.S.*, 17 Howard 442 (1854), 247, 248.

59. Ibid., 251 –53; Leon Friedman and Fred L. Israel, eds., *The Justices of the United States Supreme Court, 1789 –1969: Their Lives and Major Opinions* (New York, 1969), 1:635–54, 737– 49, 795– 805.

60. *Ritchie v. U.S.*, 17 Howard 533 (1854); *Frémont v. U.S.*, 17 Howard 442 (1854).

61. *Gunn v. Bates*, 6 Cal. 263 (1856), 270. The California Supreme Court formally embraced Taney's reasoning in *Ferris v. Coover*, 10 Cal. 589 (1858). In that opinion, the court ruled that only an action by the Mexican government for non-compliance could limit a land grant. Judge Ogden Hoffman of the U.S. District Court for the Northern District of California, which heard land cases on appeal from the land commission, shared this view. Initially, he had required Mexican claimants to comply with Mexican law and the terms of their grant. After the Frémont case, according to Hoffman's biographer, the judge "adhered to a policy of liberal confirmation of land claims." Of the first ninety that reached him on appeal after the Frémont decision, all but five were confirmed, and in nearly half the cases the federal attorneys offered no argument, assuming their efforts were pointless. Fritz, *Federal Justice*, 135, 153.

62. *Democratic State Journal* (San Francisco), January 26, 1855; *Daily Alta California*, March 1, 21, and 23 and April 12, 1855; *Cal. Stats.* (1855), 109. This act also won support from some Mexican grantees who hoped that if the land commission rejected their claims, they could still maintain a right through possession.

63. *Democratic State Journal*, March 6, 1855.

64. Paul W. Gates has argued that the 1855 law was actually pro-settler because it "seemed to make the statute [of limitations] applicable to Mexican grants." However, since statutes of limitations do not run against the federal government, and since title to public land remained in the federal government until a formal title was issued to a claimant, this interpretation is questionable. The 1850 law simply refers to "real property." See *Cal. Stats.* (1850), 344; Gates, "California's Embattled Settlers," *California Historical Review* 41 (June 1962): 110.

65. See, for example, Bigler's messages to the California legislature of January 4 and May 8, 1854, in *Journal of the Fifth Session of the Legislature of the State of California, 1854* (Sacramento, 1854), 11–33, 492.

66. *Daily Alta California*, June 23, 1855. The 1855 settler conventions agreed that the law should favor actual occupants of land—if they entered it peaceably and without fraud. It should prohibit the sale or transfer (except by descent) of any contested real estate. No action by the lawful owner for recovery of property should be allowed if the squatter had occupied the land during the year prior to the ejection suit, and no action should be permitted against parties who

had held the property for five years. In all cases where property was recovered, and the defendant had entered without fraud or deceit, the lawful owner should be barred from collecting rent for the period of occupation. On the other hand, recovery should be permitted only after the lawful owner paid the trespasser for improvements. Other demands included repeal of the 1855 limitation bill, shifting the entire burden of taxation to land and away from improvements, and the extension of preemption rights to all the public domain outside the mining districts, including swamp and overflowed lands. (Squatters were most likely to take up land along streams. Since relatively few Mexican grants had been made in the San Joaquin Valley, many settlers who located there were subsequently expelled by swamp land claimants.) Most of these principles were ratified at the state settlers' convention held in Sacramento on August 8, a convention whose main purpose was to nominate candidates for the fall election. *Daily Alta California,* June 18 and 25, July 20, and August 14, 1855; *San Joaquin Republican,* June 20 and August 10, 1855; *Sacramento Daily Union,* June 16 and August 1, 2, 9, 10, and 11, 1855.

67. *Daily Alta California,* June 8, 1855.

68. *San Francisco Daily Herald,* January 27 and 30, 1856.

69. *Nevada Journal* (Nevada City), March 28, 1856; *Spirit of the Age* (Sacramento), February 2, 1856; *San Francisco Daily Herald,* February 4, 13, and 22, March 16 and 21, and April 7, 1856; *Democratic State Journal,* February 28, 1856. For an eloquent attack on the constitutionality of the proposed legislation, see Senator French's speech, as reprinted in the *Democratic State Journal,* March 20, 1856.

70. *Journal of the Seventh Session of the Senate of the State of California, 1856* (Sacramento, 1856), 331. Senator Shaw offered a series of amendments to strengthen the substitute, all of which were rejected by overwhelming votes. For example, he proposed that in eviction actions the defendant should be able to purchase the land for its value *at the time he took possession*—to be determined by the same jury that set the price of improvements. He wanted to give any squatter who, without protest from the actual owner, occupied land for more than one year the right to buy that land. He urged the senate to repeal the April 11, 1855, statute of limitations but also asked that actions be barred against anyone who had held a parcel of land for five years or more. He proposed that out-of-state companies that dealt in land should have no standing in California courts and that such companies be regarded as "immoral and against public policy" (see *Journal of the Seventh Session,* 525–32).

71. *California Chronicle,* March 14 and 18, 1856; *Democratic State Journal,* March 18 and 20, 1856; *Daily Evening Bulletin* (San Francisco), March 20, 1856; *Journal of the Seventh Session,* 525–32.

72. *Cal. Stats.* (1856), 54–57. The law was summarized and reprinted in many journals including the *California Chronicle,* March 24, 1856, and the *San Francisco Daily Herald,* March 25, 1856. Also see Gates, "Land Business," 338.

73. *Billings v. Harvey,* 6 Cal. 381 (1856); *Billings v. Hall,* 7 Cal. 1 (1857).

74. *Billings v. Hall,* 7 Cal. 1 (1857), 15.

75. Ibid., 12.

76. Ibid., 26. Terry also noted that occupancy laws had been repeatedly ruled constitutional by state supreme courts.

77. For a description of an important squatter war in the 1860s, see Paul W. Gates, "The Suscol Principle, Preemption, and California Latifundia," chap. in *Land and Law.*

78. *Cal. Stats.* (1858), 345.

79. Joint Resolution 6, dated January 29, 1858, *Cal. Stats.* (1858), 350 –51; Joint Resolution 14, dated March 28, 1858, ibid., 354.

80. H. G. Wood, *A Treatise of Actions at Law and in Equity* (Boston, 1901), 6 (quote), 564, 697–704, 711–13, 744–50. Although most western states adopted shorter statutes of limitation, there were exceptions. For example, at the end of the nineteenth century the Dakotas and Oregon retained the traditional twenty-year limitation, and Wyoming adopted a twenty-one-year term. Obviously, local economic conditions—such as the dominance of the grazing industry in many parts of the West—conditioned the actions of lawmakers.

81. Arthur Maass and Raymond L. Anderson, . . . *and the Desert Shall Rejoice: Conflict, Growth, and Justice in Arid Environments* (Cambridge, Mass., 1978), 228 –29.

82. For a thoughtful discussion of the concept of the "pioneer" and regional identity, see Clyde A. Milner II, "The View from Wisdom: Four Layers of History and Regional Identity," in *Under an Open Sky: Rethinking America's Western Past*, ed. William Cronon, George Miles, and Jay Gitlin (New York, 1992), 203 –22.

83. Dillon, *Fool's Gold*, 333.

84. Schoonover, *Life and Times*, 211–17, discusses in detail the "squatter outrages."

85. Gudde, *Sutter's Own Story*, 234–35.

86. Zollinger, *Sutter*, 313.

87. Dillon, *Fool's Gold*, 348 – 49.

88. Zollinger, *Sutter*, 312.

89. William Prince to Charlotte Prince, August 18, 1850, Prince Letters, Bancroft Library; Marguerite Eyer Wilbur, trans., "A Frenchman in the Gold Rush: The Journal of Ernest de Massey," *California Historical Quarterly* 5 (March 1926): 36 –37.

90. Zollinger, *Sutter*, 307. Brannan's career is surveyed in Paul Bailey, *Sam Brannan and the California Mormons* (Los Angeles, 1943).

91. Hubert Howe Bancroft, *Literary Industries: A Memoir* (San Francisco, 1891), 461– 65.

92. Hubert Howe Bancroft, *California Pioneer Register and Index, 1542 –1848* (Baltimore, 1964), 347. Josiah Royce, in *California*, 41– 42, offered a fairer appraisal of Sutter: "In character, Sutter was an affable and hospitable visionary, of hazy ideas, with a great liking for popularity and with a mania for undertaking too much. A heroic figure he was not, although his romantic position as pioneer in the great valley made him seem so to many travelers and historians. When gold-seekers later came, the ambitious Sutter utterly lost his head and threw away all his truly wonderful opportunities. . . . If he was often wronged, he was also often in the wrong; and his fate was the ordinary one of the persistent and unteachable dreamer."

93. Zollinger, *Sutter*, 308.

CHAPTER 5. LAND MONOPOLY IN NINETEENTH-
CENTURY CALIFORNIA

1. Charles A. Barker, "Henry George and the California Background of
Progress and Poverty," *California Historical Quarterly* 24 (June 1945): 97–115; *Sacramento Daily Record-Union*, August 4, 1877; *Report of the Joint Committee to Inquire into and Report upon the Condition of the Public and State Lands Lying within the Limits of the State* (Sacramento, 1872), 5–7; *Report of the Committee on Land Monopoly* (Sacramento, 1874), 193, 195.

2. As quoted in Paul W. Gates, "Public Land Disposal in California," *Agricultural History* 49 (January 1975): 168.

3. Gerald D. Nash, "The California State Land Office, 1858–1898," *Huntington Library Quarterly* 27 (August 1964): 348.

4. For introductions to Gates's work see his "An Overview of American Land Policy," *Agricultural History* 50 (January 1976): 213–29, and his monumental *History of Public Land Law Development* (Washington, D.C., 1968). Gates's essays on California have been collected in a volume entitled *Land and Law in California* (Ames, Iowa, 1991), for which Lawrence B. Lee has written an excellent introduction. The pieces include, in chronological order: "Adjudication of Spanish-Mexican Land Claims in California," *Huntington Library Quarterly* 21 (May 1958): 213–56; "California's Agricultural College Lands," *Pacific Historical Review* 30 (May 1961): 103–22; "California's Embattled Settlers," *California Historical Society Quarterly* 41 (June 1962): 99–130; "Pre–Henry George Land Warfare in California," *California Historical Quarterly* 46 (June 1967): 121–48; "The Suscol Principle, Preemption, and California Latifundia," *Pacific Historical Review* 39 (November 1970): 453–71; "The California Land Act of 1851," *California Historical Quarterly* 50 (December 1971): 395–430; "Corporate Farming in California," in Ray A. Billington, ed., *People of the Plains and Mountains: Essays in the History of the West Dedicated to Everett Dick* (Westport, Conn., 1973), 146–74; "The Frémont-Jones Scramble for California Land Claims," *Southern California Quarterly* 56 (Spring 1974): 13–44; "The Land Business of Thomas O. Larkin," *California Historical Quarterly* 54 (Winter 1975): 323–44; "Carpetbaggers Join the Rush for California Land," *California Historical Quarterly* 56 (Summer 1977): 98–127; "Public Land Disposal in California," *Agricultural History* 49 (January 1975), 158–78; "California Land Policy and Its Historical Context: The Henry George Era," in Eugene C. Lee, *Four Persistent Issues: Essays on California's Land Ownership Concentration, Water Deficits, Sub-State Regionalism, and Congressional Leadership* (Berkeley, 1978), 3–30; and *Land Policies in Kern County* (Bakersfield, Calif., 1978).

5. The following essays offer useful perspectives on Gates's work: John Gjerde, "'Roots of Maladjustment' in the Land: Paul Wallace Gates," *Reviews in American History* 19 (March 1991): 142–53; Harry Scheiber, "The Economic Historian as Realist and as Keeper of Democratic Ideals: Paul W. Gates' Studies of American Land Policy," *Journal of Economic History* 40 (September 1980): 585–93; Donald L. Winters, "Agricultural Tenancy in the Nineteenth-Century Middle West: The Historiographical Debate," *Indiana Magazine of History* 78 (June 1982): 128–53; Margaret B. Bogue and Allan G. Bogue, "Paul W. Gates,"

Great Plains Journal 18 (1979): 22–32; and Frederick Merk's foreword to David M. Ellis, ed., *The Frontier in American Development: Essays in Honor of Paul Wallace Gates* (Ithaca, N.Y., 1968).

Gates was a Progressive historian who saw the past as a morality play characterized by persistent clashes between the haves and have-nots, the powerful and the powerless. His passionate commitment to equality and fairness resulted in a moralism and presentism that sometimes blurred the complexity of issues and personalities. Virtually all large land speculators appear as selfish, socially pernicious types, while speculation by farmers—probably the most pervasive form of gambling in the nineteenth century—is forgiven or justified as a necessary adjunct to agriculture in a highly volatile market economy. The law, courts, and judges generally appear as servants of property and privilege, and corporate farms are invariably portrayed as sinister and repressive. Gates concluded his 1973 essay, "Corporation Farming in California," with the following indictment: "They [agribusiness companies] have long conducted a vendetta against organized labor and through the Associated Farmers of the nineteen thirties used their power to deny civil liberties to labor leaders by a combination of crude vigilantism and pliant local officials and courts. They have successfully resisted the enforcement of the 160-acre excess-land provision of reclamation legislation [abandoned in the early 1980s] and are partly responsible for the huge California Water Project that promises much to the large land owners at the expense of the tax payer. . . . [T]hrough their alliance with the utilities, the railroads, the real estate lobby, and the oil companies, the great land companies are in effective political and economic control of California" (p. 169). This, in Gates's mind, was the painful legacy of nineteenth-century California land policies.

6. Gates, "California Land Policy and Its Historical Context," 7; W. W. Robinson, *Land in California: The Story of Mission Lands, Ranchos, Squatters, Mining Claims, Railroad Grants, Land Scrip, Homesteads* (Berkeley, 1948), 70 –71; Joseph Ellison, *California and the Nation 1850 –1869: A Study of the Relations of a Frontier Community with the Federal Government* (Berkeley, 1927), 8 –24.

7. Gates, "Adjudication of Spanish-Mexican Land Claims in California," 3 –23; Gates, "The California Land Act of 1851," 24– 63.

8. In a brilliant exposé, Gates pointed out that the legislation's leading sponsors, William Carey Jones and John C. Frémont, had received grants of their own or had purchased land from Mexican grantees. Frémont claimed the infamous Mariposa grant, which had never been occupied, improved, or even located (all of which Mexican law required to perfect title). Frémont's claim was approved by the U.S. Supreme Court after the district court rejected it. Since it was the first case to reach the highest tribunal, it set an important precedent for the approval of other questionable claims. For the full story see Gates, "The Frémont-Jones Scramble for California Land Claims," 64–93. Also see William E. Ellison, *A Self-Governing Dominion: California, 1849 –1860* (Berkeley, 1950), 103 –5.

9. Gates, "The California Land Act of 1851," 399; Gates, "California's Embattled Settlers," 102; Gates, "Pre–Henry George Land Warfare in California," 122–23.

10. Gates, "Adjudication of Spanish-Mexican Land Claims in California," 214–15; Gates, "California Land Policy and Its Historical Context," 8.

11. Gates, "California's Agricultural College Lands," 106 –7. In the 1850s, most California farms were located in the coastal valleys, and most Mexican grants were within thirty miles of the Pacific. Since the grantees were responsible for surveying their own claims, and since the General Land Office did not want to waste money surveying *private* land, it began work in interior California.

12. The California legislature requested that the national government withdraw all land sold by the state to prevent duplicate entries at state and federal land offices. The General Land Office refused because federal statutes permitted the states to select only surveyed land and only with the approval of the secretary of the interior. In other words, to honor the legislature's request, officials in Washington would have had to accept California's illegal acts. Furthermore, they knew that the state was selling "swamp land" that was high and dry, in violation of the 1850 legislation granting flood lands to certain states. California defied and subverted federal land law in many ways, as other states had done, and in 1866 Congress confirmed all entries previously made under state law, legal or not. In all, the federal government granted about 9 percent of California to the state. School sections comprised two-thirds of the total, and swamp or overflow sections another one-fourth. See Gates, "Public Land Disposal in California," 166 – 67; Gerald D. Nash, "The California State Land Office, 1858–1898," *Huntington Library Quarterly* 27 (August 1964): 347–56; Nash, *State Government and Economic Development: A History of Administrative Policies in California, 1849 –1933* (Berkeley, 1964), 126 –28, 211; and Ellison, *California and the Nation 1850 –1869*, 52. On swamp land policy see Richard H. Peterson, "The Failure to Reclaim: California State Swamp Land Policy and the Sacramento Valley, 1850 –1866," *Southern California Quarterly* 56 (Winter 1974): 45– 60, and Robert Kelley, *Battling the Inland Sea: American Political Culture, Public Policy, and the Sacramento Valley, 1850 –1986* (Berkeley, 1989).

13. Gates, "Corporation Farming in California," 156 –57; Gates, "California's Land Policy and Its Historical Context," 14; Gates, "Public Land Disposal in California," 170 –71; Gates, *Land Policies in Kern County*, 4 – 6.

14. Settlers who continuously occupied land and paid taxes for five years could acquire title through adverse use, *if* the legal owner failed to improve the land and let taxes fall into arrears. Unlike other states, however, California did not require legal owners to reimburse rival claimants for their improvements following ejectment proceedings. See Gates, "Tenants of the Log Cabin," *Mississippi Valley Historical Review* 49 (June 1962): 3 –31.

15. Gates, "The Suscol Principle, Preemption, and California Latifundia," 209 –28; Gates, "Public Land Disposal in California," 169; Gates, "The California Land Act of 1851," 414.

16. Gates, "California's Agricultural College Lands," 229 – 49; Gates, "Public Land Disposal in California," 169; Gates, *Land Policies in Kern County*, 6, 25.

17. Gates, "Public Land Disposal in California," 172.

18. Gates, "California's Land Policy and Its Historical Context," 19; Gates, "The Suscol Principle, Preemption, and California Latifundia," 471.

19. Gates, "Pre–Henry George Land Warfare in California," 141.

20. Gates, "Public Land Disposal in California," 177 (quote); Gates, "California's Land Policy and Its Historical Context," 21; Gates, "Land Warfare in California," 142– 43.

21. This is not to say that Gates lacked an understanding of California agriculture during its formative years. See his perceptive, brief monograph *California Ranchos and Farms, 1846–1862* (Madison, 1967). However, he assumed that California's "land problem" was closely related to that experienced by other states, and, like his hero, Henry George, he never carefully defined "monopoly" or clearly identified the monopolists. In some places they appear as speculators, in others simply as large land owners—despite the fact that without irrigation a 5,000-acre ranch used for grazing in the Central Valley would support no more than 140 or 150 cattle.

22. See, for example, Gates's *Fifty Million Acres: Conflicts over Kansas Land Policy, 1854–1890* (Ithaca, N.Y., 1954).

23. The growth of agriculture was inhibited by an 1852 law which permitted farmers to claim damages from livestock *only* if they had fenced their land. Enclosing land was enormously expensive in the 1850s and 1860s, before barbed wire offered a cheap alternative to plank and post fences. Only with the passage of "no fence" laws in the 1870s, the construction of railroads into the San Joaquin Valley, and the increasing use of irrigation did farming begin to displace the grazing industry in the Central Valley.

24. On the wheat industry in California see Gates, *California Ranchos and Farms, 1846–1862;* Rodman Paul, "The Beginnings of Agriculture in California: Innovation vs. Continuity." *California Historical Quarterly* 41 (Spring 1973): 16–27; Paul, "The Wheat Trade Between California and the United Kingdom," *Mississippi Valley Historical Review* 45 (December 1958): 391–412; Osgood Hardy, "Agricultural Changes in California, 1860–1900," American Historical Association, Pacific Coast Branch, *Proceedings, 1929* (Eugene, Ore., 1930), 216–30; and Donald J. Pisani, *From the Family Farm to Agribusiness: The Irrigation Crusade in California and the West* (Berkeley, 1984), 5–11 and 286–89. The production of wheat increased from 6,000,000 bushels in 1860 to 16,000,000 in 1870, and to 40,000,000 in 1890, in which year California ranked as the second-largest wheat producing state in the nation. Output peaked at 45,000,000 bushels in 1896 but quickly declined thereafter, largely because of international competition and soil exhaustion. In 1916 California produced only 4,000,000 bushels.

25. *Abstract of the Twelfth Census of the United States, 1900* (Washington, D.C., 1904), 35. Colorado grew by 387.5 percent in the 1870s, by 112.1 percent in the 1880s, and by 30.6 percent during the 1890s. During the same decades, Washington's population increased by 214, 365, and 45 percent, and Wyoming's by 128, 192, and 47.9 percent.

26. Warren S. Thompson, *Growth and Changes in California's Population* (Los Angeles, 1955), 11, 12, 13, 36, 41; Pisani, *From the Family Farm to Agribusiness,* 3, 299.

27. See Gates, "The Frémont-Jones Scramble for California Land Claims," 32; Arthur Maass and Raymond L. Anderson, . . . *and the Desert Shall Rejoice: Conflict, Growth, and Justice in Arid Environments* (Cambridge, Mass., 1978), 210–11.

28. During the 1860s the state's miners fell from 83,000 to 36,000 while the number of farmers increased from 20,000 to 48,000. During the 1860s, the only large canal was the Moore Ditch that tapped Cache Creek in Yolo County. It was completed during the drought of 1864. Dry-farmed wheat remained the state's dominant crop during the 1870s, but irrigated land increased from 90,000 to 256,000 acres. See *Eighth Census of the United States, 1860* (Washington, D.C., 1864), 662,

Ninth Census of the United States 1870 (Washington, D.C., 1872), 3:820, and *The Country Gentleman* 40 (November 4, 1875): 699–700.

29. "Census Figures on Irrigation," *Irrigation Age* 3 (November 1892): 193; *Thirteenth Annual Report of the United States Geological Survey [1891–1892]* (Washington, D.C., 1893), Part 2, "Irrigation," 30–31.

30. Wheat farming was a risky business because the rainfall in many parts of the San Joaquin Valley left little margin between an "average" year and a drought. At least ten inches of rain well distributed throughout the winter and spring were needed to produce a good crop, and crops failed every second or third year. Initially, drought protection was far more important than the promise that irrigation would produce higher value crops by allowing farmers to select the time of planting and harvesting. See the report on the state's first major irrigation convention in the *Daily Express* (Los Angeles), October 25, 1873.

31. This was the principle, well established in California by the end of the 1850s, that water could be turned from the natural channel of a stream so long as the diverter put it to good use. In the West, prior appropriation became immensely popular because it was based on a simple principle and required no expensive bureaucracy to administer. The first to use water, if that use was "continuous," held the paramount right. The courts ranked remaining rights on a stream according to chronology. However, California also recognized riparian rights to parcels of public land patented before 1866, rights that were part of the title to land adjoining streams and lakes. They were independent of time or use. In theory, any individual riparian owner could demand the full flow of a stream by his land.

32. Gates, *Land Policies in Kern County* (Bakersfield, 1978); Gates, "Corporation Farming in California," 162–69; Gates "Public Land Disposal in California," 172, 174.

33. Margaret Aseman Cooper Zonlight, *Land, Water, and Settlement in Kern County, California, 1850–1890* (New York, 1979), 143, 174–75, 297–98, 300; John S. Hittell, *Commerce and Industries of the Pacific Coast* (San Francisco, 1882), 406; *Transactions of the California State Agricultural Society, 1900* (Sacramento, 1901), 89–95; *Fresno Weekly Expositor* (Fresno, Calif.), December 29, 1875.

34. *San Francisco Chronicle,* January 29, 1878.

35. *Bakersfield Californian,* May 20, 1880.

36. *Lux v. Haggin,* 69 Cal. 255 (1886). In 1877, diversions through the Kern County Land Company's canals resulted in the death of 10,000 cattle pastured downstream in the Buena Vista Slough, between Bakersfield and Tulare Lake, on land owned by the cattle company of Miller & Lux. Miller & Lux asked that upstream water users permit one-fourth of the stream to reach their lands. Haggin and his associates refused, setting the stage for a protracted court battle not decided until 1886. Ultimately, the California Supreme Court ruled that the riparian rights held by Miller & Lux took precedence over the appropriative claims of Haggin, Tevis, and Carr. The two sides reached an out-of-court accommodation in 1888. See Pisani, *From the Family Farm to Agribusiness,* 191–249, especially 243.

37. Most leases were for five years. The company charged nothing during the first year, but thereafter lessees had to buy the water they used and turn over 25 percent of their annual crop. *Bakersfield Californian,* March 1 and May 3, 1877, and March 19, 1881.

38. Zonlight, *Land, Water, and Settlement in Kern County California, 1850 –1890,* 174–75, 259, 316.

39. F. H. Newell, *Report on Agriculture by Irrigation in the Western Part of the United States at the Eleventh Census, 1890* (Washington, D.C., 1904), 234.

40. William Preston, *Vanishing Landscapes: Land and Life in the Tulare Lake Basin* (Berkeley, 1981), 97.

41. In 1868, four years before the Southern Pacific reached Fresno, William Chapman and Isaac Friedlander, two speculators in San Joaquin Valley land, persuaded a group of San Francisco capitalists to purchase agricultural college scrip and use it to claim an 80,000-acre block of land. This was done *before* any substantial number of settlers had entered the Kings River Basin. By locating the parcel upstream, the promoters headed off many of the water conflicts that occurred on the Kern. Maass and Anderson, . . . *and the Desert Shall Rejoice,* 157–58.

42. On the Fresno colonies see Virginia E. Thickens, "Pioneer Colonies of Fresno County" (M.A. thesis, University of California, Berkeley, 1939); Thickens, "Pioneer Agricultural Colonies of Fresno County," *California Historical Quarterly* 25 (March and June 1946): 17–38, 169 –77; Paul Vandor, *History of Fresno County California* (Los Angeles, 1919), 262–65; Maass and Anderson, . . . *and the Desert Shall Rejoice,* 157– 69; and Pisani, *From the Family Farm to Agribusiness,* 122–24.

43. William L. Kahrl, ed., *The California Water Atlas* (Sacramento, 1978), 5, 8. The larger supply of water permitted Fresno farmers to cultivate such thirsty, high-value crops as grapes and cotton, rather that the alfalfa raised around Bakersfield. Consequently, irrigation was much easier to pay for in the Fresno region.

44. Maass and Anderson, . . . *and the Desert Shall Rejoice,* 161– 63 (quote p. 162) and 236. It is important to note that in Fresno County, where many irrigated farms were twenty acres, large-scale wheat farming and ranching survived to the end of the century. For example, from 1875 to 1890, the number of landowners with 5,000 acres or more declined only from forty-four to forty-one, and those forty-one held 943,557 acres, about 100,000 *more* than the forty-four claimed in 1875. See ibid., 289.

45. The pueblo of Los Angeles contained about 18,000 acres at the time of statehood. The Mexican government granted it absolute title to the Los Angeles River. In 1873 the state legislature confirmed the city's exclusive control over the stream from its headwaters to the point at which it left the city limits. In 1877, the river watered 9,000 –10,000 acres in and adjoining the city, about half within the city limits. However, the city's rapid growth following completion of the Southern Pacific line into town in 1876 led to the subdivision and sale of the town farms. See Pisani, *From the Family Farm to Agribusiness,* 40, 44– 45.

46. *Pacific Rural Press* 6 (October 11, 1873): 232.

47. See, for example, Governor Newton Booth's speech to the California Grange at San Jose, as reported in the *Pacific Rural Press* 6 (November 1, 1873): 278, and the *Sacramento Daily Record-Union,* October 30, 1875.

48. Pisani, *From the Family Farm to Agribusiness,* 129–53.

49. *San Francisco Chronicle,* January 17, 1887.

50. *Weekly Colusa Sun* (Colusa, Calif.), October 29, 1887.

51. *Fallbrook Irrigation District v. Bradley,* 164 U.S. 112 (1896).

52. For an overview of the Wright Act see Pisani, *From the Family Farm to Agribusiness*, 250 – 82.

53. *Report of Irrigation Investigations in California*, U.S.D.A. Office of Experiment Stations, Bulletin 100, 57 Cong., 1 sess., 1902, S. Doc. 356, 22.

54. Ibid., 19.

55. Ibid., 170, 190, 195, 232.

56. Donald J. Pisani, "Water Law Reform in California, 1900 –1913," *Agricultural History* 54 (April 1980): 295 –317; Pisani, *From the Family Farm to Agribusiness*, 335 – 80.

57. Statistics can be deceiving. The size of California's farms declined from 1900 through the 1920s. For example, Tulare County farms shrank from an average 460 acres in 1900 to 242 acres in 1910 to 159 acres in 1925. However, this occurred mainly because the huge wheat farms so characteristic in the 1870s and 1880s were subdivided during the early decades of the twentieth century. See Preston, *Vanishing Landscapes: Land and Life in the Tulare Lake Basin*, 170, 200; *United States Census of Agriculture: 1935* (Washington, D.C., 1936), 1:944– 47.

58. Frank Beach, "The Economic Transformation of California, 1900 –1920: The Effects of the Westward Movement on California's Growth and Development in the Progressive Period" (Ph.D. diss., University of California, Berkeley, 1963), 106. These statistics must be used carefully. Although California farmland increased dramatically in value during the first two decades of the twentieth century, prices advanced rapidly during World War I—as they did throughout the nation—and in most parts of the state slumped badly during the 1920s.

CHAPTER 6. GEORGE MAXWELL, THE RAILROADS, AND
AMERICAN LAND POLICY

1. J. M. Hannaford to C. S. Mellon, April 18, 1899, President's Office Subject Files, 1.C.1.4F, file 19-D (George Maxwell Correspondence), Northern Pacific Papers, Minnesota Historical Society, St. Paul.

2. For this story see Donald J. Pisani, *To Reclaim a Divided West: Water, Law, and Public Policy, 1848 –1902* (Albuquerque, 1992), 285 –94.

3. *Report of the Secretary of the Interior, 1896* (Washington, D.C., 1896), vi; *Reno Evening Gazette*, October 31, 1893.

4. William E. Smythe, *Constructive Democracy: The Economics of a Square Deal* (New York, 1905), 367.

5. John N. Irwin, "A Great Domain by Irrigation," *Forum* 12 (February 1892): 749.

6. Surprisingly little has been written about Maxwell. The only overview of his life is superficial. See Andrew Hudanick, Jr., "George Hebard Maxwell: Reclamation's Militant Evangelist," *Journal of the West* 14 (1975): 108 –19. On his work in California, see Donald J. Pisani, *From the Family Farm to Agribusiness: The Irrigation Crusade in California and the West, 1850 –1931* (Berkeley, 1984), 273 –78, 290 –93, and 347–50.

7. *California Advocate* 1 (December 1896): 88.

8. Pisani, *From the Family Farm*, 271–73.

9. George Maxwell to William Newport, August 13, 1900, box 9; Maxwell to

E. W. Risley, September 8, 1900, box 4; and Maxwell to H. E. Phillips, December 3, 1903, box 3, George Maxwell Collection, Louisiana State Museum, New Orleans.

10. The Carey Act (1894), a modified land cession bill, promised each western state up to one million acres if it reclaimed the land or arranged to have it reclaimed by private companies. Enacted at the depth of the depression, when the western flow of capital and settlers had ceased, the legislation had little success, at least in the nineteenth century.

11. Elwood Mead to Maxwell, December 21, 1898, box 12, Maxwell Collection.

12. Hiram Martin Chittenden, "Preliminary Examination of Reservoir Sites in Wyoming and Colorado," 55 Cong., 2 sess. (1897), H. Doc. 141, serial 3666.

13. *The Citrograph* (Redlands, Calif.), July 30, 1898, and January 7 and October 28, 1899; George H. Maxwell, "The Irrigation District System," *Irrigation Age* 12 (June 1898): 250–53; Maxwell, "Annex Arid America," ibid., 13 (November 1898): 51–55; *National Advocate* 5 (October 1900): 2; Maxwell to V. S. McClatchy, August 6, 1900, box 13, Maxwell Collection.

14. Maxwell to Paris Gibson, December 8, 1900, box 1, Maxwell Collection.

15. Maxwell to Gibson, January 9, 1900, box 1, ibid.; *Republican* (Rawlins, Wyo.), January 13, 1900; *Sheridan Enterprise* (Sheridan, Wyo.), February 24, 1900; *Casper Tribune*, January 4, 1900; *Newcastle News Journal* (Newcastle, Wyo.), February 2, 1900. Mead's influence became obvious when the *Report of the Secretary of Agriculture, 1899* (Washington, D.C., 1899), lix, approved most of the principles contained in Mondell's bill.

16. Maxwell to Gibson, December 8, 1900, box 1, Maxwell Collection.

17. Pisani, *To Reclaim a Divided West*, 309–11.

18. See, for example, Pisani, *To Reclaim a Divided West*, 273–325, and Donald Worster, *Rivers of Empire: Water Aridity and the Growth of the American West* (New York, 1985), 156–69.

19. K. Ross Toole, *Montana: An Uncommon Land* (Norman, 1959), 92; Mary W. M. Hargreaves, *Dry Farming in the Northern Great Plains, 1900–1925* (Cambridge, Mass., 1957), 329, 402–3.

20. James J. Hill to Jonathan S. Kennedy, May 16, 1902, Personal and Private Correspondence, James J. Hill Library, St. Paul, Minn. Also, see Hill to Paris Gibson, July 29, 1902, ibid.; Hargreaves, *Dry Farming in the Northern Great Plains*, 75, 136–37; and Michael P. Malone and Richard B. Roeder, *Montana: A History of Two Centuries* (Seattle, 1976), 183.

21. Albro Martin, *James J. Hill and the Opening of the Northwest* (New York, 1976), 333–35. Gibson and Hill jointly speculated in real estate adjoining Great Falls in the middle 1880s. No one had closer ties to Hill than Gibson. For example, despite his own friendship with Hill, on February 1, 1903, Maxwell wrote to Gibson: "If you should see Mr. Hill and there is any way in which he can help Reeder [secure the chairmanship of the House Irrigation Committee instead of Frank Mondell] I wish very much that you would get him to do it. It is a subject upon which I hesitate to write him, because I could not by letter satisfactorily explain the situation." See Paris Gibson File, box 1, Maxwell Collection.

22. Gibson to Maxwell, January 20, February 28, and November 15, 1900, ibid.

23. Montana was not the only state in which the Desert Land Act was heavily

used in the early twentieth century. In the Imperial Valley of San Diego County, about 200,000 acres of government land were taken up from 1901 to 1903 when private individuals reclaimed that valley. See L. M. Holt (Imperial Land Company) to George H. Maxwell, July 1, 1903, box 7, ibid.

24. Gibson to Maxwell, May 30, 1903, box 1, ibid.

25. *Cong. Rec.*, 58 Cong., 2 sess. (March 24, 1904), 3607.

26. Maxwell to Gibson, March 28, 1903, box 1; Maxwell to H. C. Plumley, December 7, 1903, box 8, Maxwell Collection.

27. Maxwell to Gifford Pinchot, December 2, 1903, box 2, ibid.

28. Maxwell outlined his views in letters to Harry Brook, August 7, 1903, box 1, and Gifford Pinchot, November 17, 1903, box 2, ibid.

29. U.S. land policy in the late nineteenth and early twentieth centuries has not received the attention it deserves. However, for brief treatments of the Public Land Commission of 1903, see E. Louise Peffer, *The Closing of the Public Domain: Disposal and Reservation Policies 1900 –1950* (Stanford, Calif., 1951), 45–53, and Paul Wallace Gates, *History of Public Land Law Development* (New York, 1979), 488 –91.

30. H. C. Hansbrough to Gifford Pinchot, December 24, 1903, box 698, Gifford Pinchot Collection, Library of Congress, Washington, D.C.

31. C. J. Blanchard to F. H. Newell, June 20 [quote] and 24, 1904, Central Files 1902-19, file 275, box 148, Records of the Bureau of Reclamation, Record Group 115. Also see S. B. Robbins to F. H. Newell, July 1, 1904, ibid. Mary Hargreaves notes that the public lands covered by the Minot Land Office were reduced from 6.25 million acres in 1901 to less than 1 million in 1906, and the same was true of land offices throughout the upper Great Plains (*Dry-Farming*, 375).

32. Public Lands Commission to the President, March 7, 1904, Central Files 1902-19, file 275, box 147, RG 115.

33. "Report of Public Land Commission, 1905," *S. Exec. Doc.* 189, 58 Cong., 3 sess.; Peffer, *Closing of the Public Domain*, 46.

34. J. D. Whelpley to Maxwell, January 9, 1903; and Maxwell to Whelpley, January 18, 1903, box 2; Maxwell to Harry Brook, March 4, 1903, box 1; Gibson to Maxwell, January 9, 1903, box 1; Maxwell to Gibson, March 28, 1903, box 1, Maxwell Collection.

35. Gibson to Maxwell, December 7 and 30, 1903, box 1, ibid. See also Gibson to Maxwell, July 10, August 17, and December 7, 1903, and Maxwell to Gibson, October 10 and December 20, 1903, ibid.; Maxwell to Gifford Pinchot, November 17, 1903, box 2, ibid.; Maxwell outlined his objections to the president's policy in his letter to Theodore Roosevelt, October 19, 1903, box 4, ibid.

36. Gates, *History of Public Land Law Development*, 489.

37. Apparently, in 1904 a bill passed the Senate promising to the Reclamation Fund all proceeds from timber sales on government land. See *Cong. Rec.*, 58 Cong., 2 sess. (March 25, 1904), 3668.

38. Maxwell to Pinchot, November 17, 1903, box 2, Maxwell Collection.

39. On the relationship between Pinchot and Newell, and the tension between federal reclamation and forestry policies, see Donald J. Pisani, "Forestry and Reclamation," *Forest and Conservation History* 37 (1993): 68 –79. For Maxwell's views on grazing, see his letter to R. H. Forbes, September 23, 1904, in Central File 1902-19, file 275, box 147, RG 115. On June 7, 1904, Newell advised Pinchot that the Public

Lands Commission ought not "to put all of our reforms into one law, but endeavor to gain each point in succession. . . . It will necessitate our commission continuing its operations for many years, but in my opinion this is the only [safe?] way in which reform of ancient abuses can be accomplished by uprooting them one at a time." See Central Files 1902-19, file 275, box 148, RG 115, and also the Gifford Pinchot Collection, box 696.

40. Elwood Mead to Charles F. Manderson, December 16, 1901; Mead to George S. Walker, April 12, 1902; Mead to C. E. Wantland, April 24, 1902, Office of Experiment Stations, General Correspondence, 1898–1912, box 1, Records of the Bureau of Agricultural Engineering, RG 8. *Salt Lake City Telegram,* April 10, 1902; *Salt Lake City Tribune,* April 11, 1902; *Cheyenne Daily Leader,* April 25, 1902.

41. *Montana Daily Record,* September 25, 1903; *Helena Daily Independent,* September 26, 1903. For a brief history of the Milk River Project see George Wharton James, *Reclaiming the Arid West: The Story of the United States Reclamation Service* (New York, 1917), 180–85.

42. James J. Hill to F. H. Newell, October 1 and 8, 1904, and Hill to C. D. Walcott, June 5, 1905, Personal and Private Correspondence, Letterbook June 1, 1902–June 7, 1905, Hill Library; F. H. Newell to Hill, October 4, 1904, C. D. Walcott to Hill, December 31, 1904, and B. Campbell to L. W. Hill, March 6, 1906, President's Subject Files, 4013, Great Northern Papers, Minnesota Historical Society, St. Paul.

43. F. H. Newell to George H. Maxwell, March 19, 1904, President's Subject Files, 4013, Minnesota Historical Society.

44. For example, C. S. Mellen, president of the Northern Pacific, consistently opposed Maxwell's subsidy. In an April 13, 1903, letter to J. Kruttschnitt, assistant to the president of the Southern Pacific, he noted: "My opinion has not changed, that there is no occasion for the railways to continue payments of this character; and but for the fact that Mr. Huntington, at the time [1899 or 1900], made a personal appeal to me to join him in this matter, our company would never have entered into such an arrangement. There is less reason now than in the beginning, and I shall be glad to further any efforts you may make for its discontinuance." See Northern Pacific President's Office Subject Files, file 19-D, George Maxwell Correspondence, Minnesota Historical Society. Also see C. P. Huntington to C. S. Mellen, February 15, 1900, ibid.

45. Louis W. Hill (vice president, Great Northern) to D. Miller, March 10, 1904, President's Subject Files 4013, Great Northern Papers, Minnesota Historical Society. See also Louis W. Hill to J. W. Blabon, August 22, 1904, ibid.; F. L. Whitney to Blabon, April 5, 1904, ibid.; Thomas H. Carter to W. M. Wooldridge, December 27, 1906, ibid.; and Thomas Cooper to Howard Elliott, September 29, 1904, Northern Pacific President's Office Subject Files, 1.C.1.4F, file 19-D, George Maxwell Correspondence, Minnesota Historical Society.

46. James J. Hill to George H. Maxwell, March 17, 1905, Personal and Private Correspondence, Letterbook June 1, 1902–June 7, 1905, Hill Library. George Maxwell was quick to respond to criticisms of his work. In a preachy July 1904 letter to Louis Hill he remarked: "You must never overlook the relation between cause and effect. *Everything* that is now being done in your territory under the National Irrigation act or which will hereafter be done in that territory under that

Act, in North Dakota or elsewhere, is the result, first of my *conception* of the plan of campaign which we have carried out, and second, of the work which we have done in co-operation in carrying it out; and if we go back to first causes, the *idea* which I originated" (Maxwell to Hill, July 26, 1904, Great Northern President's Subject Files, 4013, Great Northern Papers, Minnesota Historical Society).

47. S. 5168, 58 Cong., 2 sess.

48. *Cong. Rec.*, 58 Cong., 2 sess. (March 24, 1904), 3606.

49. Ibid. (March 25 and April 4, 1904), 3666, 4214–16. Hansbrough did not argue that all support for reform came from the railroads. He also claimed that large timber companies wanted to repeal the Timber and Stone Act so that they could eliminate competition from small sawmill operators.

50. *Cong. Rec.*, 58 Cong., 2 sess. (March 25, 1904), 3675 (March 31, 1904) 4032. The Clark statement is on p. 4029.

51. Ibid., (April 2, 1904), 4140, 4143 – 44, 4147.

52. Ibid., (March 25, 1904), 3663 – 64.

53. Ibid., (April 27, 1904), 5682 and 5684.

54. Peffer, *Closing of the Public Domain*, 56 –57.

55. Hargreaves, *Dry Farming*, 148, 224.

56. Ibid., 108 –9, 124. On the dry-farming boom at the turn of this century, see also John A. Widtsoe, *Dry-Farming* (New York, 1911).

57. Hargreaves, *Dry Farming*, 16 –19; Peffer, *Closing of the Public Domain*, 134 –37.

58. See, for example, Wallace D. Farnham, "'The Weakened Spring of Government': A Study in Nineteenth-Century American History," *American Historical Review* 68 (1963): 662– 80; Farnham, "Railroads in Western History: The View from the Union Pacific," in Gene M. Gressley, ed., *The American West, A Reorientation* (Laramie, Wyo., 1966), 95 –109; and Robert Harrison, "'The Weakened Spring of Government' Revisited: The Growth of Federal Power in the Late Nineteenth Century," in Rhondri Jeffreys Jones and Bruce Collins, eds., *The Growth of Federal Power in American History* (Dekalb, Ill., 1983).

PART THREE: FORESTS, CONSERVATION, AND
BUREAUCRACY

1. Samuel P. Hays, *Conservation and the Gospel of Efficiency: The Progressive Conservation Movement, 1890 –1920* (Cambridge, Mass., 1959), 3.

2. Although most studies of conservation begin in the so-called Progressive Era, two notable exceptions are John Reiger, *American Sportsmen and the Origins of Conservation* (Norman, 1986), and Alfred Runte, *The National Parks: The American Experience* (Lincoln, 1979).

3. Michael J. Lacey, "The World of the Bureaus: Government and the Positivist Project in the Late Nineteenth century," in Michael J. Lacey and Mary O. Furner, eds., *The State and Social Investigation in Britain and the United States* (New York, 1993), 132. On government science in the late nineteenth century, also see A. Hunter Dupree, *Science in the Federal Government: A History of Policies and Activities to 1940* (Cambridge, Mass., 1957); Michael J. Lacey, "The Mysteries of Earth-

Making Dissolve: Washington's Intellectual Community and the Origins of American Environmentalism in the Late Nineteenth Century" (Ph.D. diss., George Washington University, 1979); James K. Flack, *Desideratum in Washington: The Intellectual Community in the Capital City, 1879 –1900* (Cambridge, Mass., 1975); Wilcomb Washburn, *The Cosmos Club of Washington: A Centennial History, 1878 –1978* (Washington, D.C., 1978); and George Brown Goode, ed., *The Smithsonian Institution, 1846 –1896: The History of Its First Half Century* (Washington, D.C., 1897).

4. The Powell quote is as reprinted in Arthur Ekirch, *Man and Nature in America* (New York, 1963), 85.

5. For example, Donald Worster argues that many scientists attributed the Dust Bowl of the 1930s to drought, rather than to environmentally destructive patterns of agricultural land use, because such an explanation absolved them from criticizing the destructive elements in capitalism (see *Nature's Economy: A History of Ecological Ideas* [New York, 1994], xii [quote], and 221 –53).

6. Stanley M. Guralnick, "The American Scientist in Higher Education, 1820 –1910," in Nathan Reingold, ed., *The Sciences in the American Context: New Perspectives* (Washington, D.C., 1979), 128 –29, 132.

7. The conflict involved more than ideas. The U.S. Geological Survey had cornered the market on government research in the sciences. Until its stranglehold on appropriations could be broken, existing natural resource agencies had no way to expand their own work.

8. Jay N. Darling, "Desert Makers," *Country Gentleman* 105 (October 1935): 5.

CHAPTER 7. FORESTS AND CONSERVATION

1. There is no overview of conservation after the Civil War, though many books and articles cover the years from 1890 to 1940. The main focus of these surveys has been relatively narrow—federal resource policies in the trans-Mississippi West. The South and East, individual states, and private conservation groups have received far less historical attention, even in the twentieth century. Samuel P. Hays, *Conservation and the Gospel of Efficiency: The Progressive Conservation Movement, 1890 –1920* (Cambridge, Mass., 1959); Donald C. Swain, *Federal Conservation Policy, 1921 –1933* (Berkeley, 1963); A. L. Riesch Owen, *Conservation Under F. D. R.* (New York, 1983). See also J. Leonard Bates, "Fulfilling American Democracy: The Conservation Movement, 1907 to 1921," *Mississippi Valley Historical Review* 44 (June 1957): 29 –57; Dodds, "The Historiography of American Conservation: Past and Prospects," *Pacific Northwest Quarterly* 56 (April 1965): 75 – 81; Dodds, ed., "Conservation and Reclamation in the Trans-Mississippi West: A Critical Bibliography," *Arizona and the West* 13 (Summer 1971): 143 –71; Thomas LeDuc, "The Historiography of Conservation," *Forest History* 9 (October 1965): 23 –28; Timothy O'Riordan, "The Third American Conservation Movement: New Implications for Public Policy," *Journal of American Studies* 5 (August 1971): 155–71; Donald Fleming, "Roots of the New Conservation Movement," *Perspectives in American History* 6 (1972): 5–91; James L. Penick, Jr., "The Resource Revolution," in *Technology in Western Civilization*, ed. Melvin Kranzberg and Carroll W. Pursell, Jr., 2 vols. (New York, 1967),

2:431 – 48; Robert O. Beatty, "The Conservation Movement," *Annals of the American Academy of Political and Social Science* 281 (May 1952): 10 –19; Grant McConnell, "The Conservation Movement—Past and Present," *Western Political Quarterly* 7 (September 1954): 463 –78; and Lawrence Rakestraw, "Conservation Historiography: An Assessment," *Pacific Historical Review* 41 (August 1972), 271– 88.

2. Hans Huth, *Nature and the American: Three Centuries of Changing Attitudes* (Berkeley, 1957); Arthur A. Ekirch, Jr., *Man and Nature in America* (New York, 1963); Alfred Runte, *National Parks: The American Experience* (Lincoln, 1979); John F. Reiger, *American Sportsmen and Conservation* (New York, 1975); James B. Trefethen, *An American Crusade for Wildlife* (New York, 1975); Roderick Nash, *Wilderness and the American Mind* (New Haven, 1967); Donald Worster, ed., *American Environmentalism: The Formative Period, 1860 –1915* (New York, 1973); Worster, *Nature's Economy: The Roots of Ecology* (San Francisco, 1977); Roy Robbins, *Our Landed Heritage: The Public Domain, 1776 –1936* (Princeton, 1942); Paul W. Gates and Robert W. Swenson, *History of Public Land Law Development* (Washington, D.C., 1968). See also, for example, Arthur A. Ekirch, Jr.'s chapter "Conservationist Ideology," in which he concludes: "Conservation did not become an important American ideology until the 1900's" because the United States was "too much a land of plenty to be worried over alleged or impending scarcities. . . . Only the so-called closing of the frontier—at least in the sense of free and easy exploitation of the West—made conservation the serious concern of some Americans" (*Man and Nature in America*, 81–99, esp. 81–82).

3. Andrew Denny Rodgers III, *Bernhard Edward Fernow: A Story of North American Forestry* (Princeton, 1951), 9, 42, 100, 154–58, 206 –26; Gates and Swenson, *History of Public Land Law Development*, 550 –52, 565 –70. Hans L. Trefousse's biography of Carl Schurz devotes only one paragraph to Schurz's pathbreaking forest and conservation policies (see *Carl Schurz: A Biography* [Knoxville, 1982], 241– 42). John Ise and Jenks Cameron focus almost entirely on federal and state legislation. Like most students of natural resource policies in the late nineteenth century, they emphasize the laissez-faire anticonservation spirit embodied in such wasteful, shortsighted legislation as the Timber Culture Act (1873) and the Free Timber Act (1878). The arguments of the scientists and popular writers who opposed such laws receive scant consideration. See Ise, *The United States Forest Policy* (New Haven, 1920), 42–44, 52–53, 55–78, 112–18, 120 –29, 141– 42, and Jenks Cameron, *The Development of Governmental Forest Control in the United States* (Baltimore, 1928), 201–10.

4. James Fenimore Cooper, *The Pioneers* (New York, 1964), 20, 100, 103, 218 –19; Cooper, *The Prairie* (New York, 1964), 19, 24 –25, 69, 122, 206; Gilbert Chinard, "The American Philosophical Society and the Early History of Forestry in America," *Proceedings of the American Philosophical Society* 89 (July 1945): 469; Samuel Trask Dana, *Forest and Range Policy: Its Development in the United States* (New York, 1956), 74–75; Ise, *United States Forest Policy*, 26 –27. For a recent discussion of James Fenimore Cooper's view of the shrinking wilderness, see Lee Clark Mitchell, *Witnesses to a Vanishing America: The Nineteenth-Century Response* (Princeton, 1981), 42– 47.

5. Michael Williams, "Products of the Forest: Mapping the Census of 1840," *Forest History* 24 (January 1980): 6, 10, 14 –15.

6. Frederick Starr, Jr., "American Forests; Their Destruction and Preservation," in *Report of the Commissioner of Agriculture for the Year 1865* (Washington, D.C., 1866),

210–34, esp. 210–13, 221. Starr urged the establishment of nurseries throughout the nation to study tree culture. He maintained that because Americans had little respect for public property, the creation of state or national forests would do little to avert the famine. He favored, instead, inducements to cultivate trees on cutover lands close to the cities, though a second proposal to plant timber trees on every treeless quarter-section throughout the nation anticipated the Timber Culture Act of 1873 on a much larger geographical scale (ibid., 210, 223–25, 226–27, 229).

7. Starr, "American Forests," 212; United States Census Office, *Abstract of the Twelfth Census of the United States, 1900* (Washington, D.C., 1902), 34–35. On the history of the nineteenth-century lumber industry in the United States, see James Elliott Defebaugh, *History of the Lumber Industry of America*, 2 vols. (Chicago, 1906–1907).

8. Sherry Hessler Olson, "Commerce and Conservation: The Railroad Experience," *Forest History* 9 (January 1966): 3; Olson, *The Depletion Myth: A History of Railroad Use of Timber* (Cambridge, Mass., 1971), 8–29; "The Rapid Destruction of Our Forests," *Scientific Monthly* 32 (December 1887): 225–26.

9. N. H. Egleston, "Methods and Profits of Tree-Planting," *Popular Science Monthly* 21 (May 1882): 1–2.

10. Ise, *United States Forest Policy*, 31–32; J. M. Tuttle, "The Minnesota Pineries," *Harper's Magazine* 36 (March 1868): 409–23; *Report of the State Board of Agriculture for 1868 and 1869* (Sacramento, 1870), 28; *Biennial Report of the State Board of Agriculture for the Years 1870 and 1871* (Sacramento, 1872), 21; *Report of the Commissioner of Agriculture for the Year 1872* (Washington, D.C., 1874), 442; A. W. Chase, "Timber Belts of the Pacific Coast," *Overland Monthly* 13 (September 1874), 249; *Sacramento Daily Union*, June 19, 1878; *Garden and Forest*, December 4, 1895, 490; "Destruction of Forests in California," *Scientific American*, December 14, 1895, 377. See also *Sacramento Daily Union*, November 25, 1869; ibid., February 1, 1870; *Pacific Rural Press*, August 26, 1871, 118; and *Report of the Commissioner of Agriculture for the Year 1883* (Washington, D.C., 1883), 448.

11. *Report of the Secretary of the Interior*, House Reports, 45 Cong., 2 sess., no. 1, November 1, 1877, 2 vols. (Washington, D.C., 1877), 1:xvi; *Report of the Secretary of the Interior*, House Reports, 45 Cong., 3 sess., no. 1, 1878, 2 vols. Washington, D.C., 1878), 1:xii; Charles S. Sargent, *Report on the Forests of North America (Exclusive of Mexico)* (Washington, D.C., 1884); Sargent, "The Protection of Forests," *North American Review* 135 (October 1882), 386–401; *Forest and Stream*, April 13, 1882, 223; ibid., January 31, 1884, 2; ibid., December 25, 1884, 422; ibid., January 15, 1885, 482; "The Forest Census," *Nation*, April 2, 1885, 284–85; Fernow, "Our Forestry Problem," *Popular Science Monthly* 32 (December 1887): 231; "United States Division of Forestry," *Popular Science Monthly* 39 (September 1891): 714; Frederic Bancroft, ed., *Speeches, Correspondence, and Political Papers of Carl Schurz* (New York, 1913), 5:24. In 1903 Bernhard E. Fernow predicted that the nation's forests would be exhausted within thirty years "and . . . most important coniferous supplies in a very much shorter time" ("Outlook of the Timber Supply in the United States," *Forestry and Irrigation* 9 [May 1903]: 230). For a discussion of how standards used to estimate the timber supply changed through time, see Martha A. Dietz, "A Review of the Estimates of Sawtimber Stands in the United States, 1880–1946," *Journal of Forestry* 45 (December 1947): 865–74.

12. *Forest and Stream,* September 25, 1873, 104; "Forests," *Scientific American,* September 19, 1891, 181; "A Forest 3,000 Miles Long by 1,700 Miles Wide," ibid., March 2, 1895, 139; Charles E. Bessey, "Are the Trees Advancing or Retreating upon the Nebraska Plains?" *Science,* November 24, 1899, 768 –70. The assumption that all land could produce forests under the right circumstances had implications not lost on Great Plains farmers. One wrote to *Science* in 1888 maintaining that before the forests of western Michigan had been destroyed, "all the delicate fruits of temperate climates were successfully grown [here]" (H. D. Post, "The Influence of Forests upon Rainfall and Climate," *Science,* January 27, 1888, 50).

13. Noah Webster, Jr., "On the Effects of Evergreens on Climate," *Transactions of the New York Agricultural Society, 1799* (New York, 1799), 51 –52; Howard W. Lull, "Forest Influences: Growth of a Concept," *Journal of Forestry* 47 (September 1949), 700 –705.

14. *Report of the Secretary of the Interior, Part I,* House Reports, 40 Cong., 2 sess., no. 1, November 18, 1867 (Washington, D.C., 1867), 159 – 60; Franklin B. Hough, "On the Preservation of Forests and the Planting of Timber," in *Cultivation of Timber and the Preservation of Forests,* House Reports, 43 Cong., 1 sess., no. 259, March 17, 1874 (Washington, D.C., 1874), 90 –101; *Pacific Rural Press,* June 13, 1874, 376; "Influence of Forests on Climatic Conditions," *Scientific American,* August 25, 1888, 118; "The Influence of Forests on Climate," *Nature,* June 4, 1885, 115; *Science,* November 23, 1888, 241. For overviews of the influence of forests on rainfall, see Henry Nash Smith, "Rain Follows the Plow: The Notion of Increased Rainfall for the Great Plains, 1844–1880," *Huntington Library Quarterly* 10 (February 1947): 169–93; David M. Emmons, "American Myth: Desert to Eden; Theories of Increased Rainfall and the Timber Culture Act of 1873," *Forest History* 15 (October 1971): 6 –14; and Charles R. Kutzleb, "American Myth: Desert to Eden; Can Forests Bring Rain to the Plains?" ibid., 14 –21.

15. *Biennial Report of the Board of Agriculture of the State Agricultural Society for the Years 1866 and 1867* (Sacramento, 1868), 13, 14; *Popular Science Monthly* 7 (June 1875): 207–9; P. F. Schofield, "Forests and Rainfall," ibid. 8 (November 1875): 111–12; "How Woods Preserve Moisture," ibid. 28 (January 1886): 429–30; "Forests and Climate," ibid. 47 (May 1895): 139; Fernow, "Our Forestry-Problem," 229; *Forest and Stream,* August 19, 1875, 21; Abbot Kinney, "The Forest: Forestry in California—IV," *Garden and Forest,* October 17, 1888, 405– 6; B. E. Fernow, "Climatic Influence of Forests," ibid., March 29, 1893, 147– 48; "The Influence of Forests on the Quantity and Frequency of Rainfall: Mr. Gannett's Paper," *Science,* November 23, 1888, 242– 44; ibid., June 5, 1891, 313 –14.

16. Those who questioned the assumption that forests promoted rainfall included John Wesley Powell, director of the United States Geological Survey (USGS), Henry Gannett, chief geographer of the USGS, and Charles S. Sargent. J. W. Powell, *Report on the Lands of the Arid Region of the United States with a More Detailed Account of the Lands of Utah. With Maps* (Washington, D.C., 1878), 1– 4, 14–19, 71–73; J. W. Powell to F. H. Turnock, February 12, 1890, letterbook December 10, 1889–April 15, 1890, "Outgoing Correspondence," Records of the United States Geological Survey, RG 57, National Archives; Henry Gannett, "Do Forests Influence Rainfall?" *Science,* January 6, 1888, 3 –5; Gannett, "Is the Rainfall Increasing upon the Plains?" ibid., March 2, 1888, 99 –100; Gannett, "Influence of Forests

on the Quantity and Frequency of Rainfall," 242– 44; Charles S. Sargent, "The Rainfall on the Plains," *Garden and Forest,* June 6, 1888, 169; Sargent, "Protection of Forests," 386; "American Forestry," *Nation* 28 (January 1879): 87– 88 ; Daniel Draper, "Has Our Climate Changed?" *Popular Science Monthly* 1 (October 1872): 665–74; "Relation of Elevation and Exposure to Rainfall," ibid. 18 (March 1881): 714–15; "The Laws of Rain-Fall," ibid. 21 (July 1882): 423; "Forests and Climate," ibid. 21 (August 1882): 562; George E. Curtiss, "The Rainfall on the Plains," *Garden and Forest,* October 24, 1888, 411–12; *Forest and Stream,* November 11, 1875, 212; ibid., October 2, 1884, 183.

17. *Forest and Stream,* January 1, 1885, 441; "Forestry," *Popular Science Monthly* 9 (September 1876): 632; "The Preservation of Forests," *Scientific American,* March 8, 1879, 145. See also the memorial to the state legislatures adopted by the American Association for the Advancement of Science at its August 30, 1880, meeting in Franklin B. Hough, *Report on Forestry, Submitted to Congress by the Commissioner of Agriculture* (Washington, D.C., 1882), 59 – 60.

18. *Report of the Secretary of the Interior,* House Reports, 40 Cong., 2 sess., 159– 60; Felix L. Oswald, "The Preservation of Forests," *North American Review* 128 (January 1879): 41; N. H. Egleston, "The Value of Our Forests," *Popular Science Monthly* 19 (June 1881): 176; Egleston, "What We Owe to the Trees," *Harper's New Monthly Magazine* 64 (April 1882): 682; Fernow, "Our Forestry Problem," 233; George Perkins Marsh, *Man and Nature* (Cambridge, Mass., 1965), 113–280, esp. 254, 258.

19. Chinard, "American Philosophical Society and the Early History of Forestry in America," 453; Jeremy Belknap, *The History of New Hampshire,* 3 vols. (Boston, 1813), 3:171–72.

20. Kenneth Thompson, "The Australian Fever Tree in California: Eucalyptus and Malaria Prophylaxis," *Annals of the Association of American Geographers* 60 (June 1970): 230 – 44; *Forest and Stream,* September 24, 1874, 101; "Trees and Health," *Popular Science Monthly* 12 (April 1878): 758; "Sanitary and Climatic Influence of Forests," ibid. 44 (January 1894): 426; "The Sanitary Value of Trees," *Scientific American,* June 12, 1886, 375; B. E. Fernow, "The Forest: Hygienic Significance of Forest Air and Forest Soil," *Garden and Forest,* January 18, 1893, 34–35. The *Scientific American* argued that forests purified water as well as air: "Where the water of a stream has been polluted, as by sheep washing, for instance, after having passed for a few miles through a shady and dense forest, the water appears as clear as it was previously" ("Influence of Forests on Climatic Conditions," 118).

21. *Forest and Stream,* April 13, 1882, 204; ibid., April 17, 1884, 221; "Influence of Forests on Climatic Conditions," 118; F. L. Oswald, "The Climatic Influence of Vegetation—A Plea for Our Forests," *Popular Science Monthly* 11 (August 1877): 385–90; "The Forest," ibid. 38 (November 1890): 143 – 44; J. B. Harrison, "Forests and Civilization: The North Woods—VII," *Garden and Forest,* September 11, 1889, 442; [C. S. Sargent], "Forests and Floods," ibid., November 4, 1896, 441. The influence of forests on stream flow—almost an article of religious faith in the 1870s and 1880s— became a hot issue during the early years of the twentieth century. Gordon B. Dodds, "The Stream-Flow Controversy: A Conservation Turning Point," *Journal of American History* 56 (June 1969): 59 – 69.

22. "Waste Land and Forest Culture," *Scientific American,* March 13, 1875, 161;

"Timber Waste a National Suicide," ibid., February 12, 1876, 97; "Forests and Civilization," *Garden and Forest*, December 19, 1888, 505; C. E. Norton, "Forests and Civilization," ibid., July 10, 1889, 333.

23. Sylvester Baxter, "The Forestry Work of the Tenth Census," *Atlantic Monthly* 48 (November 1881) 682; *Forest and Stream*, August 21, 1873, 26; ibid., December 25, 1884, 442; William Hammond Hall, "Influence of Parks and Pleasure-Grounds," *Overland Monthly* 11 (December 1873): 527; Egleston, "What We Owe to the Trees," 686; *Pacific Rural Press*, April 19, 1884, 380.

24. Marsh, *Man and Nature;* Charles Sprague Sargent to Robert Underwood Johnson, November 25, 1908, box 6, "Incoming Correspondence," Robert Underwood Johnson Collection (Bancroft Library, University of California, Berkeley).

25. David Lowenthal, *George Perkins Marsh: Versatile Vermonter* (New York, 1958). See also Jane Curtis, Will Curtis, and Frank Lieberman, *The World of George Perkins Marsh, America's First Conservationist and Environmentalist* (Woodstock, Vt., 1982); Ekirch, *Man and Nature in America*, 70–80; and Charles E. Randall, "George Perkins Marsh: Conservation's Forgotten Man," *American Forests* 71 (April 1965): 20–23.

26. Marsh, *Man and Nature*, 29, 279–80; Charles Darwin, *On the Origin of Species by Means of Natural Selection; or, The Preservation of Favored Races in the Struggle for Life* (London, 1859).

27. Marsh, *Man and Nature*, 9. The forests surrounding the Mediterranean area are much smaller today than they were several thousand years ago, and deforestation and overgrazing have seriously altered the landscape, contributing to erosion and siltation. The basic cause was probably climatic changes beyond human control, but at least two modern writers essentially agree with Marsh's man-centered judgment; see J. Donald Hughes, *Ecology in Ancient Civilizations* (Albuquerque, 1975), 128, and J. V. Thirgood, *Man and the Mediterranean Forest: A History of Resource Depletion* (London, 1981), 158–62.

28. Starr, "American Forest," 225–26; *Report of the State Board of Agriculture for 1868 and 1869*, 32; Oswald, "The Climatic Influence of Vegetation," 386–87; "Tree Waste and Its Sequence," *Scientific American*, March 30, 1878, 193; *Forest and Stream*, September 7, 1876, 73–74; Egleston, "What We Owe to the Trees," 683–84; *Pacific Rural Press*, September 20, 1884, 241; ibid., March 7, 1885, 230; Francis Parkman, "The Forests and the Census," *Atlantic Monthly* 55 (June 1885): 835–39; John Muir, "The American Forest," ibid. 80 (August 1897): 155; "Observations in the Sahara," *Popular Science Monthly* 27 (September 1885): 715; Abbot Kinney, "Our Forests," *Overland Monthly* 8 (December 1886): 619; *Third Biennial Report of the State Board of Horticulture of the State of California for the Thirty-eighth and Thirty-ninth Fiscal Years* (Sacramento, 1889), 118. Not all scientists agreed with Marsh's view that human actions were responsible for the conversion of once fair lands to deserts. Sargent concluded that the process of desiccation "must be traced to gradual geological changes . . . entirely beyond the reach of human control, and not to the mere destruction of forest" ("Protection of Forests," 395). See also J. D. Whitney, "Are We Drying Up?" *American Naturalist* 10 (September 1876): 513–20.

29. *Forest and Stream*, April 12, 1877, 146; Oswald, "Preservation of Forests," 36. See also "Forests and Drought," *Scientific American*, January 18, 1873, 14; *San Fran-*

cisco *Evening Bulletin,* January 5, 1878; "Deforestation and Floods in China," *Popular Science Monthly* 24 (November 1883): 142–43; and "Forest Devastation in Japan," ibid. 29 (September 1886): 714–15.

30. *Forest and Stream,* September 7, 1882, 102; ibid., December 13, 1883, 381; ibid., January 31, 1884, 1; Felix L. Oswald, "Changes in the Climate of North America," *North American Review* 138 (April 1884): 365; Henry Michelson, "Forests in Their Relation to Irrigation," *Forester* 5 (January 1899): 9–10; J. Blatchford Collins, "The Relation of Forest Preservation to the Public Welfare," ibid. 5 (June 1899): 127–29; "Alarming Forest Conditions in Colorado," ibid. 7 (November 1901): 280–90; *Report of the Lake Bigler [Tahoe] Forestry Commission* (Sacramento, 1884); *Sacramento Daily Union,* September 21, 1878; California State Board of Trade, *Eleventh Annual Report, 1900* (San Francisco, 1901), 10.

31. *Garden and Forest,* December 29, 1897, 518. On rainmaking experiments, see Clark C. Spence, *The Rainmakers: American "Pluviculture" to World War II* (Lincoln, 1980). For dry farming, see Mary Wilma M. Hargreaves, *Dry Farming in the Northern Great Plains, 1900–1925* (Cambridge, Mass., 1957).

32. Olson, "Commerce and Conservation," 13–14; Paul F. Sharp, "The War of the Substitutes: The Reaction of the Forest Industries to the Competition of Wood Substitutes," *Agricultural History* 23 (October 1949): 274–79; *The Lumber Industry: Message from the President of the United States,* Senate Reports, 61 Cong., 3 sess., no. 818, February 14, 1911 (Washington, D.C., 1911), 15.

33. For the "multiple purpose" concept, see Hays, *Conservation and the Gospel of Efficiency,* 100–105. Historians have neglected the artificial propagation of fish during the last decades of the nineteenth century. The pisciculturists introduced a second basic concept usually attributed to the Progressives. Fish culture, not scientific forestry, contributed the idea of "sustained yield," or "continuous yield," to the conservation of renewable natural resources. During the 1860s and 1870s, a decline in the population of some species of food fishes off the Atlantic coast, in northeastern streams, and in the Great Lakes—due partly to industrial pollution, soil erosion, destructive commercial fishing techniques, and the construction of dams that prevented spawning—led to the formation of numerous state fish commissions, the American Fish Culturists' Association (1870), and the United States Commission on Fish and Fisheries (1871). Ironically, the nineteenth-century emphasis on fish farming for profit using hatcheries, and the rudimentary state of pisciculture, limited the scientific attention paid by the new commissions to the destruction of existing fisheries. Fish diseases and parasites, predators, nutrition, habitats, and the effects of various pollutants on marine life received scant attention until the twentieth century. Norman G. Benson, ed., *A Century of Fisheries in North America* (Washington, D.C., 1970); Donald J. Pisani, "Fish Culture and the Dawn of Concern over Water Pollution," *Environmental Review* 8 (Summer 1984): 117–31; Dean C. Allard, Jr., "Spencer Fullerton Baird and the U.S. Fish Commission: A Study in the History of American Science" (Ph.D. diss., George Washington University, 1967); Reiger, *American Sportsmen and the Origins of Conservation,* 52–56.

34. Donald J. Pisani, "Reclamation and Social Engineering in the Progressive Era," *Agricultural History* 57 (January 1983): 46–63; Hays, *Conservation and the Gospel of Efficiency.*

35. *Forestry and Irrigation,* one of the leading conservation journals during the first decade of the twentieth century, carried many articles and editorials warning of impending timber shortages. See, for example, Raphael Zon, "The World's Demand for Timber and the Supply," *Forestry and Irrigation* 7 (February 1901): 41–44; "Our Waning Forests," ibid. 7 (June 1901): 142; B. E. Fernow, "Outlook of the Timber Supply in the United States," ibid. 9 (February and May 1903): 74–78, 226–29; "Ostriches vs. Wise Men," ibid. 14 (February 1908): 61–62; "The Woods We Have," ibid. 14 (May 1908): 249–50; and W. J. Wallace, "Startling Words of Timber Expert," ibid., 255–56.

36. *Forest and Stream,* January 31, 1884, 1; Ekirch, *Man and Nature in America,* 71.

37. Roderick Nash, *Wilderness and the American Mind* (New Haven, 1973), 129–30, 135–40; Hays, *Conservation and the Gospel of Efficiency,* 122–98; Swain, *Federal Conservation Policy,* 6–7, 124–25.

38. There is no comprehensive study of the "land question" after the Civil War, but Paul Wallace Gates provides indispensable background. Gates and Swenson, *History of Public Land Law Development.* For surveys of agriculture in this period, see Gates, *Agriculture and the Civil War* (New York, 1965); Fred A. Shannon, *The Farmer's Last Frontier: Agriculture, 1860–1897* (New York, 1945); and Gilbert C. Fite, *The Farmers' Frontier: 1865–1900* (New York, 1966). Although much has been written about federal land policies in the nineteenth century, attitudes toward the use of land—apart from parks and wilderness areas—have received scant attention. After the Civil War, a dramatic increase in wheat cultivation, the spread of tenant farming, ballooning farm mortgages, the acquisition of large blocks of agricultural land by European investors, an explosion in the number of farms larger than five hundred acres, declining crop yields, exhausted soils, and a host of related problems all implied that American farmers were killing the land (as well as the family farm). Some writers recognized that the old American custom of "using up" farmland and abandoning it for virgin land farther west resembled the "cut and run" mentality exhibited by loggers. They suggested that in both cases the process of destruction ultimately led to desertification and reversion to a pastoral economy. Thomas Magee, "Overworked Soils," *Overland Monthly* 1 (October 1868): 329, 330; Eugene W. Hilgard, "Progress in Agriculture by Education and Government Aid," *Atlantic Monthly* 49 (April 1882): 532; Oswald, "Preservation of Forests," 42; *California Farmer,* June 10, 1864, 148; T. H. Hoskins, "New England Agriculture," *Popular Science Monthly* 38 (March 1891): 700.

CHAPTER 8. FORESTS AND RECLAMATION

1. Samuel P. Hays, *Conservation and the Gospel of Efficiency: The Progressive Conservation Movement, 1890–1920* (Cambridge, Mass., 1959). The book was reprinted in 1974 with a new preface by the author.

2. George Perkins Marsh, *Man and Nature; or Physical Geography as Modified by Human Action* (Cambridge, Mass., 1965). For the influence of forests on the physical environment, see pp. 113–280.

3. "Waste Land and Forest Culture," *Scientific American* 32 (March 13, 1875):

161. Also see Felix Oswald, "The Preservation of Forests," *North American Review* 128 (January 1879): 35–46, and N. H. Egleston, "What We Owe to Trees," *Harper's New Monthly Magazine* 64 (April 1882): 683–84.

4. Donald J. Pisani, "Forests and Conservation, 1865–1890," *Journal of American History* 72 (September 1985): 340–59. The literature on forests and stream flow is vast. Key articles are cited in "Forests and Conservation, 1865–1890," but for an extended discussion of stream flow arguments see Abbot Kinney, ed., *Forest and Water* (Los Angeles, 1900). Also see Michael Williams, *Americans and Their Forests: A Historical Geography* (New York, 1989).

5. Herbert A. Smith, "The Early Forestry Movement in the United States," *Agricultural History* 12 (October 1938): 334–35; *Third Biennial Report of the California State Board of Forestry, for the Years 1889–90* (Sacramento, 1890), 1.

6. Ronald F. Lockmann, *Guarding the Forests of Southern California: Evolving Attitudes Toward Conservation of Watershed, Woodlands, and Wilderness* (Glendale, Calif., 1981); Douglas H. Strong, "The Sierra Forest Reserve: The Movement to Preserve the San Joaquin Valley Watershed," *Southern California Quarterly* 46 (June 1967): 3–17.

7. On the Powell irrigation survey see Donald J. Pisani, *To Reclaim a Divided West: Water, Law, and Public Policy, 1848–1902* (Albuquerque, 1992): 127–68. The best biographies of Powell are Wallace Stegner, *Beyond the Hundredth Meridian: John Wesley Powell and the Second Opening of the West* (Boston, 1953), and William Culp Darrah, *Powell of the Colorado* (Princeton, 1951). On federal reclamation policies in the late nineteenth and early twentieth centuries, also see Donald Worster, *Rivers of Empire: Water, Aridity, and the Growth of the American West* (New York, 1985); Marc Reisner, *Cadillac Desert: The American West and Its Disappearing Water* (New York, 1986); and Robert G. Dunbar, *Forging New Rights in Western Waters* (Lincoln, 1983). The historiography of western water use is discussed in Lawrence B. Lee, *Reclaiming the Arid West: An Historiography and Guide* (Santa Barbara, Calif., 1980); Lee, "Water Resource History: A New Field of Historiography?" *Pacific Historical Review* 57 (November 1988): 457–67; and Donald J. Pisani, "Deep and Troubled Waters: A New Field of Western History?" *New Mexico Historical Review* 63 (October 1988): 311–31.

8. John Wesley Powell, *Report on the Lands of the Arid Region of the United States* (Washington, D.C., 1878), 17. In his annual report for 1877, Secretary of the Interior Carl Schurz predicted that at its current rate of use the United States had only a twenty-year supply of timber left. See *Report of the Secretary of the Interior, 1877* (Washington, D.C., 1877), xvi–xvii.

9. "Trees on Arid Lands," *Science* 12 (October 12, 1888): 170–71.

10. John Wesley Powell, "The Lesson of Conemaugh," *North American Review* 149 (August 1889): 150–56, and "The Non-Irrigable Lands of the Arid Region," *Century* 39 (April 1890): 915–22. In an untitled, undated statement to the press probably issued in the 1890s, Powell tried to clarify his position on the forests: "The fact is that I have written and urged with all vigor possible that the forests should be preserved from fire, which is the chief agency of destruction, and on the other hand that the forests should be opened by proper means for the use of the people—that to protect the forests from proper use is bad policy, but to protect them from fire is good policy; and I have further urged that the best way of protecting

the forests from fire is to put them in the hands of the people for use" (see Record Group 57, U.S. Geological Survey, Irrigation Survey, box 1, D-121, National Archives, Washington, D.C.). Powell's views were not unusual, particularly in the West. See J. M. Anders, "Forests—Their Influence upon Climate and Rainfall," *American Naturalist* 16 (January 1882): 20.

11. Walter Rusinek, "Western Reclamation's Forgotten Forces: Richard J. Hinton and Groundwater Development," *Agricultural History* 61 (Summer 1987): 18 –35.

12. As reprinted in Andrew Denny Rodgers III, *Bernhard Edward Fernow: A Story of North American Forestry* (Princeton, 1951), 154.

13. *Report of the Commissioner of Agriculture, 1888* (Washington, D.C., 1889), 603 –19; Henry Gannett, "Do Forests Influence Rainfall?" *Science* 11 (January 6, 1888): 3 –5; Henry Gannett, "The Influence of Forests on the Quantity and Frequency of Rainfall," *Science* 12 (November 23, 1888): 242– 44; "The Timber-supply of the United States," *Garden and Forest* 6 (April 26, 1893): 181– 82; Harold K. Steen, *The U.S. Forest Service: A History* (Seattle, 1976), 41.

14. C. S. Sargent, "Irrigation Problems in the Arid West," *Garden and Forest* 1 (August 8, 1888): 277–78.

15. C. S. Sargent, "The Danger from Mountain Reservoirs and Irrigation," *Garden and Forest* 2 (June 19, 1889): 289; Sargent, "Mountain Reservoirs and Irrigation," ibid. 2 (July 13, 1889): 313 –14.

16. C. S. Sargent, "The Forests on the Public Domain," *Garden and Forest* 3 (January 8, 1890): 13 –14.

17. C. S. Sargent, "Forests and Irrigation," *Garden and Forest* 3 (June 18, 1890): 293.

18. J. B. Harrison, "Forests and Civilization: The North Woods, VII," *Garden and Forest* 2 (September 11, 1889): 441– 42.

19. J. B. Harrison to Benjamin Harrison, September 18, 1889, Record Group 57, U.S. Geological Survey, Letters Received August 5 – October 30, 1889.

20. Bernhard Edward Fernow, "The Relation of Irrigation Problems to Forest Conditions," in *Report of the Special Committee of the United States Senate on the Irrigation and Reclamation of Arid Lands* (Washington, D.C., 1890), serial 2708, part 4, 112 –24. The quote is from p. 120. Fernow made the same points in the *Report of the Secretary of Agriculture, 1889* (Washington, D.C., 1889), 276. Many if not most dams were intended to extend the growing season of existing farmers rather than to open virgin land to cultivation.

21. On Powell's career see Darrah, *Powell of the Colorado;* Stegner, *Beyond the Hundredth Meridian;* and Stanley R. Davison, *The Leadership of the Reclamation Movement, 1875 –1902* (New York, 1979).

22. *Garden and Forest* 4 (July 1, 1891/October 21, 1891): 301, 493 –94; Rodgers, *Bernhard Edward Fernow,* 158 –59; Steen, *The U.S. Forest Service,* 27–28; *Report of the Secretary of Interior, 1893* (Washington, D.C., 1893), 78 –79.

23. *Official Proceedings of the Third National Irrigation Congress, Held at Denver, Colorado, September 3rd to 8th, 1894* (Denver, n.d.), 47–49; Lockmann, *Guarding the Forests of Southern California,* 102.

24. During the first years of the 1890s, the amount of irrigated land in the West doubled to over seven million acres. Paul W. Gates, *History of Public Land Law Development* (Washington, D.C., 1968), 647.

25. In 1893 the irrigation congresses became annual events advertised as "international" meetings.

26. Unfortunately there is no book-length study of the irrigation congresses. The best single treatment is Lawrence B. Lee, "William Ellsworth Smythe and the Irrigation Movement: A Reconsideration," *Pacific Historical Review* 41 (August 1972): 289–311. Also see Lee's excellent introduction to Smythe's *Conquest of Arid America* (Seattle, 1969); A. Bower Sageser, "Los Angeles Hosts an International Irrigation Congress," *Journal of the West* 4 (July 1965): 411–24; and Davison, *The Leadership of the Reclamation Movement, 1875–1902*. On the irrigation district see Donald J. Pisani, *From the Family Farm to Agribusiness: The Irrigation Crusade in California and the West, 1850–1931* (Berkeley, 1984).

27. Maxwell has not received the attention he deserves. The best single study is Andrew Hudanick, Jr., "George Hebard Maxwell: Reclamation's Militant Evangelist," *Journal of the West* 14 (July 1975): 108–19.

28. *Garden and Forest* 10 (October 27, 1897): 420.

29. George Maxwell, "Irrigation and the Forest" *Forester* 7 (September 1901): 233. Also see Maxwell, "Nature's Storage Reservoirs," ibid. 5 (August 1899): 183–85.

30. In January 1899 the drought prompted agricultural and horticultural societies, chambers of commerce, boards of trade, state mining associations, and many other organizations to create the California Society for Conserving Waters and Protecting Forests. A few months later southern California groups followed suit and elected Kinney president of their organization. See Pisani, *From the Family Farm to Agribusiness*, 294–99, and C. Raymond Clar, *California Government and Forestry: From Spanish Days Until the Creation of the Department of Natural Resources in 1927* (Sacramento, 1959), 169–76.

31. "The American Forestry Association," *Forester* 5 (August 1899): 171–79.

32. Michael J. Lacey, "The Mysteries of Earth-Making Dissolved: A Study of Washington's Intellectual Community and the Origins of American Environmentalism in the Late Nineteenth Century" (Ph.D. diss., George Washington University, 1979).

33. On the relationship between Frederick H. Newell and Pinchot, see the Newell diaries in the F. H. Newell Papers, Library of Congress, Washington, D.C. There is no biography of Newell, but Donald J. Pisani, "Reclamation and Social Engineering in the Progressive Era," *Agricultural History* 57 (January 1983): 46–63, assesses his character. The best biographies of Gifford Pinchot are Harold T. Pinkett, *Gifford Pinchot: Private and Public Forester* (Urbana, Ill., 1970), and M. Nelson McGeary, *Gifford Pinchot: Forester-Politician* (Princeton, 1960). Also see Char Miller, "The Greening of Gifford Pinchot," *Environmental History Review* 16 (Fall 1992): 1–20. On Davis, see Gene M. Gressley, "Arthur Powell Davis, Reclamation, and the West," *Agricultural History* 42 (July 1968): 241–57. Henry Gannett also lacks a full-scale biography, but see the article "Henry Gannett," *National Geographic Magazine* 26 (December 1914): 609–13, and Nelson H. Darton, "Memoir of Henry Gannett," *Annals of the Association of American Geographers* 7 (1917): 68–70.

34. Newell subsequently taught a course in forest hydrography at the Yale Forestry School. For his ideas see the annual reports of the USGS, Hydrology Section, for the years 1896–1901. Also see Newell's "The National Forest Reserves,"

244 NOTES TO PAGES 149–51

National Geographic Magazine 8 (June 1897): 177–87, and "Forests and Reservoirs," *Forester* 7 (September 1901): 225–28. Pinchot described his relationship with Newell in *Breaking New Ground* (New York, 1947), 316.

35. Pinchot, *Breaking New Ground*, 123, 250. For Gannett's work see the reports of the USGS.

36. By 1907, more than two dozen reclamation projects had been launched, but at no time before World War I did they water more than 3 million acres—a small fraction of the land irrigated in the West. The most reliable survey of federal reclamation is Gates, *History of Public Land Law Development*, 635–98.

37. "Report of the Commissioner of the General Land Office, 1902," in *Annual Reports of the Department of the Interior* (Washington, D.C., 1902), 320. Also see Edward A. Bowers, "The Future of Federal Forest Reservations," *Forestry and Irrigation* 10 (March 1904): 132.

38. "Report of the Forester, 1903," in *Annual Reports of the Department of Agriculture, 1903* (Washington, D.C., 1903), 497.

39. See, for example, House of Representatives, *Power of Federal Government to Acquire Lands for National Forest Purposes*, 60th Cong., 1st sess., 1908.

40. See map showing land reserved for forests and reclamation in *Fourth Annual Report of the Reclamation Service, 1904–5* (Washington, D.C., 1906), plate 1.

41. C. J. Blanchard, "Mutual Relations of the Forest Service and the Reclamation Service," *Forestry and Irrigation* 12 (January 1906): 42.

42. For Frederick H. Newell's attitude toward grazing and watershed protection see his *Irrigation in the United States* (New York, 1902), 36–49.

43. F. H. Newell to secretary of the interior, March 17, 1905, Record Group 115, Records of the Bureau of Reclamation, General Administrative and Project Records, 1902–1919, "783—Establishment and Extension of Forest Reserves," New Mexico file, box 241. Also see A. P. Davis to Gifford Pinchot, June 17, 1905, in the same file; Newell to secretary of the interior, February 16, 1905, Colorado file, box 240; John Whistler to chief engineer, November 18, 1903, Oregon file, box 241; and *Official Proceedings of the Thirteenth National Irrigation Congress* (Portland, Ore., 1905), 72.

44. Gifford Pinchot to F. H. Newell, September 19, 1903, Gifford Pinchot Collection, box 994, Library of Congress, Washington, D.C. Also see Pinchot to F. H. Newell, April 17, 1907, Record Group 115, Records of the Bureau of Reclamation, General Administrative and Project Records, 1902–1919, "783—Establishment and Extension of Forest Reserves," Montana file, box 241, and in the same file, A. P. Davis (acting director, Reclamation Service) to secretary of the interior, November [date illegible], 1906.

45. Overton Price, acting chief forester, to F. H. Newell, January 4, 1904, in Record Group 95, Records of the Forest Service, Division of Operation, box 1, Reclamation Service file, and Gifford Pinchot to F. H. Newell, April 26, 1905, Record Group 95, Records of Letters Sent by the Office of the Associate Forester, 1905–1908; E. A. Sterling, "Forest Planting About Reservoirs and Along Canals," in *Official Proceedings of the Thirteenth National Irrigation Congress*, 82–86. On March 2, 1907, the *Washington Star* reported: "The forestry bureau is not only preserving and cultivating the standing forests on government land, but is beginning to plant trees in different parts of the west. It is undertaking a vast scheme of creative work and will restore, so far as possible, the timber that has been stripped from the mountain sides, where are the sources of the streams that

are needed to irrigate the arid plains below. The bureau is working in co-operation with the reclamation service and is also advising, encouraging and assisting private individuals, railway corporations, lumber companies and others to reclothe the denuded hills." The bureau assumed that planting new forests or increasing the stands in old forests would increase the irrigable area of the West by augmenting the water supply.

46. Gifford Pinchot, "What the Forest Service Stands For," *Forestry and Irrigation* 13 (January 1907): 27–28; Hays, *Conservation and the Gospel of Efficiency*, 72. Pinchot's interest in assuming the leadership of the conservation crusade has convinced many recent historians that the chief forester was more of a publicist than a scientist. "As a popularizer," Stephen Fox has written, "Pinchot aimed for the lowest common denominator of public opinion; actually he spent most of his adult life not in forestry but in politics. . . . Pinchot ultimately turned out to be a consummate politician" (see *The American Conservation Movement: John Muir and His Legacy* [Madison, 1981], 113). Also see Stephen Edward Ponder, "News Management in the Progressive Era, 1898–1909: Gifford Pinchot, Theodore Roosevelt, and the Conservation Crusade" (Ph.D. diss., University of Washington, 1985).

47. F. H. Newell to D. C. Henny, May 1, 1908, Record Group 115, Records of the Bureau of Reclamation, General Administrative and Project Records, 1902–1919, "Sacramento, 340–991," box 831. Newell's idea had been expressed as early as 1903 by national reclamation's chief publicist, George H. Maxwell. In a November 17, 1903, letter to Gifford Pinchot, Maxwell observed: "The fact is that if the sale of the stumpage is judiciously conducted, instead of selling forest lands, [it] would yield a larger sum which would be used for irrigation works than would be provided by all the present laws put together." At the time, the reclamationists hoped that Pinchot would make this concession in exchange for their political support in getting the national forests transferred to Agriculture.

48. *Annual Report of the Secretary of Agriculture, 1905* (Washington, D.C., 1905), lvii.

49. William D. Rowley, *U.S. Forest Service Grazing and Rangelands: A History* (College Station, 1985), 47.

50. For example, a memorial from Colorado in May 1909 charged that less than one-third of the 16 million acres within national forests in that state was actually forested. See *Congressional Record,* Senate, May 14, 1909, 2019–20. Even after Congress cut off this source of Forest Service income in 1907, Pinchot and his lieutenants kept close track of the revenue generated by grazing and timber cutting permits to remind congressional committees that the Forest Service largely paid for itself.

51. As quoted in E. Louise Peffer, *The Closing of the Public Domain: Disposal and Reservation Policies, 1900 –1950* (Stanford, Calif., 1951), 74.

52. Rowley, *U.S. Forest Service Grazing and Rangelands,* 33.

53. Ibid., 81. Also see Gregory Randall Graves, "Anti-Conservation and Federal Forestry in the Progressive Era" (Ph.D. diss., University of California, Santa Barbara, 1987), 180 –81.

54. James L. Penick, Jr., *Progressive Politics and Conservation: The Ballinger-Pinchot Affair* (Chicago, 1968), 4.

55. Rowley, *U.S. Forest Service Grazing and Rangelands,* 63.

56. In 1905, the sale of timber from the national forests returned less revenue than grazing permits. Many reserves were inaccessible or poorly served by trans-

portation. Pinchot was reluctant to permit extensive logging because to do so might depress lumber prices and alienate the support of many private companies.

57. Peffer, *The Closing of the Public Domain*, 186; *Annual Report of the Secretary of Agriculture, 1906* (Washington, D.C., 1907), 52–53; *Annual Report of the Secretary of Agriculture, 1907* (Washington, D.C., 1908), 62, 64.

58. "Report of the Forester, 1908," in *Annual Reports of the Department of Agriculture, 1908* (Washington, D.C., 1908), 426.

59. *Fourth Annual Report of the Reclamation Service, 1904–5* (Washington, D.C., 1906), 30–31.

60. Henry S. Graves, "Shall the States Own the Forests?" *Outlook* 102 (December 28, 1912): 937.

61. James R. Garfield to secretary of agriculture, February 20, 1908, and James Wilson to secretary of interior, March 13, 1908, Record Group 115, Records of the Bureau of Reclamation, General Administrative and Project Records, 1902–1919, "783—Establishment and Extension of Forest Reserves," box 240.

62. "Report of the Forester, 1909," in *Annual Reports of the Department of Agriculture, 1909* (Washington, D.C., 1910), 391; A. P. Davis to chief forester, November 30, 1909, and Charles A. Van der Veer (secretary of the Salt River Valley Water Users' Association) to the director of the Reclamation Service, July 6, 1912, both in Record Group 115, Records of the Bureau of Reclamation, General Administrative and Project Records, 1902–1919, "783—Establishment and Extension of Forest Reserves," Arizona file, box 240; J. B. Lippincott, "Relation of Stream Flow and Suspended Sediment Therein, to the Covering of Drainage Basins," in Kinney, *Forest and Water*, 234. On the Salt River Project, see Karen L. Smith, *The Magnificent Experiment: Building the Salt River Reclamation Project, 1890–1917* (Tucson, 1986).

63. "Report of the Forester, 1911," in *Annual Reports of the Department of Agriculture* (Washington, D.C., 1912), 349.

64. Gifford Pinchot, "The Upper Ohio Flood," *Forestry and Irrigation* 13 (April 1907): 169; *Cincinnati Enquirer*, March 27, 1908.

65. *Washington Post*, March 3, 1907, 6.

66. Steen, *The U.S. Forest Service*, 127–29; Ise, *The United States Forest Policy*, 207–23; Gates, *History of Public Land Law Development*, 595; Roy Robbins, *Our Landed Heritage: The Public Domain, 1776–1970* (Lincoln, 1976), 368; Edwin A. Start, "How the House Voted," *Forestry and Irrigation* 15 (June 1909): 348–57.

67. Gordon B. Dodds, "The Stream-Flow Controversy: A Conservation Turning Point," *Journal of American History* 56 (June 1969): 59–69. The most important literature on this "scientific" debate is cited by Dodds. In particular see *American Forestry* 16 (1910).

68. Chittenden's criticisms resulted in the first sustained effort to test the stream flow hypothesis, made by the Weather Bureau and Agriculture Department at Wagon Wheel Gap, Colorado, in the Rio Grande National Forest. This story is told in Jenks Cameron, *The Development of Governmental Forest Control in the United States* (Baltimore, 1928), 276–77, 367–69. Also see the "Report of the Forester," in *Annual Reports of the Department of Agriculture, 1910* (Washington, D.C., 1911), 393.

69. Hiram Martin Chittenden, "Forests and Reservoirs in Their Relation to

Stream-flow with Particular Reference to Navigable Rivers," *Proceedings of the American Society of Civil Engineers* 34 (September 1908): 924–97; Chittenden, "Sentiment Versus Utility in the Treatment of National Scenery," *Pacific Monthly* 23 (1910): 29–38.

70. As quoted in Cameron, *The Development of Governmental Forest Control in the United States*, 215.

71. For example, in 1891 Fernow predicted, "Once let woods be spread over the now arid plains of the West and there would be rain in plenty there" ("Forests," *Scientific American* 65 [September 19, 1891]: 181).

72. As quoted in Rodgers, *Bernhard Edward Fernow*, 128–29. At least one official within the Bureau of Forestry conceded that many factors influenced stream flow besides the existence of trees, including precipitation, topography, geology, and the character of vegetation. See W. B. Greeley, "The Effect of Forest Cover upon Stream Flow," *Forestry and Irrigation* 11 (June 1905): 163–68.

73. *Irrigation Age* 22 (December 1906): 39; 23 (February 1908): 105.

74. Thomas R. Cox, Robert S. Maxwell, Phillip Drennon Thomas, and Joseph J. Malone, *This Well-Wooded Land: Americans and Their Forests from Colonial Times to the Present* (Lincoln, 1985), 149. This is essentially the same conclusion Samuel P. Hays reached in *Conservation and the Gospel of Efficiency; see* particularly pp. 199–218.

75. "Trees on Arid Lands," *Science* 12 (October 12, 1888): 170–71.

76. John Wesley Powell, *Report on the Lands of the Arid Region of the United States* (Washington, D.C., 1878), 20.

77. Gifford Pinchot, "The Conservation of Natural Resources," *Outlook* 87 (October 12, 1907): 291–94.

PART FOUR: FEDERAL RECLAMATION

1. W. T. Sherman to C. Delano, November 7, 1871, in Records of the Bureau of Indian Affairs, Record Group 75, Irrigation Division, General Correspondence, entry 653, box 52, "Ft. Apache, 1871–1918"; L. W. Cooke to Commissioner of Indian Affairs, October 20, 1893, RG 75, Special Cases, entry 190, "Blackfeet" box; *Report of the Commissioner of Indian Affairs, 1902* (Washington, D.C., 1903), 63–64; *Report of the Commissioner of Indian Affairs, 1909* (Washington, D.C., 1910), 10.

2. *Report of the Commissioner of Indian Affairs, 1906* (Washington, D.C., 1907), 13–15; *Report of the Commissioner of Indian Affairs, 1908* (Washington, D.C., 1908), 58. Also see *Report of the Commissioner of Indian Affairs, 1897* (Washington, D.C., 1897), 29; *Report of the Commissioner of Indian Affairs, 1911* (Washington, D.C., 1912), 14; *Report of the Commissioner of Indian Affairs, 1916* (Washington, D.C., 1917), 41, 44.

3. *Report of the Secretary of the Interior, 1882* (Washington, D.C., 1882), ix; *Report of the Commissioner of Indian Affairs, 1895* (Washington, D.C., 1896), 26; R. Douglas Hurt, *Indian Agriculture in America: Prehistory to the Present* (Lawrence, Kans., 1987), 109.

4. *Report of the Commissioner of Indian Affairs, 1891* (Washington, D.C., 1892), 51; *Report of the Commissioner of Indian Affairs, 1896* (Washington, D.C., 1897), 29; *Report of the Commissioner of Indian Affairs, 1897* (Washington, D.C., 1897), 33; *Report of the Secretary of the Interior, 1892* (Washington, D.C., 1893), liv; *Report of the Secretary of the Interior, 1896* (Washington, D.C., 1896), xlvi; *Report of the Secretary of the Interior, 1898* (Washington, D.C., 1898), xlvii.

5. Three notable exceptions are Hurt, *Indian Agriculture in America;* Daniel McCool, *Command of the Waters: Iron Triangles, Federal Water Development, and Indian Water* (Berkeley, 1987), and Janet McDonnell, *Dispossessing the American Indian, 1887–1934* (Bloomington, 1994).

6. *Winters v. United States,* 207 U.S. 564 (1908).

7. *Kansas v. Colorado,* 206 U.S. 46 (1907).

8. One characteristic of prior appropriation was that it required "continuous" as well as "beneficial" use. Courts throughout the West defined this requirement quite differently, however.

CHAPTER 9. IRRIGATION, WATER RIGHTS, AND THE BETRAYAL OF INDIAN ALLOTMENT

1. Alvin M. Josephy, Jr., "Here in Nevada a Terrible Crime," *American Heritage* 21 (June 1970): 93–100. See also Martha C. Knack and Omer C. Stewart, *As Long as the River Shall Run: An Ethnohistory of Pyramid Lake Reservation* (Berkeley, 1984); Lowell Smith and Pamela Deuel, "The California-Nevada Interstate Water Compact: A Great Betrayal," *Cry California* 7 (Winter 1971–1972): 24–35; and Donald J. Pisani, "The Strange Death of the California-Nevada Compact: A Study in Interstate Water Negotiations," *Pacific Historical Review* 37 (November 1978): 637–58.

2. *Winters v. United States,* 207 U.S. 577 (1908).

3. *Arizona v. California,* 373 U.S. 546 (1963). In 1973 the Paiutes pressed suit against the Truckee-Carson Irrigation District to define their Winters doctrine rights. They wanted sufficient water to stabilize the level of the lake and create a new fishing industry. Their case found its way to the Supreme Court in 1983 only to be rejected on grounds that Winters doctrine rights were subject to existing "executive agreements" allocating water. The Supreme Court shows less sympathy for Indian claims today than it did in the 1960s and early 1970s, and its decision may have far-reaching implications for the claims of other tribes in the arid West. See Knack and Stewart, *As Long as the River Shall Run,* 351–58.

4. Francis Paul Prucha's *Indian-White Relations in the United States: A Bibliography of Works Published, 1975–1980* (Lincoln, 1982), 66–68, included a special section on water rights with forty-seven citations. However, virtually all were articles published in legal journals. The one notable exception, discussed later in this chapter, was Norris Hundley's superb piece in the October 1978 issue of the *Western Historical Quarterly.*

5. The best broad surveys of Indian land policy in the late nineteenth and early twentieth centuries are J. P. Kinney, *A Continent Lost—A Civilization Won: Indian Land Tenure in America* (Baltimore, 1937); Frederick E. Hoxie, *A Final Promise: The Campaign to Assimilate the Indians, 1880–1920.* (Lincoln, 1984); Leonard A. Carlson, *Indians, Bureaucrats and Land: The Dawes Act and the Decline of Indian Farming* (Westport, Conn., 1981); and D. S. Otis, *The Dawes Act and the Allotment of Indian Lands* (Norman, Okla., 1973). The three most useful surveys of federal reclamation pay almost no attention to the effect of government irrigation projects on Indian water rights. See Michael Robinson, *Water for the West: The Bureau of Reclamation, 1902–1977* (Chicago, 1979); Paul Gates's chapter in his magisterial survey, *History of*

Public Land Law Development (Washington, D.C., 1968), 635–98; and William Warne, *The Bureau of Reclamation* (New York, 1973).

6. This chapter is meant to suggest to historians of Indians and natural resources an important and neglected field. A broad history of the federal trusteeship of Indian resources—including hydroelectric power sites, timber, coal, oil, and uranium, as well as water—is badly needed.

7. Robert G. Dunbar, *Forging New Rights in Western Waters* (Lincoln, 1983), 3. Ethnohistorians have greatly expanded our understanding of the deep cultural differences that separated Euro-Americans and Native Americans as they thought about time, religion, the land, labor, and technology. However, we must be careful not to fall into the trap of concluding that cultural differences alone prevented Indians from adapting to settled agriculture. Not only did some tribes practice irrigation long before contact with the Spanish, but many showed a remarkable capacity to absorb new tools and values from other Indians as well as non-Indians. There are many reasons Indians questioned the value of irrigation. On Montana reservations, for example, the growing season was too short and the soil incapable of producing those high value crops—such as beans, cotton, and melons—raised in the American Southwest. Stock-raising promised a greater return with less labor. On other reservations, Indians lacked the implements and knowledge to farm. In still other cases, they feared that improving land would invite further white greed.

8. The classic statement on the value of irrigation is William Ellsworth Smythe, *The Conquest of Arid America* (New York, 1900). See also Donald J. Pisani, *From the Family Farm to Agribusiness: The Irrigation Crusade in California and the West, 1850 –1931* (Berkeley, 1984).

9. Porter J. Preston and Charles A. Engle, "Report of Advisors on Irrigation on Indian Reservations," in *Hearings Before a Subcommittee of the Committee on Indian Affairs*, Senate, July 8, 10, 11, 12, and 17, 1929 (Washington, D.C., 1930), 2217, 2229.

10. *U.S. Statutes at Large*, 26:1011, 1039.

11. Commissioner of Indian Affairs, *Annual Report*, 1893 (Washington, D.C., 1893), 50, hereafter report year only is cited; "Message from the President of the United States, Transmitting Certain Reports upon the Condition of the Navajo Indian Country," S. Ex. Doc. 68, 52 Cong., 2 sess., serial 3056, 1893.

12. Commissioner of Indian Affairs, *Annual Report* (1891), 50 –52; *Annual Report* (1893), 47–50; *Annual Report* (1894), 24 –26; *Annual Report* (1895), 28 –32; and *Annual Report* (1900), 70, 267.

13. Commissioner of Indian Affairs, *Annual Report* (1895), 26.

14. Commissioner of Indian Affairs, *Annual Report* (1900), 59.

15. The commissioner observed in 1898 that on the Crow Reservation a $6 payment made to the Indians twice a year for land ceded to the government had been spent on frivolous items, while money earned in wages "they regard much more highly and expend with much more care and discretion." Commissioner of Indian Affairs, *Annual Report* (1898), 49. See Also *Annual Report* (1897), 29, 33; and *Annual Report* (1906), 14 –15.

16. Commissioner of Indian Affairs, *Annual Report* (1895), 28; *Annual Report* (1900), 58; and *Annual Report* (1901), 63; "Irrigation Projects on Indian Reservations, Etc.," H. Doc. 1268, 63 Cong., 3 sess., serial 6891, 1914; and "Indian Irrigation Projects, 1919," H. Doc. 387, 66 Cong., 2 sess., serial 7769, 1919, 10.

17. Ray P. Teele, *Irrigation in the United States* (New York, 1915), 218; Commissioner of Indian Affairs, *Annual Report* (1914), 38; *Annual Report* (1915), 44; *Annual Report* (1916), 42; *Annual Report* (1919), 38; and *Annual Report* (1920), 23.

18. *U.S. Statutes at Large*, 33:224; Department of Interior, *Thirteenth Annual Report of the Reclamation Service, 1913–1914* (Washington, D.C., 1915), 73–80. In fairness to the Reclamation Service, government engineers expected the members of Indian families to pool their individual allotments so that in most cases farms would be much larger than five acres. However, because a white husband and wife could each file on a farm, the Indians still received much less land.

19. Commissioner of Indian Affairs, *Annual Report* (1906), 148–50; and *Annual Report* (1909), 42; "Truckee-Carson Irrigation Project, Etc.," H. Doc. 211, 59 Cong., 2 sess., serial 5152, 1907, 3; *Forestry and Irrigation* 13 (June 1907): 288–89; and *Churchill County Standard* (Fallon, Nev.), October 20 and December 1, 1906, and May 18, 1907. The policy of permitting Indians to sell part of their allotments before the twenty-five-year trust period elapsed was extended to all Indian land within the proposed Reclamation Service projects boundaries by *U.S. Statutes at Large*, 34:327.

20. *U.S. Statutes at Large*, 33:302–5, 325, 360; Department of Interior, *Third Annual Report of the Reclamation Service, 1903–1904* (Washington, D.C., 1905), 83, 328–29.

21. *U.S. Statutes at Large*, 34:53. Congress authorized allotment of Yakima lands in December 1904 (*U.S. Statutes at Large*, 33:595). At that time proceeds from the sale of surplus land were used to pay for irrigation works constructed by the Indian Bureau, not the Reclamation Service. The 1906 statute permitted the Reclamation Service to take over the Indian Bureau's canal system. This and related legislation added valuable arable land to the public domain.

22. Commissioner of Indian Affairs, *Annual Report* (1906), 89, and *Annual Report* (1907), 50–51; Department of Interior, *Ninth Annual Report of the Reclamation Service, 1909–1910* (Washington, D.C., 1911), 32; and *Fifteenth Annual Report of the Reclamation Service, 1915–1916* (Washington, D.C., 1916), 547. On the three Montana reservations, the Reclamation Service planned to irrigate 423,000 acres. See the *Eighth Annual Report of the Reclamation Service, 1908–1909* (Washington, D.C., 1910), 90–96.

23. Commissioner of Indian Affairs, *Annual Report* (1905), 7.

24. Commissioner of Indian Affairs, *Annual Report* (1896), 30, and *Annual Report* (1900), 63. In 1895, the company promised to provide sufficient water to irrigate about 120,000 acres. However, its "ditch" was little more than rough embankments of sandy, porous soil. It quickly washed out. The commissioner reported that Fort Hall Indians branded the scheme a "deception and fraud" (p. 61).

25. Department of Interior, *First Annual Report of the Reclamation Service from June 17 to December 1, 1902* (Washington, D.C., 1903), 81–82; Commissioner of Indian Affairs, *Annual Report* (1900), 59; *Annual Report* (1904), 7–21; *Annual Report* (1906), 87; *Annual Report* (1916), 37, 43; and *Annual Report* (1919), 41. For a good summary of the violation of Pima water rights and the Indian reaction, see "Letters and Petition with Reference to Conserving the Rights of the Pima Indians, of Arizona, to the Lands of Their Reservation and the Necessary Water Supply for Irrigation," 62 Cong., 1 sess., U.S. Congress, House Committee Print H-3840, 1911.

26. For an overview of the Reclamation Service's position on state as opposed to federal water rights see Donald J. Pisani, "State vs. Nation: Federal Reclamation and Water Rights in the Progressive Era," *Pacific Historical Review* 51 (August 1982): 265–82.

27. Department of Interior, *Third Annual Report of the Reclamation Service, 1903–1904* (Washington, D.C., 1905), 268, and Commissioner of Indian Affairs, *Annual Report* (1906), 83.

28. Commissioner of Indian Affairs, *Annual Report* (1906), 83; *Annual Report* (1907); *Annual Report* (1908), 31–32; and *Annual Report* (1913), 12–13; "Irrigable Lands on Uintah Indian Reservation, Utah," S. Doc. 414, 66 Cong., 3 sess., serial 7794, 1921, 4.

29. *Winters v. United States*, 207 U.S. 564 (1908); Norris Hundley, Jr., "The Dark and Bloody Ground of Indian Water Rights: Confusion Elevated to Principle," *Western Historical Quarterly* 9 (October 1978): 445–82; and Hundley, "The 'Winters' Decision and Indian Water Rights: A Mystery Reexamined," ibid. 13 (January 1982): 17–42.

30. *U.S. Statutes at Large*, 25:113–33. For summaries of the conditions that led to the suit see pp. 1–13 of "Brief of the Appellee in United States Circuit Court of Appeals for the Ninth Circuit," in box 221, file 58730, Record Group 60, Records of the Department of Justice NA/RG60), National Archives, and *Winters v. United States*, Fed. Rep. 740, at 740–42 (1906).

31. Hundley, "The 'Winters' Decision and Indian Water Rights," 39; U.S. Supreme Court, "Brief for the United States in *Winters v. United States*," *Records and Briefs, v. 207*, Library of Congress Law Library; *Winters v. United States*, 207 U.S. 564 (1908).

32. *Kansas v. Colorado*, 206 U.S. 46 (1907).

33. "Memorandum: Conflicting Attitude Dept. Justice on Irrigation Matters," December 8, 1905, in Record Group 115, Records of the Bureau of Reclamation, General Administrative and Project Records, 1902–1919, "(762) Legal Discussions—General," National Archives. See also the undated position paper prepared by the Indian Bureau, "Memorandum Relative to Cases Involving Water Rights of Indians in Montana and Washington," in box 231, "Legal Discussions—General, thru Dec. 31, 1907," and Pisani, "State vs. Nation," 278.

34. Attorney general to the president, December 18, 1905, box 221, file 58730, NA/RG60.

35. Ethan Allen Hitchcock to the president, January 5, 1906, box 221, file 58730, NA/RG60.

36. F. E. Leupp to secretary of the interior, April 3, 1906, box 221, file 58730, NA/RG60.

37. In this case, "cooperation" meant that the Wyoming state engineer had extended the time for "final proof" (i.e., actually using water) on Wind River Reservation water claims for several years. See Commissioner of Indian Affairs, *Annual Report* (1911), 16.

38. For example, on June 8, 1912, Yakima Indians urged Congressman John H. Stephens, head of the House Committee on Indian Affairs, to reject a bill that would have reduced the water available to Indians on the Ahtanum River in Washington. They had used the river long before the Reclamation Service opened that section of the Yakima Project. Even though the stream ran through the reservation,

the secretary of the interior had, according to the Indians, granted 75 percent of the water to white farmers. "Memorial of the Yakima Tribe of Indians," H. Doc. 1304, 62 Cong., 3 sess., serial 6500, 1913, 3. For the Supreme Court decision see *United States v. Powers*, 305 U.S. 533 (1939).

39. House Joint Resolution 250 (Stephens), *Congressional Record*, 62 Cong., 2 sess., House, February 22, 1912, 2344.

40. "Water Rights of the Indians, Etc.," H. Doc. 1274, 63 Cong., 3 sess., serial 6888, 1914, 3 – 4.

41. *Congressional Record*, 63 Cong. 2 sess., Senate, June 17, 1914, 10587–600; June 18, 1914, 10652–57; June 20, 1914, 10768 – 89; June 23, 1914, 10937– 46; and June 24, 1914, 11019 –36.

42. Ibid., June 17, 1914, 10595; June 20, 1914, 10769 –70; June 23, 1914, 10936.

43. The Reclamation Service feared that selling improved Indian land for fair market value would discourage potential white settlers who had to pay construction costs and the price of setting up a farm in addition to the charge for the land.

44. This was not a special concession. The Reclamation Act of 1902 provided interest-free loans, and when the Reclamation Service took over irrigation on the Flathead Reservation, it simply reaffirmed and extended this substantial inducement to take up government land.

45. *Congressional Record*, 63 Cong., 2 sess., June 24, 1914, 11019–34.

46. Ibid., 11023.

47. Ibid., 11034.

48. Ibid., June 20, 1914, 10773 –74, for Robinson's comments.

49. Ibid., June 24, 1914, 11024, 11027.

50. Ibid., 11028.

51. On June 24, 1914, the Senate approved a compromise amendment limiting federal irrigation expenditures on the Flathead Reservation to $100,000 unless the attorney general certified that the Indians "are protected and confirmed in their water rights." This amendment failed in the House. That most senators had little understanding of or interest in Indian water rights was revealed in the vote: 29 for, 20 against, and 47 not voting. Ibid., 11019, 11036.

52. "Report of Commission to Investigate Irrigation Projects on Indian Land," H. Doc. 1215, 63 Cong., 3 sess., serial 6888 (Washington, D.C., 1914), 38 – 40, and Commissioner of Indian Affairs, *Annual Report* (1914), 39.

53. Commissioner of Indian Affairs, *Annual Report* (1915), 47. In 1915, the Reclamation Service claimed to be able to irrigate nearly 89,000 acres on those three reservations, but less than 4,000 acres were cultivated, mostly by whites. Department of Interior, *Fourteenth Annual Report of the Reclamation Service, 1914 –1915* (Washington, D.C., 1915), 117, 122, 128.

54. For examples of the persistence of the water rights problem see "Irrigable Lands on Uintah Indian Reservation, Utah," S. Doc. 414, 66 Cong., 3 sess., serial 7794, 1921, 4; S. Rep. 706, 67 Cong., 2 sess., serial 7951, 1922; H. Rep. 624, 67 Cong., 2 sess., serial 7955, 1922; and "For Settlement of Water Rights in the Toole County Irrigation District, Montana, Affecting Indians of the Blackfeet Indian Reservation," S. Rep. 1073, 67 Cong., 4 sess., serial 8155, 1923.

55. Department of Interior, *Nineteenth Annual Report of the Reclamation Service, 1919 –1920* (Washington, D.C., 1920), 439– 40. Agricultural development on the

Flathead and Fort Peck reservations followed a similar course. See the statistics on pp. 447 and 456 of the same report.

56. Preston and Engle, "Report of Advisors on Irrigation on Indian Reservations," 2210–61. Preston and Engle were chosen to conduct the study because they could take a more detached view than engineers in Interior. For more general surveys of reservation conditions see "Survey of Conditions of Indians in the United States," Senate, *Hearings Before the Committee on Indian Affairs*, 70 Cong., 1 sess., January 10 and 13, 1928 (Washington, D.C., 1928), and *Hearings Before a Subcommittee of the Committee on Indian Affairs*, Senate, September 12–14, 1932 (Washington, D.C., 1934).

57. Preston and Engle, "Report of Advisors on Irrigation on Indian Reservations," 2217–20.

58. In most western states, water rights did not attach directly to parcels of land. They could be acquired by tenants as well as landlords.

59. Commissioner of Indian Affairs, *Annual Report* (1914), 29. For good overviews of the leasing system, but with little attention to irrigation and water rights, see Otis, *The Dawes Act and the Allotment of Indian Lands*, 98–123, and Kinney, *A Continent Lost—A Civilization Won*, 214–48. See also Hoxie, *A Final Promise*, 168, and Carlson, *Indians, Bureaucrats, and Land*, 136–38.

60. Preston and Engle, "Report of Advisors on Irrigation on Indian Reservations," 2213, 2237–38, and "Extension of Time for Payment of Charges Due on Indian Irrigation projects," S. Rep. 586, 71 Cong., 2 Sess., serial 9186, 1930, 1. See also H. Rep. 943, 72 Cong., 1 sess., serial 9492, 1932; H. Rep. 1372, 72 Cong., 1 sess., serial 9493, 1932; S. Rep. 552, 72 Cong., 1 sess., serial 9487, 1932; H. Rep. 1988, 72 Cong., 2 sess., serial 9649, 1933; S. Rep. 1197, 72 Cong., 2 sess., serial 9647, 1933; and S. Rep. 908, 73 Cong., 2 sess., serial 9770, 1934.

61. Donald J. Pisani, "Reclamation and Social Engineering in the Progressive Era," *Agricultural History* 57 (January 1983): 46–63.

62. Hundley, "The Dark and Bloody Ground of Indian Water Rights," 480.

63. Carlson, *Indians, Bureaucrats and Land*, offers substantial statistical evidence to support his case. See in particular the appendices, 181–206.

CHAPTER 10. RECLAMATION AND SOCIAL ENGINEERING
IN THE PROGRESSIVE ERA

1. On the origins of the Progressive reclamation movement see Samuel Hays, *Conservation and the Gospel of Efficiency: The Progressive Conservation Movement, 1890–1920* (Cambridge, Mass., 1959), 5–26; John T. Ganoe, "The Origin of a National Reclamation Policy," *Mississippi Valley Historical Review* 18 (June 1931): 34–52; Paul Wallace Gates, *A History of Public Land Law Development* (Washington, D.C., 1968), 635–98; William Lilley III and Lewis L. Gould, "The Western Irrigation Movement, 1878–1902: A Reappraisal," in Gene Gressley, ed., *The American West: A Reorientation* (Laramie, Wyo., 1966); and Lawrence B. Lee, "William Ellsworth Smythe and the Irrigation Movement: A Reconsideration," *Pacific Historical Review* 41 (August 1972): 289–311. Stanley Roland Davison, "The Leadership of the Reclamation Movement, 1875–1902" (Ph.D. diss., University of California, Berkeley,

1952), describes the reclamation crusade of the 1890s as a "screen of sentimental-ism" and "bombast and nonsense" based on "emotional, non-intellectual argu-ment" (pp. 22, 23, 24).

2. *Irrigation Age* 10 (August 1896): 55. For examples of the effect of the depres-sion on private land and water companies see ibid., 12 (December 1897), 76; 12 (March 1898): 160–61; and 13 (December 1898): 84–90.

3. William Ellsworth Smythe, "The Republic of Irrigation," *Irrigation Age* 5 (May 1894): 189.

4. *California Advocate* 3 (9 July 1898): 4; "Reclamation of Arid America," *Irriga-tion Age* 13 (September 1899): 407–9; and "Labor, Land and Water," *Proceedings of the Ninth Annual Session of the National Irrigation Congress, Chicago, 1900* (St. Louis, 1900), 314.

5. A. P. Davis, "The Public Domain in Its Social Aspect," *Irrigation Age* 7 (July 1894): 17. See also J. S. Emery, untitled speech, *Proceedings of the Fourth National Irri-gation Congress Held at Albuquerque, New Mexico, September 16–19, 1895* (Santa Fe, 1896), 27; *Rural Californian* 17 (September 1894): 465, and 17 (October 1894): 546; *Cit-rograph* (Redlands, Calif.), July 30, 1898; Oliver N. Goldsmith, "Colonial Life for the Common People," *Irrigation Age* 8 (December 1895): 237; D. W. Ross, "Public Opin-ion and the Irrigation Congress," ibid. 10 (September 1896): 99–100; and Nelson A. Miles, "Our Unwatered Empire," *North American Review* 150 (March 1890): 370–81.

6. The literature on the benefits of irrigation is large. *Irrigation Age, The National Advocate,* and *Forestry and Irrigation* are the best sources, along with the published proceedings of irrigation congress meetings. However, such journals such as *The Independent, Review of Reviews, Century,* and *Atlantic Monthly* also pub-lished pieces on reclamation from time to time.

7. For an excellent survey of Smythe's career see Lawrence B. Lee, "William Ellsworth Smythe and the Irrigation Movement" and his introduction to the 1969 edition of *The Conquest of Arid America* (Seattle, 1969). See also Martin E. Carlson, "William E. Smythe: Irrigation Crusader," *Journal of the West* 7 (January 1968): 41–47.

8. William Ellsworth Smythe, *The Conquest of Arid America* (New York, 1900), 31, 38–39, 44.

9. William Ellsworth Smythe, "Electricity and Water Power," *Irrigation Age* 7 (July 1894): 35, and 8 (February 1895): 63. See also W. C. Fitzsimmons, "Irrigation and Electricity," ibid. 5 (May 1893): 5, and "An Impending Revolution," ibid. 8 (March 1895): 88–89.

10. *Boston Herald,* February 17 and March 26, 1895; *Chicago Daily Tribune,* April 12, 1895.

11. Smythe, *Conquest of Arid America,* 191–93; *Irrigation Age* 8 (March 1895): 70–71, 76–81; 6 (June 1895): 186–87; "Eight Years Afterward," *Out West* 19 (Sep-tember 1903): 335–36. In 1899, Smythe also launched an unsuccessful scheme to colonize the Honey Lake Valley in northern California's Lassen County. See *Irriga-tion Age* 13 (April 1899): 222; 15 (February 1900): 155–59, 207–11; and "How to Col-onize the Pacific Coast," *Land of Sunshine* 15 (November 1901): 383–91.

12. *New York World,* March 3, 1895; *Boston Herald,* February 20, 1895.

13. Frederick Booth-Tucker, "The Relation of Colonization to Irrigation," *Forestry and Irrigation* 9 (October 1903): 499–505; U.S. Geological Survey, *Water Sup-*

ply and Irrigation Paper #93 (Washington, D.C., 1904), 122–26; *Proceedings of the Twelfth Annual Session of the National Irrigation Congress, El Paso, Texas, November 1904* (El Paso, 1904), 134–36.

14. Andrew Hudanick, Jr., "George Hebard Maxwell: Reclamation's Militant Evangelist," *Journal of the West* 14 (July 1975): 108–21.

15. For the 1902 congressional debate over the Newlands bill see *Congressional Record*, 57 Cong., 1 sess., 1383–86, 2218–24, 2276–85, 6668–6708, 6722–78. The Newlands, Patterson, Jones, and Underwood quotes are from pp. 6734, 2283, 6751, and 6672, respectively.

16. Frederick Haynes Newell has been a neglected figure in agricultural history. His papers at the Library of Congress and University of Wyoming are fragmentary and reveal little of the man's strong and abrasive personality. See his typescript "A Man's Life" in the Newell Collection, Western Heritage Library, University of Wyoming. See also Arthur P. Davis's typescript "Memoirs of the Reclamation Service" dated November 3, 1915, in the Davis Collection at the same library. For a brief sketch of Newell's life see Allen B. McDaniel, "Frederick Haynes Newell," *Transactions of the American Society of Civil Engineers*, 98 (1933): 1597–1600.

17. Edwin T. Layton, *The Revolt of the Engineers* (Cleveland: Case Western University Press, 1971), 57–59, 63–68.

18. Frederick H. Newell, "Awakening of the Engineer," *Engineering News* 74 (September 16, 1915): 568–69. Newell's view of the engineer as reformer can best be seen in his speech to the graduating class of Case School, Cleveland, Ohio, on May 29, 1912, a transcript of which is in the file "Newell, 1912," container 6, F. H. Newell Collection, Library of Congress. See also his "The Engineer in the Public Service," *Engineering News* 68 (July–December 1912): 153–55; "The Engineer's Part in After-the-War Problems," *Scientific Monthly* 8 (March 1919): 239–46; "Ethics of the Engineering Profession," *Annals of American Academy of Political and Social Science* 101 (May 1922): 76–85; and the collection of lectures published as *Water Resources: Present and Future Uses* (New Haven, 1920).

19. Francis G. Newlands, "National Irrigation as a Social Problem," *Pacific Monthly* 16 (September 1906): 296–97; Charles Wood Eberlein, comments in *Official Proceedings of the Thirteenth International Irrigation Congress, 1905* (Portland, 1905), 249–52.

20. On the Town-Site Act see F. H. Newell, "Rural Settlements," U.S. Reclamation Service (USRS), Memorandum 9, in "Establishment of Townsites and Villages," Records of the Bureau of Reclamation, National Archives, Record Group 115, Washington, D.C. (hereafter NA, RG). A map entitled "U.S.G.S. Reclamation Service Plan for Rural Settlements Authorized by Act of Congress Approved April 16, 1906" is attached to the memo. See also Newell's "Reclaiming an Empire," *Pacific Monthly* 18 (October 1907): 478.

21. B. E. Stoutmeyer to supervising engineer, USRS, June 8, 1911, and "Testimony Before House Committee on Irrigation of Arid Lands on March 13, 1912, on H.R. 10443," both in "Establishment of Townsites and Villages," NA, RG 115.

22. C. J. Blanchard to F. A. Waugh, November 7, 1912, "Establishment of Townsites and Villages," NA, RG 115.

23. F. A. Waugh to C. J. Blanchard, December 2, 1912. See also J. Horace McFar-

land to Blanchard, November 18, 1912; McFarland to F. H. Newell, December 3, 1912; McFarland to Walter Fisher, December 23, 1912, and January 11 and 27, 1913; Newell to Waugh, November 29, 1912; Fisher to McFarland, December 18, 1912, and February 18, 1913; acting secretary of the interior to McFarland, February 8, 1913; C. P. Williams to the statistician, February 19, 1913; and Blanchard to A. P. Davis, October 27, 1917. A summary of the committee's report is contained in John Nolen, Frederick Law Olmstead, Frank A. Waugh, Harland P. Kelsey, and Warren Manning to Walter Fisher, January 8, 1913. All these letters are contained in the "Establishment of Townsites and Villages" file, NA, RG 115.

24. F. H. Newell, "Progress in Reclamation of Arid Lands in the Western United States," *Annual Report of the Smithsonian Institutions, 1910* (Washington, D.C., 1911), 198, and "Irrigation Manager's Conference During 1912," unpublished report in "Irrigation and Reclamation of Arid Lands" file, John D. Works Collection, Bancroft Library, University of California, Berkeley.

25. F. H. Newell to Gifford Pinchot, October 6, 1913, General Correspondence, 1913, container 168, Gifford Pinchot Collection, Library of Congress, Washington, D.C.

26. *Eleventh Annual Report of the Reclamation Service, 1911–1912* (Washington, D.C., 1913), 5–6; F. H. Newell, *Irrigation Management* (New York, 1916), 3, 32, 35. In 1915, Newell was relieved of the directorship of the Reclamation Service largely because he was a poor administrator and insensitive to the complaints of the farmers his agency served.

27. Elwood Mead to John Works, December 24, 1912. See also Mead to Works, October 29, 1915, and April 7, 1916, Works Collection, Bancroft Library. On Mead's career see James R. Kluger, "Elwood Mead: Irrigation Engineer and Social Planner" (Ph.D. diss., University of Arizona, 1970), and Paul Conkin, "The Vision of Elwood Mead," *Agricultural History* 34 (April 1960): 88–97.

28. William Ellsworth Smythe, "A Program for California," *Land of Sunshine* 15 (December 1901): 487–98; "New Zealand Institutions," *Out West* 16 (February 1902); and "The Unfinished Task," *Official Proceedings of the Thirteenth International Irrigation Congress, 1905,* 257. On the Little Landers colony see Lawrence B. Lee, "William E. Smythe and San Diego, 1901–1908," *Journal of San Diego History* 19 (Winter 1973): 10–24; Lee, "The Little Landers Company of San Ysidro," ibid. 21 (Spring 1975): 26–51; and Robert V. Hine, *California's Utopian Colonies* (New Haven, 1966), 144–48.

29. George Maxwell, "The Growth of Socialism," *Maxwell's Talisman* 6 (July 1906): 6, and "Anarchy: Its Cause and Cure—The Remedy for Social Unrest and Industrial Discontent," ibid. 9 (March 1908): 17–19. See also Maxwell's speech before the Manufacturers Club of Philadelphia, December 19, 1904, in Records of the National Reclamation Association, Printed Booklets, NA, RG 115.

30. A "croft" was a very small farm, especially the small farms on the western coast and islands of Scotland. In the *Talisman* of July 1906 (p. 10), Maxwell noted that the first homecroft scheme originated in England in 1879 when the Cadbury brothers moved their factory four miles outside Birmingham and provided rural homes to twenty-four workmen at low rents.

31. Maxwell and Newell both recognized the value of swampland reclamation and irrigation to provide additonal farms in the East and South. See Newell's "The Undrained Empire of the South," dated March 2, 1916, in Correspondence, Newell,

1912, container 6, F. H. Newell Collection, Library of Congress.

32. On the Watertown and Arizona homecroft experiments see *Maxwell's Talisman* 6 (July 1906): 10 –16; ibid. 6 (August 1906): 3 – 4, 21–22; and *Irrigation Age* 24 (May 1909): 205– 6.

33. *Maxwell's Talisman* 6 (November 1906): 3 –7.

34. Paul Conkin, *Tomorrow a New World: The New Deal Community Program* (Ithaca, 1959), 11–58; Conkin, "The Vision of Elwood Mead"; William L. Bowers, *The Country Life Movement in America, 1900 –1920* (Port Washington, N.Y., 1974); and Bill G. Reid, "Franklin K. Lane's Idea for Veterans: Colonization, 1918–1921," *Pacific Historical Review* 33 (November 1964): 447– 66.

35. Michael C. Robinson, *Water for the West: The Bureau of Reclamation, 1902 –1977* (Chicago, 1979), 32.

36. *Reports of the Department of the Interior for the Fiscal Year Ended June 30, 1920* (Washington, D.C., 1920), 1: 8 –9; Gates, *History of Public Land Law Development,* 681.

AFTERWORD

1. James L. Penick, *Progressive Politics and Conservation: The Ballinger-Pinchot Affair* (Chicago, 1968), 17.

2. Paul Russell Cutright, *Theodore Roosevelt: The Making of a Conservationist* (Urbana, Ill., 1985), 217–18; Stephen Fox, *The American Conservation Movement: John Muir and His Legacy* (Madison, 1981), 129.

3. Susan R. Schrepfer, in "Establishing Administrative 'Standing': The Sierra Club and the Forest Service, 1897–1956," *Pacific Historical Review* 58 (February 1989): 57, wisely observes: "Indeed, in the first half of this century citizen activism was a complementary, rather than antagonistic, development in the evolution of the administrative state. Federal land agencies formally and informally invited the advice of citizen groups. They did so in part because federal law barred them from using public funds to lobby Congress directly on their own behalf." Of course, some bureaus were far more responsive to "the advice of citizen groups" than others. For a survey of water policy that emphasizes the emergence of iron triangles see Daniel McCool, *Command of the Waters: Iron Triangles, Federal Water Development, and Indian Water* (Berkeley, 1987).

4. Penick, *Progressive Politics and Conservation,* 188.

5. See, in particular, Morton Keller, *Regulating a New Economy: Public Policy and Economic Change in America, 1900 –1933* (Cambridge, Mass., 1990), and Barry Karl, *The Uneasy State: The United States from 1915 to 1945* (Chicago, 1983).

6. It should be noted, however, that states' rights arguments reappeared during Roosevelt's second term. In 1937, when George Norris introduced legislation to replicate TVA in western river basins, the entire delegation from the thirteen western states opposed it, arguing that the bill implied federal ownership of western streams, reduced the power of the states, and would reward some states at the expense of others. See Anna Riesch Owen, *Conservation Under F.D.R* (New York, 1983), 60 – 61.

7. Arthur M. Schlesinger, *The Coming of the New Deal* (Boston, 1959), 333. Also

see William E. Leuchtenburg, *Franklin D. Roosevelt and the New Deal* (New York, 1963), 148–50, 154–55, 164–66.

8. Ellis W. Hawley, "The New Deal State and the Anti-Bureaucratic Tradition," in Robert Eden, ed., *The New Deal and Its Legacy: Critique and Reappraisal* (New York, 1989), 81, 89.

INDEX

Abandoned farms, 2
Absolute rights, 2, 4, 200(n3)
Adirondack Mountains, 136
AFA. *See* American Forestry Association
"Age of the engineer," 186, 189
Agribusiness, 53, 54, 194
Agricultural college scrip, 90
Agricultural overproduction, 163
Agriculture. *See* Irrigation; *under* California;
    Indian Reservations; Prior appropria-
    tion; *individual states*
Agriculture, U.S. Department of
    (USDA), 100
    experimental farms, 116
    forest reserves (1905), 151
    Forestry Bureau, 149, 151 (*see also* Mead,
    Elwood)
    Forestry Division, 56, 110, 122, 128, 144
    and government agencies, 122, 148,
    151, 154
    grazing office, 152
    Indian irrigation agriculture report, 177–78
    secretary, 15, 153
    See also Forest Service
Alder Gulch (Mont.), 35
Alfalfa, 112, 227(n43)
Alta California, 58, 64–65
Alvarado, Juan, 68, 72, 73, 74
American Anthropologist (journal), 120
American Association for the Advancement
    of Science, 144
American Civic Association, 188
American Forestry (journal), 156
American Forestry Association (AFA), 125,
    132, 144, 145, 147, 148, 149, 156, 157
"American Forests: Their Destruction and
    Preservation" (Starr), 126, 135, 234(n6)
American Geographical Society Cullum
    Gold Medal, 189
American Heritage (magazine), 164
American Philosophical Society, 148
American River, 58, 208(n22)
Anaho Island, 164

Anderson, Raymond, 97
Annals of Trinity County (Cox), 34
Anthropological Society of Washington, 120
Anti-ditchers, 30, 31
Apaches, 159
Appalachian Mountains, 155
Aqueduct, 27, 28
Aridity. *See* West, climate
Arizona
    irrigation, 48, 154
    model rural town, 188, 192
    sheep growers, 152, 154
    statute of limitations, 79
    water rights, 10, 20, 205(n44)
Arizona v. California (1963), 38, 248(n3)
Arizona Wool Growers Association, 152
Arkansas, 79
Arkansas River, 45, 171, 203(n33)
Army Corps of Engineers, 105, 107, 156–57
Ashurst, Henry, 173
Assiniboine, 170
Associated Pioneers of the Territorial Days of
    California, 82
"Association for the Protection of the Rights
    of Property, and the Maintenance of
    Order," 72
Australia, 190

Back to the land movement, 191–93
Bakersfield (Calif.), 94, 96
Bakken, Gordon Morris, 10, 13, 21
Ballinger, Richard, 157–58
Bancroft, Hubert Howe, 52, 61, 62, 84–85
Banks, 35, 36, 93, 192–93
Bard (Ariz.), 188
Beale, Edward F., 87
Bean, Walton, 61, 83
Bear Flag Revolt (1846), 58
Bee (Sacramento), 61
Belknap, Jeremy, 131
Bennett, Nathaniel, 71–72
Benton, Thomas Hart, 66, 68, 73
Bessey, Charles E., 129

SOURCE NOTE

I am obliged to the editors and publishers for permission to reprint the following:

Chapters 1 and 4, "Enterprise and Equity" and "Squatter Law in California, 1850–1858," are reprinted by permission from *Western Historical Quarterly* 18 (January 1987): 15–37 and 25 (Autumn 1994): 277–310.

Chapter 2, "The Origins of Western Water Law," is reprinted by permission from *California History* 70 (Fall 1991): 242–57, 324–25.

Chapters 3 and 6, "State vs. Nation" and "George Maxwell, the Railroads, and American Land Policy, 1899–1904," are reprinted by permission from *Pacific Historical Review* 51 (August 1982): 265–82 and 63 (May 1994): 177–202.

Chapters 5 and 10, "Land Monopoly in Nineteenth-Century California" and "Reclamation and Social Engineering in the Progressive Era," are reprinted by permission from *Agricultural History* 65 (Fall 1991): 15–37 and 57 (January 1983): 46–63.

Chapter 7, "Forests and Conservation, 1865–1890," is reprinted by permission from *Journal of American History* 72 (September 1985): 340–59.

Chapter 8, "Forests and Reclamation, 1891–1911," is reprinted by permission from *Forest & Conservation History* 37 (April 1993): 68–79.

Chapter 9, "Irrigation, Water Rights, and the Betrayal of Indian Allotment," is reprinted by permission from *Environmental History Review* 10 (Fall 1986): 157–76.